THE BENGAL SAPPE
AREAS OF OPERATIONS A
Map: Circa 1
G000231784
S
S
R
Manchuria
Mongolia
Sinkiang
Korea
Afghanistan
C H I N A
Tibet
Bhutan
Nepal
INDIA
Burma
Hong Kong
Philippines
Siam
Indo-China
Ceylon
Sarawak
Malaya
Equator
Borneo
Celebes
Sumatra
Java
Timor
I N D I A N
O C E A N
AUSTRALIA
60º
80º
Mercator's Projection
120º
GWA

THE BENGAL SAPPERS

1803–2003

THE BENGAL SAPPERS 1803–2003

An Anthology Compiled and Edited by

GENERAL SIR GEORGE COOPER

GCB MC DL

and

MAJOR DAVID ALEXANDER

THE INSTITUTION OF ROYAL ENGINEERS

CHATHAM

First published in 2003 by
The Institution of Royal Engineers,
Brompton Barracks,
Chatham,
Kent ME4 4UG.

ISBN 0-903530-24-4

Designed and produced by DAG Publications Ltd, London
Book jacket design by Jade Design, London
Maps by Gordonwood Associates, Barton Stacey, Hampshire
Printed and bound by Biddles, Guildford, Surrey

CONTENTS

ILLUSTRATIONS

Colour Plates between pages 16 and 17

Monochrome Plates between pages 176 and 177

MAPS

This book is dedicated
to all those officers and men
who gave their friendship, loyalty
and service to the Bengal Sappers
over two centuries.

FOREWORD

by

LIEUTENANT GENERAL SIR SCOTT GRANT, KCB

Chief Royal Engineer

Over 55 years have elapsed since India gained its independence. Thus, no officer currently serving in the Corps of Royal Engineers was even alive when the new National Flag of India was hoisted on 15 August 1947 at Roorkee, home of the Bengal Sappers and Miners since 1853. It is therefore all the more important that, whilst memories are still sharp and personal records are still readily available, the long and distinguished story of the Bengal Sappers is told. It is, as this anthology graphically demonstrates, a story of service, sacrifice and courage, in both peace and war. It is also a story of friendships – born of shared experience and hardship – that transcend rank, religion and nationality. And, in a remarkably vivid manner, this anthology of the Bengal Sappers highlights the unique relationship that existed – and still exists to this day – between the people of the United Kingdom and the people of India and Pakistan. This relationship is captured perfectly in Janet Crawford's delightful vignette on her childhood in Roorkee. For Janet: *"India will always be my home. I love the people, I love the country, and there is a sense of belonging."* For me, as Chief Royal Engineer, the story of the Bengal Sappers from 1803 to 2003 also left me with a powerful *"sense of belonging"* – of belonging to a Corps with a unique range of skills, a total commitment to duty and a proud history, in which the traditions of the past provide the inspiration for the future.

ACKNOWLEDGEMENTS

In putting together this anthology, the Editors wish to thank all those who have contributed. Many people have submitted their own, often privately published, reminiscences and have been unstinting in giving permission to quote from them. Others have contributed their own recollections and given permission to the editors to omit, amend or delete as they thought fit – with so much material, this has been rather necessary if duplication was to be avoided. Nevertheless, we hope we have not offended too many contributors if we have taken them at their word and omitted some favourite tale in the interest of space. Similarly, we have omitted mention of many individual units so as to avoid cluttering up the narrative with too much detail.

The Editors have quoted liberally from Colonel Sandes's excellent histories of the Indian Engineers and are grateful to the Institution of Royal Engineers for permission to do this. Special thanks are due to George Pearson who, as a subaltern in Roorkee in 1946–7, was tasked with writing a history of the Bengal Sappers during World War II. This was compiled almost entirely from Unit War Diaries and has been an invaluable source of material. Much help has also been received from the Commandant and Officers of the Bengal Engineer Group & Centre in Roorkee and we are extremely grateful.

With apologies for any inadvertent omissions, we would like to thank the following individuals, or in some cases their families or executors, for their help: Ian Lyall Grant, Bill Adams, Aitken Lawrie, Chris Popham, Mike Rolt, Pamela and Archie Jack, Ernie Odell, Vera and Harry Grattan, Edwin Fox, Dai David, John Parfect, George Hawkins, Terence Tinsley, Leslie Beswick, R Manoranjan, Mangat Rai, Janet Balston, Désirée and 'Stu' Battye, 'Honker' Henniker, Bill Gerrie, Reggie Sfakianos, Hugh Beach, George Franklin, Alan Hiscock, Katharine Lethbridge, Joan Usher, Graeme Black and Janet Crawford.

We particularly wish to thank Desmond Henly who was kind enough to donate his artistic talents in providing the line drawings and sketches throughout the text and Sandy Alexander for proof-reading the text.

We would also like to acknowledge the article in The Sunday Statesman, Delhi, dated 22nd August 1948, entitled 'Independence Day, Roorkee, 1948'.

Lastly, but by no means least, we would like to express our gratitude to John Croft for his advice on publishing, Peter Wood for the preparation of the maps, without which it would be difficult to follow some of the narrative, and all those who have given permission to reproduce photographs, particularly the Royal Engineers Library at Chatham, the British Library and the British Association for Cemeteries in South Asia.

Col Sir Proby Cautley, KCB, FRS, (1802–1871).

Above right: Field Marshal The Lord Napier of Magdala, GCB, GCSI (1810–1890).

Right: Maj Gen Sir Henry Durand, KCSI, CB (1812–1871).

Col Richard Baird Smith, CB
(1818–1861).

Col Sir Edward Thackeray, VC, KCB
(1836–1927).

General Sir
Bindon Blood,
GCB, GCVO,
(1842–1935).

Lt Gen Sir Fenton Aylmer, Bt, VC, KCB (1862–1935).

Lt Gen Sir Ronald Charles, KCB, CMG, DSO (1875–1955).

Lt Gen Sir Clarence Bird, KCIE, CB, DSO (1885–1986).

Maj Gen William Veitch, CB, CBE, TD (1901–1969).

Bengal Engineer officers in Northern India c.1870 including (centre front row) the then Lt Gen the Lord Napier of Magdala and (third from right, front row) Maj Gen Sir Henry Durand.

INTRODUCTION

"I am not sure that I ever met anyone who arrived in [India] without great satisfaction, or who could hail the first glimpse of a world so totally new without feelings of curiosity more than commonly excited. For my own part, I was thrown into a high fever of wonder and enjoyment; and assuredly, as long as I have a trace of memory left, must retain the recollection of that happy period carved brightly and distinctly on my mind."

These words were written by Captain Basil Hall, RN, in the opening chapter of his 'Voyages and Travels' published in 1831. They could have been written with equal fervour and sincerity by countless young officers arriving in India to join the Bengal Engineers from the inception of that Regiment in 1803 to the last draft to arrive from the United Kingdom in 1946.

The 'wonder and enjoyment' are still there in all the richness and variety that make up life in India: the long history revealed in the vast array of palaces, forts, tombs, temples and mosques from dynasties that have waxed and waned over four millennia; the great myths and stories of Hindus, Jains, Buddhists, Muslims and Sikhs; the religious observances that are woven into the fabric of daily life and spoken of easily and naturally as part of the cycle of life, death and rebirth; the teaming life of the cities and plains; the sweep and variety of the landscapes from the peaks of the Himalayas to the beaches of Kovalam; the inherent courtesy and friendliness of India's peoples. All this is as available now to gladden the eye and enrich the spirit as it was in 1803.

The volume which follows is not an attempt to write a full history of the Bengal Sappers & Miners; rather it is intended to preserve some of the recollections of Bengal Sappers past and present and of their wives and families before those memories are lost. It records something of what it was like to be part of such an illustrious past : how and where the Regiment developed, some of its military exploits, its social life, the men who served and commanded, the personal recollections of officers and wives and their reactions to the strangeness of the unfamiliar environment, the beauty of their surroundings and the captivating charm of India and its peoples. It is also meant to display a little of Captain Hall's wonder and enjoyment, of the deep affection which grew up between officers and the men whom they commanded and of the experiences which enriched all their lives.

The book's further purpose is to be a memorial to the Regiment on the occasion of its bicentenary and a tribute to all the officers and men who served in the Bengal Sappers over such a long period of history and who by their dedication, professional expertise and valour built a tradition of service and comradeship which will continue to make the name of the Bengal Sappers remembered for many years to come.

1
THE FORMATIVE YEARS

EARLY DAYS

It all started with Clive's victory at the Battle of Plassey (1757). Up to then the British in the north of India had only led a precarious existence in small trading factories in and around Calcutta. Suddenly they found themselves Lords of Bengal and shortly afterwards of Bihar and Orissa, while the power of the French, their arch rivals, was eliminated. Civil Government was rapidly disintegrating as the Mogul Empire, reeling from Persian and Afghan invasions as well as the expansion of the Mahratta Confederacy, lost much of its authority. The collection of public revenues had dried up, leading to general neglect of public works and services. In central and southern India, Hyderabad and Mysore were competing for supremacy, leading to general lawlessness. The East India Company found itself not only trading but filling the vacuum in civil administration. A Corps of Engineers was formed in Bengal in 1761 not only for military duties but also to undertake Public Works and Surveying. Their principal military role was to advise commanders both on the construction of military fortifications and how to conduct operations against them.

The officers for the Bengal Engineers were recruited at first on an ad hoc basis. Major James Rennell, who was appointed Surveyor General of Bengal in 1764, had already served in the Navy for seven years. He became No 7 on the list of Bengal Engineers. He was to have a brilliant scientific career, producing the first map of India and becoming a Fellow of the Royal Society. From early in the nineteenth century the officers were trained at Addiscombe, the East India Company's College for gunners and engineers, and received their technical training at the RE Establishment at Chatham, which had been opened in 1812 to train junior officers and other ranks in sapping and mining and other military fieldworks.

Addiscombe was opened in 1809 and closed in 1861. The buildings, some miles east of Croydon, dating from 1703, were then sold and have now completely disappeared but in their day were fine buildings. The front elevation bore the family motto of the original owner William Draper: '*Non faciam vitio culpare minorem*', translatable as 'I shall not lower myself by vice or fault'. As this was judged a suitable motto for young officers it was allowed to stay. Some 500 engineer officers were to pass through the establishment out of a total of 3,500 trained there but these included the requirements of Madras and Bombay as well as Bengal.

There were no special troops in the early years to execute the commander's plan but only officers, so in 1803 Lieutenant Thomas Wood was directed to raise three companies each of 75 men at Cawnpore. Wood was a Bengal Engineer, by specialisation a surveyor, but it was envisaged that the new Corps should be officered by the Infantry, so in 1804 command passed to Lieutenant John Swinton of the 12th Bengal Native Infantry, a man whose amazing courage and fine leadership had already brought him into prominence, and the Corps was designated as the Bengal Pioneers. Swinton made a great mark and had a brilliant career. He took part in some twelve sieges where he led the assaults with great courage, retiring in 1825 lame and battle scarred but still indomitable with the rank of Lieutenant Colonel – the 'father of the Bengal Sappers and Miners.'

The Bengal Pioneers acquired such a reputation during the various struggles of the East India Company that in 1808 a substantial increase in the establishment of the Corps was authorised and it was designated the 'Corps of Pioneers or Sappers'. A company of Miners was recruited, particularly for sieges, and was placed under an officer of the Bengal Engineers, but the Pioneer element remained under infantry officers for the time being.

The Bengal Pioneer of 1809 wore a green tunic with facings of the same colour adorned with yellow lace and black buttons. On his head was a tall black hat built up on a bamboo framework to resemble the headgear of the British soldier, and on his legs the loose white trousers which had been authorised in 1808 in substitution for short white drawers. The private was shod with *chapplies* (sandals) and the Indian officer wore high boots. The accoutrements were of black leather.

At any time in Northern India there is a narrow margin between devastating floods and droughts; both conditions of course lead to famine. Therefore it is not surprising that in peace the Engineer establishment of the East India Company was used mainly on public works, especially irrigation. In view of this system it is remarkable that the Corps did so well in war. A glance at the Army List of 1846 shows that the Bengal Sappers only had a Major as Commandant, a Captain as second-in-command, a Lieutenant as Adjutant and fourteen 2nd Lieutenants. Selected Bengal

Engineers were drafted in at the last moment from civilian employment and thrust upon men who were strangers to them. Fortunately, some excellent British NCOs, who were attached permanently to units, stepped in until the officers could learn their new duties and gain the trust and confidence of their men. Financially the system was highly economical, for in peace the Engineer officers were paid mostly from the Civil Government, but from a military standpoint the system was deplorable and even dangerous.

In war most engineer work involved the capture of towns and fortresses. There were basically two methods of assaulting a fortress. The normal method was to breach the wall with artillery. In this case the sappers brought the guns forward by digging angled trenches to prepared emplacements (sapping). If there was no artillery, a weak point would have to be found, such as a gate which could be blown in by a prepared charge (as at Ghazni in 1839 and at Delhi in 1857). The other method was to mine under the wall and blow it up with a heavy charge (as at Bhurtpore in 1825). The Sappers and/or Miners then led the assault with specialised equipment such as fascines for crossing ditches and scaling ladders.

In 1818 it was decreed that a Corps of Bengal Sappers and Miners should be formed and a draft of British NCOs was sent from Chatham to provide specialist backup, a practice which lasted till 1947. It was officered mainly by Engineer Officers, though Infantry Officers could still be attached as necessary, and six companies were authorised with a total strength of 816 Indian ranks commanded at first by Captain (later Lieutenant General) Richard Tickell. The headquarters moved as necessary to fit operational requirements and it was not till 1853 that it reached Roorkee. Pioneers were formed into separate units and were not finally disbanded until 1932.

The term 'Pioneer' roughly meant an infantry sepoy who could use a pick and shovel and their main task was road making. As time went on a more technical requirement for sappers and miners arose and establishments and nomenclature changed from time to time to reflect this. At the great siege of Bhurtpore in 1825 there were six companies of sappers and miners and two of pioneers and these ratios changed as circumstances demanded.

The history of Northern India is one long succession of invasions from the north-west and of infiltrations from the South. As a result there are many tribes of mixed blood but it is remarkable to what an extent the

Aryan stock has remained pure, the Aryan races having come in as invaders. In the Bengal Sappers practically all the tribes who are enlisted come from these northern areas and comprise men drawn from the hereditary martial races including Pathans from the North West Frontier.

Bhurtpore was the first major siege in which the Corps participated. It was a city some eight miles in circumference with nine gates, enclosed by a mud wall of great height and thickness with round bastions mounting scores of guns. Around it was a wide ditch which could be filled with water. A citadel with still more formidable defences and a larger ditch lay towards the north-eastern end. A man called Durjan Lal had usurped the throne and defied the Government, so in October 1825 it was decided that strong measures were necessary and an army of some 30,000 men was mobilized for the reduction of the fortress under the personal direction of Lord Combermere, the C-in-C. The defences had been considerably improved since Lieutenant General Lake had failed to take the fortress some twenty years earlier and the siege commenced in October 1825. The nature of the fortifications was such that guns had little effect – the walls crumbled exposing the buried timber and the debris formed an insurmountable obstacle. The sappers resorted to mining on unprecedented scales burrowing day by day through the water-logged soil, gasping and sweating in ill-ventilated galleries and in constant peril from heavy falls of earth until they were in position to place several great mines which were exploded on 18th January. A mine packed with 10,000lbs of explosive destroyed the north-east corner of the fortress and this led to the surrender of the Citadel. In a graphic and stirring account of the explosion, J H Stocqueler in his book *The Old Field Officer* described how: "The massive bastion trembled from level to summit and gradually rising from its firm foundation and increasing in bulk as it rose, seemed almost to precipitate its overwhelming mass upon our heads." Earth, timber and the mangled bodies of many men killed or injured by the explosion showered on the attackers.

There was a curious old tale connected with this great fortress. It had been predicted many years before that it would never be taken by an enemy until a '*Kumbhir*' or crocodile appeared before its walls. When, therefore, defenders learnt that an army under a leader named Combermere was advancing against them, they were much perturbed and some of them lost heart. Bhurtpore became the first battle honour of the Bengal Sappers and Miners.

Perhaps as big an operation was the five month siege of Multan in 1848/49 where the young Chief Engineer, Major Robert Napier, later to become C-in-C of the Indian Army, was to make his name. He had been commissioned into the Bengal Engineers in 1826 at the tender age of sixteen and in 1845 during the Sikh War he had acted as Chief Engineer, had two horses shot under him and was severely wounded. He was wounded again at Multan and disabled for several weeks but gave such brilliant service there and at the subsequent Battle of Gujerat that he was awarded the brevet of Lieutenant Colonel.

The First Afghan War was a tragedy in which thousands of brave men were sacrificed and politics determined the whole form and shape of the operations. For the Sappers and Miners though, the crossing of the Indus, the blowing in of the Kabul Gate at Ghazni and the defence of Jalalabad are feats which will live for ever in the annals of Indian warfare. Orders were issued in August 1838 to Captain George Thomson, the Bengal Sapper Commandant, then based in Delhi, to prepare for an Engineer Department with the army in the field. He was informed that no wheeled transport would be allowed and that all tools and stores must be carried on camels. He arranged for 10,000lbs of powder for mining operations to be carried by the Artillery Park. Even without the explosives the transport for just indispensable tools and stores needed by the Engineer Park and the two Bengal Sapper Companies amounted to 178 camels and eight bullocks.

Thomson was appointed Chief Engineer and the Army of the Indus set forth from Ferozepore in December. Troubles arose almost at once when a host of 50,000 followers and almost as many camels impeded the army. One Brigadier had no less than sixty camels for his personal belongings! The supply depots along the route, which had been provided by the Political Department, failed to produce more than half-rations. Drivers deserted, animals were stolen, the troops became weak and dispirited, and thus long before the first Afghan was seen, the efficiency of the force was impaired. However, the Indus was reached at last.

Unlike in modern campaigns, major river crossings were less common as heavy loads were not usually a critical factor but the bridging of the Indus at Sukkur, during the march into Afghanistan, is a notable exception. An inept and incompetent Command and staff had managed to disperse all the boats available and with considerable difficulty more were collected. Two bridges, with spans of 133 yards and 367 yards respectively, were required to cross a torrent like a millrace. Rope, timber and nails were practically non-existent so local rope makers made 500 cables of coarse grass. Local carpenters made pyramidal anchors of wooden cribwork filled with stones. Until good timber could be floated down from Ferozepore the Sappers were compelled to use split palm trees for both road bearers and decking. Even nails had to be manufactured. To add to the problems a flash flood brought down floating trees which severed many of the cables, but in about three weeks the two spans were completed and the camel transport and army was able to cross. At that time this was the largest military bridge ever built in India.

Threading their way through the stony defiles of the Bolan Pass with only ten days rations in hand, the force arrived in Quetta with Kandahar still nearly 150 miles ahead. By mid-April 1839 the Sappers and Miners were preparing a practicable road through the Khojak Pass and the Bengal Army entered Kandahar on the 26th exhausted and incapable of moving another mile. Owing to the general disorganisation of the transport and the necessity of accumulating supplies, it was another six weeks before the advance was resumed, after leaving a garrison at Kandahar.

They moved slowly on, under the command of Lieutenant General Sir John Keane, towards Ghazni, where the General was assured he might expect no resistance. On arrival before the fortress they were surprised to find a high rampart in good repair built on a scarped mound about 35 feet high. It was flanked by numerous towers and surrounded by parapets and a wet ditch, with a garrison of 3–4,000 men, plus artillery. Mining was impossible due to the water level. There were insufficient ladders for scaling the walls and the fortifications could not be breached by artillery because the heavy guns had been left at Kandahar since resistance was not expected. There was therefore no alternative to a desperate attempt to force an entrance through a gateway. Thomson had made a reconnaissance and recommended a surprise assault after the Sappers had blown in the Kabul Gate on the north-eastern side.

Thomson arranged that an explosion party consisting of Captain Peat, of the Bombay Sappers, Lieutenants Durand and Macleod, of the Bengal Sappers, supported by 21 NCOs and men carrying 300lbs of powder should be ready to move down to the gateway at daybreak. Durand led the actual explosion party, laid their charges and successfully blew in the Gate allowing the assaulting column to enter the fortress. Fierce fighting took place with Thomson in the thick of it. In a letter to his brother he reported that "the cover of my cap was cut through but I was not touched. One of the Europeans, who fell across my leg, was killed and before I could get clear of him, a dead Afghan fell across me ... I felt exceedingly uncomfortable while struggling to get clear of the bodies above me and the timber under me, while sabres and bayonets made a most unpleasant clashing about my ears."

After much confused fighting the fortress was finally captured on 23rd July with the loss of 182 casualties to our own troops. Over 600 of the Afghans were killed and 1,600 captured. Great praise was given to the Sappers and the General paid tribute to the scientific and successful manner in which the Kabul Gate, of great strength, was blown in and praised the 'stern and cool courage' of the Sappers during the daring and dangerous enterprise of laying down powder in the face of the enemy. For their bravery on this occasion Subedar Devi Singh and thirteen Bengal Sappers were awarded the Indian Order of Merit (IOM), the first Indian soldiers to be so honoured and the highest gallantry award open to Indian soldiers at that time.

The Army was now able to advance on Kabul, some eighty miles to the north, and General Keane made a triumphant entry on 7th August 1839. A veil should now be drawn over the inefficiency which thereafter affected both the civil administration and the army itself. Durand, the senior engineer in Kabul, was unable to induce the autocratic and contemptuous Macnaghten, the Political Envoy, to take proper steps to strengthen the position and on 2nd November, 1841 the storm broke over Kabul. Macnaghten was murdered, many were taken prisoner in the siege and of the 16,000 people – men, women and children – who set off for India in the bitter cold of 6th January, 1842, only one, Dr Brydon, rode into Jalalabad, eighty miles to the east, six days later.

Jalalabad, a place of no military strength or importance, without magazines and in utter disrepair, had been occupied with a brigade by Major General Sale in November, 1841. He took possession of a quadrilateral enclosure about a mile and a quarter in circumference buried amid houses and gardens, without a ditch and with crumbling mud walls topped by small towers or bastions. After repelling an attack, he set to to repair the wretched defences and by January had raised the parapets to six or seven feet, repaired and widened the ramparts, extended the bastions, retrenched three of the gates, covered the fourth gate with an outwork and excavated a ditch ten feet deep and twelve feet in width round the whole of the walls. The engineer support was provided by three companies of "Broadfoot's Sappers" commanded by

Captain George Broadfoot of the 34th Madras Infantry. Though an infantry officer George had specialised in fortification at Addiscombe and hence his remarkable ability as an engineer. In 1840 he had been ordered to raise a corps of Sappers, consisting of 600 men. A stiffening was provided by a draft from the Bengal Sappers consisting of three British NCOs, four Indian Officers and twenty Indian NCOs to become Jemadars and Havildars, and twenty sappers to become Naiks. Three companies were lost at Kabul but the remainder performed herculean tasks, thus securing Jalalabad but on 19th February a tremendous earthquake shook down all the parapets, demolished a third of the town and reduced one of the gates to a shapeless mass. The damage was soon repaired and the garrison of some 2,500 men repulsed every Afghan assault until an 'Avenging Army' of 8,000 men marched into Jalalabad on 16th April from Peshawar.

One gleam of sunshine penetrated the universal gloom. Ghazni had fallen, but the little garrison of Kalat, 150 miles south of Kabul, held out until they were relieved on 26th May and in that gallant band were 23 Bengal Sappers and Miners.

The campaign was finally over by the end of the year after a punitive force had recaptured Kabul and burnt the principal bazaar before retiring back to Peshawar and across the Sutlej. The Baluchis of Sind and the Sikhs of the Punjab, however, were not deceived and these turbulent people saw in the results of the First Afghan War nothing but the defeat and dishonour of the Government of India and they acted accordingly. There was little to show for the sacrifice of 20,000 lives.

In December, 1845 a Sikh army of 50,000 men crossed the British frontier on the Sutlej near Ferozepore and thus precipitated the First Sikh War. The Governor-General had wisely made provision for the crossing of the Sutlej in the event of hostilities, no doubt bearing in mind the difficulties encountered in the crossing of the Indus in 1839. A flotilla of 60 boats with the necessary baulks, chesses, cables and anchors were specially manufactured in Bombay Dockyard and brought up the Indus ostensibly for the transport of grain. They were then sent on to Ferozepore where they were used for the training of 1st Company in bridging and watermanship. They were hurriedly sunk when the Sikhs themselves crossed the Sutlej in force. When the Sikhs retreated the boats were raised again; the small holes were easily repaired and in the spring of 1846 two separate bridges each about 230 yards in length were built.

ROORKEE

The Headquarters of the Bengal Sappers and Miners moved to Roorkee in 1853 where, apart from a brief absence in 1854, it has remained ever since. Some one hundred miles north of Delhi, it lies on both sides of what is now State Highway 45 linking Ghaziabad to Dehra Dun and Hardwar within sight of the Siwalik hills some seventeen miles away. It was originally, in the early 19th Century, just a small village

The Ganges Canal, which was opened in 1854, passes between the village of Roorkee and the Cantonment separated by the famous Lion Bridge guarded by its huge stone lions. The Ganges Canal was constructed between 1842 and 1854, starting at Hardwar, some eighteen miles from Roorkee, where the River Ganges, the Holy River, finally leaves the mountains. It was under the supervision of Colonel P T Cautley (a Gunner officer!) with major assistance provided by the Bengal Sappers. In 1843 Cautley was joined by Lieutenant R Strachey (later Lieutenant General Sir Richard Strachey GCSI and President of the Royal Geographical Society) who was engaged on the canal headworks below Hardwar. Lieutenant Edward Fraser was in charge of construction of the 2nd Division of the Canal in 1848 up to the 110th mile and other Bengal Sapper officers were employed further down the line as well as several civil engineers.

The Canal is over 500 miles long, rejoining the Ganges at Allahabad with over 3,000 miles of distributary channels and must rank as one of the greatest feats of engineering in the 19th Century. Between ten and twelve feet deep and between 150 and 200 feet wide, it is an engineering marvel and incorporates a number of super-passages (river over canal) and aqueducts, the most famous being the Solani Aqueduct outside Roorkee which was opened in 1854 carrying the canal over the Solani River. Its aim was the irrigation of the huge area (doab) between the Jumna and the Ganges and the whole project was an instant success with the cost being recovered in two years of extra land tax.

The canal foundry and workshops, which were established at Roorkee, formed the basis for the Thomason College of Civil Engineering founded in 1847 and named after Mr James Thomason, the Lieutenant Governor of the North-West Frontier Province, who originally mooted the idea and generated both support and funds. Lieutenant Robert Maclagan of the Bengal Sappers was the first Principal and the College mainly catered for the requirements of Overseers and Staff for the Canal, moving into its present building in 1856. It continued to be closely associated with the Bengal Sappers and became a fully fledged University in 1949. Meanwhile the village gradually expanded and by the 1930s was being referred to as Roorkee City, though it remained a fearful huddle of thatched huts and tall white tenements and shops. The main street was one long bazaar, the stalls laden with odd lemonade and soda-water bottles, fly-smothered cakes, fruit and biscuits, cheap shirts and socks.

During the First Sikh War work on the canal virtually ceased and only started again in early 1847. Shortly after, Strachey handed over to Lieutenant Yule (later Colonel Sir Henry Yule KCSI CB), a remarkable character, described as 'one of those curious racial compounds which one finds on the east coast of Scotland in which the hard Teutonic grit is sweetened by the artistic spirit of the more genial Celt.' Yule found that the unpunctuality of the workmen in the canal workshops at Roorkee upset his irritable nature. Vexed with himself for losing his temper so often he decided to impose a rigid self-discipline and each time he flew into a rage he transferred a fine of two rupees from his right to his left pocket, the accumulation being devoted in the end to the erection of a sundial to teach the workmen the value of time!

THE SEPOY MUTINY

The Sepoy Mutiny began on 10th May 1857 with a revolt by the sepoys in Meerut, so starting a cataclysm which saw the end of the East India Company and a welter of destruction in Northern India. Tragedy followed on tragedy; the fighting was bitter and to the death. The causes were complex and numerous but the mutiny was confined almost entirely to the Bengal Army where some foolish administrative decisions had persuaded the sepoys that their interests were being disregarded. When the soldiers mutinied, every ruffian in the bazaars joined them for the sake of loot and this soon antagonised the civilian population.

Eight of the twelve companies of the Bengal Sappers and Miners were at Roorkee when the unrest broke out. In the early hours of 12th May information reached Roorkee of the mutiny in Meerut and six of the companies, some 500 men, were immediately ordered to proceed to Meerut by forced marches under Captain Edward Fraser, the Commandant. On the morning of the 16th, after two companies had marched out to work, Fraser ordered the remainder to store their ammunition in a secure magazine. The men somewhat naturally objected as this was the equivalent to disarming them and showed a lack of trust. Just as the ammunition wagons were moving off an Afghan sentry rushed forward and shot Captain Fraser. A general stampede to the open country followed and they were pursued by a party of Carabineers and a troop of Horse Artillery who surrounded a party of fifty and annihilated them. The remainder escaped to Delhi and joined the mutineers. It was strongly asserted afterwards that this disastrous episode was the result of panic rather than treachery. It was certainly the only serious episode affecting the Corps, the rest of whom remained loyal to their salt.

Major Baird Smith, the Superintendent of Canals, was in Roorkee with his headquarters in the Canal Foundry Workshops and was full of apprehension for what might happen next as the community was virtually helpless. They numbered about 200 souls, of whom some 90 were males fit to bear arms, the remainder being women and children. Only about 30 were trained soldiers, the other men being assistants or clerks in the Civil offices or connected with the Thomason College; they were all widely scattered throughout the Military Cantonment and Civil Station. Furthermore there were only thirty weapons available with thirty rounds apiece.

The Workshops provided a suitable place for defence against an infantry attack and preparations were immediately set in hand. Among the materials for the use of the foundry were some old Sikh guns, spoils of the Punjab Campaign, and carriages were constructed for three of them. Being of French origin they were just too small for six-pounder ball, but this difficulty was overcome by preparing grape and canister until balls could be specially cast for them. A day or so later it proved possible to move all the spare arms, ammunition and powder from the magazine in the Cantonment into the Workshops and arrangements were completed for the supply of provisions. The whole European community was then moved into the Workshops, except some officers who remained with the sepoys.

Entrenchments in front of the gateway were completed and a gun was mounted on the roof of the sheds near the gate whereby the main street of the Town of Roorkee was completely commanded and could if necessary be swept with grape. The bridge over the canal was similarly covered and every road leading to the Station was watched. With the exception of one block in the Thomason College which was destroyed by fire on the first night, no further damage was incurred and it was not long before patrols were being sent out to the surrounding area to guard against marauding gangs who were set on exploiting the unrest. The defences of the Workshops were steadily extended and three old 18-pounders and an 8-inch mortar were mounted in front of the main Guard. Shot and shell were cast for the guns, the walls were loopholed and projecting musket-proof platforms were constructed so that flanking fire could be brought to bear.

Though the attitude of the sappers in Roorkee had been uncertain, the bulk of them remained loyal and they were made responsible for the security of their own barracks. On one occasion a large number fled from their lines and made for open country in the belief that the British were about to attack them, but this was soon righted and the majority returned. Others joined the rebel cause for the sake of excitement and possible plunder rather than disaffection to the State.

By 1st October it was possible for people to resume their normal duties though all defensive arrangements remained in place in case of further disturbances. Europeans retained their weapons and a month's supply of provisions was maintained in the Workshops. Though the Mutiny was not finally quelled until April 1859 there was no further trouble in Roorkee.

In the subsequent siege and capture of Delhi, only about 130 men of the Bengal Sappers took part formed into three small companies, each of about 40 men, supported by about 450 unarmed Pioneers. Of the eighteen Engineer officers involved initially, all were Bengal Sappers. The fortifications were nearly seven miles in circumference with walls 16 feet high and 11 feet wide at the top and a loopholed parapet wall on top of that. The British could attack only a very small part and assembled their forces on the Ridge half a mile away and running northwards for four miles. A worse locality for building defensive works could hardly be found as it was nowhere more than 90 feet high, was bare, rugged and composed of hard rock, but it lay across the route from which reinforcements and supplies could come from the Punjab.

Initially the British were not besieging Delhi: they were themselves besieged on the Ridge. Major Laughton was the Chief Engineer, a highly unpopular officer, who arrived at the front accompanied by a Persian wife whose belongings were carried on some twenty camels and ten carts! Not only was he highly unpopular but he was also incompetent and was removed from his command at the end of June 1857. His errors were soon forgotten though, in the enthusiasm for the abilities of Baird Smith, who had come down from Roorkee and taken over as Chief Engineer. The exploits of Alexander Taylor and other Engineers also excited admiration, shown by their unquenchable spirit in the face of great hardships. They were brave to a man and they had youth on their side: Baird Smith was only 39 when he became Chief Engineer and most of his officers were in their early twenties. They were a remarkable band by any standards: Alex Taylor, a considerable athlete, who could jump a line of twelve mess chairs, placed seat to back; the witty and versatile Wilberforce Greathed, known as the "Insulting Engineer", a corruption of Government Consulting Engineer for Railways; James Tennant, mathematician and astronomer, known as the "Objector-General"; Henry Brownlow, with his caustic humour; Geneste, gallant, idle and capable, the actor and linguist of the Corps; Salkeld and Home, destined to win VCs at the Kashmir Gate; Arthur Lang who, as all agreed, earned many Victoria Crosses but received none. These were just some of the gallant and capable officers who Lord Canning, about to be appointed the first Viceroy and Governor General, spoke of as "accomplished all-round men, every one of them, of clear intellect and cool courage".

At the beginning of July it was estimated that there were 15,000 trained soldiers in Delhi and an even greater number of irregulars, against a Government force of 5,500, which was gradually increased over the next two months until the attack which began on 7th September. The Sappers, assisted by Pioneers, had been working feverishly for several weeks. Stacks of siege materials had been prepared, including 10,000 gabions, 10,000 fascines, scaling ladders by the score and gun platforms by the dozen. The attack centred on the Kashmir Gate where great acts of bravery were performed at its blowing in and where three VCs and eight IOMs were awarded to Bengal Sappers. (The Victoria Cross had been instituted in 1856, though it was awarded retrospectively to 1854). In the following days the force fought itself to a standstill but by then the mutineers were streaming away from Delhi. The Sappers and Pioneers alone had lost over 300 men but the fall of Delhi broke the backbone of the mutiny.

In early 1858 half a British battalion, 1st/60th Rifles, was added to the garrison at Roorkee where it formed part of what became known as the Roorkee Field Force, one of the columns destined to take part in the Rohilkand campaign and which was present at the assault and capture of Bareilly on 6th May 1858. No Bengal Sapper units were involved in the campaign which had as its aim the clearance of rebels from the province of Rohilkund. Edward Thackeray (a Bengal Sapper) took part and was present at the capture of Fort Rooyah where his horse was shot under him. Not wishing to lose his saddle and bridle he followed the attacking party on foot carrying his saddlery on his head.

Edward Thackeray had already made a name for himself the previous year when he had acted with great coolness at Meerut after Captain Fraser had been shot on parade by a mutineer and had prevented many men of his detachment on a working party outside the cantonment from joining the mutineers. He then took part in the siege of Delhi and participated in the recapture of the Magazine where he climbed on the blazing roof, successfully extinguishing the flames, despite the rebels firing and throwing missiles at him at close range. For his great gallantry he received the Victoria Cross. Only twenty, he had been dubbed "My Lord Tall Boot", very correct in his dress.

Bengal Sapper officers were to the fore in all the subsequent engagements, including the relief of Lucknow and the clearing of Oudh. McLeod Innes earned the Victoria Cross at Sultanpur in February 1858. After the capture of Lucknow the army was split into columns, some to operate in Oudh, and the Engineer Brigade was broken up and distributed among them. It was not until 18th June, therefore, that the Bengal Sappers arrived back in Roorkee thirteen months after they had started in boats down the Ganges Canal for Meerut. Apart from the sad episode there they could look back on the whole sorry story of the mutiny with the quiet satisfaction of a difficult task well done. As Lord Canning said, in the rather stilted language of the day, "the record is very honourable to the Corps of Bengal Engineers".

Napier, another Bengal Sapper officer, who was on Outram's staff at Lucknow and was severely wounded yet again during the relief operations, had spent the previous seven years as Civil Engineer to the Board of Administration of the Punjab. During this time he had been responsible for transforming a war-ravaged wilderness into an orderly province by the construction of cantonments, civil offices, roads (including overseeing the extension of the Grand Trunk Road some 278 miles from Lahore to Peshawar), bridges and canals. There is no doubt that the excellent road system he left behind him in the Punjab was a vital factor in bringing the relief armies expeditiously to Delhi in 1857.

POST-MUTINY CHANGES

The Mutiny of 1857 was to lead to dramatic changes. Infantry officers once again became eligible for appointment to the Sappers and Miners and in the late 1860s the establishment of a company, of which there were then ten, was increased to 100 men. The Corps Headquarters was organised on modern lines and an Instructional Staff was provided.

The Bengal Sappers and Miners served the Bengal Presidency, which covered the great plain of Upper India, extending from the mouths of the

Brahmaputra to the borders of Afghanistan, and which was garrisoned by the Bengal Army and administered by the Bengal Civil Service. With its Headquarters at Roorkee, the staff consisted of the Commandant (a Lieutenant Colonel at that time), a Second-in-Command (Captain) who also acted as Adjutant, an Interpreter and Quartermaster, a Superintendent of Instruction, a Superintendent of Park and Field Train, and four 'Doing Duty' Officers who commanded the companies either in Roorkee or on detachment in the Punjab. Apart from the first two, all these officers were Lieutenants, and every officer had to serve at least one year with the Sappers and Miners before they could go into any other Department.

The Public Works Department became a civilian organisation though military officers were to be seconded to work in it right up to World War II. Officers for the Sappers and Miners were now taken from the Royal Engineers, most of whom had received their initial training at the Royal Military Academy at Woolwich. Though officers were liable to be ordered to India, as to any other Station, volunteers were invited to forward their names to the Deputy Adjutant-General, Royal Engineers, Horse Guards (the predecessor to the War Office), by whom a special roster was kept. While the ordinary tour of foreign service was about five years, it was lengthened in this case to seven years due to 'the somewhat special character of engineering' in India. Though in earlier days there were many appointments of a civil nature open to Engineer officers in India – the Lieutenant Governor of the Punjab was an Engineer at that time and another governed as a Commissioner of a large district in the Punjab – the employment of Engineer officers was henceforth restricted to the Public Works Department (Irrigation, Buildings and Roads, and Railways), Survey, Telegraphs and the Sappers and Miners.

The years up to the 2nd Afghan War passed with the headquarters still at Roorkee, though moving occasionally and temporarily to Camps of Exercise at Delhi. The units had varied employment in frontier expeditions, archaeological survey, laying telegraph lines and even wire-guided land-launched 'torpedo' work in Calcutta, but remained under command of the Commandant at Corps Headquarters. Roorkee was described as 'a very pleasant place' when Lieutenant Bindon Blood arrived there in the autumn of 1871. The climate was perfect for several months each winter, while in the hot weather the neighbourhood of the mountains caused storms which gave relief from the heat now and then and kept the rainfall in the monsoon part of the summer at a fair average, thus preventing much of the trying damp heat usual in other places at that season in India.

In 1878 the whole Corps, excluding the Corps Headquarters, went on service with various columns in the 2nd Afghan War. The headquarters followed but, with the 5th Company, returned briefly to Roorkee in June 1879. Only four months later the headquarters was sent back to the frontier and it was not until September 1880 that it returned to Roorkee under the command of Major Bindon Blood, together with four companies. While three companies remained there for the next few years others were employed elsewhere. The unsatisfactory arrangement whereby units remained under command of the Commandment in Roorkee was at last resolved in the early 1880s. Napier, by now Lord Napier, had shown what the Sappers and Miners could do in Abyssinia and when he became C-in-C in India he instituted an enquiry into their organisation and equipment which laid the seeds of future reform. Companies were increased in size, issued with modern equipment and, when on field service, came under the orders of the relevant Commander Royal Engineers (CRE) whilst the Commandant retained authority for what was termed 'interior economy' (manning, recruiting, technical training and so on).

After the Sikh wars increasing numbers of jawans (soldiers) were recruited from the Punjab, both Mussalman and Sikh. Internal campaigns throughout the Indian sub-continent ceased and the emphasis was now on frontier warfare. The Second Afghan War of 1878, for which the Corps had been poorly organised and equipped, led to reforms which lasted to World War I. In general, Sapper and Miner units had little up-to-date equipment and improvisation was the order of the day. Bridging became of increasing importance and the development of the Suspension Bridge, especially by Captain Fenton Aylmer VC (later Lieutenant General Sir Fenton Aylmer VC KCB), was of special importance on the North West Frontier.

There were many curious stories in connection with the Government account-keeping in India and one of them was in connection with the monthly muster parades which were held in every garrison. Every officer, non-commissioned officer and private was seen and counted by a paymaster or other special officer, the object being to prevent the possibility of pay being drawn for dead men or for men otherwise not entitled to it. In the case of absence from the muster, the absent individual had to find someone to certify that he saw the said individual alive on the day of the muster, the fact of the individual's returning alive later on for duty not being considered sufficient proof of his having been alive on that previous day!

Lieutenant Colonel Bindon Blood (later General Sir Bindon Blood and the first Chief Royal Engineer), who had played a major part in pushing through the plans for reorganisation, became Commandant in Roorkee in 1885 and was thus in position to implement them. As far as the Bengal Sappers were concerned the Corps was reorganized into six Service and two Depot Companies with subsequent renumbering of the various companies. While 'B' Depot Company was for training recruits, 'A' Depot Company consisted of two Pontoon Sections, two Telegraph Sections, two Field Printing Sections and a Submarine Mining Section, the last being transferred from the Corps some six years later. Under Bindon Blood and Leach, his successor, the Corps was determined that they should be recognized as engineer troops, rather than infantry with tools, and fieldworks training was carried out throughout the year. 300ft suspension bridges were constructed across the Ganges Canal at Roorkee and trestle bridges built for pilgrims across the Ganges at Hardwar. The elephants, though maintained nominally to pull the Heavy Artillery guns, were often to he seen in the shafts of huge carts laden with engineer stores and equipment. It has to be said though that when the official eye was shut they were still more often found on shikar.

A mounted detachment was raised in 1900 for service in China, but was disbanded on return to Roorkee the following year. In October 1903, the title of the Corps was changed to '1st Sappers and Miners' and on 1st January 1906 HRH The Prince of Wales was appointed Colonel-in-Chief of the Corps and its designation was changed, yet again, to '1st Prince of Wales' Own Sappers and Miners' with permission to wear the Prince of Wales' plume on Colours and Appointments.

The Roorkee Club began an uncertain existence in 1891, moving from bungalow to bungalow and in constant financial straits, but as a Gymkhana Club catering for all amusements it was at last firmly established and became a popular resort despite a rigid ban on 'poodle-faking'! A large bungalow, which used to be the Thomason College Mess, close to the race-course, became the Club House, with a good dancing room generally used as a ladies' room, Whist and Reading Rooms, and two or three suites of bedrooms and bathrooms. Many of the trees in front were removed and the jungle cut down and in their place a broad lawn and rose garden were established. Though the race-course was improved it was rarely used and the Club was sadly closed in May 1939 after a long and somewhat chequered history.

One of the more unusual units was the Experimental Balloon Section which was actually raised in Rawalpindi rather than Roorkee and went on manoeuvres in 1901. The unit attended the Delhi Coronation Durbar the following year and afterwards the balloon Achilles was used to transport troops across a canal. The Section was not altogether a success, though they had some amusing times such as when the cease-fire was ordered on one exercise and the troops were ordered to close on the balloon which could be plainly seen at about 1,000ft. Unfortunately the balloon was being towed along by the wind at a fast pace.....! The Section was disbanded at Roorkee in 1910, due to recent developments in aeroplanes, but some small signal balloons were retained. Three years later the Commandant was told that arrangements had been made with the North-Western Railway at Saharanpur to fill them with gas. Despite pointing out that coal gas is heavier than air, he was told to get on with it and the Warrant Officer sent to watch the inflation of a balloon which could never leave the ground no doubt enjoyed writing a suitable report for transmission to Army Headquarters in Simla.

In 1907 General Viscount Kitchener inspected the Corps on parade, held a Durbar and laid the foundation stone of the Corps Memorial Column, a replica of a Ghazni Tower, on the parade ground at Roorkee, to commemorate the storming of the Kabul Gate at Ghazni in 1839. Construction was completed in 1911 and two years later the tower was crowned with a small dome.

The next Coronation Durbar at Delhi in 1912 necessitated a great deal of preparatory work for Roorkee and particularly for 1st and 6th Companies. In conjunction with 11 Company of the Madras Sappers and the PWD, as well as the Military Works Services, they laid railways, bridged streams and roads, built fire-alarm stations, erected signposts, provided water-supply systems and prepared standing camps for the thousands of troops who attended. Those who were privileged to take part never forgot it: the country for miles to the north of the famous Ridge was covered with tents and illumined after dark with a myriad lights. Even church came within the Sapper orbit and the Corps Workshops made *prie-dieux* for the King, the Queen, the Viceroy and the Vicereine, and stalls for the bishops, clergy and choir. The King's *prie-dieu* was brought back to Roorkee after the Durbar and placed in the Commandant's office, but urgent telegrams soon began to fly and it had to be delivered to the Bishop of Lahore for use in his Cathedral!

Three months after its return to Roorkee from the Delhi Durbar the 1st Company received orders to mobilize for an expedition against the Abors inhabiting the mountainous and densely wooded country around the Upper Brahmaputra between Assam and Tibet. Preparations were begun at once for warfare under novel conditions and among the articles manufactured were hand-grenades and wooden bomb-guns for use against stockades. During training on the Fieldworks Ground a party of sappers was detailed to run up to an imitation stockade and light and throw three grenades, afterwards jumping into a trench for cover. The party ran forward, the fuses were lit, two grenades were thrown over the stockade and most of the men took cover, but one sapper lost his head after lighting his fuse and stood, seemingly paralysed, with the hissing grenade clasped tightly in his hand. The OC, Captain Ingram, turning back from the trench shouted *'Phenko! Phenko!'* (Throw! Throw!) and then jumped at the man to snatch the grenade from him As he did so the grenade exploded and a splinter pierced his heart killing him instantly. The sapper lost his hand and was terribly wounded in the neck.

Life with the Bengal Sappers is pleasant enough especially in one of the staff appointments, as Roorkee is a pleasant little spot and the society agreeable and genial. The life can not be called highly intellectual nor very hard, it perhaps is tinged with the colour of Tennyson's lotus-eaters, always afternoon; but an officer arriving in India cannot, for a year, do better than struggle into acquaintance with Hindustani, and into knowledge of Indian ways.

Extract from the Royal Engineers Journal, 1862.

At this time Officers in India received two kinds of pay, the ordinary military pay of one's rank, and an additional allowance varying with the grade held in the department and called 'Staff Pay'. To an officer fresh from England the scale of pay appeared liberal but the expense of living was so considerable that a Second Lieutenant's pay, even when supplemented by £6 a month, was exceedingly scant as Mess expenses were high; quarters were not provided and house rents were dear; a large number of servants had to be kept and every officer had to keep at least one horse. Nevertheless there was no shortage of volunteers and, despite the lure of becoming a 'lotus eater', life was in fact often hard and the climate difficult. In the case of the non-commissioned ranks there was a current story that on landing in India a British soldier was promptly put under stoppage of pay for the price of his coffin!

Many famous officers spent their formative years with the Bengal Sappers. The first perhaps to be worthy of mention is Colonel Sir Proby

Cautley, even though he was a Gunner, but it was not unusual in those early days of the nineteenth century for officers of other arms to be employed on Public Works and Cautley was a notable engineer in his own right. He not only built the Ganges Canal, which was the largest canal in the world when it opened in 1854, but he was also a distinguished palaeontologist and received the Woolaston Medal of the Geological Society in 1837 and presented huge quantities of fossils to the British Museum.

Another officer to achieve fame was Durand (later Major General Sir Henry Durand). He had sailed for India in 1829, was shipwrecked off the Cape of Good Hope, and came to prominence ten years later at the siege of Ghazni in Afghanistan. The Army had expected to find the fortress undefended, but instead it was fully garrisoned. It was decided that the only method of reducing the fortress was by direct assault after blowing in the Kabul gate, the explosion party being led by Durand when 300lbs of gunpowder was set off. He was a man of blunt speech and strong will who had a chip on his shoulder and made many enemies, but he was a consummate administrator and reached the goal of ambition when he was appointed Lieutenant Governor of the Punjab in 1870, a post second only to the Viceroy.

Colonel Richard Baird Smith joined the Bengal Sappers in 1839 and saw action at the Battles of Aliwal and Chillianwalah, being mentioned in despatches and commended for his gallantry. In 1854 he succeeded Cautley as Director of the Ganges Canal and became Chief Engineer of the army besieging Delhi at the time of the Mutiny. He is often referred to as the saviour of India as Delhi was the focal point of the rebellion and the assault was based largely on his advice. His enthusiasm and energy were infectious and, though attacked by diarrhoea and scurvy and wounded by a shell-splinter, he earnestly pressed his case, keeping up his spirits 'with port and peppermint, cherry brandy and calomel'. Baird Smith earned the thanks of his commanders and the Government for his services, fully justifying his award of the CB. Sadly he picked up an illness at Delhi from which he never fully recovered and having embarked for England he died on board at the early age of 43, being buried at Madras with the full military honours which he had so richly deserved.

Perhaps the most famous of all was Napier, who had cut his teeth in the Punjab and at Lucknow and who went on, after the Mutiny, to take command of the 2nd Division in the campaign in China, where he was promoted to Major General. In 1866 he was appointed C-in-C of the

Bombay Army where he devoted himself to schemes for the welfare of his troops which earned him their undying affection. He became the natural choice to command the expeditionary force to Abyssinia in 1867. This was an 'Engineer' expedition from start to finish, though no Bengal Sapper units were involved, but it was his supreme mastery of logistics that led to the satisfactory conclusion of the campaign. The trials and difficulties of the expedition were well brought out in his farewell address: "You have traversed, often under a tropical sun or amidst storms of rain and sleet, 400 miles of mountainous and difficult country. You have crossed many steep and precipitous ranges of mountains more than 10,000ft in altitude where your supplies could not keep pace with you. You have stormed the almost inaccessible fortress of Magdala. You have released not only the British captives but those of other friendly nations. Magdala has been committed to the flames and remains only a scorched rock. Your gallant exploit will live in history. The Queen and the people of England will appreciate your services."

On his return to England, he received a glorious welcome, was thanked by Parliament and became Lord Napier of Magdala. He was C-in-C India for six years and was able to continue the reforms which he had begun in Bombay. He continued to receive accolades and on returning home, he became Governor of Gibraltar and was made a Field Marshal, only the second Engineer to attain this rank. His statue stands in Waterloo Place in London while another was erected on the Maidan in Calcutta. "If a thing had to be done well there was no one like Napier for being trusted to do it."

Lieutenant General Sir Clarence Bird, who lived to the age of 101, became the Doyen of the Corps and was much admired for both his physical ability and mental alertness in his old age. His handshake never became less than vigorous and he would accompany visitors to their cars to bid them farewell, no matter what the weather. He had begun his long and meritorious career with the Bengal Sappers when he joined 4 Field Company in Chitral in 1909, where he found his company commander with the same name. To distinguish the two Birds, the Pathans nicknamed him '*Chiriya*' which is Pushtu for 'Hawk', a nickname which stayed with him and of which he was very proud. After a distinguished time in France during the First World War, where he was Mentioned in Despatches three times and awarded the DSO, he returned to Roorkee as Adjutant and was best remembered for his unfailing courteousness and tact. In 1939 he became Engineer-in-Chief in India and laid the foundation for the vast wartime expansion of the Indian Engineers. This was followed by his appointment as Master General of Ordnance (India) where he tackled the huge job of obtaining equipment for all the new units of the Indian Army, including Engineers. He retired in 1944, held various senior appointments in civilian life and was a much-loved elder statesman of the Corps until his death in 1986.

The outbreak of World War I found the Corps with a strength of some 1,400 all ranks, a slight increase from some 1,300 at the beginning of the mutiny in 1857. It was to have a larger strength at the start of World War II but, after the experiences of the first global conflict, it was realised (perhaps slowly) that modern warfare needed modern equipment, though the Sapper and Miner always remained a master of improvisation. In World War I Bengal Sappers served in France and Belgium, Iraq, Palestine and Aden, as well as the North West Frontier and Afghanistan, and reached a strength of some 8,400. In World War II they were to serve in North and East Africa, Italy and Greece, Syria, Iraq and Iran, Burma and Malaya as well as most parts of South East Asia and reached a strength of nearly 24,000 men. Few then foresaw that a much greater expansion lay not many years ahead.

The Formative Years ended with the outbreak of World War I when the Bengal Sappers could be said to have come of age.

WORLD WAR I

Prior to the start of World War I, the total number of British Officers in the Corps was twenty-three and this included two in the Defence Light Sections permanently stationed at the ports of Karachi and Calcutta. The Headquarters was composed of the Commandant (a Major or Lieutenant Colonel), Superintendent of Park (the Workshops), Superintendent of Instruction (Chief Instructor Fieldworks in today's parlance), and an Adjutant, plus a Regimental Medical Officer from the Indian Medical Service. There was no separate appointment of Quartermaster, the duties being carried out by one of the subalterns in 'B' (Depot) Company. The personnel of the Mounted Detachment, the Printing and Photo-Litho Sections and Bridge Train were, in peace time, all merged in the Depot Company for such things as pay and discipline. The Band was also in 'B' Company. There were only six Field Companies, four of them at Roorkee, one at Peshawar and one at Rawalpindi. The total strength of the Corps was 1,491 All Ranks.

At the beginning of the war the Bengal Sappers, under Lieutenant Colonel P G Twining, had only six Field Companies, a Field Troop (Mounted Detachment), a Pontoon Park and a Depot Company. Yet, by the end of the war, it included twenty one Field Companies and reached a strength of over 8,000 men. India was surprised by the outbreak of war and there were only four officers in Roorkee on 4th August 1914, yet within a few weeks of the declaration of war 3 and 4 Field Companies had set off for France. In January 1915 a small Bridging Train left Roorkee for Iraq, but no wagons or draught animals were sent with it, so the equipment could only be moved by river. Numerous other units left Roorkee during the next three years and though their activities are recorded elsewhere there is little information as to what life in Roorkee itself was like during the war years.

On the outbreak of the War on 4th August, 1914, it being the leave season, there were eleven British Officers on leave in UK, or on their way there, besides several on local leave, including the Commandant, in Kashmir. With only four officers present in Roorkee the work of mobilizing all units was somewhat strenuous, especially as the period coincided with the issue of new rifles and a new accounting system for pay and accounts. At the beginning of the War one of the great difficulties was the need for British Officers. This was met by sending officers of the 'Indian Army Reserve of Officers' to the Corps for duty, thus reverting to a very old practice of pre-Mutiny days, when officers doing duty with Sapper and Miner Corps were not invariably RE Officers. The first to arrive was called up on 4th August, having belonged to the Reserve since 1908. Before his arrival nobody in Roorkee had even heard of the IARO!

THE WESTERN FRONT

Numbers 3 and 4 Companies were quickly mobilised and set off for France as part of the Meerut Division on 1st September. Their port of embarkation was to be Karachi and their first task was to assist the Royal Indian Marine to adapt the ships to troop transports for taking soldiers, animals and weapons. Having boarded their troopships on 13th September, they remained on board, in harbour, until the 20th when the convoy was at last

ordered to sail, the delay being caused by the presence of the German light cruiser *Emden* off the west coast of India. Though crowded, they were better off than their fellow sappers in 20 and 21 Companies of the Bombay Group who had embarked nearly a month earlier on the SS *Taiyebeh*, which had been declared unfit to take pilgrims to Mecca and was about to be broken up when mobilization was ordered and only the acute shortage of shipping gained it a reprieve.

The arrival in France of the first Indian troops intrigued the inhabitants. It became clear that what at first glance seemed to be Zouaves or Moroccans or perhaps Berbers from the high Atlas mountains, were certainly not French speaking people and their European officers spoke to their men in languages that the good citizens of Orleans, Rouen and St Omer had not previously encountered. Eventually the whisper went round that they were 'Les Hindoues' from the British Empire in the East. Souvenir hunters soon gathered at every halt, anxious to swap wine for cap badges, fruit for buttons or baguettes for chapattis. Though highly trained, they were equipped for frontier operations and in no sense prepared for a war in Europe. Their equipment was woefully inadequate. They had no regimental mechanical transport, no mortars or hand grenades. The reserve organisation was unsuitable and unsound, and their first reserves were exhausted before the units reached the front. Though suitable for winter in India, their clothing was totally inadequate for the rain, wind, sleet and eventual snow of the French winter and proper warm clothing did not become available until December.

The Meerut Division arrived at Marseilles on 12th October, was in Orleans some ten days later and had taken over a portion of the line by the end of the month. Though they had no time to adjust to the conditions on the Western Front, they were fresh, up to strength and keen to get going. They were soon heavily involved in the fighting around Neuve Chapelle and on the night 11th/12th November part of the 3rd Company under Lieutenant Douie was ordered to blow up some houses standing between our lines and those of the Germans, which were less than 300 yards apart. The enemy was driven off and six houses were demolished before dawn. One remained, however, so Douie led a party of four men to it in daylight and was preparing to lay the charges when the enemy opened a murderous fire. All the party were hit, two being killed outright. Douie, severely wounded, managed to crawl back to our trenches, though hit again on the way. Then, under a hail of bullets, Jemadar Ram Rup Singh headed a rescue party and brought in the remaining dead and wounded.

Douie never recovered fully from the effects of his wounds yet he was back in the line a few months later and at Festubert, on 22nd May 1915, he and his orderly, Sapper Jiwa Singh, went out in broad daylight and rescued a wounded man under heavy fire. He was recommended for the Victoria Cross, but was awarded the DSO and Jiwa Singh received the Indian Order of Merit.

One of the greatest shortages was the complete lack of trench mortars but, being great improvisers, home-made mortars soon made their appearance. The first ones were made from lengths of cast-iron piping and used black powder to fire a shell a few hundred yards. They were highly inaccurate and tended to blow up after a few discharges, causing more damage to their own side than to the Germans, but eventually Major Patterson of the Royal Field Artillery, attached to the Indian Corps, came up with his own design which he had manufactured by No 3 Company. Known as 'Patterson's Pills for Portly Prussians', the mortar shells were made from cut-down 18-pounder shell cases filled with three and a half pounds of explosive packed round with stones, horse shoe nails and anything else that came to hand. The first two prototype dischargers were tubes made of wood and cast-iron respectively, later versions being made from steel piping. The propellant was black powder which also ignited the shell fuse, the length of which was calculated to explode the shell when it landed in the enemy trench. The first live trial was held on 19th November 1914 with Lieutenant Robson of No 3 Company as the chief gunner. Robson had only joined the Company the day before and was presumably given the task on the old Army principle of giving particularly risky jobs to the latest joined subaltern on the grounds that he was unlikely to realise the danger and would not argue anyway. Robson fired 20 rounds and to the delight of the watching sepoys two exploded in the German line. The Sappers and Miners now went into full production and soon battalions of the Indian Corps were able to make some reply to the enemy.

Similar improvisation was called for in the case of grenades, of which the Allies had none at this early stage of the war. The first home-made grenades consisted of empty tins filled with shredded guncotton and nails or rivet punchings, with a fuse inserted in the top. With a tendency to go off as soon as the fuse was lit, a certain lack of enthusiasm was shown by those in their immediate vicinity, but improvements were made and catapults made of strong elastic were used to send these 'jam-pot' bombs anything up to 300 yards, or so it was claimed. An adaptation of the clay-pigeon trap was also used with some success. Another improvisation was the 'hair-brush' grenade, a slab of guncotton attached by wires to a flat piece of wood of hair-brush shape which afforded a convenient handle for throwing. As in the jam-pot variety, the fuse was ignited by match, cigarette or pipe, both patterns being very unreliable in action. At a demonstration of the hair-brush grenade before some forty Generals and their staffs, only the stick went forward and the charge dropped to the ground. Some spectators fled, others crouched low, but no explosion took place. After an interval a search was made and the charge was eventually found beneath one of the Generals. Soon after this Captain B C Battye, a Bombay Sapper and a member of the famous Indian Army family, invented a better grenade which was made in the ironworks in Bethune and consisted of a small cast-iron cylinder, four inches long and two inches in diameter, closed at one end and with serrations on the outside to facilitate the break up of the case when the bomb exploded. The Battye bomb was considerably more reliable than the jam pot and soon superseded it.

Searchlights, widely used by the Germans in defence, were improvised by the Sappers and Miners from motor car headlights which were connected up to an electricity supply from the rear. They were nothing like as effective as the German purpose-built version but were better than nothing. Another task for the Sappers was the manufacture of periscopes for use in the front-line trenches.

In mid-November a detachment of No 3 Company, under Captain Kelly and Lieutenant Wheeler, joined 6th Jats in a raid on two saps which the Germans were digging towards our lines. This trench raid achieved complete surprise. The Jats worked their way down the trenches and the sappers destroyed the two saps, a Jemadar and Havildar subsequently being awarded the IDSM. Eight nights later, after some British and Indian Battalions had retired before a powerful attack, Kelly was sent to ascertain whether a certain trench was occupied by the enemy. Most of it proved to be still held thinly by Indian troops but towards the far end the dead alone were in possession. Picking his way between the corpses, alone and in pitch darkness, Kelly came to a traverse beyond which he heard whispering but was unable to distinguish the language spoken. As he listened a bomb exploded at his feet and he fell severely wounded in the face, neck, shoulder and hand, but rolling over he crawled back and lying on his side directed the attack till he collapsed. Such lonely reconnaissances require the utmost courage. Darkness, uncertainty and suspense add to the terror of the situation, and the stimulus of companionship in danger is lacking. This support of the infantry was to become commonplace with the Sappers helping to destroy enemy saps or digging them out towards the enemy trenches themselves. In a similar operation in March 1915 at the battle for Neuve Chapelle, a party of Sappers were giving fire and bombing support to the Garwhalis and Lieutenant Percy Hobart, who had been Adjutant in Roorkee on the outbreak of war and was to become Major General Sir Percy Hobart in World War II, was awarded the Military Cross.

The support in the trenches developed into operations below ground and the first tunnel was dug by Sappers from the trenches opposite Festubert, the target being a German sap which ran towards the Indian lines. Finding a relatively dry trench from which to drive their tunnel, they dug a vertical mine-shaft from where they began to burrow towards the enemy position. Later in the war tunnelling would become a highly technical operation with specialist tunnellers, but at this stage all they could do was dig towards the enemy keeping direction with a compass, measuring by string and shoring the tunnel as they went. At last the miners arrived at a point which they calculated was directly beneath the German sap and they began to ferry down explosives. The charges had been placed in position but the fuse had not been connected when an enemy mortar bomb landed at the entrance of the mine shaft, collapsing part of the tunnel, killing some men and burying others. The NCO in charge, Havildar Sucha Singh, withdrew his men until the shelling ceased and then entered the mine-shaft himself. Pulling out the dead and wounded he forced his way past the collapsed portion of the tunnel, reached the charge and set the fuse, despite the shelling which had started again. He then returned to our own lines and detonated the mine. Havildar Sucha Singh was awarded the IDSM for his coolness in what was a highly dangerous and claustrophobic operation. It takes little imagination to picture the courage needed to move alone, in the dark, 30 feet below the ground, along a tunnel three feet high and partially collapsed, with the threat of the remaining roof collapsing at any time and with no possibility of rescue if it did.

Just before Christmas, the 2/39th Garwhalis noticed that the water level in their trenches was rising rapidly and, despite damming the worst part and digging drainage ditches, the water continued to rise inexorably. Lieutenant Robson from No 3 Company came forward and after a close inspection of the ground realised that the Germans were pumping water from their own positions some 300 yards away. Going forward to try and pinpoint the exact position of the enemy pump, Robson was shot and killed. Though he had only been on the Western Front little more than a month, he was well known for his constant presence round the forward positions, not to mention his introduction of the home-made mortar, and his death was keenly felt by all units.

A curious incident occurred in early March. One night Major Sanders, a Bengal Sapper serving with the Bombay Group, and Captain (later Lieutenant General Sir Francis) Nosworthy found a desperately wounded German close to the enemy's wire and decided to bring him in. Sanders tried repeatedly to hoist him onto Nosworthy's back, but at each attempt the German shouted something which they did not understand and fire was opened on them by the enemy. Nevertheless, they succeeded eventually in carrying the man back to our lines. A fortnight later they were summoned to Brigade Headquarters where they were confronted by a civilian of the Geneva Convention who had been sent to enquire into an alleged "atrocity" vouched for by many Germans. It was asserted that a wounded German had been crucified at a certain spot and on a certain night by two Indians and, as Sanders and Nosworthy were implicated, they were required to give evidence on oath. It then appeared that the delirious German had shouted repeatedly to his comrades that he was being crucified. Both officers, of course, were completely exonerated; but after a full account of the incident appeared in The Times they decided that they would never allow themselves to fall alive into the enemy's hands. It is sad to relate that Sanders died of wounds nearly three years later while serving as a Lieutenant Colonel on the Staff.

After the heavy losses at Neuve Chapelle in March 1915 the possibility of moving the Indian Corps from the Western Front had been mooted. It was not because they could not cope with the requirements of modern war – far from it – but simply because their strength continued to dwindle. The reinforcement system did not work satisfactorily and the wider involvement of the Indian Army in other Theatres made it increasingly difficult to sustain those units in France. It was felt that the Indian Corps could now be spared from the Western Front and redeployed to Mesopotamia where they could more easily be supported from home and adapt to the climatic conditions and the nature of the terrain more easily than British troops. In August a formal request was made to transfer the Corps but, before this was put into effect, the Sapper Companies were heavily involved in preparations for an offensive near Loos. They built observation towers, buried telephone cables, arranged water supplies and drove mine galleries. Both 3rd and 4th Companies were engaged in the subsequent battle and afterwards excelled themselves when 140 men erected 2,800 yards of wire in a single night although the German trenches were in one place only 50 yards from our front line. In early November the Indian Corps began to be relieved and by 10th November the last unit had left the Front. As it happened the Indian Corps exchanged a bad situation for another far worse.

MESOPOTAMIA

Political expediency and the need to safeguard British oil supplies at the head of the Persian Gulf brought about the campaign in Iraq. Dashing leadership, fine troops and poor opposition in the early stages accounted for the initial successes. Rashness, bad management and lack of men and

material led to the subsequent disasters. War was not declared here until November 1914 and the victories of 1915, under an optimistic commander, gave place in 1916 to reverse after reverse. Plans were changed constantly and responsibility was shifted from shoulder to shoulder. When the Imperial General Staff at last assumed control from the Government of India, it was powerless to save much from the wreckage of the politically-inspired and Treasury-ridden operations launched by that Government. Soldiering in this theatre of war was hard and exhausting. Not for nothing was there an old Arab saying: "*When Allah made Hell he found it was not bad enough, so he made Iraq, and added flies.*"

The first Bengal Sapper unit in Iraq was a small Bridging Train of only 22 men under Jemadar Sadar Din and they reached Qurna, 40 miles north of Basra at the junction of the Tigris and the Euphrates, in the middle of February 1915. They were equipped with eighteen pontoons and a large complement of stores, but they had no transport and the equipment could only be moved by river. Enormous expansion was needed and continual improvisation. The country was scoured for anything suitable for bridging and equipment was manufactured on the spot. The unit earned much unpopularity because of its rapacious demands on all material arriving from Basra but, nevertheless, acquitted itself with credit under the greatest difficulties.

Major General Townshend, commanding the 6th Division, gave priority to bridging as his strategy was based largely on his ability to transfer troops rapidly across the river Tigris. The Turkish enemy attempted to destroy the bridges with floating mines, but these were defeated by a novel type of boom thrown across the river by the Bridging Train under Captain E W C Sandes who had arrived from Roorkee in April to take over command and who, in later years, was to write the history of the Indian Sappers and Miners. By the end of September our forces had reached Kut al Amara and pursued the retreating Turks 60 miles upstream, closely followed by the Bridging Train. Lieutenant General Sir John Nixon, who had taken over supreme command, wanted to press on still further to Baghdad and, though Kitchener and the General Staff in London initially advised against it, the Cabinet eventually gave way and the die was cast. At the same time they ordered the despatch of the 3rd and 7th Indian Divisions from France.

Lured by the prospect of capturing Baghdad, the small Indian Expeditionary Force advanced up the Tigris as far as Ctesiphon, some 40 miles south of Baghdad, the limit of its advance, where it encountered powerful Turkish reinforcements and was forced to withdraw after suffering severe casualties. Then began the long retreat to Kut, a nightmare of forced marches by land and confusion and sniping on the river. The Bridging Train was given up for lost but, by a miracle, it reached Kut, chased by Arab cavalry and losing the last of its pontoons, but it had proved its worth by constantly providing bridges and rafts, often at short notice. The men were exhausted. After numerous adventures in Kut and with its equipment destroyed, their exploits came to an untimely end, but it had bridged the Tigris no less than 17 times and had never failed the division it was supporting in its victorious advance and subsequent strategic retreat.

Another small unit of Bengal Sappers in Iraq at this time was a "Wreck Party", formed from the Calcutta Defence Light Section, which raised or demolished sunken ships in remote stretches of the Tigris, cleared the river of floating mines and assisted in electrical work.

3rd and 4th Companies did not reach Iraq from France until January 1916 and were sent initially to the Euphrates where they were employed on bridging and road construction, a decision that was difficult to understand in view of the complete lack of engineer units on the Tigris front at that time. However, after a few weeks 3rd Company was sent forward on the Tigris front and was involved in the abortive attempts to relieve Kut, which finally surrendered on 29th April with the loss of nearly 40,000 soldiers in and below the town.

Major General Sir Fenton Aylmer, who had won the Victoria Cross with 4 Field Company in the Hunza Nagar campaign of 1891 and was Adjutant General in India from 1912, had been appointed to lead the operations to relieve the beleaguered garrison. With inadequate resources and unaware that the garrison could have held out much longer, he failed in his hurried attempts to relieve them. He bore his disappointment with characteristic stoicism and it in no way affected the performance of his duties during the rest of his active career. He returned to India to command the Mhow Divisional area and retired in 1918, having attained the rank of Lieutenant General. Aylmer was endowed with a strong sense of duty and expected the same in others, but he was tolerant of ordinary human failings and endeared himself to his troops, as well as to his junior officers, as a fearless and intrepid leader.

At the end of March 1916 what became known as the 2nd Mobile Bridging Train was formed with 80 reinforcements from Roorkee. By the time the Train was fully formed it occupied two miles of road on the march and was independent of river transport. It could provide 500 yards of medium bridge and was used against the enemy's right flank and rear, helping eventually to open the way to Baghdad the following year. Another reinforcement was 1st Company, which had been stationed in Peshawar at the start of the war, was mobilized for overseas service in June 1916 and arrived on the Tigris front in August where it was joined at last by 4th Company which had been languishing on the Euphrates front since its arrival from France. By the end of 1916 the Expeditionary Force was well supplied with engineer units for the first time since the conflict had begun.

General Sir Stanley Maude, who took over the Tigris Corps in July 1916 (and supreme command the following month), was opposed by the Turkish 13th and 18th Corps under Halil Pasha. He was under pressure to advance up the Tigris but was determined to operate slowly and methodically, being only too well aware of the failure of his predecessors. He had also been instructed to avoid heavy casualties. His first objective was to clear the Turkish forces from their positions around Kut and thus give his own forces the freedom of manoeuvre necessary for defeating the enemy and advancing further. Having cleared the right bank, General Maude was determined to cross to the left bank in the vicinity of Kut, thus severing the Turkish communications and enabling his supply ships, currently unable to steam past the Turkish positions far downstream, to move upstream. On 5th February 1917 he summoned Captain Witts, commanding No 2 (Mobile) Bridging Train, to a private interview and ordered him to carry out a reconnaissance for a crossing at Kut itself. He was sworn to absolute secrecy and was instructed to make his reports in private letters addressed to Maude by name. Even Brigadier Beach, himself a Sapper, who was head of the Intelligence Branch was told nothing! "Paddling about in a boat for two or three nights with the Turks on one bank and our troops on the other was no joke," wrote Witts subsequently, "and though the river was 400 to 600 yards wide, I was not sorry when I was in a position to report the scheme impracticable."

The Tigris was eventually bridged later in the month further upstream in a carefully planned and boldly executed operation, but no Bengal Sapper units were involved, apart from the Bridging Train. Meanwhile 1st, 3rd and 4th Companies were with the 7th Division of 1st Corps supporting their advance up the river bank, while the Turkish forces withdrew to their main positions covering Baghdad. Finally, on 11th March

1917, Baghdad was occupied at last and the defeats of 1915 and 1916 were avenged.

The military situation demanded that General Maude should now strike in several directions: westward to the Euphrates, northward up both banks of the Tigris, and north-eastwards towards Khaniqin to cooperate with the Russians advancing into Iran from the Caucasus. The Bengal Sapper units moved north in support of the 7th Division and for the next few months prepared positions, bridged rivers, laid out camps, made roads, arranged water supplies and fought floods, but they rarely came under fire because it was at last recognised that to employ technical troops in the front line, except in an emergency, was the height of folly.

Towards the end of 1917 administrative considerations in Iraq and the need for reinforcements in Palestine, restricted offensive action. Allenby required replacements for British troops sent to France and consequently the 7th Indian Division was ordered to Palestine and with it went 1st, 3rd and 4th Companies. These units sailed from Basra on 4th January 1918 to earn fresh laurels in the advance to Damascus and beyond. Bengal Sapper units remaining behind in Iraq included the 2nd and 8th Companies, which had arrived from Roorkee in November 1917, and the 5th Company which arrived from Aden the following month. In addition, 5th Field Troop was raised in Baghdad. The Spring and Summer of 1918 saw little fighting but much activity. The enemy was in no shape to attack and our forces were ordered to pursue an 'active defence' as further troops were to be transferred to Palestine. 2nd Company built an elaborate suspension bridge to replace a pile bridge which had been swept away in a flood over the river Adhaim, and also did river-training work, using huge brushwood 'sausages' for the purpose, as well as improving many tracks. 8th Company carried out extensive demolitions as a reprisal after the capture of Najaf and used nearly two tons of guncotton for the purpose.

At the end of the hot weather further Sapper reinforcements started to arrive from India. The 6th and 52nd Companies left Roorkee on 12th September followed by the 54th later in the month. Though they arrived too late to see any actual fighting, as the Turks laid down their arms and signed an armistice on 30th October 1918, 6th Company and detachments of the 2nd and 8th were engaged in road-making and bridging, while the 5th Field Troop maintained a flying ferry across the Tigris. The 8th Company was stationed in Mosul after the Armistice.

54 Company, though, was involved in supporting a column marching from Bushire on the Persian Gulf into Iran in October with the aim of

suppressing the activities of anti-British tribesmen; this operation continued after the surrender of the Turkish forces. The only other Bengal Sapper unit involved was the 6th Field Troop which joined the Baluchistan Field Force in October 1918 operating in eastern Iran, but there was an ex-Bengal Sapper, Brig Dickson, responsible for maintaining the line of communication with India. During his time in command he had many curious experiences including an invitation from a new provincial Governor who, wishing to earn popularity, had invited all the prominent residents and many influential visitors to witness the public execution of four robbers. Tea was served to the guests while one robber was shot, another hanged, a third hurled from a cliff onto spikes and the last killed by having his throat cut. In the intervals between the items of entertainment a band played suitable selections.

EGYPT AND PALESTINE

In August 1914 the situation in Egypt was intricate and dangerous, for the British occupation was based only on an unwritten convention. Nominally Egypt was still a part of the Turkish Empire, though the Turks had little influence on her policy, yet her importance in a world war was immeasurable because of the Suez Canal; indeed the value of the Canal as a means of expediting the concentration of the scattered resources of the British Empire during the first year of the war needs no emphasis, and its protection was an important factor in British strategy. The peace-time British garrison in Egypt was insufficient to guard it and it was obvious that, should Turkey join forces with Germany, the situation might become critical.

When war broke out the intention was to allow the enemy to attempt the passage across the Sinai and strike him only when he reached the Canal. As for the Germans, they imagined that the mere appearance of a Turkish force on the Suez Canal would be the signal for a wholesale rising in Egypt, but events were to prove them wrong. In September 1914 the 3rd (Lahore) and 7th (Meerut) Divisions, the latter including the 3rd and 4th Companies, spent a few days in Egypt on their way to France with the aim of showing the flag and impressing the local population. The only Sapper and Miner unit involved in the early years was the 10th Company from the Madras Sappers and it was not until the fall of Jerusalem in December 1917 that the stage was set for the entry in strength of the Sappers and Miners into the war in Egypt and Palestine. The 7th Division, including 1st, 3rd and 4th Companies, led the stream of reinforcements from Iraq and reached Suez in January 1918. The Bengal Sappers were busily employed from the moment they reached the front, north of Jerusalem, as our forces were weak on the ground, so many British units having been sent to France to counter the German offensives there. Their main tasks, apart from consolidating our defensive positions, were draining marshes, digging wells and building roads. In the preparations for further advance and in order to deceive the enemy, dummy camps were set up in the Jordan area, fifteen thousand dummy horses made of canvas filled the empty horse-

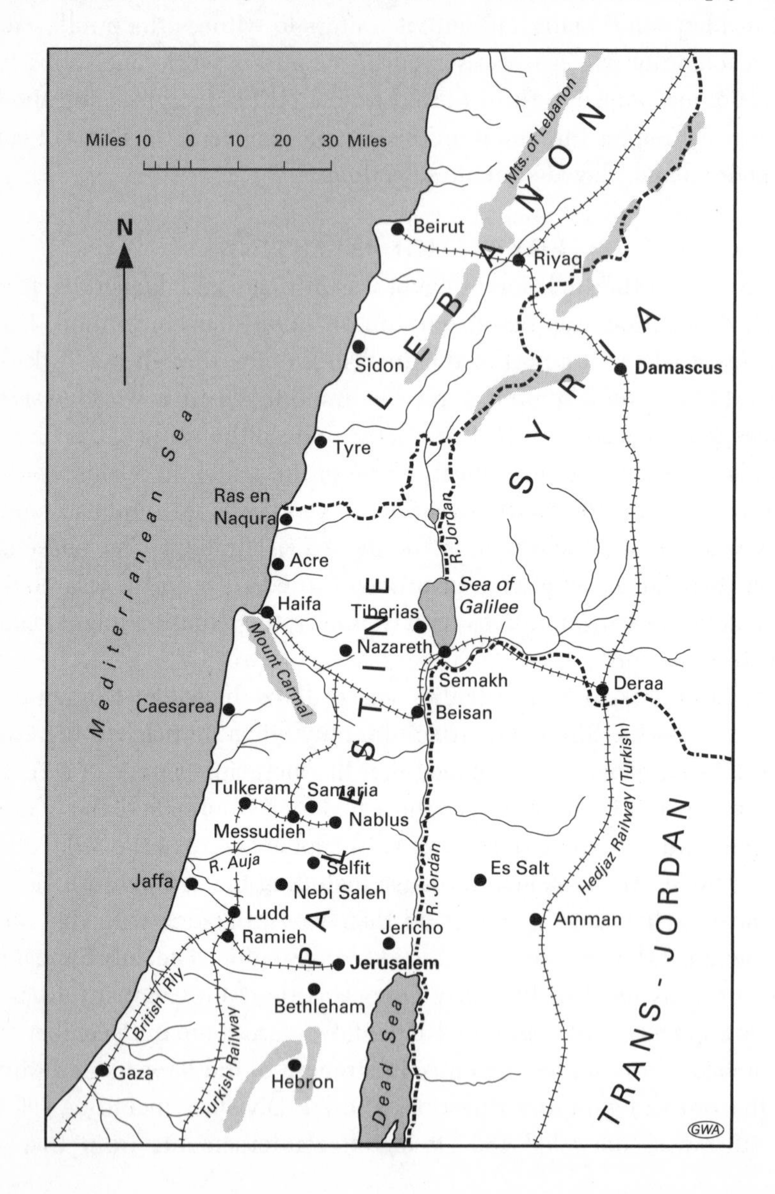

lines and sleighs drawn by mules raised clouds of dust when the horses should have been going to water. Battalions marched ostentatiously down to the Jordan by day and returned, unobserved, in lorries by night.

A tragedy occurred in the camp of 1st Company on 11th July when the Company Commander, Captain Gray, was murdered by one of his own men. A Sikh Sapper, who was in the guard tent awaiting trial by court-martial, managed to escape after dark with a loaded rifle and shot Gray, who was the soul of good nature and full of energy, in the back as he was sitting in his tent reading a letter. The murderer then shot at the Company Subadar and finally committed suicide.

Preparations continued quietly near the coast, north of Jaffa. Tube wells were sunk, existing wells improved and pumping plants installed in dug-outs, until twelve large water-supply installations were ready for watering eight divisions. As the construction of numerous bridges over the river Auja might attract unwelcome attention, a 'School of Pontooning' was established on the river banks several weeks before the attack to lull the enemy into a false sense of security. By the middle of September General Allenby was ready. On 19th September an irresistible assault was made on a seven-mile front by five divisions, followed up by three cavalry divisions, and a huge rent was torn in the Turkish defences near the coast. The task of the engineer units was to prepare two wide tracks through the enemy's positions for the advance of the cavalry, artillery and transport; and so rapidly was the work carried out that, two hours after the assault, the leading cavalry division was able to pass through on its long ride into Syria.

The advance soon developed into a pursuit. The 7th Division advanced from Acre on 2nd October along the coast road to capture the valuable port of Beirut, while the cavalry divisions were making spectacular advances inland capturing Damascus on 30th September. Speed was essential and the 3rd and 4th Companies were well to the fore to begin any necessary work on the road as soon as possible. Within twelve miles of Acre the road bent towards the coast and skirted a promontory called the Ras en Naqura for a distance of seven miles. It was a rocky track, only six feet wide, with several gradients of one in five and the last mile lay along the face of an almost vertical cliff. This stretch was known as the 'Ladder of Tyre', for here the track took the form of a series of great steps cut in the solid rock and partly covered by debris. General Bulfin, the Corps Commander, came forward to examine this formidable obstacle and was told that extensive blasting would be needed to make the Ladder fit for wheeled traffic and that, in the process, there was every possibility that the whole shelf might slip into the sea. There was no other route for many miles inland and if the Ladder were destroyed the progress of 7th Division, and perhaps of the whole Corps, would be blocked. Bulfin demanded 'time for a couple of cigarettes' and then ordered the attempt to be made. It was completely successful. The Ladder was demolished to ease the gradient and widen the road and within three days the entire length of seven miles around the headland was fit for wheeled traffic, including 60pr guns.

On 31st October an Armistice was granted and Allenby's remarkable campaign was over. In twelve days he had routed the enemy and four weeks later had occupied the whole of Syria. His pursuit of the beaten Turks was one of the most relentless in history. The 3rd and 4th Companies had fought in all the battles of the 7th Division in three theatres of war and by the time they returned to Roorkee in 1920 they had been away for more than five years.

ADEN

Aden has had many masters, but was seized by Britain in the nineteenth century and after the opening of the Suez Canal in 1869 it became the Gibraltar of the East and a coaling station and port of prime importance. It does not have an equable climate: if it is warm in Suez, it is hot in Aden, and if hot in Suez, unbearable in Aden, so much so that a Persian poet once described it as "*giving to the panting sinner a lively anticipation of his future destiny*."

The entry of Turkey into the war on 14th November 1914 brought her into immediate contact with the British land frontier at the southern end of the Red Sea. A Turkish Corps was stationed in the Yemen and constituted a direct threat to the small and isolated garrison of not much more than two battalions in Aden. Though there was a Bombay Sapper Company, there was no field or mountain artillery and in this respect it resembled the Sudan Defence Force which had only one gun and that a saluting gun! As the British Protectorate covered the territories of the Aden hinterland and as the coast of Arabia from Perim to Muscat was considered to be within the British sphere of influence, it is evident that the situation in Aden was precarious. However, the 29th Indian Brigade was landed on 10th November, while on its way to Egypt, and having pushed the Turks inland, left one battalion as a reinforcement at Perim, about 100 miles west of Aden, which secured the garrison a short respite.

There were no further hostilities during the early part of 1915 but in August the Turks pushed forward capturing Lahej, only twenty miles away, and pushing on beyond Sheikh Othman to the very gates of Aden. Reinforcements came in the nick of time, including 5th Company from Roorkee, and one of their first tasks was to carry out defence works at Maala, where the line passed through the Golf Links but tactfully avoided the Polo Ground. From September onwards the situation at Aden underwent little substantial change. Minor operations in this area could not directly affect the course of the war, so it was laid down that an 'active defence' was to be maintained and no general offensive was to be undertaken. This situation lasted for the next three years, though sharp fighting

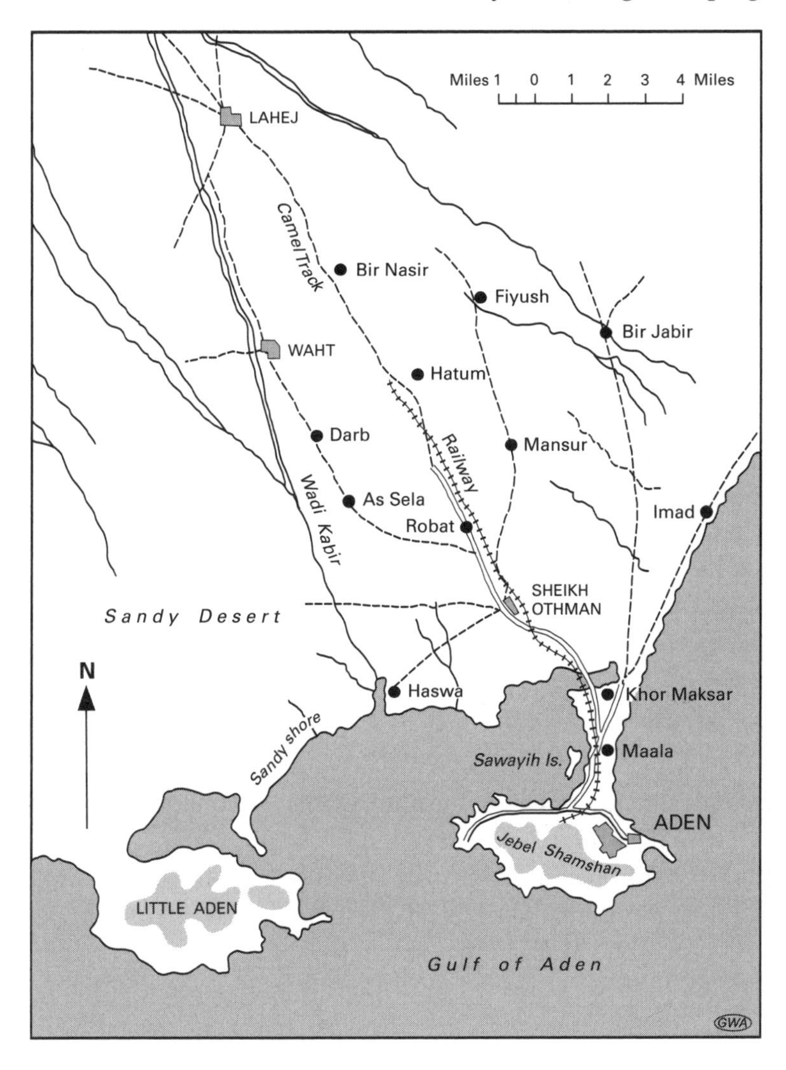

took place in the area of Waht, the 5th Company soon receiving their baptism of fire. On 25th September they set out with a column including the 4th Buffs and some Indian infantry who plodded through the sand until midday when the Buffs were immobilized by the appalling heat and lack of water. The desert heat haze had reduced visibility to 200 yards and, because of the lack of telephones and wireless sets, the units were completely out of touch with their headquarters. The British gunners began to collapse from heat-stroke. "In the early afternoon," wrote Captain Le Breton, commanding the 5th Company, "a message reached us ordering the guns to withdraw and the Sappers to remain in position to cover the retirement of the infantry. Without the Gunners the Company seemed as isolated as though on a raft in a fog in mid-ocean. The sand was so hot that it was impossible to sit or lie on it for more than a few minutes and the temperature in the hospital *tonga* was 136° Fahrenheit. The firing died down, but we could not know whether the rest of the Brigade had retired unseen by us. We held our positions until about 4pm when the haze lifted and we saw some exhausted Punjabi infantry carrying or supporting to the rear a number of the Buffs who had collapsed from the incredible heat. We continued to cover the retirement until our own positions were reached at dusk." The results of this reconnaissance in force were unsatisfactory; many of the men were incapacitated and the operation proved only that there are climatic conditions under which the range of action of even the best troops is strictly limited.

After this unfortunate venture, the normal routine of patrolling, strengthening the defences and improving living conditions was resumed. Lieutenant Salberg of the 5th Company suggested that bricks might be made from sand mixed with mule and camel droppings and straw. An experiment having proved successful, all units asked for Sapper instructors and started their own brickworks, and buildings of every sort sprang up from a mosque to an observation tower. The Sappers also repaired a number of old, wind-driven irrigation pumps found in the local date-gardens and thus secured sufficient water to enable all units to grow some wholesome, though unpleasant tasting, plants. A 'Water Column' was also formed, with help from the infantry, but the health of the garrison suffered and the frequent relief of the British units became necessary.

Early in 1916 information was received that the Turks were despatching troops to coerce the Arabs in the eastern part of the Aden Protectorate and a Mobile Column was directed to demonstrate in support of the friendly tribes. 5th Company was with the advanced guard but several hours later news arrived that the Turks were coming out in force and by that evening the column began to withdraw. In the interval the Sappers played their part as infantry but casualties were light as the enemy's rifle fire was aimed too high and his artillery shells were smothered in the soft sand. The brass fuses from his shrapnel did some damage though and one of these ricochetted with such force from the water-bottle of a Sapper that it killed a camel. There were no casualties among the Sapper officers and this small affair was typical of many excursions undertaken into the desert in pursuance of the policy of active defence, with 5th Company usually to the fore. In another of these small operations the Company was ordered to destroy a Muhammadan tomb from which enemy snipers were firing on our cavalry patrols. Ordered to undertake this in daylight, the Sapper party was saved from annihilation by a fortuitous sand-storm and were able to complete the task and withdraw before the Turkish guns opened fire.

In November 1917 the newly-raised 51st Company arrived from Roorkee to relieve the 5th Company which sailed for Iraq in December to earn fresh laurels in a wider sphere. They welcomed the change of scene and their sentiments were expressed with remarkable aptitude in the opening verses of a poem by one of their officers which was published anonymously in *The Times*:

> The hot red rocks of Aden
> Stand from their burnished sea;
> The bitter sands of Aden
> Lie shimmering in their lee.
>
> We have no joy of battle,
> No honour here is won;
> Our little fights are nameless
> With Turk and sand and sun.

The 51st Company did not have to wait long for its baptism of fire when they took part in an attack on Bir Jabir. The defences were occupied after sharp fighting and a fortified house was demolished with gun-cotton before the force withdrew to Sheikh Othman. Captain Fane was awarded a Military Cross for his gallantry in this operation. Hardly a day passed without a skirmish of some sort and on 5th January 1918 they were concerned in an enterprise against Hatum which led to some heavy fighting. In the withdrawal after the raid two battalions were cut off and a third, after suffering heavy casualties, retired rapidly through the 51st Company which then became the rearguard of the force. For two hours the company was closely engaged but it managed to retrieve the situation by its steadiness and accuracy of fire, though it was once in imminent danger of being cut off. Although the force regained its base in Sheikh Othman in safety and without heavy casualties, the company suffered the loss of its able commander, Captain Boal, who was severely wounded and invalided back to India where he received the DSO for his gallantry.

The company continued its good work, supporting the infantry in many small raids, building a hutted camp supplied with water from a 80 foot tube-well and working on extending various roads. It also sank a well 250 feet in depth in Sheikh Othman and was still there when the war ended.

BACK IN ROORKEE

By the end of the War 27 Field Units, including 21 Companies, had been raised and the strength of the Corps had risen to well over 8,000. As has been mentioned, at the beginning of the war one of the great difficulties was the need for British Officers and this was met by training officers from the Indian Army Reserve of Officers. After the War these Officers presented the RE Mess with a large bronze and marble clock, with two vases to match, as a War Memorial, while the RE Officers presented the famous 'Winged Victory'.

In 1920 a Committee decided, after canvassing present and former officers of the Corps for suggestions, that the War Memorial of the Corps for the Great War should take the form of a colonnade round the 1907 Centenary Memorial Tower (Ghazni), in front of the Quarter-Guard on the Parade Ground. Designs were obtained from Lionel Health, Principal of the Mayo School of Art in Lahore, and building began in 1921. The design is in the Mogul style and in keeping with that of the 1907 Tower: built of red brick, with red Dholpur stone pillars and '*chajjas*' on the eaves, with white domes. The units who served in campaigns, battle honours, and the names of the dead are inscribed on stone slabs fixed to the walls. The Memorial was completed in 1926 and unveiled by Field Marshal Sir William Birdwood, C-in-C India, on 26th February 1927. A Reunion of past members of the Corps of all ranks was held in Roorkee on this occasion lasting four days and being very well attended.

The total killed in the War was 11 British Officers, 1 British NCO, 3 Indian Officers, 171 Indian Other Ranks and 15 Followers. Many more were wounded. In recognition of its services, the Corps was granted the following Battle Honours (those selected to be borne on appointments being shown in heavy type):

THE GREAT WAR

LA BASSEE, 1914 **FESTUBERT 1914–15** GIVENCHY, 1914 **NEUVE CHAPELLE**
AUBERS **LOOS** **FRANCE AND FLANDERS, 1914–15** **MEGIDDO** SHARON
DAMASCUS PALESTINE, 1918 **ADEN** **KUT AL AMARA, 1915–17** CTESIPHON
DEFENCE OF KUT AL AMARA TIGRIS, 1916 BAGHDAD KHAN BAGHDADI
SHARQAT **MESOPOTAMIA, 1915–18** PERSIA, 1918
NW FRONTIER, INDIA, 1915, 1916–17 BALUCHISTAN, 1918

The Bengal Sappers and Miners served in virtually every theatre of war and covered themselves in glory. No account has been given, though, of the on-going operations on the NW Frontier, as these belong to another Chapter. Neither has any account been given of the campaign in East Africa as no Bengal Sapper units were involved, though a few individual officers did take part. Notable among these was Lieutenant Colonel SH Sheppard who was GSO I to the Divisional Commander, who recorded that 'our troops also had to contend against enemies other than German askaris and the country. Lions, rhinoceroses, hippopotami and crocodiles were encountered, sometimes with unfortunate results, and elephants and giraffes interfered with communications. Lions were dangerous in certain areas. On several occasions they attacked men and carried them away into the bush and their roaring around our camps often caused a stampede among transport animals. A rhinoceros once charged a column on a night march and threw it into such confusion that it was delayed an hour. Another charged one of our patrols while it was engaged with a German patrol. First, it scattered our patrol, then the enemy and finally turned on some Masai tribesmen who were watching the fight and killed one of them. Hippopotami attacked boats at river crossings and had to be repelled with bayonets. Crocodiles took an unceasing toll of unwary porters. Elephants wandered by night along newly made roads and left pot-holes which delayed our motor convoys. Giraffes broke our telephone lines so often that it became necessary to raise the wires to 25 feet. During a football match near the sandy bank of a river all went well until a powerful kick sent the ball into the river where it was promptly swallowed by a crocodile. Then there were the insects ...'

Perhaps it was just as well that no units were sent there from Roorkee!

2
LIFE BETWEEN THE WARS

CANTONMENT LIFE

In the period 1924–6 while the colonnade was built in Roorkee around the Corps Memorial Column, Maurice (Tubby) Broomhall, later to achieve fame by escaping from a German POW Camp dressed as a German General and subsequently becoming the senior British officer in Colditz, arrived in Roorkee to command No 7 Bridging Train. Mechanisation had not yet taken place and the establishment included two elephants and a large number of bullocks to haul the pontoon wagons. With a passion for driving fast cars, this situation caused Maurice some considerable frustration. He made determined efforts to increase the efficiency of his bullocks by trying to teach them to trot and, in the nearby Solani River, to swim. He had little success with either venture as bullocks, magnificent animals though they are, are apt to overheat and collapse if they are 'encouraged' to trot and he managed to incur the disapproval of higher authority, whose inventory of animal 'engines' was being put at risk! However, life was enlivened by the receipt of letters such as:

To: District Superintendent, Sahebjang Loop-Line, East India Railways
Beloved Sir,

I am arrived by passenger train at Ahmedpur Station and Belly is too much swollen with Jack Fruit. Therefore I went to Privy. But as I was doing the nuisance the Guard doing the whistle blew for the train to go off and I am running with Lota in one hand and Dhoti in next when I am fall over and expose my shocking to many female women on Platform and get leaved at Ahmedpur.

This is too much bad if passenger go to dung and dam Guard not wait train five minutes for him. I am therefore pray your honour to make big fine on guard for public sake otherwise I am big report to paper.

From your faithful servant
Chliley Sin
Munshiffs Court, Berhampur, Bengal

'Honker' Henniker arrived in Roorkee at 2am one morning in 1928, accompanied by another subaltern, to find that the train had outstripped the telegram announcing their arrival. Nothing daunted, and with the theory that an officer should always drive himself, they set off in a tonga, Honker driving with the driver in the rear seat. Reaching the Officers' Mess without mishap, they were shown to a bungalow where the owner, a man of commanding presence, asked them what the hell they wanted. On being addressed as 'Sir', he replied that 'even in the Orient' it was unnecessary to address a subaltern as 'Sir'. They discovered later that he inherited his commanding presence from his grandfather, Field-Marshal Lord Napier.

Next day, being a Thursday, was a holiday, so officers wore plain clothes. Proceeding to the Mess they entered the dining room; round the table sat about ten officers each intent upon a newspaper held in a rack before him. No one moved, they sat down and a silent waiter brought them each a paper-rack and a newspaper. It was a long room, the walls being covered with cream-coloured distemper. On them hung the heads of all kinds of wild animals and at one end of the room was a frame with a tiger's skin stretched upon it. From the beams of the roof there hung three electric clusters, each surrounded by a sort of red petticoat lined with white silk. All the officers but two in the Bengal Sappers were bachelors. Not a single one had a motor-car.

The Officers' Mess has been in existence since 1856 and is one of the oldest, if not the oldest, mess building in India. In the years after Partition it was described by General Cariappa, the Commander-in-Chief, as the finest Mess in the Indian Army. A notice at that time on the Mess Notice Board read "The Mess Rules were written before the War (World War II). What was good enough then is good enough now", signed by the Commandant.

The Roorkee Polo Club was founded in 1873, the game having been reintroduced in Calcutta by the Rajah of Manipur a few years earlier, after being in abeyance in India for a hundred years or more. The game is of course a very ancient one, being mentioned in a story in *The Arabian Nights* and was enjoyed, much later, by the Mogul Emperor Jahangir. When first played in Roorkee the teams used cricket balls, but these were too heavy and ultimately the bamboo root, at first chopped round with a native adze and then beautifully turned on a lathe, became the standard. For many years the Workshops pursued a roaring trade in these polo balls and other polo requisites. The game became virtually '*de rigueur*' and as each officer in peace-time had two chargers, with the Indian Government providing forage and grooms, and the Indian Polo Association imposing no height limit, it was easy enough to play. Rather than use their chargers for polo, though, officers found it was possible to buy proper polo ponies for relatively small sums and loans could he had from the long-established Corps Polo Fund, to which every officer subscribed. Polo thrived accordingly and young officers applied all their resources, both mental and physical, to the game. Every morning at sunrise, officers, singly or in rides, would be twisting and turning, halting and galloping, training their horses. After lunch, the Mess garden would ring with the strike of the ball, as some enthusiast sat on the wooden horse in a circular polo pit lashing the ball all round the compass. Three days a week they assembled in the evening and played slow, medium and fast chukkas till the shadows fell.

In case anyone should think it was all play, officers worked as well! For instance, the Assistant Adjutant was charged with the responsibility of training all the recruits in drill and musketry. Another subaltern was charged with all the administration: clothing, feeding, housing and leave. In the summer of 1930, the former combined his duties with that of the Station Staff Officer whose principal care was being treasurer of the garrison church accounts, which were in a healthy state at that time. The Parish Council therefore decided to spend funds on a wall round the church to keep out the cattle and the SSO instructed an Indian contractor accordingly, with orders to complete the job before the Sunday of the Chaplain's next monthly visit. The Chaplain and the SSO rode to the early service to find that the contractor had indeed finished the wall round the church, but it was right round and there was no way in! While the better jockeys got to church by feat of equitation, others had to climb in like thieves into an orchard.

'Honker' Henniker was posted to 2 Company, the only other officer being a Captain, with three British NCOs for technical duties and two hundred and fifty Indian sepoys divided into three sections (later renamed 'platoons'). The Viceroy's Commissioned Officers (VCOs) managed the sections and formed an important link between the sepoys and their British officers; each averaged about twenty years service. It was not long though before he was transferred to another company whose Captain went to England on eight months' leave and he was left in sole charge. The subaltern in temporary command of the next door company went sick and so he commanded his company as well. In India this spread of command was considered quite normal, while in England a subaltern at that time thought it a big day if he saw twenty men on parade. Guided by the head clerks, 'Honker' solemnly wrote letters in one company office and read them next door.

Occasionally he had to try a case, difficult enough for a young subaltern with British soldiers but all the more so in a language he did not yet understand and had to have a clerk to interpret. On one occasion when the accused seemed to be saying much more than the clerk was translating, the clerk explained "Sahib, he is telling many lies. You had better punish him severely". All this time he was taking lessons in the vernacular with an old frail Hindu, named Jagdamba Prashad. He always carried an umbrella and in hot weather he used it as a sunshade; when an officer passed he would lower it as a mark of respect. A similar situation arose in the case of the two elephants which were on the strength. These solemn monsters were intended to provide the power that in later days was supplied by bulldozers. One elephant had to go each day to the jungle to fetch fodder for the two of them. As he walked majestically through the Cantonment he would salute if he met a British officer. He raised his trunk in salutation and the officer, if in plain clothes, raised his hat in acknowledgment. Sadly, in 1930 the elephants were abolished. Lieutenant Colonel Martel, filled with reforming zeal from the Mechanised Brigade at Tidworth, came to Roorkee and saw the elephants. To a tank expert an elephant was anathema, and two were doubly accursed, so the blue pencil of financial stringency was drawn through the elephants' forage bill. The elephants, with deep obeisance, departed and the immediate effect was that elephants had to be hired from the PWD for shooting parties.

There were other rituals, too, as quaint as the elephant's. There was the ceremony of Attestation. For this the whole Corps was paraded on three sides of a square. On the fourth side was the War Memorial and under its colonnades the recruits were standing. At the signal to begin, the religious teachers of each religion would read out in the vernacular the oath of allegiance. The recruits repeated it in unison: 'I swear to obey all legal commands of the King-Emperor, his Heirs and Successors and the Officers and NCOs set over me ...', or words to that effect. The Prophet and all the company of Heaven were called to bear witness to the oath.

An equally impressive ceremony, though of a somewhat bizarre kind, was the promulgation of the sentence of a court-martial. The commonest was a Summary Court-Martial when, in effect, a commanding officer had but to put on his sword, his spurs and his medals, and hand out up to two years' imprisonment across the office table. The accused was then paraded in the presence of all, the sentence was read aloud, and the accused was led away in handcuffs. If he was an NCO reduced to the ranks, the regimental tailor (looking like Jack Snipe in a loin-cloth) appeared with a theatrical pair of scissors and snipped the chevrons from the culprit's arm. There were, of course, safeguards and if the reviewing officer thought an injustice had been done and annulled the finding and the sentence, the culprit was again paraded. The tailor, this time with a packing needle and a ball of string, shambled into the arena and stitched the chevrons on again. This rough justice appealed to the jawans as there was always more to every case than ever came to light. More often than not the accused would shrug his shoulders and say 'It is the will of God'.

The Young Officer (YO) joining the Bengal Sappers in the Thirties received plenty of useful advice before leaving England. Apart from his copy of 'Customs of the Service' on being commissioned, he would have been sent 'Notes on Kit etc for Officers Proceeding to Northern India' by the Corps Adjutant in Roorkee. This covered such vital information as:

"In the hot weather, the dress for mess is white mess jacket (without grenades), white overalls, and scarlet silk "Kamar-band" (waist belt).

On a trooper, home mess kit is always worn as far as Port Said.

Gloves – Seldom worn. Bring out your old ones, a pair or two of string gloves for riding, and a pair of motoring gloves if you have them.

Hats – The cheapest and best mufti hat is a "Bombay Bowler" which you can get at Port Said. The variety sold in England is always wrong and absurdly expensive.

Tennis Flannels – White flannels are worn in the winter.

Free allowance of baggage when travelling on warrant from a port is 15 maunds for a subaltern. (A maund = 80lbs)

Servants – Crowds of scalliwag bearers will meet the boat with bogus recommendations."

On arrival in Roorkee, the YO, on a monthly salary of about 400 Rupees (£30), received the "Officers' Bungalow and Servants Handbook" with such advice as:

"Standard Wages:

Bearer	20 Rupees (1 Rupee = approx 7.5p in today's money)

Bhisti (Water-carrier)	12 Rs
Sweeper	12 Rs
Mali (Gardener)	12 Rs
Syce (Groom)	3 Rs per horse, to include clipping, shoeing and oil for hoofs (summer only).

Clothing and Extras – Officers' personal servants should be decently turned out and the usual custom is to provide those that serve in the Mess with such things as pagris, white coats and kamarbands."

The wives and children of Indian servants were permitted to attend the Dispensary of the Sir Bindon Blood Family Hospital as out-patients, provided they had a note to the Lady Doctor from their employer. In special cases they could be admitted to the hospital for a small charge, normally 10% of one month's pay.

Aitken Lawrie was commissioned in 1934, when we still had an Empire, and was delighted when he got the only available vacancy in the Bengal Sappers. He remembered the thrill of walking back to his bungalow after dinner in the Mess with jangling spurs, trampling over huge crackling leaves as big as soup plates, listening to plaintive music coming from a lighted shrine beside the road and the sound of jackals baying at the moon. In some ways it was a tough posting as his Company was always at 24 hours notice to dash to the Frontier by the main line railway which passed through Roorkee. The officers were a rugged lot who despised the Bombay and Madras Sappers as poodle-fakers living in the sloth belt! Many of them were dyed-in-the-wool bachelors and there was an old rule that "Subalterns must not, Captains should not, Majors may and Colonels should get married". Nobody was allowed Home Leave unless he played polo for the Corps, had shot a tiger or had been on a long trek through the hills. Aitken was only a beginner at polo and had no wish to shoot a beautiful tiger so applied for two months leave to walk through the Himalayas to Tibet. Taking his bearer and five mules for luggage and provisions, he had a wonderful time among glorious scenery, doing a lot of painting and holding an exhibition in Simla on his return.

In 1935, Mangat Rai joined 5 Field Company, commanded by Bill Veitch and with Dick Connor as second in command, at Roorkee. Mangat Rai had been one of the first Indians sent to Britain for training in recognition of the part played by the Indian Army in the First World War and in response to pressure from Indian leaders. He went to the 'Shop', was commissioned from Woolwich as a 'King's Commissioned Indian Officer' (KCIO), did his

Young Officer (YO) training at Chatham and went on to Cambridge for degree training. Meanwhile, a start was being made to create cadet academies in India and in the following year the first two officers from the Indian Military Academy in Dehra Dun arrived in Roorkee as 'Indian Commissioned Officers' (ICOs) and completed their training at the Thomason College. Officers thus fell into four categories: British Officers (BOs), KCIOs, ICOs and VCOs. As Mangat Rai wryly commented, 'If the caste system originated in India, it was certainly being kept alive and flourishing in the Bengal Sappers!'

Roorkee Cantonment was a place of wide open spaces, straight roads, wide grass verges well planted with trees and 'Maidans' for polo and military parades. There was an area of rough broken ground where fieldworks and various engineering projects were carried out and of course the Ganges Canal which was used for bridging training. There were extensive workshops in pleasant brick buildings with heavy pan-tiled roofs, arcades and shady courtyards – more Spanish or Italian than English or Indian. Everything looked surprisinglv clean and green and tidy, with white concrete verandah-ed bungalows in large gardens, lines for Indian troops, and lines for British NCOs, who were trades instructors. There was a native bazaar, the Thomason College, a hospital, a church, a few civilian bungalows for college instructors, a doctor, a policeman and so on. Life for a young subaltern in Roorkee was pleasant but spartan. Roorkee had little to offer on the cultural side or of entertainment. Social life moved at a sluggish pace but the facilities for games were excellent. Tennis, golf, squash and polo were available, and hockey and volleyball could be played with the jawans. There was a swimming pool adjoining the Officers' Mess. There was plenty of shooting, particularly duck, and the bag would be distributed among the few married officers, leading to dinner invitations later. Dinner jackets were worn on these occasions.

A particular resident in Roorkee at this time was the policeman, Freddie Young. He was rarely in the Station, though, spending most of his time chasing dacoits and gaining for himself an awesome reputation for resourcefulness and courage. There was at the time a notorious dacoit called Suleiman who, together with a band of his own robber friends, haunted the wilder districts, terrorizing the villages, eluding the law for years and becoming a legendary figure of fear. On one occasion, Freddie Young met Suleiman by arrangement and alone in the jungle, in an attempt to come to terms with him. It says much for the courage of this Englishman and the thief's honour of Suleiman, that no advantage was taken by either side at this lonely meeting, though no agreement was reached. He was finally brought to book, though, tried for murder and duly hanged. However, before his sentence was carried out he asked to see Freddie Young and made one final request: that Freddie should look after his son. Despite living in a region beset with blood feuds Freddie agreed and made him his orderly.

Life was not entirely a bed of roses, though, for the early Indian Commissioned Officers and, though Mangat Rai never mentioned it, the early entrants to the Corps were subjected to a certain amount of hostility from British officers who felt that Indians were poaching on their preserve. S N Dar, speaking of his early days in Roorkee, said: "We were eventually accepted by the British but not without a few initial jolts. For example, often when we left our calling cards at their houses we received no reply, while youngsters coming from the UK were invited back for teas and dinners, so we stopped calling. Then, at one stage, we were made to move out of the RE Mess on the plea that as we were students of the Thomason College we should mess in the College. We were told that the College Mess would provide us with a more congenial atmosphere, so we pulled out and, maintaining that we were officers first and students next, we started our own Mess in a bungalow behind the College. This, in fact, was the first Corps of Indian Engineers Officers' Mess. Major Harold Williams was in charge of us and knew us all as students and friends. He would implore, argue and cajole, and did much to improve our relationship with the Royal Engineers. Later, the Adjutant General and the Military Secretary visited us and thereafter matters were righted somewhat and the relationship improved. Looking back, however, I feel that both sides were carried away – one by racial conservatism and the other by touchiness". Relations between British officers and ICOs cannot have been helped, though, by the invidious nature of the posting policy whereby ICOs were posted to field companies in command of platoons, replacing VCOs, while British officers were not required to command platoons.

Being within easy reach of hill stations, it was possible to enjoy a European temperature at the hottest time of the year, when work was slack and short leave could be obtained. Stu Battye and Mangat Rai used to go to Simla, the summer capital, for a few weekends. The former had friends up there and Mangat Rai had a widowed uncle who lived in Chota Simla, so they would pile their suitcases into Mangat Rai's old Chevrolet tourer, leave Roorkee after work on a Friday afternoon, drive through the night via Saharanpur and arrive at Kalka at dawn. Here the ascent to Simla began along a hazardous mountain road with many hairpin bends but, sharing the driving and making a few stops, they arrived in good time for Saturday lunch with their respective hosts. They used to start the journey back on Sunday afternoon and, again driving through the cool of the night, they would arrive, bleary-eyed, in Roorkee in time for first parade on Monday morning. In the early hours of one Monday morning they approached at speed the level crossing between Saharanpur and Roorkee. No train was coming but the gate was closed, with the gatekeeper asleep in his hut by the railway line, and Mangat Rai, assuming mistakenly that he would have a clear passage, smashed into the gate, bending it out of shape. The gatekeeper, having been woken up by the noise and concerned that he would not be able to repair it, was soon reassured on being given ten rupees with the suggestion that he got help from the village 'lohar' (blacksmith). He had not taken down their names and addresses or any details about the car so they continued their journey thinking that was the end of the matter, but there was an unexpected sequel. A week later, Mangat Rai was on the mat in front of Colonel Drew, the Commandant, who said that he had received a letter from the Police Commissioner saying that a car had damaged the level crossing gate, the registration plate had been found lying beside the railway line and had been traced to him. The Commandant chided Mangat Rai and said he thought it had been 'bloody careless' to leave incriminating evidence that brought 'badnam' (opprobrium) to the Bengal Sappers!

Joan Usher told of her life in No 5 Bungalow as a child in 1936. The house belonged to a Contractor in Roorkee who was paid rent by the Quartermaster. It had spacious grounds of over an acre with a large lawn in front and an orchard at the side with about forty mango trees. The house itself was single storey with a high thatched roof and wide cool verandahs on which were set tubs full of bright geraniums, canna lilies and 'mali's joy' (red salvias). There was a well from which a buffalo could draw water for irrigation and beyond the vegetable patch were the stables. The servants' quarters were at the back, with the cookhouse nearby, approached by a stone-flagged path. Every morning the khansaman (cook) produced his grubby but comprehensive exercise book, which contained all his recipes accumulated from the various memsahibs he had worked for, and would choose the menu for the day, in conjunction with her mother, Laura. He would then do all the shopping in the bazaar before working at his primitive stove and oven, little more than a hole in the ground filled with burning charcoal, to produce delicious English meals. Light came from the open fly-proof door or an oil lamp and as there was no refrigerator things like milk, butter and cold drinks were kept in an ice-box for which ice was brought daily. Other stores were kept in a 'dhoolie' which was a square cupboard with wire mesh sides all round so that air could circulate and the four legs stood in saucers of water to keep out white ants. Washing up was done by the 'masalchi', using bundles of grass and ashes.

The sun seemed to shine all the time casting deep shadows under the peepul trees with their huge leaves which crunched deliciously when they fell off the trees and dried. A short drive led from the pillared entrance covered with a profusion of pink and white bougainvillaea. There was a box for calling cards and a mounting block for her parents to mount their two horses 'Lady-be-Good', a grey polo pony, and 'Memory', her mother's horse. With her Madrassi ayah (nurse) she would he taken for a ride on her donkey before breakfast or for a walk by the canal where there would sometimes be an elephant on the edge of the water with a small boy on his back giving him a scrub as he threw water up with his trunk.

With no 'mod cons' each household employed at least ten servants. Their bearer, Shafi, took orders from her mother and served at table in clean uniform and smart turban, assisted by the 'khitmaghar' who brought the food over from the cookhouse. The table was always laid with an immaculate white damask tablecloth and well polished silver. The bearer would bring calling cards and chits (messages) from other bungalows to her mother inviting her to tea or both parents to dinner. Though sounding very grand today, this was the normal way of life and 'Form' was very important so that everyone knew what was expected. Telephones, of course, were virtually unheard of and unit offices only had them installed during the summer of 1937.

The 'bhisti' or 'paniwallah's' job was to carry water from the well in two large kerosene cans which had wooden handles to enable him to hook them up on his yoke. He brought these to a large drum under which he lit a good fire to heat up the water. At night it was the custom to shout to him 'Paniwallah hum mara gusal muncta hai!' (please get my bath ready), to which a thin voice in the distance would reply 'Bahut achha, Sahib'(Very well, Sir). The bath was a galvanised metal tub in the corner of the wash-room and was filled with 'garm pani' (hot water), with a can of cold water left nearby so that one could adjust the temperature to one's own liking. When finished, the tub was merely tipped up on the concrete floor and the water ran through a hole in the wall to water the garden. Creatures used to come in through the same hole: lizards, large spiders and sometimes even snakes if the wire gauze had come away! In another corner of the bathroom was the 'thunderbox' and the 'sweeper' emptied this by taking out the enamelled pan from within and taking it to a deep trench hidden somewhere far away from the house. He also had the job of sweeping the floors and keeping them really clean. The 'dhobi' came once

a week to collect all the household washing which was brought back next day beautifully laundered and ironed. There was also a 'flying dhobi' when something was wanted urgently and this was washed and returned the same day, regardless of the weather. Such items as uniform shorts would also be beautifully starched, the starch being applied with a short blowpipe or even by mouth!

Katharine Lethbridge, a young twenty-year old bride, was next in No 5 Bungalow, though they privately named it 'Gingerbread Cottage'. Her parents were living in India and she had married Jack Lethbridge in Simla. She described how her Indian servants took over, treated her with tolerance, cheating only in moderation, lying a little, stealing a little, never taking too much advantage, a bit here, a bit there, the custom of the country. They were kindly, hardworking, loyal and resourceful. If they pocketed a few pennies, who could begrudge them? Most of them had so little, always willing to work long hours, travel on uncomfortable journeys, wait in inhospitable places, never complaining, always welcoming, one owed them a great deal that could never sufficiently be repaid.

Like Joan Usher's parents, they had a compound full of servants and she talked about the garden dominated by huge mango trees. It had a small orchard of lychees, papayas growing by the stables, a ten foot hedge of scarlet poinsettias and neem trees whose aromatic leaves were dried and packed among the clothes to discourage pests. There were also guavas, a sweet-scented mogra, limes, pommelos, sheeshum trees, so delicate and green in spring-time and, either in the garden or just outside, jacarandas, Indian laburnum, gold mohurs, and pale-stemmed eucalyptus. Porcupines were a threat to the vegetables so a deep ditch was dug round the vegetable garden with a wire-netting fence on the inside bank. Even so these spiky creatures got into the canna-lily beds and wrought havoc, eating the roots and trampling what remained.

With its high thatched roof, the bungalow collected a strange moving population of creatures who lived between the thatch and the ceilings, which were no more than cloths painted white and stretched high up across the tall rooms to give them a flimsy kind of respectability. Civet cats sometimes set up house above the ceiling cloths and one could watch the indentations made by their paws as they walked across. They would appear outside on the roof at night, visible by their shining eyes if one flashed a torch. Snakes sometimes hibernated in the thatch and appeared when the weather got hot, and if there was a visiting mongoose it was encouraged to stay by putting out food. Of course there were the customary scorpions and centipedes, dormant in winter but appearing with the warmth. At night, there were 'Flying Foxes'.

There were rarely more than three or four wives in the station but marriage among the British officers gradually became less frowned upon and with more wives there were more social events. There was even a married Commandant to take over the bungalow overlooking the Solani river that had been so austerely inhabited by bachelors: one room, one bed, one chair, one man. There were also, of course, a number of NCOs' wives and they too would hold parties, perhaps performing 'The Lancers' and old-fashioned 'square dances'. The lot of the NCOs was not easy in India, few seemed to integrate with the country, although their lives had greatly improved since Victorian times. They had plenty of opportunities for sport, the families escaped the hot weather in hill stations, but they learned very little Hindustani and got the worst of the Indian servants and remained strangers in a strange land.

Commonly Indians of whatever religion were very private over their family affairs and it was difficult to persuade a woman to use a hospital when the age-old custom was to have babies at home attended by a 'dai' or ancient relative. Due to the initiative of Mrs Clarence Bird a maternity hospital was built and officers' wives could visit the mothers and new-born babies, although visits were not easy. But the young mothers did start coming and the habit grew.

General Sir Aylmer Hunter-Weston presented the Officers' Mess with a handsome silver table-piece "The Horn of the Hunter", the emblem of the Hunter-Westons, in 1937. This was received with delight and followed the purchase in 1920 of "Winged Victory" from a Naples silversmith as the Mess 1914-18 War Memorial, the mounting for which was completed by Mr Fripp, a London artist, and it was then kept as a centre-piece by the RE Mess at Roorkee. The Mess was famous, not only for traditions dating back to Indian Mutiny days but also for its wonderful collection of sporting trophies. These included Bison, Black Buck, Buffalo, Markhor and Sambhar, as well as Tiger.

Ian Loch became OC 5 Field Company, the first unit to be Indianised, in 1938. With his understanding, tact and sense of humour, he was able to weld them into a team that supported him with loyalty and affection. Raj Mangat Rai, his second-in-command, tells a story of the whole Company in line on a drill parade when a 'pi-dog' invaded the parade ground. Ian had a well-bred bull terrier off parade, but it could not watch such insolence. The two became locked in a fight to the finish. Ian and the Subadar stepped forward and took each dog by the tail and carried them airborne to the mule troughs, into one of which they were dropped. Not a soldier moved, though the whites of the eyes of every jawan moved to follow the happenings. Not a smile, but inwardly every one of them chuckling his heart out. Ian then returned and the parade continued.

David David joined the Corps in April 1938 and was posted to 4 Field Company in Roorkee where Harry Macdonald was OC and the other subalterns were Ken Shepheard and 'Streak' Moor. His eighteen months of peacetime life in Roorkee included a two month trek in Ladakh and Lahoul, as well as regular polo, hockey and football with the jawans, and one or two weekends to the jheels after duck. Bill Veitch was commanding the Workshops at this time, with Dick Connor as his assistant and a number of British Warrant Officers and NCOs as trades instructors. What went on behind the gates of the Workshops was largely wrapped in mystery as far as newly arrived junior officers were concerned and only gradually did they come to realise how important it was that a high standard of proficiency in all trades should be reached and maintained. In everything, Bill Veitch set and expected the highest standards so that by the time he ended his tenure as Chief Instructor in 1940 he had increased the capacity of the Workshops by sixteen-fold.

In 1940, after the family's leave in England, Joan Usher returned to Roorkee, this time to live in No 10 College Road (now a Military Nurses' Home). This was a more spacious bungalow, as by now her father was a Major, and had a flat roof, accessible by outside steps, where one could sleep in the hot weather. The old pink Chev with its running boards, horn and removable talc windows had gone, to be replaced by a car of lesser character but, with a portico across the front entrance, one could drive it between the pillars! Children went to the Army School where there was one big schoolroom for all ages: there was plenty for the thirty or so pupils to do, but little actual learning took place. Frances Adams ran the local Bluebirds, the Indian version of the Guides, while her husband, Bill, was an instructor in the Officer Cadet Training Unit commanded by Harry Usher.

I REMEMBER: AN INDIAN CHILDHOOD

by

Janet Crawford

I was born in Roorkee on 7 January 1923, the middle child of a family of five; Jean and Angus first and the twins, Mary and John, 18 months after me. Our father was a member of the Thomason College Staff and we lived in a sprawling bungalow behind the workshops. We were all baptised in the little Church of St John the Baptist in Roorkee and Jean and I were married there some 20 years later.

Our childhood days were full of sunshine and happiness and I remember picnics when we donned our solar topis and set off on our bicycles for Dhanauri, Deobund Cut or the Asfanagar Falls. The cook and bearer followed in a tonga with the tea things and while we paddled in the water or played games under the shady trees, they collected twigs and sticks for the fire to boil the kettle. A clean white cloth was laid on the grass for the spread of sandwiches, curry puffs and cakes. I don't think cook ever understood why we went to so much trouble when we could have had a perfectly good tea sitting in comfortable chairs in our own garden at home. 'But it's a picnic, khansaman', we would explain.

Our servants were part of our large family and I know that they felt the same. They brought all their cares and worries to our mother and she would give them simple medicines for a sick wife or child. We were known affectionately by our Christian names – Angus Baba, Janet Baba and so on. One of my favourite pastimes was to sneak into the kitchen and talk with the khansaman. He was a real old gentleman with a flowing white beard and spoke broken English, although I preferred to speak with him in Hindustani. He had fought in the Great War in France and had so many stories to tell. France seemed a different world and his stories of the mud, cold and snow made me shudder. It seemed so different from my beautiful golden India and I never ever wanted to go there. He didn't live in the servants quarters but had his own bungalow in the bazaar and he was much respected by the other servants. One of his specialities was 'vegeetible pups' and if I shut my eyes I can still taste them; a soft pastry filled with curried vegetables and shaped like a half moon with a fluted edge.

All children in India are brought up on a diet of dal (split pulse) and rice. One nourishing dish and a great favourite was 'Pish-Pash', rice cooked in a rich mutton stock with little pieces of meat, so the end result was rather sloshy, hence the name Pish-Pash. When you put your spoon in, it went Pish and when you lifted it out, Pash! 'Rumble tumble' as we called scrambled eggs was another popular nursery dish.

One of our bearers was called Ali Hussan and he had come to us from his village to be trained by my mother to wait at table. One day after he left us, my parents were invited to dinner by his new Master and Mistress and he embarrassed my mother by asking about us children by name and wanting to know every detail of how we were and what we were doing.

Then there was the mali, who grew beautiful flowers in the garden to fill the house with their scent and colour. In the winter, roses, sweet peas and chrysanthemums and many other English summer flowers, while in the summer, bright marigolds, balsam and zinnias with their vibrant colours.

The bhisti's job was to fill the chattis in the bathroom with water from his goatskin for our baths and also the chattis in the pantry where the water was boiled for drinking. Milk was delivered daily by the dudh wallah and ladled out from his shining brass urns into jugs. My mother had an instrument called a hydrometer which registered the water content in the milk and woe betide the dudh wallah if he had cheated! The milk was also boiled and the thick skin which formed on the top was eaten as cream, delicious with soft brown sugar sprinkled on the top!

The sweepers came and went but I remember particularly the mehtarani in her long flowing skirts and tinkling bells on her ankles. She had a large broom to sweep the paths round the house and we loved to tease her by creeping up on her and lifting her skirts to see what she was wearing underneath. She would round on us and chase us with her broom in mock anger.

She had two daughters, Cinthe and Munthe but no husband, at least we never saw one. Cinthe and Munthe were our playmates. Sadly Munthe loved playing with fire and had a tragic accident when her sari caught fire and she burned to death. Cinthe always had to make words rhyme, like 'lakri-pakri' and 'roti-toti. She was married at a very young age and had her first baby at the age of 12. It was unbelievable – at that age we were still small children.

We had our own tailor, who sat on the verandah all day rattling away on his Singer sewing machine, making clothes for us or doing repair work. He was known as the 'Boy tailor' because he was just a lad when he first came. He was with us for years and became so proficient that he went to Naini Tal for the summer, where he earned good money from all the memsahibs. In the winter he returned to us. Unfortunately he suffered from halitosis so my mother made him chew the bark of a neem tree and that did the trick!

The dhobi came once a week and was there for most of the day. The tough articles like sheets, towels and jharans (dusters) were sorted and written down on the dhobi list, tied in a bundle and sent away to the ghats to be bashed on the stones and washed in the canal. They were then spread on thorn bushes to dry and to be bleached by the sun. The more delicate articles were washed at home in large tubs of soapy water. My mother sat in a chair supervising and chatting to the dhobi. When finished they were taken away to be ironed and the soapy water was tipped on to the rose beds to kill the aphids.

My father had two chaprasis (orderlies), Nunoo, who was very tall and very dozy and Ram Chandra, who was small and very active, always dashing around carrying messages. They sat outside my father's office but, as Ram Chandra seemed to be doing all the work, leaving Nunoo to doze on the verandah, my mother decided that he should sit on her verandah instead where she could keep him occupied. There he sat in the warm sunshine, slowly polishing an endless array of brass and silver. Sometimes he was given another job to do but dozing remained his favourite pastime.

One day we witnessed something we had never seen before and have never seen since, nor are we likely to again, I suppose. We were playing in the garden when it suddenly got dark as though a cloud had passed over the sun. We looked about us, curious and surprised and then we saw a black cloud travelling very fast towards us. This was followed by a funny rushing sort of noise and then suddenly we were in the cloud, thick with grasshoppers falling all around us, or so we thought. In fact they were locusts and the servants became very excited. They filled buckets, dhotis, shawls and anything else with the insects. "Very good to eat", they told us. "Bahut achha!" I didn't think I would like to try; they looked so pretty with their green gossamer wings. I am not sure if they cook the whole thing or just eat the legs, but you would need an awful lot to make it a worthwhile meal.

I loved the vendors who came daily to our house carrying their large baskets on their heads; the fruit wallah with his bright red sweet Kashmiri apples, brown russets, oranges, guavas, pawpaws, lychees, mangoes, water melons – all in their seasons.

My grandmother had a large orchard and sold the fruit every season. This was mainly mangoes and as the fruit started to ripen the buyer would arrive with his family and set up camp in the orchard. Long ropes with tin cans dangling were arranged round the trees and by simply attaching the end of the rope to someone's big toe, they were able to sit outside their tent and smoke their hookahs, every now and then giving the rope a sharp tug, setting the tins clanging and frightening the birds away.

The fish or machhli wallah had a rod across his shoulders with a large basket hanging from either end. They were full of slippery fish gleaming with iridescent colours. They, of course, came from the Ganges Canal and it was best not to think about what they had fed on! Occasionally the Thomason College Dairy had seafood from Karachi for sale. Delicious pomfret and prawns were always a great treat.

Best of all the boxwallahs were the Chinamen, always known as 'John'. They had boxes of the most beautiful silk and satin underwear, and table and household linen exquisitely embroidered. We mooned and sighed, handling these things with longing but we were too young for such romantic garments. Sometimes my mother would buy some table linen for best occasions but for us it was a joy just to look.

The haberdashery man was another favourite with my mother. She would spend hours browsing through his box, stocked with packets of needles, pins, threads, buttons, hooks and eyes and so on. He often left his box with us over-night for safe keeping, collecting it in the morning before going on his way.

The College baker was famous for his confectionery and what beautifully decorated cakes he would make for every occasion. Pink and white meringues which melted in the mouth were one of his specialities. He was an old friend of the family and years later he made our wedding cake. He was present in his best brocaded atchkan to show Hugh exactly where to cut the cake with his sword.

Christmas began early in December when we made a trip to Dehra Dun to shop. Most important of all were the ingredients needed for several large Christmas cakes and puddings. For many days afterwards we were all roped in to chop the peel, de-seed the raisins and prepare the nuts. Nunoo, of course, the bearer and even the mali were required to help but not until my mother had examined their hands and made sure there was no mud under the mali's fingernails! When all was ready, the College baker arrived and settled himself down on the verandah in front of a large brass mixing bowl. With his hands (spotless, of course) he creamed the butter and sugar; dozens of eggs were added, followed by flour little by little, and finally the fruit, nuts and spices. The baking tins ranged from two large ones for ourselves and then diminishing in size, according to how many my mother wanted to give as presents and to whom. The tins were carefully weighed and noted before being sent away on trays to the Bakery for cooking.

As Christmas drew near the shopkeepers arrived in their best clothes followed by their servants bearing 'dollies' on their heads. These were large baskets filled with gifts of dried fruit, nuts and sugary sweets. We were all present on the verandah to receive them. They bowed and salaamed and offered us their gifts which made us feel very special. Sometimes there was a bottle of whisky for my father but that would come only from a wealthy bannia.

Thomason College held a big Christmas party for the children. The Hall was decorated with balloons and paper chains. There was a large Christmas tree twinkling with lights and an enormous paper cracker hung from the ceiling. We were told that Father Christmas would be arriving by aeroplane, which was very exciting. Rarely was an aeroplane to be seen in Roorkee and if ever one did appear everyone would rush outside shouting 'Jahaz'. We heard the sound of a plane, there was a sudden hush and then there he was, Father Christmas, red capped and bearded, waving to us from one of the skylights. We clapped and cheered and someone went out to escort him in. We sat down to a scrumptious tea and afterwards we each received a present from the tree. We were accompanied by our ayahs and when the giving of the presents was over, Father Christmas slashed open the cracker with a sharp stick and there was a cascade of puffed rice, sugar sweets and small coins. This was the ayahs' turn and they scrambled about filling their saris with goodies and searching for the lucky coins.

Christmas Day itself began with the brass band from the bazaar; the 'pooh-pooh' band as it was called, playing tunes such as 'For he's a Jolly Good Fellow' and 'Bye, Bye, Blackbird'. How they procured the instruments, let alone learned how to play them, was a mystery but we thought it was great fun to be greeted like that on Christmas morning. Of course they wanted bakhshish and we were pleased to give it to them. A whole stream of people arrived to greet us and wish us a happy day, carrying little gifts in return for bakhshish. The mali from the cemetery always came with cornflower buttonholes for us all. The postman and telegraph man (whenever did we receive a telegram?) came in full uniform and we expected them and enjoyed their visits as it was all part of Christmas Day. In the afternoon we went round visiting friends, returning home to our Christmas dinner in the evening. We never had turkey, it was always a goose with all the trimmings, followed by a plum pudding cooked by my father on his blue flame paraffin stove. We were allowed a small glass of Stone's Ginger Wine, which made us feel very grown up and sometimes the servants' families would shyly peep in and make their salaams.

If there was a visiting priest from Saharanpur, there would be a church service. To hear the bells rung on Christmas Day was something very special. There were two bells; one to remind us that the Service would soon begin and the second to tell us to hurry as there were only five minutes left. I remember one occasion when my aunt arrived late and very breathless as she slipped into the pew in front of us. She was wearing a new hat and, to our horror and amusement, the price tag was hanging down her back.

Very rarely a tamasha wallah would call with his baskets of tricks. We begged to be allowed to watch but we had to sit at a safe distance. I loved the cheeky little monkeys dressed in jackets and shorts with pillbox hats on their heads. They seemed to enjoy the fun as they danced and did all sorts of funny things to the rattle of drums. I felt very sad for the bears, who stood on their hind legs and shuffled about. It was so undignified but they appeared to be well looked after and well fed. The cobras terrified me but I was compelled to watch them as they slowly uncoiled themselves from the baskets, swaying from side to side to the tune of the pipes. Their hoods spread out, evil eyes glinting and forked tongues flicking in and out. Ugh! We were told they were quite harmless because they had been milked of their poison but I was not prepared to take any chances and I was glad when they were safely back in their baskets again.

We joined in the fun of the Indian festivals too. The beginning of winter brought Diwali, the Hindu festival of lights. Little earthenware dishes filled with oil and having a floating wick outlined every shop, house and temple and when the wicks were lit at dusk the whole place was transformed into a fairyland of flickering light. It is said that every Diwali night the goddess Kali fights a battle with the Evil One and the lights are there to help her conquer him.

As the weather warmed up, it heralded the Hindu festival of Holi. It is a festival of fun and enjoyment when people spray each other with coloured water or powder, so everyone wears their oldest clothes. My father's students always paid him a visit at Holi and he joined in the fun and let them spray him. There was much eating, dancing and drinking.

The big Mohammedan festival is Id which marks the end of Ramadan and the long fast when no food, nor even a drop of water, is consumed during the daytime, so when the weather is hot this can be very trying. As soon as the new moon appeared in the sky like a fingernail, there was great jubilation, feasting and giving of presents.

My parents had some great friends, the Mirzas, whom we often visited. They lived in a very large house close to the Canal bridge leading into the bazaar, where the two famous terracotta lions sit proudly at each end, gazing into the distance. My mother, my sisters and I had to go to the zenana where we sat on cushions eating dried fruit and nuts, surrounded by the women of the family. The conversation was in Urdu and broken English, with much giggling as the ladies tried to learn the English words. Then the pan (betel-leaf) box was brought out and Mrs Mirza prepared the pan for us, which was quite a ritual. The pan leaves were spread with a red paste of betelnut and other sweet scented spices, folded in a special way and handed to each of us in turn. It is supposed to be very good for the digestion. Meanwhile my father and the boys were entertained by Mr Mirza, who spoke perfect English and I believe drank whisky and smoked cigarettes.

When their eldest daughter was married we were invited to the wedding. We were not present at the wedding ceremony itself but went to the feast afterwards. We sat on the floor round the banquet and ate with our hands, dipping little pieces of chapatti into delicious curries. A huge dish of pilau rice covered with pure silver leaf was in the centre and, using finger and thumb, we made little balls of the rice and popped them into our mouths. There were all sorts of sticky sweets and nuts and bowls of fresh fruit as well, all beautifully decorated.

But time was passing and school was looming. We girls went to St Mary's Convent in Naini Tal, run by German Nuns of the order of Mary Ward. The boys went to St Joseph's College, also in Naini Tal. For me they were the best years of my life. I know this has been said before but in my case it was true. Amongst other things, they taught us the real meaning of Life and why we are here on earth; how we must learn to live in love and peace with everyone, regardless of class, creed or colour. For nine months we were at school, returning to Roorkee for the three glorious winter months.

After I had left school, I found Roorkee had changed. The war had started in 1939 and it was crowded with military personnel. Temporary bungalows were sprouting like mushrooms and there was great activity everywhere. It was all very gay with parties, dances, band concerts and even a pantomime. Everyone seemed to be living for the moment as one never knew what tomorrow would bring. That was when I met Hugh, who was serving in the Training Battalion. He had been put in charge of arrangements for the New Year's Eve Ball and he asked me to be 'Miss 1943'. As the old year was seen creeping out and while someone was striking twelve on the big brass gong, I was carried on in a curtained box. On the stroke of midnight the lights became brighter, the curtains were drawn back and I emerged dressed as a fairy. I stood on a table and everyone joined hands round me as we sang Auld Lang Syne. After that Hugh and I danced the night away while the poor weary bearers stood around, longing for us to go, so that they could go home to their families and beds.

On 31 July 1943, Hugh and I were married in the little Church of St John the Baptist, where I had been baptised and where my sister, Jean, was to marry Aitken Lawrie some three months later. My father was on active service at the time, somewhere in Iraq, so my brother Angus gave me away and Jean and Mary were my bridesmaids. The first face I saw as we came out of church under an archway of swords formed by six VCOs was the dear sweet face of our old mehterani. She had come to see her Janet Baba married! The guard of honour included Subadar Major Sujjan Singh and Subadar Sultan Ahmed and they were all invited to the reception so Hugh felt it only right to make part of his speech in Urdu. For our honeymoon we went to Kashmir and our houseboat was called 'Paradise Regained'. What romance.

For me India will always be my home. I love the people, I love the country, and there is a sense of belonging. I remember the early winter mornings with the mist rising from the fields, the long warm afternoons in the garden full of roses and chrysanthemums and trees festooned with bougainvillea, the evenings full of the chatter of parakeets and other birds going home to roost, the smell of wood and dung fires from the villages where evening meals were being prepared and the night sky full of bright stars, so big that you feel you can reach up and touch them and later, in the still of the night, the familiar, haunting call of the jackals. These are some of the sights and smells I shall always remember when I think back on the paradise that was my India.

Now my life was to change for ever but that is another story in another land.

NCO IN ROORKEE

by

Ernie Odell

In 1920, at the age of 23, I was posted to India and like the rest of the draft we were promoted to L/Cpl. We sailed from Plymouth in the SS *Huntspill*, a ship the Allies had captured during WWI and put into use as a troop-ship, and on arrival at Bombay we were soon housed in a transit camp at Colaha Point to await posting to a unit. Up until now we had not seriously considered the type of unit to be found in India, so it was with some trepidation that we scanned the notice boards each day for news of postings. Finally the orders came through and we discovered that the draft had been split into three, the corporal, myself and six others being ordered to the 1st KGO Sappers and Miners at Roorkee. The journey took three days but I didn't mind this as I found all the new sights fascinating. I watched vendors coming along the side of the train shouting their wares – unfamiliar fruits and bizarre-looking sweetmeats, as well as two separate containers of water, one for Hindus, the other for Moslems.

We reached Roorkee at last, about mid-morning on the third day, and we were met at the station by a Royal Engineers sergeant who arranged for us to be taken to the British Warrant Officers and Non Commissioned Officers' Mess. We were rather surprised to be met by a sergeant, but even more surprised when we were ushered into a very swish mess and greeted by a man in white flannels and a sports blazer, who was introduced to us as the regimental sergeant-major. He immediately treated us to a round of drinks at the bar and I began to feel things were looking up.

We all tried to give the impression that we thought this sort of behaviour was quite ordinary but I know I for one was astounded and the others looked equally bemused. Sergeant-majors didn't normally behave in this sort of way! We learned from this genial man that we had all been promoted to 2nd corporals and furthermore now that we had been posted to the Sappers and Miners we should all be promoted to corporals. This was then the third rank in the RE and equivalent to a lance-sergeant in the infantry, so we were certainly getting quick promotion!

Next day we were fitted out with uniform appropriate to service in the Corps. We found that we were to wear a rather attractive silver badge, depicting the Prince of Wales feathers, in our sun helmets and that the uniform was of a light khaki colour, quite unlike the rather darker uniforms used by regiments of the British Army in India. Our life here was to be very different from what we had experienced so far. The mess boasted a billiards room, a bar, a huge lounge and a good-sized dining room. The food, though initially strange to us, was pretty good and there was plenty of it. It all seemed very luxurious.

We were given a briefing by the adjutant and OC of 'H' Company during which we learned, to our considerable astonishment, that there were only about fifty Warrant Officers and NCOs in the whole of this Corps of Sappers and Miners. This detachment was one of three that went to make up 'H' Company, the parent unit. We also discovered that the Corps consisted of many field companies, field troops (mounted) and other units – including a bridging train in which the pontoons were pulled by a team of six bullocks, they being better suited to the climate than horses. Many of these units were out on service on the North West Frontier and in Mesopotamia. In the HQ at Roorkee there were workshops and fieldworks, where Warrant Officers and NCOs acted as instructors, very much on the same lines as at Chatham.

The Corps was composed of about equal numbers of Hindus, Sikhs and Mohammedans. None of these could speak English, so the first priority for newcomers like ourselves was to learn Urdu. It is a difficult language and it was a long time before I became fluent in it. Meanwhile life continued and although much impressed by everything when I first arrived, I discovered quite quickly the overwhelming drawback to such an existence – boredom. There was too much sitting about for my liking and it was really too hot to venture out exploring as I should like to have done. Hockey was popular but I had never played the game, and although football was played, there was already a team in existence so there was not much chance for newcomers. I liked billiards but then so did everyone else, so it was equally difficult to get a game.

If it hadn't been for the arrival of a major from the Bengal Lancers, I think I would have gone spare. As it was, this man was persuaded to form an equitation class for newly arrived British NCOs and I eagerly joined. What's more, I completed the course, passing out top in the riding school section, successfully fooling the examiner into believing that I was in control as I completed the jumping section. I felt quite pleased with myself and was in a good mood for several days, until I heard from some official source that all of us who had recently arrived with the Sappers and Miners were to stay in India for the rest of our service, which intelligence plunged me into gloom for several weeks. Things might be looking up at present – but India for the next fifteen years! Besides, I was a plumber by trade, and I couldn't see that in a hot country like India there would be much use for my skills with lead. Anyhow I hadn't volunteered for such service. Gradually in the face of the inevitable my grousings grew fainter, until I became quite resigned and looked about for compensations.

It was not long before we were issued with our accoutrements. These were not the same as we had been used to in England; instead of rifle and bayonet, there was a leather belt similar to an officer's Sam Browne, only wider, to which was attached a long scabbard housing, what was known in official jargon, as 'Sword, Bayonet, Pattern 97'. This was, as the name implies, a weapon about 2ft 6in long, having on its upper edge a saw. I thought this most extraordinary as the English Press had made a great fuss about the Germans using bayonets with saw edges in the war, yet here we were being issued with them! Perhaps the reason could be found in the fact that these fearsome objects wouldn't fit a Lee-Enfield and had been designed to fit the muskets of earlier and less humane years. They were actually extremely efficient as saws but they were withdrawn from use in 1930.

We were housed in a block of quarters whimsically known as 'Angels' Terrace'; the rooms were fairly large and reasonably comfortable, with a bathroom shared between two. At the end of this line of quarters sat a pankha wallah – he was the man who operated the pankha (a huge fan) by means of a rope, often attached to his big toe. At night it was this man's duty to see that the pankha waved languorously to and fro throughout the hours of darkness. Since he often dropped off to sleep, he was the object of much cursing and abuse. Sometimes sugar would be thrown round a sleeping pankha wallah, and although this may sound a fairly odd kind of punishment, it was effective enough when the ants started to swarm all over him in their search for more.

But life in the mess was fraught with lots of hidden dangers. Horseplay of one sort or another was much in evidence, and I remember one occasion when a corporal only narrowly avoided losing his ear when the glass from a picture showered down around him; the subject of the picture – Queen Victoria – was unamused, but this may have been owing to the arrow lodged in her bosom at the time. Rather more seriously there was the case of Corporal McMahon who died one day before afternoon tea, having imbibed too much alcohol at luncheon, the effect of which, when combined with the intense heat, led to a fever and cardiac arrest. We all took note of his untimely end and drank a lot less from that moment on.

Soon I became more than restless, so a friend and I decided to apply for a transfer to the Military Works Dept. The adjutant, Captain C. A. Bird, afterwards General Sir Clarence Bird, seemed a nice sort of bloke, and we were pretty sure that he would look favourably on our request. He asked me the kind of life I was looking for, and I replied that while I enjoyed leisure as much as the next man, I preferred to have bouts of activity interspersed with it. He smiled and seemingly made a snap decision.

'How soon can you get your kit together?'

'In about an hour, sir.

'Right. You're going to join the 5th Field Company at Parachinar. The train leaves at 6pm tonight. That should be enough action for you – there's a war on up there they tell me. Good luck'. He waved a hand and I was dismissed.

After seven years in India, I was eligible for home leave and got in touch again with Miss Edith Clark, with whom I had been pretty pally in my early days at Chatham, and who was now living in London. We saw quite a bit of each other. In fact we saw enough of each other to become engaged and finally married in Lyndhurst Church on 15th December 1928. Our honeymoon consisted mainly of visiting old friends and relatives before sailing to India in April 1929. It was the first time that Edie had been out of England so she was both excited and, I think, a little apprehensive.

There were sixty other families of British Other Ranks on board, and quite soon things were going with a swing. Having done the journey twice before, I felt quite knowledgeable, and was able to point out the sellers of bogus relics at Port Said, and the hundreds of thousands of mauve jellyfish that surrounded the ship while we lay docked at Port Suez. On arrival in India, we were stationed in Rawalpindi, but eventually moved to Roorkee, which Edie found a strange place. Instead of the large shops, cinemas and other comforts that we had been used to in Rawalpindi, there were some small dingy stalls and narrow, dirty alleyways. For a time I think it depressed her – I know it depressed me! We were allotted quarters in Angels' Terrace, although these were very different when furnished as married quarters to how they had been on my first arrival in India.

The WO&NCO's Mess was much the same as ever but now, being a married man, I didn't see so much of it. By this time there were about forty WOs and NCOs altogether in Roorkee and, as more than half of them were married, the question of amenities was a high priority. The only place where any functions could be held was a large hall in the single men's quarters called, optimistically, 'The Theatre'. It had actually got a stage and dressing rooms, but was normally used more for dancing than for strictly thespian activities. There were dances every Saturday night and each year there was a Grand Ball during Armistice week. The year after we arrived together in Roorkee I was elected Chairman of the Ball Organising Committee. Determined to make things a great success, I ordered decorative paper printed with birds and butterflies with which to cover the pillars. I also sent a party of sappers with a lorry to the jheels (swamps) several miles away, ordering them to fill the lorry with the huge plumes of pampas grass which grew there in profusion. These were fixed to the walls all round the theatre and onto them Edie, plus assorted helpers, tied no less than five thousand paper poppies. The whole effect was extremely attractive and at the Ball that evening I was complimented early on by the Colonel and his wife. I say 'early on' advisedly, as I think by the end of the evening it is unlikely that his wife would have been quite so fulsome in her praise. It was the pampas grass that was to blame. I hadn't appreciated that a great deal of it was ripe, meaning that anyone who brushed against it would come away with a liberal sprinkling of fluff and seeds. By the end of the evening one could see little groups of females with what I can only describe as peeved expressions, picking at each other's dresses like a group of baboons looking for fleas. In addition, one or two people suffered from hay fever and so retired early, eyes streaming, to sneeze themselves to death in private. Despite these unfortunate side effects, however, the main body of the guests enjoyed themselves tremendously. I think!

There were one or two incidents at the Ball mainly involving ladies who had unhappily arrived in a dress identical to another's. This was not so infrequent or so accidental as might at first appear. It was the work of Banarsi Dass, who lived in Roorkee bazaar and owned the only decent dress shop in the whole place. He was a complete rogue, but rather a likeable one, and although many of the ladies called him an arch-fiend, some even using (I believe) coarser expressions, many still traded with him on account of his monopoly of the market. He employed several darzis (tailors) to help him, and possessed a large battered book of dress patterns. Before the annual ball he had gone to Delhi and returned with numerous rolls of dress material; then, armed with his order book, he had sallied forth to the married quarters. Many of the women were delighted when he told them confidentially that he had, by the *greatest* good fortune, a piece of material that would be exactly right for a ball gown, and moreover, went so well with the lady's particular colouring. In some cases the ladies provided their own patterns – not that Banarsi cared. Since there was much rivalry between the ladies, not one of them had disclosed what she intended wearing for the Ball saying no more than "I am having it specially made". Came the great evening, a few found themselves paying dearly for being so secretive! Luckily, Edie was a first-class dressmaker herself, so was not among those embarrassed in this way, but as may be imagined Banarsi's name was (charitably) Mud. I did hear that several ladies descended on his shop the next morning, breathing fire and vowing vengeance, only to find that, quite by chance, Mr Dass had left that very morning for his holidays!

The cold weather of 1934-35 was a memorable time for us. I was to be promoted to Regimental Quartermaster Sergeant on 22nd November and in March of the new year I heard that I was to be further promoted to Warrant Officer Class I. I was thus entitled to serve another five years, so we were able to take a spell of leave in England. On our return we were confronted with a brand new bungalow, so Edie was soon busy adding personal touches while I got on with the garden.

Being a large compound with hedges and bushes and trees, it is little wonder that snakes were abundant. One evening, when walking round the bungalow preparatory to retiring, I saw to my annoyance that the bathroom door to the garden had been left open by the sweeper. Muttering to myself about the incompetence of the man I shut the door and then bent down to pick up the chamber-pot which was under the basin. As I did so I felt a sudden sharp pain in my index finger and jumped back with an exclamation – to catch sight of a deadly cobra slithering hastily away. I wasted precious moments trying to kill it, for the full extent of my own danger did not immediately strike me. The instant it did, my first thought was to chop off my finger, a desperate remedy rendered impossible by the lack of an axe. Hastily, I looked around for other ways of maiming myself and decided on a razor blade. I rushed to the cupboard and ripped open a fresh packet of blades – I did not want septicaemia on top of snake-bite. For one ghastly moment of indecision I rested the blade on top of the two fang marks, then I slashed down hard and almost yelled aloud with the pain. I made three incisions before I felt certain that I had touched the bone. There were tears in my eyes as I squeezed out the blood. It was unusually thick and dark. For about a minute, the only sound in the room, other than my heavy breathing, was the steady splat, splat of my blood in a tumbler. After a time, I judged I had lost as much blood as was wise and made a tourniquet from the window-blind cord. Then I woke the Bandmaster from next door and together we raced to the hospital on my motorcycle combination. There we roused the assistant surgeon. I was given an injection in the arm (jolly painful) and two in the stomach (not recommended for the faint-hearted), after which I felt happier – now I would be all right. A little later the first symptons of snake-bite poisoning appeared.

First, there was a very nasty pain in my stomach, to which was soon added a tightening of the throat and a tremendous desire to go to sleep. The finger itself became a mass of tingling pain and then went numb. I felt terribly weak. The medical officer arrived and ordered that I be given regular and enormous doses of black coffee. I can remember now how marvellous that coffee was, but it was soon accompanied by another symptom – a persistent and disconcerting double vision that made me feel slightly sick. The great desire to sleep continued and my pulse was extremely sluggish; they had applied a tourniquet to my arm and it was decided, in spite of the danger of gangrene, that this should be left on. After a considerable time my pulse had recovered sufficiently for the tourniquet to be removed and I was allowed to sleep. Although lying for several days in a ward with 'Dangerously Ill' plastered on the door, I felt sure that I was in no danger and enjoyed the visits of the Indian instructors who ignored the notice forbidding them to enter, explaining that they could not read English. I did not question this surprising statement – in fact I laughed heartily, welcoming their humour after my very grim ordeal. Had I actually succumbed to the snake-bite, Edie would not have heard about it until I had been dead and buried, for she was up in the hills and a corpse in midsummer is not kept for longer than twelve hours.

As a suitable postscript to the story, I learned afterwards that when the medical officer returned to his bungalow after treating me he found a very unwelcome visitor – a krait lying on his bed. Enraged at this impertinence, he grabbed a gun and blew its head off – doing the bed no good at all.

I was due to go on pension in 1939/40, but I now saw that it would be most unlikely that I should be retired. War was declared and I was soon busy enlarging the workshops to cater for the influx of tradesmen that was expected. A short time later, due to the ill-health of the former Regimental Sergeant Major, I was promoted to that rank but continued to spend most of my time down in the workshops. One day the Adjutant called me into his office and asked me if I would be interested in accepting a Commission. Despite some persuasion, I declined, and when I was asked why I was turning down this opportunity, I replied frankly that I was RSM of the Corps, had the best bungalow of the WO&NCOs, free rations, lighting and water, and if I accepted a Commission I would only receive a shilling or two more in pay as a Lieutenant and this would be more than cancelled out by mess bills etc. I was then told that I would be a Captain and Assistant Officer in charge of Workshops. There is a fine art in knowing when to give in and this seemed to be the moment.

FIRST WEEKS IN ROORKEE

by

Ian Lyall Grant

Unlike most newly-joined subalterns, Chris Rosher and I arrived in Roorkee in 1938 from the north-west. We had driven by car from England and entered India by the classic route through the Khyber. After a week's pause in Nowshera to get acclimatised, we drove down the Grand Trunk Road and entered Roorkee in early April by the famous Lion Bridge over the Ganges canal. First impressions were not encouraging and our hearts fell; in 7,000 miles we had seldom seen a more scruffy village. Four years here didn't seem a very jolly prospect. However a polite inhabitant directed us to the Cantonment, about a mile away, which, with its neat layout and many trees, presented a very different picture and restored our spirits.

We reported to the Adjutant, the slim and immaculate Mike Perceval-Price, and were directed to temporary accommodation in No 10 bungalow, where I met my bearer, Abdul Aziz. He had been recommended to me in the UK and proved to be a staunch, dignified and likeable companion. He had the reputation of being a competent cook when required, a very useful talent on travels, but was now getting rather too old for the more arduous journeys. He arranged for tailors and a haircutter to appear from nowhere and I was duly measured for khaki-drill uniform and white-drill mess kit. Abdul was also entitled to new clothes for acting as waiter in the Mess, and for best occasions. He indoctrinated me into the mysteries of the bungalow's plumbing facilities, or rather complete lack of them, the main mystery for me being why in a Sapper stronghold there was no running water, no drains, and no hot water. Fortunately there was electricity and a single creaking ceiling fan gave some relief from the daily increasing heat, already in the nineties.

Having smartened up as much as possible, for we had very little kit with us, we made our way to the Mess which, we had already heard, had the reputation of being rather stuffy. It was, therefore, a surprise when a large major introduced himself and asked if we would like to join his party in a forthcoming outing. He explained that he planned to watch a famous Hindu religious festival, the Kumbh Mela, which only took place once in every twelve years, and would be held the very next day at Hardwar, only a few miles away. Of course we were delighted to accept. Bill Williams, for it was he who had invited us, was a kindly man of great charm. He got on very well with Indians, and was to have a distinguished career, ending up as a Lieutenant General and being appointed the first Engineer-in-Chief of the Indian Army after Independence. He became an Indian citizen and was buried in Roorkee.

The next day we set off with Bill Williams for Hardwar, picking up on the way the Principal of the Thomason Engineering College, Mr Puri, and his very attractive wife. We drove along the road beside the canal, duly admiring its remarkable engineering features, and at Hardwar joined the Canal engineer on the flat roof of his bungalow. From here we had a splendid view of the pool of sacred water from the holy Ganges in which the pilgrims were going to immerse themselves in order to absolve themselves of their sins. I had never seen such a huge crowd, more than a million I was told, nor one of such diversity. Gradually a procession of holy men, many of them naked, formed up, led by about twenty elephants carrying the most important priests who were apparently saying prayers. As the head of the procession reached them the crowd prostrated themselves and I was astonished to see that the leading elephant carried a large wireless set operated by two uniformed British soldiers intoning their well-known prayer, "report my signals". The crowd was good-humoured, the police unobtrusive, and it was a relaxed and pleasant day. Mrs Puri was charming and lively and teased me by asking if I hadn't got any sins that I would like to wash away. India was growing on me.

The Commandant at Roorkee was Colonel Kenny Lee. The next day we reported to him in his office. He was not a very fit man and I was not much impressed. Nor was he as it turned out. He asked a few questions and then made a note in the Commandant's private journal. Long after World War II an Indian Commandant was to show me what he had written. It was: "Don't know how he will turn out. Looks cheerful."

Chris, a noted horseman, was posted to a field troop, and I was posted to 3 Field Company. The OC, Major Tom Wright, was away on leave pursuing tigers in the forests of the Central Provinces. From his camp he had written a letter in pencil to his new subaltern, whoever it might be. It contained much good advice, and stressed that I would be more or less useless until I could speak Urdu. He recommended at least four hours study every day, including one hour with the Munshi. Tom was still a bachelor and not one to waste words, but behind a rather dour front he had a good sense of humour. A good boxer and fine horseman, he had a high sense of duty, and believed that officers should play games with their men rather than play polo, which was the main evening activity in Roorkee. He ran an excellent company and I greatly respected him.

Roorkee suffered from being a single-regiment station and inevitably tended to be rather self-centred. The nearest other units were 40 miles away at Meerut to the south and about the same distance at Dehra Dun to the north. As Sappers often do, most people worked hard. First parade was at 6.30am, breakfast 8–9, and many did not come in for lunch until between 2 and 3pm. Siesta, or study, until about 5, then polo or games until 6.30. Tin bath and change for dinner around 8pm. Quite reasonable in the cold weather, but arduous when it started getting hot. It reached a peak of about 116 degrees in June.

After a short period in No 10 Bungalow, I was moved into one nearer the Mess. Like all the others it was hired by the government from an Indian landlord. There was a large central room with some antiquated furniture and three large bed-sitting rooms. Each bed-sitter had an en suite bathroom, a little concrete-floored annex with a door to the outside. It contained a tin hip-bath and a commode, commonly called a 'thunderbox', and had a hole in one corner through which the bath water could be emptied into the garden. Cobras were not uncommon in Roorkee and 'old hands' liked to tell newcomers that the snakes often came in through these holes. Each bungalow was surrounded on three sides by a wide verandah and was set in a square 'compound' of about an acre, with several trees. In front was a garden with a few flowers and at the back were the stables and a series of small hovels for the servants and their families. Each bungalow was supported by a team of a sweeper (mehtar), a mali (gardener) and a night watchman (chowkidar), as well as the bearers and syces (grooms) of its inhabitants. There were no locks on any of the doors but I never heard of anything being stolen.

The Mess had been the private residence of a Sapper subaltern in the days of the East India Company, when it was permitted for Britons to own land and property in India. It faced north and had a breathtaking view of the Garhwal and Kumaon Himalayas. Except in the monsoon months, snowy peaks could often be seen stretching from one side of the northern horizon to the other, a view so perfect that it looked almost unnatural. Sadly, increasing smog has now obscured this stunning prospect. There was a fine lawn, a tennis court and a small covered swimming pool. To sit out on the lawn and drink nimbu panies (fresh lime juice) or whisky sodas at the end of a long day was unforgettable. There was also an excellent library in the Mess and one of the first books I came across was an account of a motor race from Peking to Paris in 1904. It had been won by Prince Borghese and two companions, who had motored across Asia and Europe in two months. An extraordinary feat which made our own trip to India seem rather mundane.

An unfortunate incident two or three years previously had given Roorkee a bad name with educated Indians. When Indian officers first started being commissioned into the Indian army they went to England and had just the same training as the British. After an Indian Cadet Academy was set up at Dehra Dun, Indian Sapper officers went not to Cambridge for two years but to the Thomason Engineering College (now Roorkee University). The then Commandant had decided that, while they were students, they would be happier setting up their own Mess or 'chummery' rather than coming to the main Mess. If they had been British this would have been an excellent arrangement and much appreciated by the young officers. But they weren't British and it was an unimaginative mistake. The Indians felt that they were being excluded from the British Mess and this led to much ill-feeling.

The lack of other units and the number of middle-aged bachelors made meals in the Mess rather sedate affairs. Esprit-de-corps was high but conversation was not a strong point, or so it seemed to junior members. There was a rumour, no doubt exaggerated, that subalterns should keep quiet until they had climbed over 20,000 feet, or shot a tiger. Fortunately times were changing. There were some first-class officers around, for instance Ken Sheapherd and Stu Battye among others, and with the arrival of a brilliant and gregarious new Deputy Commandant, Colonel 'Bulger' Duke, the old shibboleths were being rapidly broken down.

There was much for a new subaltern to learn about Indian ways and religions. The Bengal Sappers had been partially involved in the rebellion of 1857, although the Sappers had not harmed their British officers. A feeling among the soldiers that their religions were under threat had been one of the reasons that many soldiers of the Bengal Army joined the rebellion. As a result, the Bengal Sappers, who apart from specialist artisans, enlisted mainly soldiers of high caste, including some from the old district of Oudh whose men had been at the heart of the mutiny, were scrupulously careful to avoid giving religious offence. I was instructed that Mahommedans must not be asked to touch or carry any product of pigs, nor Hindus any product of cows, nor Sikhs any form of tobacco. This was easy enough, but it was a surprise to learn that to high-caste Hindus the British were equated to the lowest caste, the untouchables, and if my shadow fell on the food in the Hindu cookhouse, the food would be thrown away. It seemed a long way from the "Shun! Any complaints?" of Chatham.

The basic task for British officers was, of course, to organise training. In the summer the emphasis was on individual training. Much emphasis was placed on education. The Sappers learnt, or improved, their skills in various trades in the workshops, under the instruction of British NCOs, or went on a wide variety of courses. Many Indians had considerable skill but were used to rather slapdash methods. As an Indian Commandant was to say to me later: "You know our chaps; one-thou, ten-thou, it's all the same!" However, they were quick to learn higher standards and over the years some became very good indeed. The winter, when the climate was excellent, was the time for collective training.

Although everyone worked hard, there was plenty of relaxation. Two months leave was authorised each year, and in addition there was a splendid arrangement in the cold weather by which three periods of ten days leave could be taken, without counting as leave! On Thursdays the custom was to wear mufti and only put in a short day and, of course, religious holidays were carefully observed. With four major religions to be catered for, these were not insignificant.

A bicycle was the normal means of transport around the cantonment, but every officer was entitled to keep a horse, a 'charger', at Government expense, for use on parade or (theoretically) on the line of march. In Roorkee horses were more often used for exercise or for polo. Very few officers owned cars (we had sold ours) preferring to own a second horse for polo. Polo was the standard activity for officers not engaged in playing or organising games with their troops, and was played on the fine ground in front of the Thomason College. Competitions were held with the Cavalry and Gunners in Meerut and the 2nd Gurkhas in Dehra Dun. Shikar, ie shooting or fishing, was a popular activity on weekends in the winter, and very good it was too. Not many people fished, but there were some fine mahseer in the Ganges and the higher reaches of the Ganges Canal.

On longer leaves, those who were married, or who craved a little social life, repaired to Kashmir or one of the many delightful hill-stations which had been established in the foothills of the Himalayas. As there were many 'abandoned' wives spending the hot-weather in these places while their husbands were working in the plains, the activities of bachelors were regarded with mild suspicion, and they were known as 'poodle-fakers'. More adventurous souls chose to go trekking or shooting in the Himalayas and Karakorams. This vast and sparsely inhabited area offered unlimited opportunities for travel and exploration at minimum expense. Few who travelled in the great mountains would ever forget the experience.

The pre-war Indian Army was a long-service volunteer army. In the Bengal Sappers many of the sappers, let alone NCOs and VCOs, had served for a dozen or more years. Indeed a sapper with less than four years service was often referred to as a recruit. The physical and educational standards required of would-be volunteers were high. In an admittedly exceptional year, 1935, nearly 400 Sikh would-be recruits had travelled to Roorkee from their homes in the Punjab and only five had been accepted. Regular trips to the North West Frontier kept operational skills sharp, while technical skills were in constant use. As a result, field companies were good by any standard, and it was not surprising that the Bengal Sappers had a high opinion of themselves, and were somewhat derisively referred to by the other Sapper groups as "God's Own". It was a soubriquet that they were happy to accept.

Once my uniform had been made, I was, of course, available for duty. I was detailed to attend the first parade at 6.30am one morning and told that the training for that day would be anti-gas drill. Here I felt on firm ground. Our last course at Chatham before posting had been on anti-gas. Our instructor had been the very charismatic 'Ginger' Wilkinson, and so I had absorbed something of what we had been taught. On parade, the courtesies over, I explained to Subedar Kishan Singh the main points to stress. He was an elderly Sikh, with a grey beard neatly tied up in a snood, and spoke perfect English. He listened gravely and then gave out the orders to the other VCOs and senior NCOs. When they had gone he turned to me and said: "What you told me was absolutely right, Sahib. I remember in the first gas attack at Ypres ..." *Collapse of junior subaltern*, as 'Punch' used to say. Dai David, who had arrived in Roorkee a few days after Chris and me, had a similar experience. When he asked his Pathan subedar what games he played, the Subedar drew himself up to his full height and said: "I don't play games, Sahib. I do RECONNAISSANCES!" It turned out that he had been one of those remarkable individuals who had been chosen to reconnoitre the trans-border regions of India to collect intelligence for India's defence. Both

Dai and I had begun to learn how much the very high quality of the Indian Army depended on its VCOs.

In May Roorkee began to get very hot during the day although the nights were relatively cool. It was now customary at night to move one's bed and mosquito net into the garden, which was cooler than the bungalow. If it came on to rain, as it sometimes did, shouts of "Chowkidar!" would echo round the cantonment as the night-watchmen, usually fast asleep on the back verandahs, hastened to help in carrying the beds back to the front verandahs. In the morning all the doors to the house would be shut to retain the cool air. 'Dust devils', spirals of dust-laden hot air, became frequent during the hotter hours of the day and in the company office papers were sent flying and everything was covered in dust.

At the end of May, I was called to the Adjutant's office and told that in a week's time I was to leave Roorkee and go to Wana in Waziristan. This was to enable an officer in 2 Field Company there to go on leave. This was splendid news as Roorkee was by now almost unbearably hot, around 110 degrees, and leaving one's bungalow was like opening the door of an oven. So it was with a light heart that, together with Abdul Aziz, I caught the Frontier Mail as it stopped at Roorkee at 2am and set out for the glamorous North West Frontier.

SHIKAR

A novelist, who had stayed in Roorkee with the Commandant in the mid 1930s, had caused great offence by writing later that there were only two subjects of conversation in Roorkee, 'the Bengal Sappers' and 'shikar' (hunting). One fears, however, that there was an element of truth in this comment, for the *esprit de corps* of the Bengal Sappers was very high and the easily accessible shooting and to a lesser extent the fishing was as good as, and in some respects better than, anywhere else in India and many people took advantage of it.

Hog-Hunting

'Pig-sticking', as it was irreverently called, was widely popular, though it had not flourished in Roorkee as the country was considered too difficult and the boars too fast and clever. This was rectified by the purchase of some good Arab horses as the local villages often complained that 'sounders' of wild hog had located themselves in their crops and were doing damage. Most officers at Roorkee used spears about six feet six inches long, always held underhand when in use, with three-edged army pattern heads, shafts of stout male bamboo, good lumps of lead on the butts, so that the spear balanced well back, points carefully sharpened, and neat leather cases with bits of cork at the end to keep the points in order. Described by Lord Macaulay as "the most exciting and perilous of field sports", it was certainly not for the faint-hearted. The boar, quite unlike the British pig, is a gallant fighting animal who will attack at sight. He is a handsome beast with his clean limbs, fine feet, muscular body, thin straight pencil of a tail with a tuft on the end of it and a truly fierce expression. He often has formidable tushes (tusks). The wild boar on the Commander-in-Chief's 1923 Christmas card was painted by Lord Rawlinson himself.

Bindon Blood described how "one day we met early at a village with open country to the south and west, the Ganges canal-bank cover to the east, the terai (foothills), with some of its forest land, two miles or so to the north and north-west and to the north also the glorious range of everlasting snows, rising to 23,000ft or so, a hundred miles off but looking about ten, shining in the morning sun and forming a background ever grateful to the eye. The villagers turned out in force to beat and talked enthusiastically of this and that 'burra baari jungi daant-walla' (great heavy fighting tusker) we were to see directly! So we went out into the cornfields and having formed a line of beaters some 300 to 400yds long, with a party of three spears at each end and another in the middle, we moved on through the high corn as quietly as possible. I, still a Griffin (that is, new to India), was with one of the end parties and we went on for half a mile or so without anything happening, but then suddenly a sounder of about forty pigs, headed by two splendid grey boars, with some smaller boars and sows and plenty of 'squeakers' of all sizes, the little ones striped, went away past my party heading at a great rate for the terai and jungle to the north. After giving them a start of the usual 400yds or so, we went hell-for-leather after the two boars. I was riding the best of my two Arabs and soon slipped ahead of my two friends. I had not got on terms with the boar however when we came to the terai, rode down a small nullah, crossed a shallow stream and got into rather broken ground with bushes and some thorns. Here the pace shortened a bit and I began to think of using my spear, when the boar jinked away to the right, turning without losing pace, while I was carried on some little distance before I could turn my horse. However we were soon round and on the line again, when I saw that the boar had set his stern to a big thorn bush and was facing all comers, truly a grim sight! As I turned after the boar my two friends arrived on the scene, but before they came into action I tried a slant-wise charge at the boar. When he saw me coming he charged me just at the right moment and, more by good luck than good management, I fended him off, catching him with the spear on his near shoulder and, owing to the speed and pluck of my horse, nearly turning him over. He was not much damaged however as I took him too far forward, and he succeeded in getting back to his thorn-bush before either of my friends could intervene. He was as full of fight as ever being much annoyed by the wound I had given him. He charged out when I went for him again on my gallant Arab which avoided him discreetly, leaving him to the old hand of our party who killed him beautifully with a thrust just in the right place behind his shoulder. He died game, without a sound".

God gave the horse for man to ride,
And steel wherewith to fight,
And wine to swell his soul with pride,
And women for delight;
But a better gift than all these four
Was when he made the fighting boar!

Fishing

Few records remain of the exploits of fishermen based at Roorkee and it was never a particularly popular sport. There was no trout fishing in the vicinity, although there was a good rail connection to the excellent trout streams of Kulu and Kashmir. However, the mahseer fishing in the Ganges and the upper reaches of the Ganges canal was very good; indeed the size of the mahseer in the Raiwala pool in the Ganges below Hardwar was legendary and some were said to weigh well over 100 pounds. Bindon Blood told how, on the way back to Hardwar one day after shooting tiger, he saw an otter bring a nice 7lb mahseer to the bank, "so we had fresh fish for dinner". He also related how that year, 1874, they saw great quantities of fish of about 3lbs caught by the local inhabitants using lengths of cotton cloth, normally forming part of their dress, to intercept fish trying to leap over the dam separating the Ganges river from the Canal. One day a very nice mahseer was caught with a sun-umbrella belonging to the wife of a brother officer!

Shooting

Shooting was the most popular activity, no doubt partly because the products of the chase were far tastier than the victuals supplied by local contractors. Broadly speaking there were three types of shooting available: small game or shot-gun shooting, big game shooting in the great mountains and big game shooting in the jungle. It was a sport that was encouraged, for the hunting skills that had to be acquired for success were also of military value, while the 'bandobast' (a splendid Persian word, widely used, and much more evocative than 'logistics') necessary to visit remote areas was useful military training. Moreover, half the attraction of these shooting trips was that they took a participant to the wilder parts of the country, where one could see not only magnificent scenery but a side of Indian country life unknown to those with more conventional interests.

In 1931 Colonel A H Cunningham, who had spent 28 years as a Bengal Sapper ending up as Commandant, published privately what would now be called a DIY book on big game shooting in India. While more than half the book concerned the pursuit of tigers, this remarkable book had natural history notes on all the major and unusual animals which might be encountered in the Indian jungles and mountains. Every aspect of the sport was covered in a most detailed and practical way. It was a book designed for young subalterns and any beginner who absorbed its information had a good chance of success and of avoiding dangerous blunders. The Colonel also recommended the study of natural history, plants and trees, and photography, so as to take advantage of the many opportunities which visits to unusual areas provided. Many young officers in the thirties were deeply indebted to this book for its down-to-earth advice.

Small Game Shooting

Small game shooting was widely available in India and Roorkee was no exception. Partridges, of several species, quail and snipe existed in many of the fields and uncultivated land in the neighbourhood. The local village headmen would often (but not always) agree, in return for a small *douceur*, to shooting in the village fields and would provide beaters, who were paid a very small fee, to beat through the crops. Black partridges were particularly sought after as they were delicious to eat.

In some parts of the forests in the nearby foothills, peafowl and red jungle-fowl (the original chicken) were common. In the wild both are very wily birds and far from easy to locate. Most Hindus and many British objected to the shooting of peacocks and would only shoot a peahen when required for the pot, but few had reservations about the jungle fowl which are also excellent eating.

However, the cream of the local small game shooting was the week-end pursuit of wild duck at a place known in Roorkee as "The Jheels". The jheels were some swamps, flooded annually by the Ganges and located between Roorkee and Meerut, sixty miles to the south. Between the two World Wars the only vehicles in Roorkee were two or three private cars, so shooting on the jheels, where boats were needed, was difficult to organise. At that time there were two elephants on the Corps strength, officially required for building pontoon bridges, and these made ideal transport for those interested in jungle shooting which duly flourished. However, modernisation decreed in 1936 that the elephants should be replaced by two 30cwt lorries, much to the disgust of the jungle enthusiasts and the delight of the devotees of the jheels. Flat-bottomed punts, designed to be transported in the new lorries, were constructed in the Corps workshops and were duly carried to and from the jheels at certain week-ends in the cold-weather shooting season.

The swamps belonged to no-one and the whole subject tended to be shrouded in secrecy, whose main purpose was to conceal the excellence of the shooting from rival parties from other stations, notably Meerut, who sometimes had the effrontery to want to shoot there as well. The ability to provide punts and then remove them was, of course, a vital link in this strategy. For a junior officer an invitation to shoot on the jheels was much prized and indeed it was an unforgettable experience.

The area was inhabited by a small tribe of Indians who lived in three hamlets on the fringes of the swamp and eked out a living by fishing and hunting. They were a curious people, unusually tall and addicted, supported by a long pole, to standing on one leg like the storks and herons that were their neighbours. The leading members of the largest hamlet were important cogs in the organisation. In return for a weekly retainer and an extra gift when shooting took place, they set up the camp, positioned the punts and acted as guides. Their duties were also supposed to include discouraging other wildfowlers, although there was a doubtless well-founded suspicion that the simple villagers were astute enough to keep in with both the rival stations.

The winter climate in North India is wonderfully good and those weekend visits to the jheels are not easily forgotten. First there was the long drive down, much of it across country and passing through several of those remote villages where the heart of India really beats. On arrival at the camp the guns would each be escorted by a villager and punted to some pre-arranged location in the jheels. Then the evening flight would start as the duck flew into the marsh for their night's feeding and for twenty minutes or so there were duck coming at all angles. One participant records that his chief memory of these evening flights is of teal coming very fast and low over the tall reeds and being missed behind by yards, inspiring the advice from his guide: "Bik par maro, sahib!" (Aim at its beak!)

Although these evening flights were sometimes very successful and were followed by a memorable supper in a moonlit camp, they never possessed the fascination of the morning ones when a guide, muffled from the knees up in a homespun cotton sheet, would appear at the entrance to the tent in the dark of the early hours. With him one would trudge out under the stars along a narrow path twisting erratically through the reeds. Suddenly a punt would emerge from the gloom and the guide, having deposited his sahib and gun in it, would push and paddle it out into the swamp. Deciding whether to shoot from a sitting position, or to try standing, always hazardous, or to get out of the punt and stand in the waist-high water, was a difficult decision, especially for newly-joined and inexperienced subalterns who had a feeling anyway that they were only there to act as bird-scarers, ensuring that the duck could not settle. In the dark the air would be full of the cries of the swamp-dwellers, the croaks and quacks, the groans and sighs, all suddenly getting quieter in that short cold period before the first glimmer of daylight appeared. Then one would begin to hear the rustle of invisible wings beating overhead; to be followed a few minutes later by an occasional glimpse of small dark bottle-shaped objects moving swiftly across the eastern sky. About this time would come the first distant shot, followed by a few minutes of high excitement when the duck could be clearly seen. Soon, however, most of the duck would have flown off to spend the day on the wide reaches and sandbanks of the Ganges, while the sun rose, red and round in a cloudless sky, giving the glorious promise that the cold, fresh morning would with absolute certainty turn into a hot sunny day. Now the day-dwellers of the swamp, the fresh water terns, the coots, the herons and the black-and-white kingfishers, took over. This was the cue for the great brown marsh harriers to quarter the swamp, causing flurry and panic wherever they appeared.

After the light was fully up, the bag was collected and taken back to camp where the final rite took place, the consumption of a whole roast duck each for breakfast. Breakfast was in the open air and looking across the swamp one could sometimes see, beyond the clumps of palm trees surrounding the three villages, a great range of snowy peaks stretching right across the northern horizon. How could one forget such week-ends?

Shooting Big Game in the Mountains

Roorkee was also well placed for a second type of shooting, the pursuit of the many varieties of wild deer, goats and sheep in the great mountains to the north. The aim of this very strenuous sport was to obtain a trophy with the largest horns, such beasts normally only being found in the remotest and most inaccessible areas. The allotment of licences to shoot in various areas was strictly controlled and it was illegal to shoot hinds, or stags with horns below a certain size. It was thus a challenge for the hunter and, as only the oldest male beasts were culled, not damaging to the wildlife. That it had been a popular activity for very many years was apparent from the amazing variety of horns which adorned the Roorkee Mess and many of the names below the trophies were of young officers later to become famous, such as Bindon Blood, Hunter-Weston, Nosworthy, Neame, Hobart, Lethbridge, Bird, Broomhall and many others.

In some areas, also, black and brown bears were a great nuisance to villagers as they robbed the few fruit trees, damaged the sparse crops and occasionally killed the village animals, as well as terrorising anyone who chose to move along village paths at night. Consequently hunters were often implored to shoot some particularly tiresome beast and, when shot, their skins were preserved and made a useful floor covering for a sparsely furnished bungalow.

Much of the interest of this form of shikar was in the visit to little-known, and sometimes unexplored, parts of the great mountain ranges which stretch for 2,000 miles along India's northern border from Chitral to Assam. But the more distant parts took many days to reach and needed a long spell of leave, so Kashmir, and some of its neighbouring States, were most commonly visited. At Srinagar, the capital of Kashmir, it was possible to hire a Kashmiri guide or shikari, as well as the tents, gear, food and transport required for what was, in effect, a minor expedition. A march of a week or more was often required to reach a suitable area and this was valuable preparation for the arduous climbing required to stalk the big deer, called barasingh, in the higher forests, and the wild goats and sheep in their rocky fastnesses far above the tree line. These animals are endowed with wonderful eyesight and an acute sense of smell. To get close enough for a shot was far from easy and required much knowledge of their habits and much skill in assessing which way the wind was blowing in the vicinity of the game.

Summer was the individual training season when fewer officers were required with their units and in peacetime most leave was taken then. Shooting trips to the cool of the hills were a wonderful break from the oppressive summer heat of the northern Indian plains and the hard exercise involved made its participants very fit. It was unsurprising, therefore, that many bachelors, and some married couples, found it a splendid way to spend a summer leave. In wartime, of course, leave was shorter and had to be taken when opportunity offered.

Archie Jack was a keen shikari and kept well-illustrated diaries of his trips. Here is an extract from a day on his march up to a shooting area in Kashmir in the autumn:

"7 Oct 40, Mungil, 8,400ft. Chota hazri (light breakfast) at 0300hrs and away an hour later with the shikari, tiffin coolie (man acting as cook), and a local man who was to show us barasingh. Climbed up to 10,500ft in the dark and when it got light worked through the top of the forest on the north side of the slope, ending up about 500ft below [point] 13,209 at 0930hrs. Plentiful tracks in the snow but not a barasingh to be seen or heard. Very disappointing. Climbing back on to the top of the ridge, had to indulge in some rock climbing ... had a delightful stand-easy there, ate a capital breakfast and continued reading *Pride and Prejudice*. At 1115hrs started the 3,000ft descent of the extremely steep north slope to the Kuzuz nala".

There he met his coolies, who had come the long way round with his gear and with them marched for two hours up the "steeply rising nala bed" to a campsite at a place called Nimalwas, "just below the snow" at 11,000ft. Here he learnt from a herdsman that there was an old red bear causing trouble further up the nala. In the last few days it had attacked a man and killed two ponies. So at 1700hrs he went up to look for the bear, but was unsuccessful and returned to the camp in the dark. During the course of the day he had climbed about 6,700ft and descended 3,000, all carrying a rifle. It was not a sport for wimps. Admittedly even Archie Jack, who had represented Great Britain as a pentathlete in the 1936 Olympics, found this day rather tiring and rested the following day before moving on to his next campsite at 14,000ft.

The following year, on a similar trip in November, Archie Jack had the risky experience of spending a night at 10,000ft without any bedding. Out hunting in the high forest with only the tiffin coolie and an old local, he realised as dark descended that the old man would never find his way back to the camp through the steep forest in the dark, so decided to spend the night in a luckily-found herdsman's shack. He gives an amusing account of this night:

"The tiffin coolie and I collected some fire-wood and we got an excellent fire going ... I split up all the rations I had left in my haversack with the other two. They were willing to share everything with me except the sandwiches, the potted meat of which, they quite rightly asserted, had not been 'halaled'. At about 2000hrs we settled down for the night on the floor of the hut. The rest of the night was for me an experience which must be similar to that of a joint being roasted on a spit ... with this big difference that I had to replenish the fire myself every clock hour throughout the night. The others took no notice of the fire once it was lit, but I would have died, I think, had I not kept it going well. As one lay on the floor, one part of one's body was red hot and the other extremely chilly. The tiffin coolie went straight into a deep sleep with vocal accompaniment, but the old local stayed awake and succeeded in keeping me awake for the first three hours with his enthusiastic and systematic scratching. I think he must have covered every portion of his anatomy and in setting about his work he adopted a series of the most acrobatic postures imaginable. The noise of his scratching was quite unbelievable; exactly like a 'bastard file' being cleaned with a wire brush. It was impossible to get any sleep while he was on the job. He at last came to a grating conclusion like a gramophone running down and I think we were both very relieved that this big work had been finished and had been so well done ... At first light we stamped out the fire and set off, and as we went along I realised how wise we had been not to attempt the route at night ...".

Hill-shooting was always full of incident and appealed greatly to those with an adventurous turn of mind. Not the least of its attractions were the local people encountered and the wonderful scenery of the great mountains, enhanced at every dawn and sunset. Kipling had noted its fascination:

'Do you know the world's white roof-tree – do you know that windy rift
Where the baffling mountain eddies chop and change?
Do you know the long day's patience, belly down on frozen drift,
While the head of heads is feeding out of range?
It is there that I am going where the boulders and the snow lie ...

It was a call that appealed to many in the formidable Roorkee hot weather.

Jungle Shooting

The third type of hunting was the pursuit of tiger and deer in the 'reserved forests' which were managed in British India by the Indian Forest Service. There were two main areas of reserved forest accessible from Roorkee. The first was in the extensive forests of Central India, where the jungle was mainly dry and open, and shooting was permitted day and night throughout the hunting season. The other was in the United Provinces, where forests adorn the Siwalik foothills of the Himalayas for two hundred miles from Dehra Dun to Nepal. Here the forest is more dense and shooting was only permitted in the winter and then only in two weeks of each month and never after dark. Hence the former was favoured for longer leaves and the latter for short ones. In each area the forest was divided into 'blocks' for administrative purposes. In the UP each block was about 50 square miles (more in the CP) and in each block there was a wooden bungalow for the use of the Divisional Forest Officer (DFO) on his travels. These bungalows, very basically furnished and usually sited by a stream or lake, could be hired very cheaply when not being used by the DFO and made splendid jungle 'camps'.

Much of the attraction of jungle shooting lay not only in the hunt but in being the temporary owner of a large slice of country containing a wonderful diversity of wildlife. In some areas there were wild elephants and in all there were tigers, panthers and bears, many species of deer and antelope, wild pig, large pythons, a host of smaller animals and a wide variety of birds. It was fascinating to watch and identify them. However, as only such nabobs as the Viceroy, or Maharajahs, had elephants at their disposal, the ordinary person had to move around and hunt on foot. Now tigers hunt by night and normally prefer to rest and avoid humans by day. But not always, so walking around in a forest with tigers in it, even by day, was not without its interest.

In those days the main aim of most jungle shikar parties was to shoot a tiger. Nowadays, when tigers have become an endangered species, the idea of shooting one causes shudders of horror. But 75 years ago it was very different. There were then an estimated 40,000 tigers in India. A tiger kills around 80 animals a year, most of them deer. Where forests were conserved, some culling was necessary to maintain the deer/tiger balance and to prevent the tigers from turning their attention, as they did, not infrequently, to the cows and villagers who shared their habitat. Tiger shooting was a traditional sport in India, it was exciting, difficult and not without danger. The switch from shooting to photography was only just beginning and colour photography and long range lenses were still a dream.

Tigers have acute sight and hearing and unless a rare chance occurred, considerable skill was needed to locate one; many shooting parties never even saw one in their two or three weeks in the forest. Tigers hunt by roaming large areas of the jungle at night in search of prey and often use the footpaths and dry river-beds which allow a silent approach. Where they have passed is betrayed by their pug marks in the dust or sand, so it was customary to spend two or three days deducing from footprints in which area a tiger was active and then to tie up a live bait, usually a buffalo calf, at several likely places where he might pass. If the bait was taken it would be dragged into some thick cover to conceal it from the vultures. The tiger would then eat part of it and return the following night for the rest, thus giving a hunter a choice of three methods of making contact.

The first method was to stalk a bait at first light and hope to find that a tiger had killed it and was still there before dragging it off. As this sometimes involved approaching round a corner at very short range it could be an exciting business but it was rarely successful.

The second method, if a bait had been taken, was to follow up the 'drag' in the hottest hours of the day when the tiger, if nearby, was likely to be asleep. A machan (platform), usually an improvised chair, would be tied up in a tree close to the kill. The hunter would then sit up in the tree and wait for the tiger to return. In the UP shooting at night was prohibited and so only if the whole operation had been quickly and quietly done and if the hunter remained absolutely still and quiet, was there any chance of the tiger returning in the three or so hours of daylight remaining. Whether successful or not, it was a fascinating experience. About 4pm the shouts of villagers herding their animals in for the night would cease and the possession of the forest would return to the animals. Tigers and panthers always do a careful reconnaissance before returning to a kill. Often the alarm call of one of the larger deers would be the first indication that a predator was near. Then a little barking deer, which could clearly see something dangerous, might bark excitedly close by. Finally, if the kill was in or near long grass there might be the rustle of a large animal's movements accompanied by footfalls and heavy breathing. Often the tiger would now wait until dark before actually approaching the kill and so in the UP the hunter had to call up his support party and return to camp. However in a very quiet place events might take a different turn. Both tigers and panthers can move absolutely silently when they choose. The hunter might suddenly see, as though it had arrived in a puff of smoke, a tiger lying down and observing the scene only twenty yards away. A male tiger in the wild is an amazing sight. Its brilliant orange, black and white colour, the huge shoulders and fore-paws and the big white ruff round its head are a quite stunning spectacle. Only if the hunter kept absolutely still might the tiger, after ten minutes or so, move on to the kill and give a chance for a shot.

The third method was the beat. This involved anticipating into which area of thick cover a tiger would drag the bait after killing it and hoping that it would lie up close by. A reconnaissance would show to the experienced eye in which direction the tiger would choose to retreat if disturbed. One or more machans would be tied in trees covering this line for the guns and trees chosen for 'stops' to cover any other possible exits. The task of the 'stops' was to tap the trunk of their tree and simulate woodcutting, thus guiding the tiger towards the silent area where the guns were. In the heat of the day the beaters, plus one or two guns, would walk in small groups in line abreast through the dense cover talking to each other. If there was a tiger present it would usually walk away from the noise towards a quieter part of the forest. This method was most successful if the beat was laid out beforehand, improvised platforms put in place, trees marked for 'stops' and a path clear of leaves swept round the perimeter to give quiet access. If a kill occurred, a party of beaters, usually woodcutters from a local camp, would be assembled at the bungalow, 'stops' were chosen and a rehearsal would take place. One of the sahibs would imitate the tiger, wake up, rub his eyes, and growl at one or two 'stops' before walking out past the guns. This part was always played for laughs, which it invariably received, but there was a serious side, for a rehearsal was essential for a properly run beat and the safety of the beaters.

Of course things could easily go wrong. The tiger might become alarmed if too much noise was made and come out at a gallop. If so it might well be missed or wounded. Worse still an inexperienced gun might fire too soon and turn the tiger back into the beat, when it might burst through the line of beaters mauling anyone in his path or, if wounded, go to ground in thick cover. It was a point of honour to follow-up a wounded tiger, for such an animal might be crippled and resort to the easy option of man-eating. Following-up a wounded tiger on foot was the most dangerous part of tiger-shooting, for a male tiger will conceal himself in thick cover and almost invariably charge anyone who gets close. In two or three bounds he will be on them. It was for this reason that heavy double-barrelled rifles were favoured.

Over the years many officers from Roorkee went shooting in the jungles. Philip Neame (later General Sir Philip Neame) was a noted shikari, once shooting a charging tiger dead at muzzle-point. Before expiring it knocked him down and mauled his right arm so badly that he nearly lost it. It was a legend in the Mess that, from the UK, he had announced to Roorkee his engagement to be married with the telegram: '*Returning next boat. Have secured tigress*'. Another notable shikari was Bindon Blood who was reputed, during his time in India, to have shot no less than forty-two tigers. Some jungle shooting parties would be small and these were often accompanied by half a dozen volunteer jawans to help lay out the beats. Everyone liked this as the informal atmosphere of a jungle camp enabled both officers and men to get to know each other. Larger parties did not need such help and tended to be mixed and more social. However, to record all the stories of tigers seen, tigers killed, and wounded tigers followed up, would be tedious, so here are three short excerpts to give the flavour.

In the 1930s Stuart Battye was perhaps the most experienced of those from Roorkee who enjoyed jungle shooting and his preference was for the forests of the Central Provinces. Stuart often went with family parties and, in spite of many sit-ups and beats, it was not until 1935 that he was successful one night in shooting a tiger himself. Meanwhile he had carried out many stalks and acquired a great deal of jungle lore, and later that year he spent two weeks trying to catch up with a large old tiger. On the last day of his leave, when his baggage had already left, he sensed that this tiger was lying up in a particular patch of jungle. There was no time to arrange a proper beat, so he walked round the area putting up pages of the Times newspaper, impaled on sticks, as stops, climbed into a tree at the far end and got his bearer, suitably armed, and four locals to do a beat. It was successful and the tiger walked out past his tree giving an easy shot. It was a very skilful piece of shikar. Three years later, in the same area, he had the rare experience of encountering a tiger on foot and shot it dead. Like many hunters, however, once successful, his interests turned to photography. He had already taken good photographs of deer and antelopes and, but for the war, photographing game would have become his main interest.

Several of the British NCOs who trained the Sapper and Miner tradesmen in Roorkee were keen shikaris, and would sometimes take blocks in the nearby UP forests for deer and small game shooting. One of the keenest of these was Ernie Odell and he had an alarming experience one day when stalking a small barking deer. He was only about twenty yards away when a tiger seized the deer. Armed only with a shot-gun, useless against such a large animal, Ernie started to withdraw, but the tiger saw him and followed, growling. It began closing the gap so, seeing a tree easy to climb, he dropped his gun and scrambled up and fortunately, after a nerve-racking half-hour, the tiger, which had been clawing the foot of his tree, gave up its vigil and returned to its kill.

One of the last of the Roorkee shooting parties in the UP jungles took place in December 1941, a week after the Japanese war had started. This was a trip to a famous jungle block called Bijrani (now part of the Corbett National Park), by a large mixed party and the aim was as much enjoyment of the jungle atmosphere as shikar. The block was (is?) a most attractive one and the forested hills and patches of grass were full of birds and animals. It was an experience to sit outside the bungalow after dark and to hear and identify the many different cries of the jungle animals living out the dramas of their normal lives.

In Bijrani it soon became clear that there were several tigers hunting in the block and the first few days were taken up with deploying baits and laying out beats. The first excitement was when Dai David and Mike Rolt, returning from preparing a beat, turned a corner to see a tiger fifteen yards away in the knee-deep grass beside the path. Unusually the tiger (which was eating a monkey) displayed no intention of moving off, indeed quite the reverse. After a hasty conference they wisely decided to take another route, for shotguns loaded with pellets, which was all they were carrying, are ineffective against tigers.

On this trip only two baits were killed. The first was nowhere near a beat and Mike Rolt sat up over the kill. However, the tiger did not return and, shooting being permitted only in daylight, Mike returned at dusk empty-handed. The following day a 'natural' kill of a deer was spotted and Bill Adams duly sat up over it that afternoon, but again the tiger failed to put in an appearance. Meanwhile, others had shot a black bear and a thirteen-foot python for their skins. An effort was made to eat steaks from the bear but they were tough and tasteless and no-one fancied trying the python.

A day or two later, another bait was killed and dragged into one of the beats. As two couples had to return home that afternoon, it was decided to try a beat at mid-day. It was too early, however, and the beat drew a blank, the tiger, not yet asleep, slipping out while the beat was forming up. Guessing that it would probably return that night, a dawn beat was planned for the next day. This needed some organisation as the beaters needed to spend the night camping at the Forest Rest House (FRH). However, they had been well rewarded and were game to do this, so the next day the party started off in the dark before dawn to repeat the beat.

Power, Rolt and Holmes, the latter only having arrived in India two weeks previously, were to be the guns, while Ievers and Lyall Grant accompanied the sixteen beaters. Shortly after dawn the beat started. Nothing happened until the beaters were about a hundred yards from the guns when a single shot rang out, followed after a pause by three more. There were then some fearsome roars and the noise of a heavy animal crashing back towards the beaters, the signal for all the beaters to get smartly up the nearest tree. After the recommended wait for half an hour, the two guns with the beaters went round to join the other guns. It transpired that Nigel Holmes had shot the tiger at about 80 yards as it was passing out of the beat. It fell down but sprang up and bounded back into the beat and subsequent shots were thought to be misses. Following-up a wounded tiger on foot with one or two people can be very dangerous, but the party followed up the trail, throwing stones ahead and anticipating a charge at any moment. Suddenly there was a growl and some movement in the bushes a few yards ahead. Mike Rolt climbed a tree and a rifle was passed up to him. He fired two or three shots answered by growls and then silence. A cautious approach revealed a large tigress lying dead.

The rest of the day was spent skinning the tigress and the following day the party marched back to roadhead and returned to Roorkee for Christmas. The Japanese war had just started and the hunters on this trip would shortly find themselves in other jungles, pursuing an even more dangerous quarry.

DISCIPLINARY DILEMMAS

A Court Martial

Subedar-Major Sajjan Singh was a thick-set, sturdy Sikh of land-owning stock, hailing from the Punjab. His thirty years of Service sat lightly on his broad shoulders. His beard, showing hardly a streak of grey, was neatly rolled, the ends being led up his cheeks to disappear under his turban. Restlessly active by temperament, he had in his younger days been a physical training instructor, an accomplishment still evident from the spring in his gait. He paused for a moment outside the Commanding Officer's office before entering to make his morning report, then, lifting the bamboo matting which covered the doorway, he entered and saluted.

'Salaam, Subedar-Major Sahib', I returned. There was a moment's pause before he spoke and in that moment I detected an unusual gleam in his eye. Then, with a dramatic gesture, he thrust his left hand in front of me. It clutched a crumpled sheet of newspaper. As he relaxed his grip the paper unfolded, revealing the pathetic remains of a man's fingers. The small brown digits had been neatly severed near their bases and now lay like the shrivelled remains of some long dead mummy.

I started back in my chair and the gleam in Sajjan Singh's eyes transferred itself to his mouth in a broad grin. His sense of the dramatic had not been mistaken.

'It concerns Recruit Gurbachan Singh, Sahib. You may remember that he recently failed part of his recruit's training and was relegated to the next squad. Last night, requiring some poles to support his mosquito net, he obtained them from the quartermaster's store and then borrowed an adze with which to sharpen them ...'

There followed a tale of dizziness and a terrible accident resulting in the loss of the fingers of the left hand.

'Did anyone see what happened?' I interjected.

'No one, until he staggered into his barrack-room where he collapsed onto his bed. There were others there who quickly wrapped a pagri round the wound and then took him to the hospital. The doctor sahib has sewn up the cuts and he will soon recover.'

'Let us go and see the place where this happened', I suggested. What I hoped to discover from looking at the scene of the accident I do not know, but there was something at the back of my mind and I wanted to try and work things out for myself. I looked again at the evidence in front of me, probing for an explanation to this unusual accident. An adze was a common tool among the carpenters and many a man was skilled in its use, but an accident such as this was unheard of. I noted the angle of the cuts on the bones and counted the fingers. It was a plausible story, too plausible perhaps, and something did not quite seem to add up.

'Take good care of this, Subedar-Major Sahib.' I said, indicating the contents of the newspaper in front of me. 'There will have to be a court of inquiry and the fingers will be required for evidence.'

'Have no concern about that, Sahib, I will look after it myself.' And he screwed up the newspaper and stuffed it into his trouser pocket.

We crossed the parade ground and made our way between the barrack blocks. Presently we came to a spot indicated by Sajjan Singh. There were some wood shavings and the dark stain of dried blood.

'It was here that Gurbachan Singh was sharpening his pole when dizziness overcame him. He then went round the end of this block.' We followed a trail of drops of blood which led us unwaveringly back to Gurbachan Singh's barrack room and bed. It seemed a pretty steady course for one suffering from dizziness and I said as much to Sajjan Singh. He paused and for the first time I think he began to wonder as I had been doing.

There was for the time being nothing more to be done but I ordered a court of inquiry to be held, though it would be some time yet before Gurbachan Singh would be fit enough to attend.

The court of enquiry found that the incident had been an accident but it seemed to me that one vital piece of evidence had escaped. This set me in a quandary. Should I confirm the finding or not? It was only a hunch that I had and in any case Gurbachan Singh was no more use to the service. Yet I felt my deduction was correct and that the only way in which it could be tested was by confronting Gurbachan Singh with the evidence and a court martial was the place to do it.

Gurbachan Singh had by now returned from hospital and he was marched in front of me the next day. He stood to attention the other side of the desk, his left arm bandaged and carried in a sling. I read out the charge and remanded him for Summary Court Martial He looked surprised and slightly puzzled but said nothing and was marched out. The law dictated that he must have a minimum of twenty-four hours in which to prepare his defence.

A Summary Court Martial was in some ways a unique affair. The procedure was introduced into Indian Military Law shortly after the Mutiny. The new procedure was simple and the powers of the Commanding

Officer were greatly enhanced. In fact, by present day standards they would have been considered outrageously dictatorial, but if harsh in retrospect they suited the needs of the period, were well understood and undoubtedly contributed to the very high standard of discipline in the Indian Army of pre-World War II.

The court consisted of the Commanding Officer flanked by two other officers who took no part in the judgement but were there to see fair play. The maximum punishment which could be awarded was substantial, being twelve months imprisonment and discharge with ignominy. Quite rightly it stopped short of the death sentence or penal servitude for life!

The court duly assembled to try Gurbachan Singh. Two Indian officers joined me to be witnesses to the fairness of the proceedings. The accused was marched in with his 'friend'. He was not entitled to a defending officer or counsel, nor could he object to being tried by me, his Commanding Officer. When all the witnesses were assembled we stood and I took the oath to administer justice truly and without partiality to the best of my ability. The witnesses were then required to take an oath of affirmation according to their own religious practices, to tell the truth, the whole truth and nothing but the truth.

I now assumed the roles of judge, jury, prosecuting counsel and, paradoxically, defending counsel when the cross-examination of a witness so required. There were no preliminaries and I opened with the charge.

'Number ... Gurbachan Singh ...'

'Han, Sahib.'

'Under Indian Army Act Section ... you are accused of wilfully causing a self-inflicted wound, in that you ...' (and here followed details of the charge) '... in order to avoid further service.'

'Do you plead guilty or not guilty?'

'Not guilty, Sahib.'

'Call the first witness, please.'

The first to enter was my Subedar-Major, Sajjan Singh. He saluted. He had already taken the oath so I went straight ahead.

'Subedar-Major Sahib, do you recognise the accused Recruit Gurbachan Singh?'

'Ji han, Sahib.'

'He is accused of wounding himself on purpose in order to avoid further service. Please tell me what you know about the matter.'

'Very well, Sahib. On the evening of 3rd inst I received a report that Recruit Gurbachan Singh had had an accident and cut off his fingers. I immediately gave orders to be taken to the spot where I found these.' And with the same dramatic gesture as before he produced the roll of newspaper which he unwrapped and spread out on the desk in front of me for everyone to see. The same shrivelled digits, small, pathetic, lonely and useless lay there before us. It all seemed so tragic and unnecessary and I wondered, not for the first time, if it wouldn't have been better to accept the opinion of the court of inquiry and let the man pass sadly on his way out of the army, whither he had come of his own accord, without more ado.

Sajjan Singh finished his evidence and I asked Gurbachan Singh if he wished to ask any questions,

'Ji nahin, Sahib.'

Other witnesses followed, each adding his little bit to the story, but still it could have been nothing but an accident. Nobody had actually seen the incident so nobody could provide any direct evidence as to how it happened.

Finally I turned to Gurbachaan Singh. He need not give evidence on oath but he was required to answer any questions I put to him.

'Tell me, Gurbachan Singh, in your own words how you came to lose your fingers.'

'It was like this, Sahib. I needed some poles to support my mosquito net so I went to the quartermastery and obtained them from the quartermaster havildar. They were bamboo poles and I wanted to place them in the ground round my bed where we sleep outside in the hot season. So I also borrowed an adze from the havildar to sharpen them.'

So far, so good. The story was plausible enough and accorded with all the witnesses had said.

'What happened then?' I asked.

'I went round to the open space between the two barracks and started to sharpen one of the poles. But dizziness overcame me and the adze slipped and cut off my fingers.' He finished his tale by describing his return to his barrack room and collapse onto his bed.

I waited for a few seconds and there was silence in the room while I looked at Gurbachan Singh. Then I started to cross-examine him.

'Do you remember just how you were holding the pole with your left hand when the adze slipped?

'Yes, Sahib, it was like this.' And he took my proffered swagger cane in his left hand, his fingers and thumb encircling it to grip it tightly.

'The adze then chopped down from above and cut off all your fingers but not your thumb?' I queried.

'That is so, Sahib, you see I still have my thumb.' And he held up his stump of a left hand devoid of fingers but with the thumb intact.

'That was very fortunate that the thumb escaped when it was also gripping the pole like the fingers, wasn't it?'

'Yes, Sahib, it was very fortunate indeed that I still have the use of a thumb on that hand.'

'The adze only slipped once, didn't it?'

'Yes, only once,' replied Gurbachan Singh most emphatically.

I had led him to the point of no return. I felt sure now that the charge was proved but I had to make it abundantly clear both to the accused and to the officers on my right and left, so that there could be no shadow of doubt in their minds of the verdict when it came.

'Gurbachan Singh,' I continued, 'you have heard evidence that these are the remains of your four fingers. Do you dispute that evidence?'

'No, Sahib.'

'Will you count the pieces?'

'Ek, do, teen, char ... panch, five, Sahib,' he concluded, and a puzzled fear showed in his eyes.

I went on without a pause.

'You have just told me that the adze slipped only once and that you lost four fingers at one cut. I suggest that that story is untrue and that you deliberately laid your hand on the ground and chopped the fingers off but you had to cut twice because the adze is not broad enough to chop them off in one cutting and at the second chop you cut one of the severed fingers into two pieces. Is it not so?'

There was absolute silence in the room and I could feel the tenseness in the atmosphere. Gurbachan Singh seemed to be having difficulty with his breathing. Finally he croaked:

'You know all things, it was even as you say. When I failed my recruits' course I could not bear the shame and laughter of my friends till madness overcame me and I cut off my fingers so that I could be discharged and sent home. The madness is gone now, Sahib, but there is little that I can do with my hand. I am very sorry.'

There was silence for a moment but for the laboured breathing of the culprit. I felt suddenly flat and out of humour. Whilst the case had lasted there had been tension and excitement. Now that was over but what had been achieved? A judgement which tore out a man's soul brought no satisfaction and at that moment justice without mercy would have cried unto Heaven.

I let him go, as he would have gone but for my hunch: discharged from the service as unfit for further duty.

Summary Justice

I knew nothing about the powers of the Commanding Officer when I first arrived in Roorkee. I suppose I had done some Military Law at OCTU, but it must have gone in one ear and out the other; all I remembered was my father's admonition when I joined the Army that 'A Court Martial is a Court of Justice not a Court of Law'. Would that that was so today!

Young officers in India had some pretty hefty summary powers, but I was not to exercise mine until some time later. I did, however, pass the garrison detention centre every day and was only too aware what a jawan faced when he was sentenced to a term of 'rigorous imprisonment': dressed in Field Service Marching Order, he underwent a monotonous routine of carrying a heavy stone on his head from one end of the compound to the other and then a similar load back again. In full view from the road, it was a good deterrent.

Some eighteen months later, by a quirk of fate, I found myself commanding a field company at Insein, just north of Rangoon. After several years in Burma with very little leave, we were looking forward to returning to India, even though there was much despondency at the prospect of the company being disbanded. However, on arrival in Roorkee we were greeted with the news that we were to be re-formed from a three-caste company into an all-Muslim unit destined for Pakistan after Partition and I was promoted to Major. We had to wait another three months before we moved across the new border to Sialkot and with all the civil unrest following Independence no leave was possible until then.

With huge movements of population families had been split up, many had perished in the mass slaughter of that period and it was important to get the men on leave as soon as possible. But there was a mass of work to be done in Sialkot to turn it into an Engineer Centre and it was only possible to send people on leave in batches. I briefed every leave party personally and stressed the importance of returning from leave on time so that another party could go in their place. I emphasised the point that if someone couldn't trace their family within their allotted leave, they must return to Sialkot and we would alert the civil authorities.

All went well with the first two parties and everyone returned on time, many with harrowing tales to tell. Then there was one absentee from the next party. Abdul Aziz returned a week later and was promptly put in the Guardroom and remanded for my Orders the following day.

He was charged with 'absence without leave' and marched in front of me: 'You remember that I stressed the importance of returning on time?'

'Yes, Sahib.'

'As a result of your absence, another jawan has been unable to go on leave. You have let the company down and I am extremely disappointed.'

'Yes, Sahib, and I am very sorry.'

'Tell me why, having gone absent, you decided to come back.'

'Sahib, because I found what happened to my family.' He was obviously very emotionally disturbed so I asked him 'What did you discover?'
At this he burst into tears and between his sobs I established that not only had his wife and children been murdered, but his house had been burnt and his grandparents had also been killed. He had lost everything.

I realised I faced a ghastly predicament. Today he would have been given counselling but this was 1947, the mail had not returned to normality, soldiers had no news of their families, nobody had had leave for many months, if not years, and everyone wanted to get away as soon as possible. If I failed to make an example of this absentee there was a distinct likelihood of a breakdown of discipline: not only would I face having more absentees, but there was a danger that soldiers would go absent from Sialkot itself. Morale had been wonderfully high up till now, but in these circumstances it could change overnight and I was very conscious that I had no other British officers to help me and I placed enormous reliance on Jemadar Mohd Khan who was acting as my company Subedar.

All this flashed through my mind as the accused quietly sobbed in front of me. I glanced at Mohd Khan and could see that he was as worried as me. I looked Abdul Aziz straight in the eyes and said: 'You know what I said before you went on leave. You have let the Company down and you will serve twenty-eight days Rigorous Imprisonment. March out.'

I felt ghastly and was ready to burst into tears myself. Jemadar Mohd Khan came back to the office and quietly said: 'Sahib, you did right'.

Justice? I suppose so, but I was just 22 years old and I hated myself, even though I knew I had had no alternative. Abdul Aziz's face haunts me still.

An Error of Judgement?

I joined my Field Company in Java on 31st December 1945 direct from a British Parachute Field Squadron. The Company had been in Batavia for some months and was well-established and enjoying a more relaxed regime compared to that in Burma. It was engaged on the usual engineering tasks: support to infantry patrols, the installation of, and repairs to, electricity and water supplies, the repair of roads and bridges and so on. There were also less usual tasks, such as stopping and searching trains, raiding local hotels and brothels, as well as helping at the local brewery with the production and distribution of 'Bintang' beer!

I took over the Sikh platoon but was soon involved in auditing accounts, dealing with the Company's mail and filling in for the Second-in-Command when he was posted to Singapore at short notice, leaving me with little time with my jawans. Three months later the Company moved closer to Bandung leaving my platoon behind. I enjoyed this time alone with my Sikhs, improving my Urdu and getting to know them better. I have never been looked after so well. At the weekly issue of rum I was always given the first tumbler, three-quarters full, which, fortunately, I had no difficulty dealing with! In any kind of physical contest, though, I always came last. Also I was never allowed to be alone, even when 'courting' in the evenings (a rare event!) – "Just pretend we are not here, Sahib. We look the other way!"

Having no previous experience with Indian troops I had asked Jemadar Khem Singh to let me know whenever I made mistakes or took wrong decisions. One morning a havildar (sergeant) asked for leave to return to India as his sister was very ill. Knowing the pressure on transport I expressed my regret but said this would not be possible, adding that I would have supported his request if it had been his wife who was ill. When he had saluted and left, Khem Singh suggested that I had been wrong in my thinking. He knew the havildar's family, he had only one sister and as his mother was past child-bearing age he could never have another sister. On the other hand a wife could be replaced without difficulty! I therefore arranged for the havildar to return to India where he saw his sister before she died.

I never discovered whether I had made an error of judgement or had been gently conned!

4
TRAVELS IN THE GREAT MOUNTAINS*

We are the Pilgrims master; we shall go
Always a little further: it may be
Beyond that last blue mountain barred with snow,
Across that angry or that glimmering sea.
James Elroy Flecker – The Golden Journey to Samarkand

Several ranges of the greatest mountains in the world divide India from Central Asia and in the days before air travel they were a potent attraction to officers contemplating leave. Some went there to climb mountains, some to fish or shoot, some to trek and admire the beauty of the scenery and some to visit remote and little-known areas.

Frivolity, or 'poodle-faking', in hill stations was not in the Roorkee tradition, so every Spring tents were taken out and aired, ropes were tested, rifles examined, rods repaired, maps studied, plans discussed. Which passes shall we cross this year, which glaciers, which rivers shall we ford, climb which mountains, pursue what quarry? There were numerous forays, mounted mainly from Roorkee, before World War II and those of Katharine and Jack Lethbridge, Stu Battye, Archie Jack and Ian Lyall Grant were perhaps typical.

HONEYMOON IN SPITI

by

Katharine Lethbridge

Jack and I were to be married on 15th August 1925. We had wanted to go to Kashmir for our honeymoon but cholera had broken out there and my family advised strongly against it. Why not then the Hindustan-Tibet road? We were ambitious to climb and explore but people shook their heads. This is a honeymoon they warned Jack. Find somewhere nice and stay there or your wife will be back in Simla within a week.

All on deaf ears. If we moved fast and far enough we could leave the monsoon behind; it only reached the top of the Himalayan range then petered out. We started to arrange for stores, for yakdans and kiltas to

* *Maps on pages 196, 199 and 204 cover the areas of these travels.*

carry them in, for suitable clothes, for boots, for crampons, for an orderly, a cook, for guns so that we could feed ourselves and bring back trophies of the chase, for tents and ropes and blankets. The room started to become lumbered with all kinds of things that had nothing to do with a trousseau. The great day arrived and passed with all its protocol and magnificence leaving little impression on my mind that was not one of unreality; one of those dream-like days when in spite of everything that happens one is the same person at the end as one was at the beginning.

Still not trusting the vagaries of the monsoon we double-marched next day to Narkunda, riding part of the way and taking a short cut over the hill from Mattiana, where we passed an unforgettable spring surrounded by wine-red potentillas, the water tasting far better than the champagne of the day before. We arrived at Mr Kitchingman's doorstep next day at Kotgarh where he had his headquarters (we had warned him of our coming). Surprised to see us so soon, he presented us with a great bunch of roses, an ice-axe and apples and apricots, as many as we could carry, and sent us on our way down, down, down, into the valley of the Sutlej where we bathed our weary feet in the river at Nirth. We had chosen to come by this lower road rather than by Baghi and Kadrala because it was shorter and so we could be more quickly away from the monsoon.

Kotgarh, which we had just left behind us, was a little centre of civilization where there were gardens growing gooseberries, raspberries, apricots and peaches and where small quantities of jam were made which was sold in Simla. As well as the Forest Officer's Headquarters there was a Mission House where hill girls were trained. They learned knitting and sewing and other crafts and had made for me, by my mother's instructions, some splendid long woollen stockings, for use in the higher hills, knitted with separate big toes like the thumbs on mittens so that they could be used with hill sandals. Kotgarh was temperate at about 6,000ft so pleasantly habitable all the year.

The Sutlej river rushed in a deep gorge several thousand feet below Kotgarh and a road ran along the valley which was tropical in its closed-in heat and alive with enormous butterflies, the like of which I had never seen before or since; peacock blue with swallow tails, sulphur and orange and black, sulphur and blue and black, orange and black. There were huge lizards that ran across the road shivering their long tails – all these I note in my diary and add them to the forty-three different wild flowers I had found high up the day before and the lammergeyers, griffon vultures, kestrels and white-headed eagles.

We were now in the native state of Bashahr and because of the heat hired ponies to help us on our way. Unwisely I wore shorts exposing my knees to the fierce sun. The consequence was painful in the extreme. My thighs and knees swelled till they looked like legs of mutton, they were bright red and trembled as I walked. Never since have I shown disrespect to the sun. We reached Rampur which was the winter capital of the little state, a picturesque village of grey slate roofs, a small bazaar, a Buddhist temple and a gigantic prayer wheel past which anyone could walk and give it a turn, thereby acquiring merit. Hinduism and Buddhism met in peace in this remote place and people respected the tenets of both religions.

At Sarahan, the summer capital of Bashahr, two marches on and a good many thousand feet up, we received a gift from the Raja of apples, pears, nuts, vegetables and grapes carried to us ceremoniously by a group of court servitors dressed in round hats and duffle cloaks. Jack paid a courtesy visit in return. Friendship with the Raja was not only pleasant in itself but could ease the problems of travel through his lands. Our baggage from Simla as far as Rampur had been carried by mules with their own muleteers. From here we had to employ local coolies under the system of '*begar*' which made every village responsible for hiring out a number of its inhabitants, men or women or animals for the purpose of carrying loads. One village carried as far as the next village and then the loads were handed over. Sometimes the system worked smoothly and the people were pleased enough to do the job for good payment in hard coin. They would not accept paper money which they considered worthless. But sometimes no one wanted to go because it was harvest time or there was a festival or just an argument about whose turn it was.

High passes, or long distances without habitation, brought complications. Loads had to be repacked and made lighter and extra men taken on to carry food for the porters themselves. But once the arguments were over and everyone was on their way they did their job cheerfully. Women carried as much as men and occasionally a donkey was thrown in, so it was a motley collection of bearers upon whose backs one's possessions were transported. Most of these discussions, arrangements and decisions rested on Jack. He spoke Hindustani so well that I became idle and left it to him. He had the right touch of firmness and tact, was friendly with everyone from coolie to Raja and cared for everyone's welfare before his own. To help on this trip we had an excellent orderly called Padma Datt, a hill Brahmin much respected and obeyed because of his high caste.

It was on this road that I first saw a postal runner, one of those remarkable men who carried the mails into some of the remotest regions of British India. They worked in relays but the individual runners covered huge distances, fifty or sixty miles sometimes, travelling steadily at a fast trot up and down these mountains hardly varying their pace, lean, long-legged and brown, eyes glazed on the distance in front, looking neither right nor left, mail bags slung at their backs, long spears in hand with bells at the top to scare away wild animals. It seemed uncanny and almost unbelievable to arrive at some tiny shack which was the local post office where there was nothing else but a cow shed and a cot and a babu basking in his own importance, perhaps able to read two words of English; and there was your letter, carefully wrapped in a grubby cloth, handed over with bows and smiles and all the ceremony due to an object of world-wide importance.

Not wanting to break into our stores while we were still on the Hindustan–Tibet road, we got the custodians of the forest bungalows where we stopped for the nights to provide us with meals. Chickens (still pecking round at four o'clock in the afternoon and eaten by seven), eggs, bread of a sort, sweet potatoes, ordinary potatoes, sweet corn known as *bhoota*, were sometimes to be had. We asked for porridge at Sarahan and were given a stew of unhusked grain which tore me in shreds so that I could not walk more than a few hundred yards at a stretch. We had a steep zigzag hill to climb from Sarahan to Taranda next day. Padma Datt regarded me with dismay. "I will arrange a kamarband (waist cloth) to attach to the memsahib to pull her up the hills," he announced, and Taranda hill became a byword between Jack and myself meaning an almost insurmountable difficulty.

As we travelled up the Sutlej valley, whether a few feet above the river or thousands of feet above that, the mountains became grander, the cliffs more precipitous, the country wilder and more sparsely inhabited. Some side valleys were extensively cultivated as at Sarahan where there were hillsides of carefully terraced fields irrigated by channels led off from the smaller streams and with climates varying from temperate to tropical according to their height and crops varying from millet and barley to swamp and heat-loving rice. The forests were magnificent and wherever timber could be extracted the trunks were pushed down steep slides into the Sutlej river which was swift and deep and carried them down to the plains. Marches between stages varied between eight and sixteen miles and every mile was either an up or a down, the road following the hillsides as best it could, crossing side torrents on stone bridges, or cut into the cliffs or built out from the vertical rock on wooden supports. Landslips were frequent, often carrying away large sections of the road, but they were always bypassed or mended again in some way and the process of repair was continuous.

Forest bungalows afforded roof shelter, charpoys to sleep on, a chair or two, a rough table and not much else. One used one's own bedding and often the wooden furniture was full of bed-bugs which must have enjoyed a frugal existence, visitors being so rare. Hung up in each bungalow was a framed chart showing a cross section of the road from its start at Simla to its end at the Shipki Pass which led into Tibet. The chart was not to scale and made the road look even more alarming than it was. The stages were marked like points on a graph, names and heights and distances given so that one knew from stage to stage what was awaiting next day, level ground (never), X number of thousand feet up, X number of thousand feet down or ups and downs in confusion. In addition, points were marked where accidents had taken place and the dates on which these accidents had occurred – where so and so had gone over the cliff on horseback, where somebody else had received a rock on his head, where the road had collapsed and sent them all to kingdom come.

That road remains in my dreams: craggy, remorseless, awesomely beautiful, shoulder after mountainous shoulder, tempting one on towards the unknown. We did not at this time reach its arid end on the Tibetan border, which missed the monsoon, but crossed the Sutlej on an iron bridge at Wangtu. We were now on the right bank of the river at the foot of those huge hills on which we had gazed from Simla. We turned northwards up a side valley towards the Babeh Pass (15,700ft) and the country of Spiti.

About ten miles on and 3,000ft above Wangtu was a village called Yangpa. There was no road to it only a stony path which crossed and recrossed the roaring Babeh stream on bouncy wooden bridges with no rails. I was frightened, which I had not been on the Hindustan-Tibet road. The village, in a grove of walnut trees, was picturesque and dirty with solidly built grey-tiled houses. The people all dressed in home-made brownish duffle were shy and duffle coloured themselves but friendly and hospitable too, offering us fresh walnuts and a camping site under the walnut trees. It was here that I first met the tall pink bells of the Himalayan balsam and triggered off their pods of black seeds which scatter themselves at a touch like little guns. Some seed gatherer must have brought these seeds to England because this balsam now grows along the banks of our west country rivers and I can still explode the pods to remind myself and watch the bees struggling out of the bells smothered in ghostly white pollen.

At Yangpa we put up our tent for the first time and opened our stores. Himalayan villages had food for themselves but seldom could they spare much for the traveller except perhaps a little milk or fruit or a whole sheep to be divided up between everyone in the camp. We began to appreciate the necessity for meticulous organization in our commissariat. All yakdans were numbered and had lists of their contents pasted inside their lids with duplicate lists in the log-book which we carried. So if one packet of tea was needed it was not necessary to open every yakdan to find it. Then, taken out, it was crossed off the relevant lists. But here in Yangpa another complication arose. As the following three marches were very rugged and steep and would take us over the pass, all loads had to be re-sorted and repacked to make them lighter. As there was no further habitation before the pass, extra coolies would have to be engaged to carry food and firewood for those already carrying our possessions. Shoes (mostly home-made sandals) would have to be provided, warm clothes and sunglasses against snow blindness. As sunglasses of a civilized kind did not exist, everyone provided himself with a thick tuft of black hair – usually yak's hair – and tackled the snow looking rather like a bearded collie.

These arrangements took a day or two to complete and were made in view of the whole village who took up their positions quietly and politely on the rim of our little camp watching enthralled at all the comings and goings and the extraordinary contents of our boxes and bedding rolls. Two villagers took charge of their side of the business and became the go-betweens, Ram Saran and his assistant Asmani. They agreed to come with us as Shikaris. Ram Saran was no more than 4 feet 6 inches in height, very small and meek, a kind of mountaineering mouse with wonderful eyesight and endurance. Asmani was a slightly bumbling and larger replica of his friend, anxious to please everybody as long as it did not require too much effort. Ram Saran had crossed the pass on many occasions and could speak Tibetan as well as his own native patois.

We started off on the second day with what looked like a truly monstrous cavalcade stringing out through the village fields of barley, millet, potatoes and peas, soon leaving these behind and entering a magnificent forest of tall blue pines with mossy floor and blue cranesbill and wild garlic among the mosses, climbing, climbing until the trees thinned and gave way to rhododendrons with greenish ice-like flowers and stony bogs where the little three-petalled trilliums grew. Then there were no more pines at all, only birches, the air became wispy and thin and we stepped out above the tree line at 11,000ft having passed by stages from sub-tropical Sutlej valley to sub-arctic alp. We had reached a camping place called Moling where the valley widened out into an expanse of boulder-strewn and flower-bedizened meadow. On either side of the swift grey stream were mountains like waves about to break, some snow-tipped, some blown bare, each descending in great sweeps and fans of stony detritus, scoured and scraped by wind and snow but forming the perfect abiding place for hundreds of flowers. Although it was August, this was their spring and September would be their autumn and the profusion of growth and blossoming was a race against time. Here was a cave to shelter the porters, formed by great tumbled rocks and enough birch wood to make a roaring fire. There were flocks of sheep about and big black shepherd dogs and shepherds perched upon rocks making simple shepherd music on their plaintive wooden pipes, filling the valley with haunting sound above the hurrying water. These men spent the short summer on the mountain pastures with their flocks, leading them down again to the villages before the first snow fell. The sheep grew fat on the sumptuous feeding and mutton had the aromatic taste of flowers.

Opposite this camp at Moling a great pinnacle of rock dominated the valley. We had gazed on this from Simla beckoning as it did like a distant finger. Now we had obeyed its command. Under this peak around a grey rock in a bed of grey gravel I first saw a blue poppy. In my mood of joy, on my feet of wind, this flower seemed to me unearthly, not belonging to this world. For a time I hardly believed that what I had seen was true until I found it again in the garden at St John's College, Oxford. But not that blue – not quite. And not that setting of grey rock. That was reserved for the high hills.

One more march to go to Poshtirang at 13,500ft before ascending the pass. The rocks grew wilder, the flowers smaller, hugging the ground. There was a half moon that night and standing outside the tent one lost all sense of distance, mountains within arms' reach, the slope up to the pass no more than a garden bank. Shy whisperings between Padma Datt and Ram Saran and passed on to Jack told that the kamarband was ready, two kamarbands in fact, knotted together – to pull the memsahib up the pass, but it would have taken more than two kamarbands to hold my feet on the ground. Shortly after midnight we were up and ready to go, racing to get to the top before the sun rose and melted the surface of the snow. At the first glint of light we were gone, strung up along the white slopes like a row of ants, no one pulling anybody. My reputation was redeemed.

The Babeh Pass lies at 15,700ft (some maps say 16,000ft) with no great hazards except for crevasses in the glacier on the Spiti side. But any pass of that height must be treated with respect. It crosses the main Himalayan range which exhausts the monsoon so that little rain penetrates to the arid countries beyond. The pass opens in May or June and closes again in September or October and during the few months in which it is open it is busy with traders bringing their flocks of sheep and goats across loaded with borax and salt and returning with flour. Each animal carries a pair of small pannier bags on its back and there is much gossip and passing of news between the travellers going north and the travellers coming south. Sometimes there are yaks grunting their sure-footed way across the snow, but yaks cannot penetrate far into the heat of Bashahr or they become sick with the rich grazing and humid warmth. At the top of the pass two great snow cornices lean over from either side forming a kind of gateway and in the middle is a cairn of stones. Everyone here must contribute a stone or a coin or a prayer flag to assure the mountain spirits that travellers are grateful for a safe passage. Tibetans or Spitimen chant a prayer – "The gods are triumphant, the devils are defeated" and pass round the cairn clockwise to acquire merit.

So far, so good. It had just been a matter of slogging up the steep hill, but on the Spiti side was a glacier and the glacier was full of crevasses. At this time of year they were open and easy to see and avoid but if covered with snow were dangerous. We met one party who had lost a man and a yak. There is something final about a crevasse, its green lips answer nothing. And how many years, hundreds perhaps, before those frozen bodies are spewed out from the icy mouth to the wonder of anyone who may be present to behold them?

So quickly down off the ice on to the tumbled moraine and into a new country.

Spiti is a high-up country with valley floors at about 11,000 to 13,000ft, arid, precipitous, with hills like the teeth of wolves, cliffs striped in a multitude of colours, blue, sulphur, magenta, pink, fearsome rushing rivers, no trees and a wind that cuts like a saw. Some quirk of history joined it and its neighbouring land of Rupshu to British India but in nature it was Tibetan. The people were apple-cheeked and slant-eyed like Tibetans, they spoke Tibetan, they were Buddhists, they kept yaks, they drank the awful brew of brick tea, peaflour, soda and mutton fat. They were poor, dirty, cheerful, courageous and intelligent. They endured one of the harshest climates in the world, they had few prejudices, were easy to live with, full of unselfconscious charm, and had a sense of humour which accorded with our own.

Their houses, grouped in small villages, were tucked under the hill-sides for shelter, flat roofed, broad at the base and sloping back as though setting their feet firmly against tempests to come. Lower floors were for animals, upper floors reached by notched logs – all wood was laboriously imported. Windows were small or non-existent because of the cold, fires open, the smoke escaping according to its own pleasure. Fuel was either animal dung or *burza*, a woody shrub which grew on the hillsides, which was gathered in summer and stored on the flat roofs. Yaks and *djomos* (a cross between a yak and a cow) were their cattle, they had donkeys, sheep and small biangi goats whose coats produced the beautiful under-pashm, warmer and softer than any sheep's wool. Yaks produced hides, meat and milk, long hair for rope-making and long tails for ceremonial banners. They were also the chief draught animals and load carriers. Occasionally one saw a large fierce dog and there were a few sure-footed ponies.

Where the land allowed and the smaller streams could be guided and tamed, terraces were carved out of the rocky soil and irrigation channels run among them, and there tiny fields of barley and peas grew and brilliant strips of summer flowers along the water courses, cranesbill, buttercups and dwarf blue aconites which were worn in the hat or presented as good luck tokens. Plants on the stony hills were small, intensely aromatic like spikenard or woolly like edelweiss. If there was a tree at all, it was a flattened willow in a sheltered valley, if there was a bush other than the burza, it was a wild rose, brilliant pink and clinging to a precipice.

Roads were no more than stony means of getting to places. Screes of loose pebbles slid from the upper slopes remaining at the angle of repose until one crossed bringing the whole incline down in a stony torrent. Here one learned the value of the long iron-shod Khud stick, used uphill and leant on to take one's weight and minimize the sliding. Icy streams had to be crossed and recrossed often waist-high with stones rumbling and rolling underfoot. The depth could be tested by throwing in a rock.

If the rock said: 'Duck!' you could go ahead and cross, if the rock said: 'Donk!' – don't! Even the 'Duck' crossings must be treated with respect and taken arm in arm so if one person slipped he could be pulled up by the others. No stream was far from a glacier so the cold was intense and to regain one's circulation was unbelievably painful. Early in the year some snow bridges remained over the streams but these had mostly melted by midsummer. There were a few wire bridges on which a seat for one passenger was slung on a cross-wire and pulled backwards and forwards. But the indigenous bridge was the *jhula* made of twisted willow-twig rope. Three of these ropes were slung between stone towers, one for the feet, two for the hands, the three ropes joined by lesser ropes. Climb the stone tower, grip the hand ropes (they were usually too thick), shuffle your feet gingerly on to the lower rope and start, trembling, down the slope. The relentless water below came nearer, dizzying your senses. Don't look down, stare ahead or you will lose all sense of balance and uprightness, just grope and hope. The hand ropes spread away wider and wider, now you were crouching and clinging, the rushing water came nearer and nearer – then thankfully you started on the upgoing slope, the hand ropes drew together, the far tower was under your feet and you were across. What a fuss! The Spiti men would run over carrying sheep on their shoulders and the yaks would plunge into that turbulent water and swim over, unperturbed, even if they did arrive a mile or more downstream!

One oddity about the streams often dictated the crossings. They were fed by glaciers and snow-fields and the volume of water varied according to the temperature, much larger under a hot sun and dwindling to a trickle during a freezing night. So crossings were often possible or impossible according to the time of day and the distance from the glacier mouth and the melting snow-field. This was not travel for the faint-hearted or for the ignorant.

Scrambling down off the glacier moraine we reached this strange land about which we yet had much to learn. Quickly the Bashahri coolies dumped their loads, received their pay and turned for home hoping to recross the pass that day. On the opposite side of the valley was a small village called Mudh. By means of loud shouting an order was sent across for milk and firewood, "Homa! Shing!" which arrived together with a little crowd of villagers come to investigate. The tent was pitched, not with tent pegs to hold the ropes because the ground was so hard and stony that no tent peg could be knocked in and all the ropes had to be attached to heavy stones. Ram Saran went off to hire yaks for the next day so that we could continue our journey down the valley.

The stream which had flowed out of our glacier mouth was now an imposing river called the Peen. We followed the right bank then turned up a valley to a village called Ensa where there were rumoured to be ibex. The shooting of game in the hills as in the jungles of the plains was strictly regulated, only so many animals being allowed on a permit. Trophies from animals such as ibex, burrhel and ammon were greatly sought after. Long journeys and arduous climbing were involved and as so few people went, there was no shortage of game and everybody respected the rules. No carcass was ever wasted, every scrap of meat, every square inch of hide was used by the local people and the sahib carried back the horns as proof of his journey. No one in those days thought that the world's animals would become so rare, pushed out of their homes by increasing populations, hunted with machine-guns or killed and wasted 'for sport'. An animal for us was much needed meat, shot dead quickly and consumed on the spot.

Ensa village was a tiny settlement on the apex of four precipitous snow-filled valleys reaching up to jagged black peaks of about 19,000ft. There were only two or three houses but even so there was a village headman called San-to-pa and a small herd of yaks, each with its own distinct character, and although we only wanted one yak to carry a light bivouac to camp higher up, they all had to come because they would not be parted. A yak is docile, hardy and sure-footed on the worst ground and as long as he is not taken into the heat or deprived of the hours in which he must chew the cud, he will accomplish marvels. He is also a steady mount, although on ascents one tends to slip off his tail end, and on descents off his head end, in other ways he is satisfactory if slow. Here I sometimes rode a yak whom we named Ptolemy. He had a beautiful white face and bushy tail and was led by a Spiti man whom we had named Napoleon on account of the shape of his hat. When Ptolemy was halted he was tethered to a pebble, the knowledge that he was expected to stand still being a stronger restraint than any iron shackle.

After four days of precipitous climbing we shot three ibex. The carcasses were brought down to the village and an orgy took place. The Spiti man's first act when confronted with a carcass is to remove the liver and eat it raw. It was never possible to obtain even one small slice of this doubtful delicacy for oneself. "Wonder of wonders!" they said. "That animal had no liver! Would you believe such a thing?" Anyhow the liver had gone and it was best not to ask questions. Ibex meat in any case was awful, tough, smelly, black, very unpleasant, they were welcome to the lot and took it. Forty-eight hours of feasting and every scrap had gone and the villagers and our camp followers lay about distended and miserable. Until the banquet had been worked through and digested no one would rise to his feet or lift a finger to do anything.

I say every scrap had gone but that is not quite true. Our cook, a plainsman, took part of his share and hid it under the saucepans hoping to get it all the way back to Hindustan and impress his relations with this unusual delicacy. But noses betrayed him and as soon as this illicit treasure reached the comparative warmth of Bashahr it was discovered and buried. Also we laid a claim to a part of the hide because by that time my boots had worn through on the jagged rocks and I had nothing to wear on my feet. The Spiti men made for me a remarkable pair of ibex skin shoes with the hair on the outside which lasted for the rest of the trip. Anxious in general about my feet, San-to-pa presented me with a highly coloured and embroidered pair of felt knee-boots with yaks' leather soles which I kept for years and buried with tears under an oak tree.

The clothes of the Spiti people, although woven of home-made duffle like the Bashahri clothes, were often coloured and gay and embroidered. The chief garment was a loose knee-length coat tied round the waist with a broad sash or kamarband. Treasures were tucked into the folds of the sash or inside the voluminous front of the coat. Their caps were fur-lined with ear-flaps against the wind and usually very dirty. They wore felt knee-boots soled with yaks' leather and sometimes old Army boots or old Army greatcoats picked up on their travels, but these looked absurdly incongruous and were only prestige objects being far too clumsy for the kind of climbing they had to do. The boots were a positive handicap, great causes of blistered feet and more profitably carried than worn.

It was when we were at Ensa village, still feasting on ibex meat, that the great man of Spiti arrived – no doubt rumours of all that plenty had travelled far. His name was Labh Zang. He walked into camp one evening in the quiet way of the born hillman, a few long strides up the hill, then subsiding unobtrusively, legs crossed, back upright, bright dark eyes taking in ourselves, the whole scene, its possibilities. He had in some minor way an official standing, partly as servant of the Nono or ruler of Spiti, partly as liaison between the Commissioner of Kulu and its little satellite province of Spiti. He sat there smiling, argus-eyed, one of the eyes on his job as an official and the position it brought him among his fellows, another eye on this new sahib and the sort of chap he might be, another eye on the weather, another on the shikar, an important and immediate eye on all that meat and still another eye on the perfectly delightful state of being alive in this best of all possible lands. The talk ran to travel, to the future, to shikar, to all the distant lovely places we could visit in his company and to illustrate the layout of the mountains and their passes and the stony ways he knew so well, he held up one clenched fist and with the fingers of the other hand traced along his wrist and knuckles and bent-up fingers the way to the Parang-la, the Tsho Moreri Lake, the great downs of Chumurti where dwelt wild asses and Marco Polo's sheep, using his hand like a relief map, showing where the road was '*maidani maidan*' (flat, according to him), '*salamisalami*' (slopey-slopey, in other words jolly steep), or '*bilcul tang*' (cliffs and gorges of fearful aspect). He spoke Hindustani and nearly tempted us to stay and visit his village of Mani but Jack had a wise eye on the Babeh Pass and its unpredictable way of closing early in autumn, so regretfully we refused, but engaged him without fail to come with us the following year.

From Ensa, sadly, we turned for home. Our time was drawing to a close, the sky was black as we recrossed the Babeh Pass. It was September, the shepherds were collecting their flocks on the other side and we halted for a day or two above Moling, exploring the nearby nullahs, one of which, Yusku, was haunted and full of strange noises. The men said ducks and chickens of a ghostly sort lived there; I suspected goblins. A few stray birch trees provided splendid camp fires whose flames flew up in showers of golden sparks. There were two great glaciers in the nullah called Tusku, striped with dark crevasses like spread tiger skins. Water still flowed by day, but thin sheets of ice formed across the stones at night, making little hothouses for tiny mountain flowers, buttercups and blue dwarfs and little stunted daisies. Sadly I did not know the names of these beautiful alpine treasures and never found a book to help me. The first snow fell, etching the stony hills in grey and white. Time to go.

JOURNEYS TO THE HIGH PLATEAUX

by

Katharine Lethbridge

We made four journeys to Spiti, and beyond to the high plateaux of Central Asia, during those years based on Roorkee, approaching either along the already familiar route of the Hindustan–Tibet road from Simla, or through Kulu. In this year of 1926 we repeated our journey of the year before travelling further and profiting from experience gained. We no longer allowed ourselves to depend on servants from the plains who felt the cold and tended to get ill at high altitudes. We did take a Kumaoni orderly, Bacchi Chand, but in our final trips dispensed with everyone except the men from Spiti. This made for a homogeneous and contented camp and made it possible to form trusting friendships with these fascinating people, previously prevented by go-betweens.

On this second occasion Labh Zang, who joined us in Spiti, news having gone before, brought with him a remarkable companion, a boy called Tshulim Tomonandan who agreed to take on the camp cooking. I was supposed to teach Tshulim how to cook but knowing so little about it myself the results were odd. He did not lack initiative and if he thought porridge was rather dull stuff which could be improved with onions, he added onions. But cooking for him was a side line. He was the bard and the story-teller, he spoke Hindustani well, could read and write and had a store of riddles and tales and legends to pass the long hours as many peoples have who live simply with few possessions, long memories and harsh climates.

High up among the rocks and screes or huddled inside the tent or crouched over the fire stirring the cooking pots or just to pass the time as we walked along beside our motley cavalcade, he kept us entertained. He told us the story of Alchung the naughty boy who ran away from home because his mother nagged him and he did not like work. He lived in a cave on the mountainside hunting wild sheep and lining his cave with their skulls. He robbed the villages too, stealing the flocks and herds so that soon he was hated by man and beast alike. He paid no attention at all to the local godlings, just took what he wanted with never a thank you.

But all those skulls! He sat in his cave gnawing bones and they looked at him with their empty reproachful eyes. At last he could bear it no longer so he came down the hill to the villages and asked the people to forgive him and in the tolerant way of the Buddhist faith they did so. He entered a lamasery and learned to meditate and pray so in the end he became a holy man, much revered. A hillside and a valley were named after him recalling his good deeds rather than his bad.

One day, waiting for a snowstorm to clear away, Tshulim with another Spiti boy called Tantup sang a song to which they danced, slowly then quickly, question and answer:

Where are you going?
  To the country between two passes.
What will you find there?
  I will find three hills.
What names have the hills?
  One Gold, one Silver, one Copper.

What grows on the hills?
  A sandal tree and a poplar tree
And the third has grass upon it.
  What birds sit there?
On one sits a vulture
  On one sits a peacock
On the other a parrot.
  What do the birds say?
The Vulture says: I am he that flies over the Passes!
  The Peacock says: I am he that flies over the Temples!
The Parrot says: I am he that flies over Speech!

Or sometimes they would sing a lament like the love song of Oorgyn Bootée whose lover was far away.

Though the apricot trees are in blossom,
  They give me no joy, for you are not here.
Though I live with my father and mother
  I am not happy, for you are not here —

... and so on for many verses, the threnody from every land of every lonely lover.

And tales too of Mila Repa (Cotton shirt), the saint who could fly through the air or under the earth or pass through stone walls and make rain by licking his finger and whose bones after his death were found to be studded with pearls. When the good spirits came to take away the bones and the holy pearls the people begged them to leave just one pearl hidden in Tibet which they did, but no one has ever found it.

It pleased them to see that we listened to their tales and we honoured their observances, progressing on all occasions clockwise round the holy places, respecting the chortens which were the tombs of their saints and the stone cairns which were built for their debis or local godlings. This apparently empty land was filled for them with a ghostly crowd of invisible beings, kindly if respected, hostile if ignored and living their own mysterious lives apart from the world of men. Every hill and valley had its local spirit. Offerings of prayer flags or coins or little cakes were made at the cairns, prayers were chanted, and if one wished to shoot some particular animal, a dough or butter image was offered in exchange for the real creature of flesh and blood. It was Alchung's sin that he offered no substitute for the lives of the animals he took but just snatched them arrogantly without a by your leave as Westerners do. No wonder that the dark empty eyes of the skulls so disturbed him and turned him to repentance as no human agent could do. Here was a lesson in respect for life as something containing within itself a sacred mystery belonging not to man but to the universe in which he lived.

Passing through Spiti again on our way to the Parang Pass and Rupshu in 1926 we met the Nono who was ruler of Spiti, although at the time he was only a boy and his mother, the Shema Sahib, was acting as regent. The Nono came to our camp with a small retinue of courtiers having crossed a roaring stream on his stout little pony to reach us. He was about fourteen years old, dressed in a gold cap, a red coat, a pink shirt and embroidered boots and he was not more than about four feet high. He brought a turquoise, a yak's tail, some wheaten flour and some yak's butter as a present. He wanted a rifle in exchange but we gave him our electric torch which fascinated him but which he broke almost at once. Having no grasp of the world's bureaucracies, he asked us to restore to him the power of beating recalcitrant subjects. Later we met his mother, a domineering old lady, bent on the same restoration of rights. We held court inside our small tent sitting on boxes and pillows while the local babies crawled round us and Labh Zang directed affairs and acted as interpreter. The Shema Sahib brought a jar of arak which she shared round, not into mugs but into our cupped hands so that we had to swallow it down immediately in one gulp or lose it, and fiery it was, making one choke and gasp.

Because Spiti was sparsely inhabited, difficult to reach and on the far edge of British India, it got very little government attention. The only substantial benefit it enjoyed was an iron bridge at Lingti over the Spiti river and one practical thing that Jack could do for the people was to inspect this bridge as an engineer and report on its condition. It was also possible on our journeys to discover and correct discrepancies in maps of the inner Himalayas which were sometimes quite inaccurate, showing rivers running in one direction when in reality they were flowing in another – and so on. This information was then passed on to the Survey of India.

Heights marked on maps were often inaccurate as well and we tested these where possible by taking the temperature of boiling water whose boiling point varies according to its height above sea level. The inability of water to reach a high temperature at high altitudes, but to boil before it did so, made it impossible to cook certain useful foods such as rice and lentils, a fact which Marco Polo discovered long before, only he put down the difficulty to cold rather than height. 'And I assure you that because of this great cold, fire is not so bright here, nor of the same colour as elsewhere, and food does not cook well.' (*Travels of Marco Polo*)

We reached the capital of Spiti, Dankhar, built on a precipitous spur of rock, a kind of martin's nest-cum-honeycomb-cum-goblin place, glued to the cliffs, full of cells and dark passages and according to Labh Zang built in part by *debis*. Half-way up the cliff was a Lamasery with a temple where within three wall niches was a Buddha image flanked by two companions. In front of a nearby altar a lamp burned, a simple wick in a dish of butter enclosed by an open-work brass lid. This lamp was never allowed to go out and in order to supply enough butter to keep it alight pious pilgrims presented a sheep or goat to the Lamasery flock and in recognition of this act prayers were said in perpetuity for the donors, or, as Labh Zang added in a practical way, for as long as the Lamasery lasted. Jack and I presented a goat and I wonder now, after all these years of change and confusion, whether they still pray for us in that high-up haunting place where the mountains tower above among the hurrying clouds and the river roars thousands of feet below, the loose rocks rumbling along its bed with a thunder like muffled drums.

On either side of this temple altar were box shelves containing the library brought from Tibet. Each volume, consisting of loose leaves of grass paper written by hand and measuring about twenty inches by six, was wrapped in white cloth and placed between two wooden boards and put in a partition by itself, a tab of red, yellow and blue silk hanging from it. On the wooden pillars around the walls of the temple were panels of silk tapestry painted with pictures of gods and saints, an ambience of Buddhism, a hint of Hinduism, a confusion of mythical and supernatural beings.

Up a dark staircase was a little door opening on the private room of a special godling where only the most favoured lamas were allowed to go. It smelled sweet and oily and was hung with banners and there another lamp was burning. If this lamp burned low (so said Labh Zang) the godling 'growled like a yak'. The floor of this room was covered with grain of which Labh Zang took a handful – he seemed a most favoured person in this place. If cast upon his fields it would keep away misfortune, so perhaps this particular god was in charge of agriculture. Higher up and across a roof courtyard was the chief lama's room where there were more tapestries and sacred paintings around the walls and a window looking sheer down into the gorge below.

On our perambulation around this strange city we had been accompanied by a group of lamas some of whom could speak Hindustani. They were friendly thoughtful men with fine intelligent faces and now we all sat down together upon the floor of the abbot's room and held a discussion upon the meaning of God, for them no personal approachable being but rather a dimension in eternity pervading creation, part of the sky, the hills, the waters, the rocks, the lives of all creatures and the soul of man. Surely that same vision which came to the initiators of the great religions, though their disciples dragged it down different ways, arguing with each other at the crossroads, not seeing that each rocky path led in the end to the same home.

'Part of myself is the God within every creature,' said Krishna. *(Bagavadgita)*

'I am in my Father and ye in me and I in you,' said Christ. *(St John XIV)*

Language is at best a clumsy instrument with which to discuss abstruse and mystical ideas, but how much more difficult if the discussion is held in three languages, sitting on a stone floor in a howling wind at 13,000 feet! How much easier to abandon cosmic thought in favour of the saint, the godling and the supernatural friend! So with our discussion unfinished and our thoughts still struggling for understanding we stepped out of the abbot's sanctuary into the warm sun and climbed to the topmost pinnacle of the city.

Here there was a high fort, the uppermost rooms of which were kept for the Nono when he was in residence. A young lama escorted us to this place having put on his best clothes for the occasion, a red coat and a tall yellow hat. He then led us down through dark passage-ways to a small hovel where an Englishman, 'Hay Sahib', had lived for a time and spent a winter. How cold he must have been on that pinnacle with no heat and probably only sattu tea (tea and peaflour) for nourishment! Why he came there we could not discover, perhaps he had just succumbed to the spell as we were doing. In any case he had become a legend and would no doubt in time appear among the *debis*.

In spite of its fortress ring of mountains, Spiti had at times been invaded, so they told us, both from Ladakh and by Sikhs from the Punjab. Perhaps there were Gurkha marauders too but the history they could recount was dateless and vague. An invading army had at one time been inveigled into Dankhar perhaps to make a treaty or some such thing. In a room overlooking the precipice the marauders were feasted and filled with Chang (beer) and arak (spirits) and when they were all satisfactorily gorged and drunken the Spiti men shovelled them all out through the window down that shuddering drop. No hope for any of them but perhaps they deserved it.

North of Spiti lay Ladakh, the easternmost province of Kashmir. To reach it one must cross the Zaskar range of precipitous peaks and come down on the other side to a country of great sweeping downs, the valleys of which did not drop lower than 15,000ft. There were no great peaks here but the tops of the downs stood at about 21,000 to 23,000ft, mostly swept clear of snow because of the wind. To get to this place and the province of Rupshu to which we were bound, Labh Zang led us out of Spiti by the Parang-la (*la* means pass) a more formidable passage than the Babeh. First a descent into a narrow gorge, a gash in the hills with a roaring stream along its base, yellow beaked choughs overhead and wild roses clinging to its sides, then a precarious path along the fierce water, jumping from side to side, from rock to rock till a narrow way led upwards towards the pass itself which stood at 18,000 or 19,000ft (discrepancy again in the maps). There was a night halt at Dokpo Tar where a small tent could be pitched and which was ringed with rocks of weird shapes like petrified monsters and trolls. These came to spectral life when the moon rose, threatening the trivial presence of humankind so that one was relieved to struggle out at dawn, cold as an icicle, handkerchief frozen hard in pocket, to gaze on the incredible bewilderment of jumbled peaks below just touched by the early light. So up the last climb before the sun started to melt the high snow, a prayer to the *debi* at the top then down, down to this quite different land of sweeping rounded hills, lost lakes, nomad herdsmen, wild asses and Ovis Poli.

This huge wild sheep is named after Marco Polo who passed in his journey rather further north and wrote: "There are great quantities of wild sheep of huge size. Their horns grow to as much as six palms in length and are never less than three or four. From these horns the shepherds make big bowls from which they feed and also fences to keep in their flocks. There are also innumerable wolves which devour many of the wild rams. The horns and bones of the sheep are found in such numbers that men build cairns of them beside the tracks to serve as landmarks to travellers in the snowy season."

Even though not so numerous in Rupshu as Marco had found in the Pamirs we saw many of them, sometimes as many as fifteen together. At first we saw no big rams but families of small rams, ewes and lambs and were able to take photographs, although these with our second-rate equipment were poor. Travelling, searching, exploring, we finally found the big rams and Jack was able to procure the prized trophies and the camp was able to feast on the hoped-for meat.

In describing this huge wild sheep I sometimes wonder if I am telling the truth but fortunately we took measurements at the time and those measurements are there to read. The horns, immensely thick and heavy and shaped like a conch can measure from 40–45 inches in length round the outer curve and 17–18 inches in circumference at the base. The height of the animal at the shoulder is about twelve hands and the body size can be compared to a large long-legged donkey although the quarters are more lightly built, sloping away from the shoulders. They have thick greyish-brown hair rather than wool, are swift and agile, preferring open country to rocks and cliffs. Eyesight and hearing are wonderfully keen and they would use the unevenness of the downs to disappear in an uncanny way as though they had never existed. Sometimes called Ovis Poli and sometimes Ovis Ammon, I would be tempted to think of him as one of earth's mythical beasts if I had not tried to lift his enormous skull and sampled his strong, dark meat.

On the same kind of ground but living rather higher up and more addicted to precipitous climbing were large herds of burrhel or blue wild sheep. These were smaller than ammon but large as sheep come, of a blue-grey colour with sweeping rather than curled horns. It was easier to watch these burrhel than watch the ammon as they were less shy and more numerous. Through a telescope I once watched a prolonged battle between two rams standing on their hind legs and plunging at each other so that the crack made by the impact carried across more than a mile of valley between us. Both ammon and burrhel sometimes sat on their hindquarters like dogs which makes them in retrospect more unlikely than ever. It was a source of wonder that such large creatures were able to feed so well on the sparse herbage underfoot. Herds of these wild sheep grazed at a smart walk, making up for the sparseness of the feed by moving across it quickly and certainly the animals we saw were sleek and well-looking. There was never enough snow to cover the grass for long as the fierce winds dispersed it into the dry air and this must have proved to be the case in winter-time as well.

Wild asses or *kyang* abounded. Full of curiosity they galloped to and fro in front of our tent snorting at our intrusion and pawing the ground indignantly with their hoofs, their reddish brown coat and white bellies and legs glistening with health and ardour.

> 'Who hath sent out the wild ass free? Or who hath loosed the bands of the wild ass?
> Whose house I have made the wilderness, and the barren land his dwellings.
> He scorneth the multitude of the city, neither regardeth he the crying of the driver.
> The range of the mountains is his pasture, and he searcheth after every green thing.'
>
> (*Job 39:5-8*)

They were in truth a little bombastic, making a great show of themselves, ready to fly if you approached too close, but never able to resist the temptation, inquisitive as they were, of coming back again and having another look.

Once we found a dead kyang with no marks on him to show how he had died. His bulk was impressive, a great barrel body, thick neck and heavy aquiline nose, comparable in size to a stocky mule. The stallions fought each other fiercely in far-flung galloping battles, biting, kicking and snorting to exhaustion, so perhaps this animal's heart had failed. If we had not been lucky enough to find him so soon after death and examine him in detail, no doubt wolves, snow leopards and vultures would have soon demolished him to the last bone. Wolves were numerous and hunted kyang, although it must have taken a pack of them to pull down so large a prey. We witnessed a hunt one day, five wolves after a kyang, one wolf playing in front of the kyang to divert his attention while four crept up behind. This kyang escaped because the wolves caught our scent and fled.

Snow leopards were rare and we only once or twice saw one at a distance although we often saw footprints. The Spiti men never lost a gruesome opportunity when Jack shot an animal of strewing the guts over a wide area in order to tempt a leopard and this with songs and incantations and very bloody hands. A snow leopard was called a *jadpo* and a headman was called a *gadpo*, which led to a deal of amusement and confusion as we so frequently muddled the words. There were small light-footed gazelles in the more open places called *goa*, very shy and swift of foot, whose meat tasted of the aromatic herbs on which they fed. There were marmots in plenty, upright sentinels above their holes, disappearing like magic at any sign of danger. And blue hares, as wispy and ghostly as shadows, swift and nearly invisible against the grey rocks.

A march or two from the Parang-la down the Pare River which ran northwards into Rupshu, we came upon a lake, clear and blue in its peaceful setting of downs and marshland and snow-flecked hills. This was the Tsho Moreri lying at a height of 15,000ft. Here on the shores of this lake was the summer encampment of the ruler or chief nomad of Rupshu who was called the Gova. His herds of yaks and sheep and goats were scattered around in great numbers and not far off was the Lamasery of Kanzok, founded and built as a pious act by the Gova's grandfather. This Lamasery was, as far as I know, the only building in Rupshu and remarkable for the fact that nearly all the materials used in the building had come long distances over the roughest of ways.

The nomads, including the Gova, lived in black tents woven of yaks' hair and dug into the ground to the depth of about three feet so that in the distance they looked squat and low like fat black mushrooms with flags and yaks' tails waving from their roofs. Labh Zang who, needless to say, was a friend of the Gova's, arranged for us to visit the camp and meet the great man which we did outside his tent among a crowd of retainers and relations. We could not enter the tent because of his family godling inside who might have objected to our intrusion. We could however look in through the doorway.

It was surprisingly spacious with an altar opposite the entrance upon which burned a lamp. Under the altar were spread freshly cut grass turfs and round the walls of the tent were bags of provisions, cooking pots, ropes, blankets and all the miscellaneous gear needed for this peripatetic existence. The nomad women wore fine headdresses studded with turquoise stones, all the older people wore long homespun garments down to the ankle, the children wore scarcely anything at all despite the cold, and everybody was dirty. But how could they be otherwise? The camp was grubby with skins and scraps and bones lying around but perhaps not even Abraham was over particular on this score knowing how short a time he would spend in each halting place.

It was not so easy to feel a closeness to these nomads as it was with the Spiti people. They seemed one step further back in history and the extreme harshness of their existence prevented them doing much at all except survive and see that their flocks survived as their only means of subsistence. It was all the more to the credit of the Gova's grandfather that he had founded this Lamasery which stayed in one place, possessed a few books, educated a few boys, carried on some traditions and formed a tenuous link with the more cultured Lamaseries of Tibet.

But who then destroyed those more cultured Lamaseries of Tibet? The 'civilized' Chinese. Perhaps some of those beautiful hand-written books, despoiled later in Tibet proper, have survived in these remote and unknown Lamaseries in far-away Rupshu and Spiti.

The Gova was rightly proud of his Lamasery at Kanzok and invited us to visit it. He instructed the lamas to perform a Devil Dance for our benefit and escorted by Labh Zang and Tshulim we went to witness this, acted out in the courtyard of the two-storeyed building, a kind of miracle play in which good and evil were opposed, and there was a great deal of leaping about and sword clashing and blowing of great horns. The costumes were magnificent: long silk-embroidered cloaks and kilted skirts, fantastic masks depicting animals and devils and supernatural beings. We were able to look closely at these after the dance was over and found them beautifully cared for and maintained, kept in a great chest and only taken out on special occasions. A service in the temple followed and although women were not supposed to attend, Labh Zang and Tshulim smuggled me in and nobody objected. We sat on the floor cross-legged and chanted and rang bells and blew gigantic horns while small acolytes came round with a large brass teapot and handed out cups of Sattu tea. The atmosphere was relaxed and casual and I could not feel there was as much reverence as at Dankhar, but looking round at the faces of the young lamas and remembering that all they knew beside this was the harsh life of the mountain herdsman, I could not but respect them and feel chastened by their simple devotions.

Occasionally one met a saint and had the feeling of having entertained 'angels unawares'. One old, old lama came to our camp carrying a bundle of letters which he wanted to show us. He was wearing a tall red hat and had a beautiful contemplative face like an angel from a medieval cathedral. The letters were written by an Englishman who had visited Rupshu 100 years before and it would have been interesting to study these, but to the old man they were not historical but magical and he did not want to be parted from them even for a short time, only for us to see and hold his treasure.

To return to the Gova and his encampment, it was not long before we tired of being a permanent entertainment for rows of well-behaved nomads sitting cross-legged just in front of our tent watching round-eyed our every movement and all the extraordinary objects that came out of or were put back into our boxes. Only the Gova's young son was a nuisance. Like all people who had power without responsibility, he did not know how to behave and when we had exhausted our small stock of presents he came back for more and more. The only way to get rid of him was to leave ourselves, so we instructed Labh Zang to hire for us a small herd of yaks from the Gova to carry our belongings and to buy a little flock of biangi goats to supply us with milk, and set off on our journey again.

The biangi goats gave very little milk but a great deal of amusement. They were silky and white and looked like angel goats but were as wicked as goats come. They knew exactly when milking time was due and would seek out some high pinnacle of rock from which the combined efforts of the whole camp could not dislodge them. When they were ready for milking, they came for milking but not before. On the march they would turn right if we wanted to turn left and all hands were needed to change their minds. Obviously their promised land was not our promised land and this led to many arguments. But their mischief was perpetrated with such grace and good humour that more was gained in entertainment than lost in nourishment. These charming little creatures with their smiling mischievous faces produce the soft undercoat known as *pashm* from which the famous 'Pashmina' shawls of Kashmir are woven. To help care for the flock we engaged a man called Dorjé ('the Thunderbolt') from the nomad camp. He was small and slit-eyed with no more than two or three hairs to his chin and the merriest grin ever. At the age of about eight or ten he must have plaited his hair and donned his sheepskin cap with earflaps, since which time he had never disturbed the arrangement.

We walked round the Tsho Moreri on its white shores covered with some saline deposit which made the water brackish and undrinkable. The lake was shallow, shining and blue, ruffled to a darker blue when the wind passed across it, reflecting the sky and clouds and the snow-sprinkled hills around it when the wind was still. The brightness and beauty of this lake gave rise to an expression used by Labh Zang who, when he had cleaned the barrel of a rifle assiduously and was satisfied with the result, would say with a grin: "The Tsho Moreri has come!" On this lake were numerous ducks and geese, all at the time in eclipse plumage and unable to fly. They had come from the plains, made their nests and brought up their young and would fly back again in a few months' time. If surprised they would scuttle away with great quacking and splashing neither young nor old able to take to the air. From one high rock not far off we looked down upon two more lakes, smaller than the Tsho Moreri, called the Kyun lakes, one sapphire blue, one emerald green and from this high place we could see Hanlé in the distance with its Lamasery tucked in among the painted rocks lying between us and the upper waters of the Indus.

Alas! No time to go there, no time to dip our hands in Indus water, but if we had, there would have been still another peacock-coloured distance, still another rocky pass, still another shining range of hills —Karakoram, Tien Shan, Kuen Lun – names to dream of. One needs another life. "Out of the hills I came, out of the hills and the high winds. Just is the Wheel!"

So much wind, such desiccation, so little snow, such freezing cold, there was little encouragement for plants to grow, but to lie on the stony earth and peer into the furrows made by wind, was to discover a multitude of tiny growing things, so low down, so tenacious and so unperturbed by weather that they formed a little silver world of their own. Silver I say because most of the leaves were silver rather than green, everything had the aromatic smell of artemisia, many had wool like edelweiss. If there was a flower it was clear and bright as the sky. Rocks were splashed and mottled and spread with many-coloured lichens, blood red, orange, grey, white, dark green. We came to Alchung's hillside where he had lived in his skull-lined cave and acres and acres of sweeping downs were purple with the blossoms of a small plant like rest-harrow. Alter one's scale of vision and there were the gardens underfoot, miniscule but exquisite. I felt as I wandered across these vast uplands with their huge skies and hidden lakes, their fabulous animals and tiny shining flowers, how happily I could spend my life here, but I would be more careful than Alchung had been to keep on the right side of the local *debis*. I had not experienced a winter, only high summer which to us seemed cold enough but to the people who lived there, quite hot. Once, scaling the Bodpo Pass which was roughly 19,000ft in height, we fell in with a company of traders and their yaks passing over into Tibet. One man had discarded all his clothes except for a sort of kilt made from his coat. Pleasantly breezy weather but evidently too hot.

A glimpse into Tibet, a then forbidden land, determined us to visit the place and on our last journey we did so. But first I will descend to the plains again and describe an approach we made to Spiti through the states of Mandi and Kulu and across the Hampta Pass. We travelled by train from Roorkee to railhead at Pathankot and then by lorry through Mandi as far as motor transport could go. This drive was alarming; up and down and round, a demon Sikh driver who cared for nobody, our lorry on two wheels and no hope of retaining food or drink of any kind. When thankfully we reached the end of the motor road and transferred to the peaceful company of mules, we stopped at a place called Jatingiri and had a meal.

At one time when he was very young and had not long been in India my father had been resident counsellor to the Raja of Mandi and the bungalow at which we stopped, beautifully placed on a hillside overlooking forests and hills, had been built there under his instructions for the use of travellers. I never forgot that meal. Emptied out and battered by the long lorry drive, we were disappointed to find that the cook had taken a holiday. But the village headman and the night watchman stepped into the breach and cooked us rice and chapattis and dhal (lentils) flavoured with herbs from the garden. There are many kinds of dhal in India and many kinds of herbs but I never tasted anything so good as the Mandi dhal and the Mandi herbs eaten in that bungalow at Jatingiri. Perhaps there was even something left of my father's presence of long before to add to the memory and the flavour.

From here we crossed the Bubu Pass into Kulu, a zigzag up to 9,000ft and a zigzag down into the beautiful rather enervating valley of orchards through which runs the River Beas. All round the valley are mountains whose slopes are clothed with oak and pine and alpine meadows. Sturdy villages of stone and timber are tucked among groves of walnuts and poplars. A number of English people had bought land and settled here, growing apples and pears and other fruits and sending them out packed in baskets carried on coolie-back to supply the markets of Simla and the plains. My father's memory again intervenes. He had, while travelling in Kulu during his young days, offended the wife of one of these rather powerful landowners by not paying her his respects. He had also unwisely sent his laundry to her dhobi (washerman). She forbade the return of the laundry until he had made the correct approaches. No kowtow, no clean clothes. He capitulated.

We had arranged for Labh Zang to meet us in Kulu with one or two other Spiti men to help us across the Hampta Pass which he faithfully did. But cholera had broken out and we ran into a crowd of troubles. People were fleeing from the infected villages, spreading the infection, corpses were being buried along the water courses, medical care was sparse and in those days little could be done for the victims who generally died within a few hours of being struck down. No attempt was being made to contain the disease and I remember a gruesome pot of cherry jam offered to us at one bungalow which held more flies than cherries. Along the roadside were beds of wild strawberries delicious to behold but we dared not eat them. We must leave as quickly as possible, especially as we were now responsible for the Spiti men, but to gather coolies to carry our belongings was nearly impossible because of the prevalent panic.

Jack's diplomacy and Labh Zang's persistence extricated us and we struggled across the Hampta Pass into the little country of Lahoul which lay between Kulu and Spiti. We had with us a motley collection of load carriers and invalids escaping from the heat and in the confusion on the way we lost the box which contained all the money for the trip. One Kula man had changed his mind half-way up the pass, dumped the box under a rock and returned home. This box was vital, as the money inside was all in small coins, exact change, which enabled us to pay each porter the precise sum owed him as no one was rich enough to carry change. The box was miraculously retrieved intact but we learned the lesson never to put all the small change into one box again.

Among the stray people who had joined our caravan was an old Spiti man already very ill with jaundice which he had contracted in the humid heat of the Kulu valley. In spite of all the help our men gave him it looked as though he would never have the strength to regain his home but once up in the thin cold air he started to recover and we met him again sometime later in his home village full of thanks and gratitude.

Along the banks of the Chandra river in Lahoul were no human habitations at all but so many flowers that the hillsides looked like fallen rainbows and spreading downwards from the peaks above were two glaciers, the Big Shigri and the Little Shigri, which we had to cross. The glacier ice lay under shifting layers of loose stones which slipped and rolled away underfoot. A Kulu man dropped his stick which slid to the lip of Big Shigri above the spewing mouth. Wisely, the man abandoned the stick, but one of the Spiti men named Tshering Tshobell, longing to show off in front of the men from Kulu, scrambled to the glacier lip, rescued the stick and returned it airily to its owner. No doubt a tale repeated many times on winter nights in the smoky comfort of his home.

These marches across the Shigri glaciers were some of the hardest I remember for not only did the smaller stones shift and roll but huge boulders lay across the ice which either had to be climbed or circumvented. Everything was in movement, no path could ever be formed and every traveller had to make his own. But, the glaciers passed, we came to a camping place of softest green, a little dell among rocks, starred with small mauve primulas. And so onwards to the easy Kunzam Pass, the upper villages of Spiti and their friendly inhabitants.

It is not often that I look back upon these journeys and recall fear. But the incident of the dropped stick on the Shigri glacier still brings a shudder, as does another incident also connected with rolling stones in the Peen valley of Spiti. Benighted on a steep hillside in pouring rain above a grey rushing river, stones rolling underfoot, stones loosened by the rain hurtling from above, the absolute relentlessness of that hungry turbulent water – one slip! Then a little light in the distance as of some star. The kindly people from the village of Mudh, knowing that we were on our way, had left the shelter of their houses to go out and light a bonfire to guide us. They took us in and we spent the night in an upper room listening to the storm and wondering at the hospitality of the very poor. Our transport had also been benighted but had wisely halted until daylight.

I will go back now to that resolution made by us to enter Tibet when we had gazed over that inviting land from the heights of Rupshu. Because officially to enter Tibet was forbidden, when travelling near the border one had to sign a declaration to say that one would not cross it. However if one did not ask for the papers nothing was signed so there was no perjury. The risk of meeting Tibetan officials was slight. They did not wish to be troubled with small border incidents any more than we did and the vagueness of the border made arguments unlikely.

The difficulty lay in transport. For one thing the land was almost uninhabited and one could hardly enquire and search for transport in a place where one was not supposed to be. So it was necessary to take one's own. Labh Zang suggested that we should buy ponies in Spiti which would accompany us all the way and this we did.

To buy six suitable ponies was quite a long business so we decided to hand it over to Labh Zang and give him plenty of time to carry it out. To make final arrangements and to give him the money necessary to buy the ponies we asked him to come to Roorkee in the winter and stay awhile. One day on my return from an early morning ride on 7th January 1929 I found Labh Zang and Tshulim standing at our gate, exceedingly travel worn and disreputable, watched over suspiciously by one of our Indian servants who could not believe that the Sahib would want to see two such grubby rapscallions. The trust and friendship that brought them on this long journey was remarkable. It had taken a month and a half to cover the distance, being continually turned back by snow or blocked roads, and then finally having to brave the railway, neither of them even having seen a train before. Labh Zang looked ruefully at his boots and said he was ashamed because the dust came up between the cracks.

We settled them into a little house in the compound, gave them some new clothes and showed them the sights of Roorkee. Not that one had to go far for this, even the flatness of a parade ground was a wonder. The Indian servants did not approve, but when they had gone to bed we had Labh Zang and Tshulim into the house, showed them our china and silver, our lampshades and books and bric-à-brac, astonishment on astonishment. They stayed for a week but then grew restless and homesick and wanted to start back on the marathon journey to their hills. Before they left we had been able to pay over the money for the ponies and make the final arrangements for our journey to Tibet.

Labh Zang had come to Roorkee argus-eyed, and the details that he took in came out in conversation later on. He had not liked to disparage Roorkee at the time, that would not have been polite, but he did not think much of the place: too flat, too hot, too dusty and the people unfriendly. But, "You people, the Sahibs are a wonder," he said. "Sometimes you crouch under rocks in snowstorms suffering discomfort and cold. Sometimes you sit in soft chairs dropping the ashes from your cigarettes into silver dishes." He returned to his own people in the mantle of a sage.

The following July as arranged, Labh Zang and Tshulim met us on the Hindustan–Tibet road with six sturdy Spiti ponies. We crossed the Babeh Pass and turned down the valley of the Spiti River reaching Labh Zang's village of Mani which was close to the Tibetan border. Here Labh Zang enjoyed much admiration and we were feasted and put on show. Passing on, we came to a place where Tshulim assured us that not long ago one hundred and eight saints had lived peacefully in their *chortens*, but when a woman sinned there a hundred of them fled in disgust to China and now there were only eight remaining.

What would have happened if the sinner had been a man? I suspect that the saints would have just turned their heads away and stayed put. The disappearance of these prudish holy ones had left four ruined temples with neglected images and frescoes stained by weather. One of these images sat, not in the lotus position as Buddha images do, but with his legs down in the European way. There is a legend that a 'Messiah' or 'Bhodisatva' would come from the west so this perhaps was an image looking forward in anticipation of that coming.

We were now on a strip of disputed territory and perhaps it was arguments over the border that led to the ruins as much as the desertion of the hundred prudish saints. We crossed an insignificant mountain stream with a small stone bridge at a place called Kara-ti and this, Labh Zang assured us, was the real border.

A few miles on we reached Chusa where there were hot sulphur springs flowing out from under a cliff. I have never enjoyed a bath more than I did at this place and as Labh Zang aptly remarked: "Not even the English could keep the water so hot." A series of stone basins had been hollowed out under the spring, the water led from one to the other becoming cooler as it grew further from its source, so you could choose your temperature. A few days previously I had injured my back and the relief this sulphur water gave me was inestimable. In the old days, so Labh Zang said, the different pools were inscribed with instructions as to their use, but then a jealous doctor came and smashed the inscriptions because he thought the baths were taking away his patients. So there was nothing to tell me I was staying in far too long and when I finally crawled out I could hardly stand. But the back was cured and after a long sleep I was well again.

We turned eastwards into the Chumurti province of Tibet and followed the Samlakhar water towards its source. Rumour had it that some Tibetan officials were on the prowl so every day Labh Zang would scout ahead to bring us warning. He met one of these men who questioned him closely about our intentions. What blarney Labh Zang exercised and what stories he invented we never knew but cunning diplomacy was what he was good at. Perhaps he represented our ragtag and bobtail camp of two English people, six ponies and half a dozen Spiti men as a dangerous invading army. I do not know. But the officials were warned and cautiously kept away. We pitched camp at Samlakhar in a grassy cup under a great rock looking out over the ammon downs and the endless rise and fall of the land on the way to Tashigong, and if one's searching eye could have spanned the distance, towards the sacred mountain of Meru or Kailas and the lake of Manasarawar where, so legend had it, four great rivers rose from the mouths of four great beasts: the Indus from a lion's mouth, the Brahamaputra from a horse's mouth, the Sutlej from a bull's mouth and the Karnali from the mouth of a peacock.

In order to rest the ponies we stayed in one camp. We climbed to 21,000ft, we wandered across the windswept downs, we stalked ammon and burrhel, we lay on our backs and watched the silent lammergeyers sailing like dark specks thousands of feet above us, and wondered at the blown snowdrifts sprawled like huge question marks across the hills. All this must end. What next?

The ponies had done us well. They were docile and friendly as animals are who spend the winters indoors being hand fed. Black Beauty, Bucephalus, Mineroo, Sergeant Murphy, Yarkandi and Little Sorrel, I do not now remember how they got these names. But they were an anxiety too. On the stony ground they cast shoes, but we brought a store of shoes and one of the Spiti men was a blacksmith. Two of them developed sores but our loads had dwindled so we sent them back to Spiti with two men to recover at home. There was a danger from wolves and snow leopards when they were grazing outside the camp. Labh Zang was vigilant, often sitting up among the ponies at night to guard them. Without them we could not have travelled in Tibet as searching for transport would have announced our illicit presence.

Sadly our time was up. We left Samlakhar with the four remaining ponies, Labh Zang and Tshulim and an odd Spiti man or two who still wanted to come with us. We took our way down the Spiti river to its junction with the Sutlej under the great peak of Leo Porguil. Now we were on the upper reaches of the Hindustan–Tibet road near to the Shipki Pass, an arid country beyond the monsoon where pine trees with edible seeds took the place of the deodars to come. Gradually our cavalcade dwindled as we could hire transport again and the Spiti men took the remaining ponies home. Only ourselves and Labh Zang and Tshulim remained.

Not many marches down the road we came to Chini, to that part of the land which had seemed so wild at the beginning of our journeys and we felt as though we had surely reached the fringes at least of civilization. It was at Chini that the Viceroy, Lord Dalhousie, who could not stand the rains in Simla had built a house and ruled India by remote control in the nineteenth century. This house was now the municipal offices of the district. There was also a forest bungalow where we stayed and two Moravian Mission houses. We now could wash our clothes and scrub ourselves and eat like kings as the garden of the forest bungalow was full of vegetables and apricots and peaches.

Looking back on our wild wanderings I watch in my mind, as though from the tent doorway at evening, the full moon rising behind jagged cliffs and moving slowly across its shining face, two ibex with their scimitar horns and hoary beards passing from darkness to darkness; or lie on my back at 20,000ft and gaze into the high up sky and see far above the motionless wings of a lammergeyer, sailing, sailing, looking down on his vast jumbled world of peak and ravine and hidden lake; or sit with Dorje the goatherd, huddled under a rock lost in a snowstorm and share with him not talk, because we had no common language, but a matchbox full of pear drops and a friendship beyond words; or stoop down low on the moraine beside a glacier and see under a thin sheet of ice the brightest, most delicate and perfect flowers, their feet in running water, their heads protected by this little private hothouse of their own; or gaze silent and amazed across the pale blue waters of the Ysho Moreri in its circle of pearly hills; these and a hundred other pictures which nothing can despoil or diminish in times of dullness or distress. But come to an end they must and the briefness of their duration preserved their clarity which otherwise might have been dimmed by the retelling.

'And lo, I am parched with thirst and I perish.

Give me quickly the cold water flowing forth from the lake of memory.' (*Orphic tablet*)

On this our last return journey Labh Zang and Tshulim came with us almost to the end and only turned home when the heat closed in upon us. On the last stretch of stony road, to the last of all the *debis* in his little rocky shrine, Labh Zang prayed: "May the Sahib be made Commander-in Chief, may I be made Government Treasurer and Tshulim a Sirdar!" But that prayer was never answered.

NEPAL VISIT, 1934

by

Stuart Battye

Pick up a Sunday paper and study the travel section. It won't be long before you find Nepal's capital, Katmandu, in the headlines. Worldwide tourism has penetrated this Himalayan kingdom; in fact you can join an Everest expedition on a tourist ticket. But it was not always so. In the days of the British Raj, Nepal was an independent kingdom in treaty relationship with India. Yet Nepal remained a closed country to Europeans. No roadway existed from the network of India over the lower Himalayas to the valley in which Katmandu lies. There, however, life was a little less rugged with some twelve miles of roadway linking the various townships, roads that carried a few official motor-cars and some country buses laboriously transported over the mountains in pieces and assembled in the capital. There was also a cableway running over the heights and spanning the gorges carrying some of the day-to-day essentials for life in the valley, a somewhat tenuous but vital lifeline. The rest, furniture, trade-goods, pianos, kerosene, petrol, people – in fact, what you will – were carried over the mountains on the sturdy backs of the Nepalese. But this is to anticipate.

Under the original treaty the Government of India maintained a representative in Katmandu who went by the imposing title of Envoy Extraordinary and Minister Plenipotentiary. In the years of which I write the incumbent was a British Officer of the Indian Political Service. With him was a doctor and an educational adviser who together formed a minute British community. One further civilian, an engineer, was employed by the Nepalese Government to be responsible for public utilities including the mountain cableway.

It is curious that Nepal should have remained an isolated country for so long. The Indian Army at that time contained ten Gurkha Regiments. These regiments were officered by British officers but only occasionally was one permitted to enter Nepal for recruiting purposes. This then was the state of affairs in the 'thirties', virtually a closed shop, and no young officer bent on adventure could hope to get permission to enter the Kingdom.

But then Vi, a sister by marriage, came over the horizon. Vi knew everybody, at any rate everybody who counted for anything. And well she might. Her father had been one of the 'Heaven Borns' who numbered amongst his more senior appointments Foreign Secretary to the Government of India, and Resident in Kashmir. Vi and her sister had, twenty years previously, been known as the 'Rosebuds of Kashmir', a well deserved compliment to two gorgeous young things in the years before the Kaiser's war.

Vi returned to India after a lapse of a dozen or so years for a second visit and deftly made use of her contacts which ranged from Mysore in the south to the Himalayas in the north. It was whispered that the British Minister in Nepal had in his younger days sought to gather nectar from the Kashmir rosebud but found no response to his advances. Nevertheless a friendship had continued and so it came about that Vi received an official invitation to visit her old friend in Nepal, "but" he added, "since my wife is at home in England, perhaps you should be accompanied by an escort in order to maintain the proprieties". Vi wrote to me suggesting that I accompany her as ADC. I needed no second bidding.

The hot winds of April were now sweeping across the Gangetic plain, raising dust from the parched fields and blanketing the trees in a haze which seemed to accentuate the sun's heat. I paced the platform at

Gorakhpur whilst Nasru, my bearer, squatted by the baggage. Presently the overnight mail came panting in, an even thicker dust haze shrouding its passage. There was Vi in khaki shirt and jodhpurs, terai hat and all, hot foot from watching the final heats of the Kadir Cup. We bundled on to a metre gauge railway which had conveniently waited for the mail train. Presently we were clanking and swaying over the shimmering plain heading for Raxaul and the road to Katmandu.

How long this part of the journey took I cannot now remember. The sun declined, the shadows lengthened and the hot wind ceased, giving way to a clear rose-tinted twilight which rapidly darkened into night. Vi had been generously supplied with a hamper by her erstwhile hostess and this was unpacked as we rattled along. Later, Nasru came through from the servant's compartment to unroll our bedding along the lower bunks.

Sometime early the following morning we crept across the River Gandak, the steel bridge girders reverberating hollowly to the clinkety-clunk of the bogies. Hoping to find a restaurant on the station at Raxaul we patiently waited for breakfast. Alas, we had miscalculated the devastation caused by the Bihar earthquake which some three months previously had suddenly rocked the lower Himalayas and the Terai, bordering Bihar and Nepal. Raxaul station was there but the buildings were not. Instead, *chattai* screens had been erected for the most essential offices. These did not include a restaurant, so Vi's hamper was again investigated, whilst Nasru, ever resourceful, produced tea and some tinned milk from somewhere. Refreshed, we took stock of our situation. A narrow gauge line connected Raxaul with Amelkganj, just inside Nepal, but the earthquake had dealt that a very nasty side swipe and no trains were running.

The alternative was a country bus. Country buses, whether in India, Pakistan, Persia or Afghanistan tend to be of a type. The basis is a sturdy, if old, 30cwt engine and chassis. On to this is built an openwork body, partly of wood and partly of metal. A substantial roof rack crowns the lot and substantial it has to be. But the real glory of the bus is the paintwork. Varied in hue and ornamented with a portrait or two and the most alluring slogans in Hindi, Urdu, Persian or whatever, there is no mistaking its ownership and the superlative service offered. Inside there are usually two classes; alongside the driver in front is first class, the rest is anybody's guess, for seats athwart or lengthwise are occupied by all and sundry, well-to-do *bannias*, *burqa*-clad females, snotty children and lesser live stock, whilst outside, when the driver is not looking, mount the ticketless outriders to be shouted at and thumped into scurrying departure at the next stop.

Vi and I travelled first class. Somewhere up above Nasru had stowed our gear in amongst the bundles, tin boxes, bicycles, wicker baskets, chickens and inevitable paraphernalia of the passengers below. We left Raxaul in the cool of the morning but it was not long before the sun climbed and the hot wind started to wisp its way across the road stirring up dust and leaves until the air was thick with haze. Behind us the pall was impenetrable for several hundred yards but fortunately there was little traffic and we rattled merrily along. Merrily at first but gradually the heat and dust had its effect and we tied scarves round our faces in an attempt to filter the worst. What it was like behind us in the main body defied description. Yet everyone seemed to take it as a matter of course, accepting discomfort as part of life. Most of them had never known anything else. Gradually the track rose through the lower hills, dry cultivation gave way to stunted thorn bushes dotting the crevices and rutted hillocks eroded by past monsoon rains. The cross-wind was actually a blessing for it dissipated both body heat and the more foetid effects of compact humanity.

We drowsed through the day, somehow the fifty-mile journey ticked away and as the afternoon light lengthened we crossed the border and came to a halt at Bhimpedi. Once inside Nepal, Vi became a VIP and I basked in some of the reflected glory. A reception committee was there to welcome us, willing hands seized our impedimenta, stalwart backs shouldered our baggage, whilst two ponies were led forward for us to mount. We had traversed hundreds of miles of India on broad gauge railway, then metre gauge, to be followed by country bus; now the real stuff was to come, four legs or two.

I looked at the track ahead as it rose steeply round the curve of a hill. This was the beginning of the lower Himalayas proper. Our destination for the night lay several miles ahead. I looked at Vi's slender figure as she mounted a white, shaggy little pony and I looked at Nasru's thick set, rather stout, unathletic torso. Nasru, bearer, camp cook, waiter at table, tiger skinner, general factotum, was too valuable an asset. Motioning him to mount the second pony, I took my khud stick and set off on foot.

Some hours later and two thousand feet higher we arrived at the Government Guest House as dusk was falling. It is very comforting at the end of a long and tedious journey to find everything is laid on. Vi's friend, Clendon, had ordered in food, firewood and such essentials as were necessary to our comfort. The Guest House was a simple affair with a living room, one bedroom and a bathroom, zinc bath, washhand stand, thunderbox and all. Outside, a tent had been pitched for me with (what luxury) a brass-bound iron bedstead and mattress. No canvas camp stuff here.

In no time drinks were carried in by Nasru (the pony ride had been a wise precaution) then supper, served in this case by the *chowkidar*. He was garrulous to a fault, regaling us with talks of travellers long since gone, of 'high-borns' padding by on elephants up the winding track over the passes and down into Katmandu. This occupied the meat course. For sweet and dessert the real *pièce-de-résistance* were those terrifying minutes when fissures opened, water spouted, villages subsided, trees cracked and fell, all the horrifying details of that terrible earthquake. I found it a stimulating account but Vi said, somewhat tartly, that he had been indulging, possibly with some of the drink supplied by Clendon. She was not a little bored with this voluble henchman but since she could scarcely understand a word of what he said it was not surprising.

The sun was just touching the treetops when we breakfasted next morning. Far behind lay the dust and heat of the plains. All was cool and clear, with the stimulating call of the dawn birds. We were still in the region of the rain forests, straight-backed sal trees marched alongside with cotton trees; flame of the forest made a vivid splash of scarlet in the olive greens and browns of the lower slopes. Presently, on our upward way, we came in sight of terraced cultivations, layer upon layer rising from the valley to ridge, an incredible feat of agriculture which had taken years to accomplish. Gradually rain forest gave way to chir pines, whilst higher still we came upon mountain oaks, wild cherry, wild pear, with here and there a glistening magnolia, interspersed with the sudden crimson flash of a giant rhododendron.

All morning we toiled upwards, the porters now strung out behind us. Vi's terai hat came out as the sun rose higher, warming our backs. The temperature was delightful and the air clear enough to reveal the unfolding view as we topped the first pass about midday. To our right the cable hummed its quiet way over the mountains. Pigeons fluttered and jostled for the grain spilled from the sacks loaded on the freight platforms. In one stupendous sweep the cable spanned a two-thousand foot gorge. Later, when I met Mr Lilburn, the engineer, I asked him how the continuous cable had ever been hoisted into position. "Quite simple", he replied, "it was carried over the heights by coolies and laid in place beneath the pylons". I had visions of a monstrous millipede traversing the mountains to string out this thread-like cable.

We were now above the tree line and having lunched we started on a decline to the next valley. Vi kept to her pony, I to my two legs, Nasru quietly slipping off the second pony on the easy slopes in order, I suspected, to keep up appearances. Other travellers passed us making for India whilst we overtook hillmen carrying the heavy loads which earned them a living. One had a pack of six two-gallon petrol cans balanced on his back, the rope head-band taut against his forehead, his leg muscles bulging and straining at every step. Another supported a cradle in which sat, facing rearwards, a smartly dressed Indian gentleman, umbrella and all, incongruous but somehow not surprising.

In places the track resembled the Giants' Causeway, rocks were worn smooth by the passage of countless bare feet. Soon we were down in the trees again, the heady scent of pine trees warmed in the sun surrounding us. Then we were skirting a ridge, the pathway running horizontal for a mile or two. In the afternoon we climbed to another pass and finally descended wearily to the welcome Guest House as evening was coming on. That was the longest stage of the journey, seventeen miles over a couple of passes with a two-thousand foot gorge in between. Again Clendon had stocked the larder and arranged for our comfort. We sat looking out on the deepening shadows creeping up from the valley below, chasing the last of the sun's tints from the tips of the trees till all were in shadow. As the stars came out and the chill of evening set in, Nasru discreetly announced that supper was ready. This time we never saw the *chowkidar*, he was a very different chap from the previous one and let Nasru do the waiting.

The final stage was largely downhill as the track dropped away into the main valley of Nepal, gradually broadening out into a road and there on the outskirts of Patan was Clendon with a car to meet us. Soon we were threading our way through narrow streets stacked with rubble from shattered buildings, then on to the plain and so up a slope to Katmandu.

The British Legation was like an English home, a double storied house set in a delightful garden which was clearly Clendon's pride. His official duties being light, he was able to devote time to his garden. Day after day bowls of fresh flowers would appear in the house, his speciality being the matchless rose-buds that he cultivated. What a contrast it was to relax in such comfort after the arid bachelor bungalows of the plains. Early mornings saw me out on a pony kindly provided by our host, whilst after breakfast Vi and I made the most of our time sight-seeing. We visited the nearer townships, Katmandu and Patan in more leisurely fashion, Bhatgaon and Swayambunath, all now to be found in the tourist guides. But in those days they were a unique privilege for European eyes. Everywhere there was evidence of the earthquake. Villages had subsided, roads shifted, houses collapsed in rubble.

Katmandu sprawled across a valley and over low ridges on either side. In the valley lay the old town, temples and bazaar, while climbing the ridge to the east lay the Government buildings. Tucked away further still was the Royal Palace and the Prime Minister's residence. On the western ridge was the British Legation which looked across the valley towards the Government buildings.

The *Hanuman Dokha*, the Royal Council Chamber, was cracked across and across. In contrast the Legation had hardly been affected, which carried some significance to the superstitious and greatly enhanced the prestige of the British. Down below, in the old town area, the bazaar was a fascinating place of narrow streets and open shop fronts. These seemed to have survived with only minor damage. Shopkeepers were cheerful and eager to do business. We wandered along looking for small presents to take to friends at home. We haggled over this and that and soon discovered that it was prudent to enquire for two prices – one price was local the other "Company". The "Company" price was a relic of the East India Company days when goods from India carried a "Company" mark up.

Adjoining the bazaar, the damage was greater. Temples had been torn apart revealing to profane eyes, perhaps for the first time, the deities enshrined. But the magnificent *stupa* at Swayambanath, with its all-seeing eyes gazing to the four points of the compass, mercifully remained intact. Erotic frescoes, bas-reliefs or carvings leapt at us from doorways, the walls of ancient buildings portraying voluptuousness in many forms. Sex seemed to vibrate in the air. Clusters of tall stone *lingams* sprouted from temple precincts encircling *yonis* clinging to their bases. At first I was embarrassed but not so Vi, "Oh, you must expect this sort of thing," she said, taking it in her stride, "it's all part of their religious mystique."

Even the earthquake had its lighter moments; when rescuers reached a Hindu and a Muslim buried together but still living, a feeding tube was passed down to relieve their suffering but an altercation immediately arose as to who should have first suck. The Brahmin wailed that he would lose caste if the Muslim first defiled the tube and the Muslim refused to touch it if an infidel had sullied it. Then there was the fruit seller who was entombed with his stock in trade. Nine days later he was released none the worse, orange peel everywhere.

In the evenings it was usual for the other English families to come round to the Legation for a drink and a chat or a game of billiards, rather like dropping in at the Club. The doctor was a keen entymologist. I have never seen such a superb collection of butterflies and moths, some as big as fig leaves. This set Vi off on another line. "What about a few specimens for a nephew?" Next afternoon we set off like a couple of schoolchildren into the countryside armed with butterfly nets. At first we wandered along without seeing much, then we got into *lantana* country and things began to liven up. "Muffed", from Vi as I missed a forehand swipe only to retrieve the game with a deft backhander. Childhood enthusiasm awoke and soon we were scampering after swallowtails, camberwell beauties, maps, purple emperors and hosts of other exotic specimens. Our eventual bag was over fifty different species which was so well received by the nephew in due course that they were set up professionally.

The days passed quickly and it was time we paid our respects to the Maharaja, the hereditary Prime Minister of Nepal, who virtually ran the country. (The King, Maharaj-di-Raj, was revered in godlike isolation far removed from mundane affairs of State). We duly presented ourselves, were introduced by Clendon and received in audience. The conversation was somewhat desultory being conducted through an interpreter, for although Urdu was freely understood, custom decreed that such a vulgar language was not to be used. The Maharajah kindly inquired about our journey, comfort and welfare, to which we made suitable replies, thanking him for this unique opportunity of visiting his fascinating country. As a parting gift he presented Vi with a complete Nepalese costume, whilst I received a silver embossed ceremonial kukri, one of my most prized possessions. Finally he invited us to visit his "Jew". We took our leave mystified as to what this meant. However next day we were driven to the outskirts of the city and into an enclosure which turned out to be the Zoo. It was rather a pathetic affair with a few antelope, *bara sinqha*, and some tsarus cranes. Two spitfire tiger cubs retreated snarling to the back of their minute cell-like cages and I came away saddened at their miserable existence.

Soon it was time for us to pack up and go. Clendon bade us farewell as we mounted the ponies and ascended the track from Patan. We reached the Guest House without undue fatigue being by now accustomed to the heights. Next day we faced the long seventeen miles stage. It was a glorious day and the panorama of Himalayas, whichever way you looked, was superb. The same forest, the same terraced cultivation, all looked different in a different angle of light.

Late in the afternoon clouds gathered over the nearer ridges. Soon lightning began to flicker and thunder to rumble. Suddenly there was a blinding flash, a roar like a barrage exploding and a tree split asunder in a pall of smoke just to the right of the track. This sent us scampering and slithering down the last hundred yards as great drops began to turn the dust into mud and we ran panting into the Guest House just as the clouds burst in a torrent of rain.

That evening we supped with a log fire hissing in the hearth while the storm outside gradually rolled away. The *chowkidar* never uttered a word. Perhaps Vi had been right and the drink had long since dried out of him.

We set off next day under a clear sky down the last steep slopes to Bhimpedi and into the bus. The sun was ten days higher in the sky and the atmosphere that much hotter. At Raxaul in the railway carriage the fans hummed and whirred, stirring the stifling air as we continued our journey southwards. Our next stop was Lucknow where, unbeknown, a further adventure awaited us. But that is another story.

TIBETAN TRANSIT, 1937

by

Stuart Battye

Peaceable, silent and remote, Tibet in the years before World War II was a closed country, little known and little understood except by a few who were fortunate enough to obtain permission to cross its border. It is many years since I wended my way through Sikkim up onto the Tibetan plateaux and even then it had its Chinese problem, but a problem of mere local importance compared to those of later years.

It all began with a file, one of those khaki affairs beloved of Government Departments; silvery fish insects scuttled between its pages, and the tattered evidence of their depredations signified their contempt for Government property. The file reached me in Roorkee one stifling day in the Indian hot weather. The sight of it alone produced an inward groan but the note from the Adjutant pinned to the outer cover was somewhat startling. Briefly, it appointed me to a mission at the British Trade Agency in Gyantse on the road to Lhasa. That was all. The object of the mission I was left to discover from the file, whose proportions were distinctly middle-aged. In fact, as the correspondence showed, it had started life over seven years previously and to obtain the information I required necessitated ploughing through its pages one by one. The minute sheets were revealing; depicting only too faithfully the indecision of one prevaricator after another and their ability to 'pass the buck.' Eventually I pieced together a story from its pages. A year or so previously, a certain British Trade Agent in Gyantse, whom by singular coincidence I had known since my earliest days, had continued the long fight of his predecessors and submitted a comprehensive report on the Agency buildings, emphasizing the need for extensive and urgent repairs. The answer should have been obvious, but the bill for such repairs made the financiers wince. Thus the contest of procrastination and hedging indecision was joined. It covered the minute sheets and a stalemate was threatening when someone remembered an obscure regulation whereby the Agency should be inspected every few years or so by an engineer officer. This had offered a golden opportunity to defer the irksome decision to open the treasure-chests and a suitable engineer officer was duly sought. This much I gathered from that musty file.

Paradoxically the opportunity of visiting Tibet did not at first elate me. I did not feel flattered at being considered 'a suitable engineer officer'; I knew only too well that I was chosen *faute de mieux*. It was during a period when the Faqir of Ipi was being more than usually troublesome and most officers were away on the Frontier dealing with him. I went to the Adjutant and told him I did not want to go. There was a long argument with some sarcastic remarks flying about till eventually he murmured something about the honour of the Corps and I capitulated.

Several months were to elapse before I could start my long trek onto the roof of the world. For one thing there are only two periods in the year when travel in that region can be undertaken on a reasonable basis. From November to March, ice and snow and a wind that seems to start at the North Pole, petrify every moving thing; during the summer months the lower Himalayas, which guard the southern frontier of Tibet, are drenched in torrential monsoon rain. Only the periods between these two extremes are fit for normal travel. I chose the autumn; it was then or not at all.

In the meantime much correspondence fluttered to and fro. Permits to enter Sikkim and permits to enter the forbidden country were required. Everyone had to be informed of my exact whereabouts on any given day. Stores, transport, kit, a servant who could speak the language and, most important, a large bag of money, all had to be collected. Moreover I had to learn more about the job. I obtained books and essayed some desultory reading in between my ordinary work. I found Sir Francis Younghusband's account of the 1904 expedition and pored over that. Then there were maps. The Survey of India produced some sheets. For the most part they were blank, with the enlightening word 'unsurveyed' printed across the area. My personal file grew fatter and fatter. Eventually by a day in early September the last letter had been received and the final arrangements completed. I worked till late that night to wind up my job and leave it ship-shape for my temporary successor. Back in my bungalow the floor was a jumble of pack-loads, food, bedding, cooking-pots and clothing. However, all seemed to be ready and I wearily stretched myself out for a few hours' sleep.

In the grey dampness of early dawn I stumbled onto the station platform as the Calcutta Mail arrived hissing and puffing. My faithful bearer Nasru, himself roused by the syce who had in turn been roused by the chowkidar to light the early fire, had awakened me with *chota hazri* to catch the mail at the grizzly hour of 4am. As the train pulled out of the station bearing me on the first stage of my journey, Nasru stood rather dejectedly on the platform salaaming deferentially. I felt very much alone.

Twelve hours later, idly reclining in a first-class compartment, I turned over in my mind the events of the past few days: the checking of stores, the packing of boxes, the bag of money, the frontier permits – yes, the permits – by heavens above! The PERMITS. Where was that bulging file with all my correspondence and the vital passports? Feverishly I thought of each package in turn, knowing, without examination, its contents. The growing realisation that the most vital item of all had been forgotten jerked me out of my erstwhile composure. That file had been my chief clerk's *chef d'oeuvre* and he had forgotten to give it to me before I left the office. Or had I forgotten to ask him? Cursing myself, cursing him, grinding my teeth, boiling with frustrating thoughts of arriving at the frontier only to be turned back, I sat down again. The train had drawn up at a largish station and my ideas were beginning to clarify. Hurriedly calculating time and space, I realised that the file could not overtake me by post till I was well inside Tibet, even if I dawdled at each stage as long as my time-table would permit. Blast everything! Yet somehow I would get across those frontiers. I remembered enough details to compose a variety of telegrams. There was just time and I sped down the platform to the station office, scribbled the necessary messages, and regained my compartment as the train was moving out. There was nothing more to be done. I felt resigned. Surely the Deputy Commissioner could fix the Sikkim frontier guards for me? There was time enough for that. In the event he did nothing but at the time I comforted myself with the thought of the telegrams I had despatched and with what I would do to my chief clerk on my return.

Calcutta was like a steam oven. Overhead, monsoon clouds, billowy, soft and moist, drifted on their unhurried way. I can recall little else during my twelve hours' wait in that city and was thankful to board the night-mail, bound for Siliguri.

Next morning there was a breath of freshness in the air. We were now in the foothills of the Himalayas and the train could carry me no farther. A hundred miles away to the north the rising sun had caught a snow-capped peak which glistened and scintillated in the fresh atmosphere. "This is it!" I thought. Behind me was the damp sapping heat of the plains. Before me lay the ragged crests of the lower mountains, and beyond, who knew! It was like the dawn of a new life, 'the soul's awakening ...' I was brought back to earth by a figure salaaming in front of me.

Was I Battye Sahib? He had a car to take me to Gangtok which the Resident Sahib had ordered. My long-planned arrangements were working well. Soon we were winding up the road into the forests of the lower hills. Months of rain had decked out every tree and shrub in its greenest foliage. Here and there iridescent butterflies flitted or a bronze-winged dove would flap away from the road in front of us. We ascended the gorge of the River Tista, swollen to a porridge-coloured torrent from which a thin mist was rising at this early hour. The road led to Darjeeling but at the Tista bridge it forked and we took the right-hand track for Sikkim. I had long since ceased to worry about the frontier guards. The fresh air, the scenery, the anticipation of high adventure had all eclipsed any lurking sense of difficulties. I felt I could surmount anything, bluff my way past anybody. At that moment the car drew up at one end of a very narrow bridge and there, guarding the access, was a tough-looking man with an inverted saucer hat (presumably to keep off the rain) and a rifle. This was the frontier. Another rifleman then approached the car and began to address me in an unknown tongue. I assumed he was asking for my pass so I replied in Urdu explaining that the 'Deputy Sahib' had accorded me permission to enter. This meant nothing to him and he beckoned me to come inside the guard-house. I followed feeling less confident than a few moments before. Inside, other guards were squatting or standing. They all grinned. This was encouraging, and once more my pass was demanded and again

I harangued the guard in Urdu. What a lame story it would have sounded to them had they understood! We were getting nowhere, till presently the guard commander produced a sheaf of counterfoils. He flicked through them, cocking an inquiring eye at me as much as to ask if mine was there. Taking my cue I suddenly pointed to one. There was an "Ah!" from seven smiling guardsmen and honour was satisfied. The driver meanwhile had been nonchalantly chewing betel-nut and expectorating the red juice from time to time. Now he restarted the car, I took my place, and as the sentry presented arms we trundled forward over the bridge. We were past the first frontier – inside Sikkim.

Gangtok, the capital of Sikkim, sprawls over a ridge in the hills. We had climbed steadily from Siliguri and the air at this height was invigorating. On a promontory by itself stood the Residency. I arrived there about lunch-time, to be welcomed by Clive Richards, the British Trade Agent, who was acting for the Resident, then on furlough. His welcome could not have been more cordial, untinged by any resentment at my particular mission and we were soon discussing our mutual problems without any restraint. Clive had succeeded to the post only recently and was not the originator of the letter now reposing in the middle-aged file.

From the comfort of the Residency I gazed at the scenery outside. It might have been a picture from an Alpine holiday. Mist still clung to the valleys, eddying slowly upwards as the day wore on. The hills were grass-covered and dotted with low shrubs, with here and there a clump of conifers. The house itself was far removed from the traditional Indian bungalow. There were wooden floors, beautiful panelling and stairs to mount to one's bedroom. Such things lay in the limbo of home leave but here one could enjoy the delights of an English country house half the world away. I would gladly have lingered in such a spot for a week or two. Reluctantly I banished these thoughts. There was still a lot to be done. I had reached road-head and tomorrow my trek would start in earnest. On foot, or on pony? I had always used my own two legs on previous expeditions and rather despised those who borrowed four. There was, however, the matter of prestige to uphold and I acquired a shaggy-looking animal, rather larger than the average run of Mongol pony. This was an advantage as, being forewarned of the local saddlery, I had brought my own, which had been built for a hunter. Next I was introduced to Pemba Dorje who was to function as cook-bearer. A Bhutani by nationality, he spoke both Urdu and Tibetan. We soon settled terms and off he went with a handful of money to buy the fresh essentials of the larder.

As we chatted over our coffee that night I diffidently mentioned to Clive my horrid gaffe over the frontier permits into Tibet. He waved the matter aside. He had, he said, issued the permits himself and there were no frontier guards anyway. My fears had been groundless; nevertheless I kept quiet regarding my method of entering Sikkim.

Next morning Pemba Dorje saw to the loading of baggage on to the pack-mules. After a leisurely breakfast I ordered a start to be made. Nothing happened. I glanced at Pemba Dorje sensing trouble. He was standing looking evasive. I told him to get moving. Then it all came out. Pemba was a man of some substance and had no intention of walking. I bristled. Never had any previous bearer of mine required transport other than his own two legs. I was going to walk; the shaggy Brutus was only for prestige. Pemba could something well walk. He remained obdurate, subtly pointing out that he could not have sahib's meals ready ahead of him unless he, Pemba, rode a horse. There was undoubtedly some strength in this argument. At that moment Clive appeared and I turned to him for advice. What was the local *dustoor*, I inquired. He favoured Pemba's counsel and I gave in. Pemba must have anticipated some such scene; for with oriental diplomacy he had already arranged for himself a horse which was led round almost immediately from the direction of the stables. Over the saddle he slung two filthy goatskin bags and mounted. I inquired what he carried therein. I should have remained silent.

"*Sahib ka tiffin*," he replied.

I turned hurriedly away and the cavalcade started. As a parting gift Clive presented me with a bottle of beer; it might, he suggested, serve to sweeten the contents of the goatskin bags.

My journey that day lay up a rugged mountain track which climbed a few thousand feet in about ten miles to Karponang. I will not dwell on that first day's journey. It was not a success. The sky had become overcast soon after we started and presently the rain came crashing down, solid heavy rain such as is only known in those regions. When I rode Brutus, doleful and uncomplaining, I became cold and miserable. When I walked I was less cold but more miserable; for the only watercourse lay down the track we were ascending. Soon I was squelching along in waterlogged boots which hurt anyway and my precious saddle was being ruined. I passed some rinderpesty-looking cattle with bloated leeches hanging from their muzzles and ears. Others streamed with blood where these loathsome creatures had been rubbed off. I shuddered. The exhilaration had died out of me, and, like the Israelites of old,

I inwardly moaned at leaving the fleshpots of the plains to come to this soaking hell. Only an idiot would have agreed to undertake such a venture and why had I not stuck to my guns in the first place refusing to be coerced? So ran my gloomy prognostications as I trudged or sometimes rode with the incessant rain hissing down. It was the longest ten miles I have ever known but just when everything seemed to be at the lowest ebb I rounded a corner to see the dak bungalow at Karponang, standing on a bluff above me. I staggered onto the verandah only to be menaced by an enormous black dog. He really meant business; for he came at me with eyes and teeth flashing, only to be brought up short by a chain I had not at first seen. Somewhat relieved, I stood back and let out a bellow for the chowkidar, who was the probable owner. Fortunately the chain held and in a very few minutes after the dog had been led away, docile as a lamb, there was a roaring fire blazing inside. With the steam rising I discarded my dripping garments one by one, picking off the leeches which were nosing their way through any opening they could find.

For the next two days my route led on upwards but now the sun shone and all was well in the garden: all except one thing – my boots hurt more and more. Before leaving I had had them resoled, 'made over' the local *mochi* called it. During the process he stripped sole, welt, and everything from the uppers. The latter were then wrapped round any convenient last and new welts and soles were fixed. The result was a pair of boots beautifully repaired but bearing little resemblance to the original size. Alas, I had failed to test them out before leaving base. After a few days I could stand their chafing no longer. I was painfully lame with swollen tendons which squeaked in protest at every step, so packing the boots away in disgust I took to shoes.

Changu, the next port of call, was delightfully situated overlooking a large natural lake. Hearsay had it that this lake was once stocked with rainbow trout but like many another fishy story there appeared to be little substance in the tale. On arrival it was discovered that one of the mules was suffering badly from colic. I had brought a few medical supplies but nothing suitable for a mule. There was, of course, my cherished bottle of beer. Reluctantly I made the decision to apply the precious fluid as a drench. First, however, I swallowed a largish sample just to make quite sure it was all right, then holding the mule's head up I poured the remainder down its gullet. The mule gave a knowing wink, the beer frothed, and by next morning the colic had gone with the wind.

Our ascent continued still favoured by the weather. At the top of the Nathu La pass I placed a votive offering on the cairn marking the frontier. To the southward, range upon range of hills, some still covered with patches of cloud, lay between me and the plains of India.

Turning my back on the scene, I stepped forward into Tibet. The track now traversed ridges and valleys clothed in alpine flora. Here and there sky-blue gentians opened their star-shaped flowers towards the sun; aconites and foxgloves lined the pathway; tall fir trees lent their shade. The pungency of many herbs filled the air; so strong was it, in fact, that soon I had a headache and felt sick. At least I put it down to this, although at that height, over 14,000ft, mountain sickness could not be ruled out. Fortunately it passed off later in the day and never recurred. Across a shallow valley a herd of yak sprawled, grazing or contentedly chewing the cud. They were prize beasts. Their massive horns, sturdy backs and straight hams looked very business-like and being ignorant of their temper I was glad they were no nearer.

I spent two days at Yatung, in the Chomo valley, where there was much of interest to see and some local notables to visit. I was bidden to take tea with a Tibetan lady of some standing. She lived in European-style retaining only the traditional dress of red silk blouse and long striped skirt reaching to the ankles. Both were amply filled. Her smiling face was crowned by black hair swept back into a pigtail reaching to her waist. Tea was served from a set heavily decorated with the facsimile of our own King and Queen. Unfortunately my presence must have upset the serving wench for, on clearing away, there was a devastating crash from just outside the door and pieces of royal china were scattered in tragic confusion. My hostess took the incident in good part and I took my leave to avoid further embarrassment.

Two more days saw my little party up at last on top of the world. On all sides stretched wide plains rimmed by unnamed mountains. In the clear atmosphere they seemed close at hand, yet miles and miles separated the nearest from where we travelled. Short grass or dwarf sedges formed a carpet underfoot muffling our steps and we moved in silence, for the vastness of these uplands had a queer subduing influence. I ceased to wonder at the tales I had heard of curious phenomena in this strange world.

The next staging post was Phari Jong. Set in the middle of the plateau between two ranges of mountains, it stood out four-square, a bastion against all comers. By now I had become accustomed to the height and marches grew longer. I doubled each stage without undue fatigue. Pemba, too, had things well in hand. He would have breakfast ready for me at 7am. At 7.30, the remains would be packed away in his noisome saddlebags: then Pemba would mount, and, wielding a piece of thong, urge his pony into that curious running trot which eats up the miles with the least discomfort to both man and beast. I followed more leisurely, timing my arrival at each intermediate post so that lunch would be laid out ready for me. After lunch the same performance as at breakfast was repeated and I would arrive at the final stage in time for tea. It was an excellent arrangement and there was seldom a hitch.

Traversing endless plains can be monotonous. After we left Phari Jong the first nine miles of the road led up to the Tang La, over 15,000ft high, the highest pass along the route. Thence the track lay straight as a die for twelve long miles, the end obscured in shimmering mirage. I rode and walked alternately, stopping now and again to gaze at the beauty of Chumalhari, a 23,000ft giant, which lay across the plain to the right. The intervening level was dotted with grazing yak. Others lay nearer to the track and it was no unusual thing to have to pick our way through a herd of these sturdy beasts which showed neither fear nor undue curiosity.

Occasionally I met a traveller. There was a monk who asked for alms. I made my offering, receiving no thanks in return. At first I was annoyed till I learnt that merit thus acquired should more than recompense the giver. Next I was offered a dagger by a wandering bagman.

It had a useful blade and a sheath covered with sharkskin. It smelt strongly of rancid fat, a scent which seems to pervade all Tibetan instruments that have any connection with food. I closed the bargain and the knife changed hands for a few rupees. Later I met an Italian professor accompanied by a young German doctor. They had spent more than a year in the country studying books, paintings, and in fact every aspect of Tibetan life. The long train of pack animals testified at any rate to their acquisitive efforts. The professor told me he intended to publish an account of his researches. We met again on my return to Gangtok and I have often wondered since if that book has ever been written. Ahead of us the route traversed the western shore of the Bam Tso, a lake of considerable size. Numerous wildfowl fed and preened in the shallows. I was without a gun and indulged my interest in bird-life by watching them through my binoculars. One other species prominent in those uplands was the snow-bunting. Bold, rather bad-tempered little birds, they picked about on the ground and would hustle and bicker at the lemmings which also fed in their vicinity.

As I neared my journey's end the open plain gave way to narrower gorges. The pathway was a well-defined single track, but presently branched each side of a prayer shrine, a stone building carrying an assortment of prayer-wheels. Observing Buddhist custom I kept to the correct side and broadcast many a prayer by rotating the wheels as I passed. I was still debating the improbable result of this twiddling when, rounding the corner, I came face to face with an enormous stone effigy painted blue which scowled most unpleasantly, its arm raised menacingly, barring the way to all-comers. So had it stood in 1904 to repel the advancing Gurkha regiments. The tide of battle had swept by, leaving this giant defying imaginary invaders till sun and frost eventually do their worst.

On the seventeenth day the valley we had been traversing debouched on to an open plain and there at last in the distance stood Gyantse, scene of much fierce fighting more than thirty years previously. The Agency was hidden by some poplars; behind it, running up a ridge, was the Tibetan Fort which had proved such a hard nut to crack. I mounted Brutus and rode in the last few miles.

The two officers of the escort made me very welcome. In those days a company of Indian infantry garrisoned the Agency at Gyantse and acted as escort to the Agent, with a platoon at Yatung, through which I had passed ten days previously. Together with a doctor we filled the small comfortable Mess, and when Clive arrived a few days later I moved into the official rest-house to make room for him. There was a full programme to complete, so next day I set-to to survey the buildings which made up the post. One part composed the officers' quarters, another the escort lines, married quarters and the Agency offices. It was a compact layout and in a few days I had collected the information I required.

Outside the walls were a football ground and a tennis-court. We spent most enjoyable evenings playing one or other game. The effect of height on the behaviour of a football is ludicrous. The ball never seems to be on the ground but sails about like a child's balloon. Our tennis was even more hilarious. The balls had already lost weight and with the reduced effect of gravity they played a game of their own above our heads. But the high-light of sporting activities was a polo match played between Clive's team and the escort. Clive invited me to play for his side, the other two members of which were local gentlemen, a postal packer with a homburg hat perched above his pigtail and a storekeeper similarly clad. They could both hit a shrewd ball. On the day appointed we trotted out to the polo ground which was a flat expanse covered by naturally short grass. Brutus was roped in to play and I borrowed two more ponies from the doctor. All three did me proud. Brutus was phlegmatic and played as if he had been foaled with a polo-stick in his crib. In three chukkers we had the escort twelve goals down, but since their ponies suffered from a mild form of glanders perhaps they started with an unfairly long handicap.

The days slipped by all too quickly but I could not leave Gyantse without paying my respects to the Abbot who ruled the local monastery with stern discipline. There was concrete evidence of this in the two rawhide whips that stood in the corner of his parlour. The escort boys and myself made up the party and a clerk from the Agency conducted us to the monastery where we found our host awaiting us with tea prepared. This was served in exquisite jade bowls as we squatted on the floor, oriental fashion. Tibetan tea resembles our own in colour only. It is darkly brewed and served strongly laced with salt and yaks' butter. I gulped down a mouthful or two of this fearsome beverage and nibbled a biscuit which, in strong contrast to the tea, was of pure European descent. I turned to smile at our host; immediately an attentive minion refilled my cup. The Abbot sipped his tea: we all followed suit but no sooner had we replaced our cups than they were refilled. I began to sweat and my stomach to surge. Conversation through an interpreter was desultory. Presently our host produced a watch from the folds of his chuba. It had Russian numerals and he was obviously very proud of it. Looking more closely at him, I then realised why he displayed such an expansive smile. He had a fine set of false teeth; presumably also 'made in Russia.' We admired the watch and taking our cue from its evidence we thanked our host and withdrew, carrying with us his permission to pay a visit to the Gompa.

It would take me many pages to describe this temple in detail. We passed into a dim interior where there was a strong impression of being watched by unseen eyes in shadowy forms that peeped and muttered. But our attention was immediately directed to the two central figures of Buddha sitting in contemplative attitude. Their feet, surrounded by offerings, were lighted by wicks floating in yaks' butter in massive silver bowls delicately embossed with Chinese dragons. The light from these lamps also illuminated the Buddhas' lower limbs, while their heads were revealed by rays of light from clerestory windows cunningly set for just such a purpose. Looking up at the figures above me I caught something of the sculptor's intention: there was a benignity in the expression of each face and an inward peace evident from the introspective set of their glance. But most striking of all was the simple beauty of their hands; the craftsmen who fashioned them were true artists.

We moved on after placing our offering of scarves upon their feet. Through the library, its walls stacked with books written on parchment or papyrus, we passed on to lesser temples and balconies; we scrutinised murals depicting the 'wheel of life' cornered by the 'four winds,' or a portrait of the Dalai Lama. Presently we came to a low door set at the end of a dark passage. The guide seemed disinclined to enter but overcoming his uncertainty he stooped down and we passed inside. It was little wonder that he hesitated. This was the shrine of Kali, the black goddess of death. So fearful is she that her image is kept covered. I had a peep behind the veil and approved of that custom. Never have I felt the power of evil so oppressively close to me as in that shrine. It was like a magician's den. A stuffed yak hung from the ceiling; there were clay effigies standing here and there with pins stuck in them, and the glassy eyes of other nightmare creatures stared up from the corners. I moved hurriedly on but could not for the moment see our guide. Looking back, I caught him in the act of prostration before the black image of death. I have seldom been so glad to get outside four walls.

By the end of a week my work was completed. On Sunday, Clive took me out to look for a rare dwarf rhubarb. We found these little plants in fair quantities at a height of 16,000ft and gathered handfuls of seeds. We continued our climb to the top of a ridge standing at nearly 17,000ft. There we sat to have our lunch. It had been a stiffish climb and I found my breath coming very short. Forgetting the height for the moment we opened a can of beer. As the cap came off a jet of frothy liquid shot into the air and it was with difficulty that we rescued any at all. Sitting over our lunch we had a magnificent view. It was a peerless day with a few light clouds about and on all sides range upon range of mountains stretched as far as the eye could see. And in the midst, standing out, a giant among giants, was the massive outline of Everest. It was dead into the sun and try as I would I could not get a photograph from that angle. I had to content myself with recording lesser views but the symmetry of that great mountain is printed indelibly on my memory.

That evening I packed up my belongings, collected my papers together and ordered some baggage mules. Early next morning I bade farewell to the garrison, turned Brutus southward and set out for India. As I hurried homeward the weather which had been so good up till then began to deteriorate. Towards evening the sky to the south-eastward turned to a leaden colour and the usual pastel shades of approaching night were absent. I passed a peasant working on a small patch of cultivation. The rays of the dying sun lit up a striking picture. The peasant was dressed in the customary dull-red *chuba*, a sort of cloak with sleeves. He had his hand on a wooden plough to which were yoked four yak. They plodded to and fro in the same unhurried manner as beasts of burden do the world over. At each turn of the small field the farmer encouraged his team with a yodelling song. I gazed wonderingly at this scene, a scene that had remained unchanged down the centuries, and passed on with the yodel ringing in my ears. Wind and weather seemed to trouble that man not at all.

Next morning the sky was overcast and a biting wind had sprung up. I pulled my fur hat down over my ears and urged Brutus to a faster pace. I doubled and trebled my marches and the weather did not improve. The shores of the Bam Tso were now crusted with ice and over its waters Chumalhari loomed black and forbidding, for the most part shrouded in lowering cloud. We came to a Tibetan encampment sheltering in the lee of some folds in the ground and as we passed some children came running out to gaze at the unusual sight of a white-skinned traveller and to clamour for backsheesh. What astounded me was that they were stark naked and apparently thought nothing of the biting wind or the snowflakes which by now were beginning to fall.

I woke next day to a white world. The wind had increased to gale force and blew straight in our teeth as we struggled towards the Tang La. My fur hat was in full use leaving only a small triangle for nose and eyes. Fine snow crystals stung as they whirled in the wind. Eventually the cairn marking the top of the pass came in sight. Tattered scarves, the offerings of many travellers, floated like wraiths in the blizzard. The sightless eyes of two skulls stared ghoulishly from the stone heap adding to the eeriness of the scene and we hurried on bending our heads to the storm. At last I staggered into Phari Jong, my face burning and my eyes blurred. But before I could relax a limping figure appeared at my door. His eyes rolled and his head lolled. I looked to Pemba for enlightenment. It turned out to be the village idiot who seemed to have come off worse in an encounter with a dog; for his leg, on examination, was fast approaching a state of gangrene. I set him down on a chair. Pemba grasped his head and turned it firmly away while I performed an emergency operation with a pair of scissors and a syringe of perchloride of mercury. I bandaged up the leg and stood back. Tears rolled down my patient's cheeks: tears not of gratitude but of self-pity and as he staggered to his feet his only remark to me was "Backsheesh, Sahib?"

During the night the storm abated and I woke to a Swiss-like scene. Snow lay sparkling in the morning sunshine. The sky was blue and some alpine choughs whistled as they flapped overhead. I looked out at the undulating lower hills, regretting the skis I had not thought to bring. But I was brought back to reality by my smarting face. It hurt like hell and the skin was already beginning to peel. In the days that followed it sloughed completely but I had other worries to think about. Snow at that height had been rain lower down and I squelched into Yatung tired and wet. The sunny weather had not held and we struggled over the Nathu La through snow up to our knees. It was still raining down in Sikkim and I walked the last twenty miles into Gangtok in weather as drenching as when I had left it a month before.

It had been raining for a fortnight and the state of the road to Siliguri was uncertain as I was soon to find. After spending a night in the rest-house and bidding a final farewell to Pemba and Brutus, I took a car and set off for the plains. Hardly had we left the town before we came to a subsidence in the road. Nothing daunted my driver plunged into the lower surface and up on to the other side. He was obviously a man of daring and resource which he more than proved throughout the rest of the journey. Time after time we negotiated stretches of roadway covered with debris from landslides higher up. At one point the track was so tenuous that we had to scrabble with our hands before a passage could be attempted. Presently my driver said he could get by. I thought he could not and, not daring to ride, walked on. On the right hand the soggy mass of earth still oozed and trickled obscuring the road; to the left the hill dropped sheer. As the car lurched forward, for one sickening moment a wheel dangled over the edge; then the engine roared, the wheel spun, and in some miraculous fashion it gripped the quaking mess of earth. With another lurch the car was back on the track and over the landslide. I lost count of the slips we negotiated and we still had many miles to go. It was well on in the afternoon by now and I felt our chances of getting through before dark were slender. These thoughts were confirmed a moment later when on rounding a corner we were confronted by a blockage as big as a house. The car stopped. There was nothing more it could do. There was no going back over that road behind us, and I turned to the driver, who seemed to take everything as a matter of course. Blithely he suggested the light railway, which ran parallel to the road fifty feet below. "But it is closed." I argued. "No, Sahib, it was opened today for first time since two weeks," he replied.

A knot of coolies had collected round the car. They had been working in desultory fashion clearing the blockage and were glad of a more interesting diversion. At that moment I heard a whistle from up the line. Telling the coolies to follow with my baggage I plunged down the *khud* and arrived on the track in time to signal the train. Obligingly the driver applied his brakes and an empty goods wagon drew up opposite me. This seemed too good to be true and I was about to step inside when I remembered the baggage. I shouted to the coolies to hurry but the engine-driver was growing impatient. He blew a blast on his whistle, opened his steam-valve and the train drew away before I could assemble my cortège. First down the hill came my intrepid driver. I paid him handsomely and wished him luck – he would need it on that road. Presently I heard another train approaching and frantically I signalled it to stop. Its driver was anything but obliging and passed on with a wave of his hand.

Slowly we trudged down the line to reach the next Station some twenty minutes ahead of the last train of the day. I bought a ticket and waited. The train arrived, a funny little affair hardly bigger than the Hythe–Dymchurch model at home. As I entered a compartment I felt all hazards were now behind me. I was wrong. The steel bridge outside the station had been swept away by floods and the rail track was now laid on a stone causeway. Over this causeway a foot of water poured. The train started and we hissed our way into the flood led by a coolie carrying a hurricane-lantern. Looking back on this fantastic scene, the wading figure in front, the engine bubbling behind, water swirling round the wheels, heads craning out of every carriage window,I have always wondered whether the lantern was for the benefit of the engine or the brave man in front. It was pitch dark when we drew into Siliguri and the station looked very different from the morning of my arrival five weeks previously. With a flood of thankfulness I stepped out on to the platform.

And what of the real object of the mission? My report, when completed, ran into a good many pages and, so I heard later, provided the key to unlock the treasure-chests. That no one suspected collusion is perhaps surprising; for unwittingly the powers that be had assigned me the task of testing the opinions held by a British Trade Agent who was also my elder brother.

ON TO LHASA

by

Archie Jack

In 1938 Archie Jack, at that time a Lieutenant, undertook a three month trek from Gangtok in Sikkim to Gyantse in Tibet, on to Lhasa and back to Gangtok. The rationale for his journey was to carry out an official visit, effected every few years by an Engineer officer, to ensure that the Indian Army garrison at Gyantse had all the necessary facilities. Accompanying him was a friend, Captain (later Major General) Ken Shepheard, Jack's excellent Baluchi orderly (Khan Gul) and a Sikkimese cook (Man Bahardur) who had taken part in several climbing expeditions, including Nanga Parbat. They were two of the very few Europeans ever to have visited Lhasa before World War II.

The diary he kept provides a fascinating and detailed record of the rigours of the journey, the remoteness of the terrain and the courtesy with which he was received by the British representatives in Sikkim and Tibet. However, the highlights of the diary are his descriptions of the monasteries at Gyantse and Lhasa and his meetings with the Tibetan spiritual and political leaders in the capital city.

It is these aspects of his expedition which are covered in the following extracts from his diary.

On 21st August we came to a splendid view of the Tibetan fort at Gyantse five miles away, on its huge rock, dominating the extensive plain. We visited the British fort with its small garrison of Indian troops and called on the British Trade Agent Hugh Richardson, who gave us a most warm welcome. He was most interesting to talk to, for he was a considerable expert in Tibetan matters and actually spoke the language.

I was at work most of the time we were there as the Tibetan contractors had done a pretty poor job in recent years, so far as the British fort was concerned, despite the report submitted by Stu Battye in the previous inspection. Richardson arranged for us to make a formal visit to the monastery, mounted, as only the lower classes in Tibet pay calls on foot. The monastery occupies a crescent shaped area, at the northern end of the town with the horns pointing south. The hill behind it carries a defence wall with towers every 150m or so. The pagoda-like roof is in the form of the classical '*chorten*', the geometrical figures of which represent the various elements. The square base represents the earth, the circular portion above, water. The spoke represents fire, the crescent, air, and the small prick on the top, ether. There are some variations on this design, the Gyantse pagoda, for instance, instead of being based on a perfect cube has a series of plinths. Small bells are rigged on the outside which tinkle prettily in the wind. At the entrance to the Dukang there are the usual statues of the great gods of the North, South, East and West, twelve feet high when sitting down. We were followed round by four little beggar boys from Kham who constantly made the customary polite gesture, an outstretched arm with fist clenched, thumbs pointing upwards and the tongue sticking right out. The painting of the Wheel of Life was just inside the porch and the chapels with their statues and valuable porcelain ornaments were most attractive. I was able to take photographs though it was rather dark and a service was taking place. We made an official call on the two 'Jongpens' (Governors); it is always customary to have two as a single Governor could not be trusted. We visited the Tibetan fort, the only occupant being the charming monk caretaker who showed us round the chapel and the former refectory. The view from the fort over the town and the monastery below was magnificent. On our way back we were shown a small temple which contained the first bearded Buddha we had seen, with on each side a statue of an armed guard; on the altar there slowly revolved a delicate prayer-wheel driven by the hot air rising from a lit candle below.

We visited the Nyang Tokipu monastery some 15 miles down the valley leading to Shigatse, where we were received by the Reincarnation Abbot, a rather awkward looking lad aged about fifteen. This Monastery is known as the 'Monastery of Happy Musings on Misery'; it is an establishment for voluntary solitary internment of succeeding periods of six months, three years three months three days, and then for life. At each stage the occupant may opt out if he so wishes. The monks are incarcerated in small stone cells which are built on the hillside, food and drink being passed daily to each occupant through a 'guichet'. To begin with a small hole in the wall provides the light they require to study their religious books, but later this is blocked up and they live thereafter in absolute darkness until their death. To recover the victuals passed through the 'guichet' the inmate's hand must be gloved. From one cell came loud cries and long groans. We were told that the inmate had only just achieved levitation and that he was floating about in an uncontrolled way, knocking into the walls and ceiling.

On our return we passed a herd of white 'burrhel', quite unconcerned, at a distance of only thirty metres. In the streets of Gyantse we came across a convict with feet in iron gyves connected by a steel chain to another chain around his waist. He was sitting in the street begging. It appears that this is the Tibetan custom. Rather than sending prisoners to jails, they gyve them and turn them out telling them to come back in ten years or so to have the gyves removed. This system has two advantages, firstly it is vastly cheaper than the normal jailing system and secondly the appearance of a gyved convict in the streets does tend to deter others: a good idea for the Western World?

Richardson was informed that the Tibetan Government had approved our application to visit Lhasa. No one could understand how this had come about since all applications made by private individuals had for many years been refused. There were possibly two explanations: firstly my application had been made through the British Government and not through the Indian Government, which was the general rule; secondly I happened to have learned through the Royal Geographical Society in London that a certain Tibetan called Ringang, an important government servant in Lhasa, had attended the same school as me in England, though ten years previously, so I had written to Ringang asking him for his help in this matter. Anyway we were both absolutely delighted by this decision on the part of the Tibetan Government; one problem remained and that was that a number of official calls on important personalities in Lhasa would have to be made and on such occasions presents of some importance have to be offered. Fortunately Richardson had a stock of such presents which he put at our disposal and which we could replace on our return to India. He offered us a pair of binoculars, a fine camera, thermos flasks, Homburg hats, hunting knives, toilet sets and bottles of scent and packets of elegant soaps for the ladies.

Leaving Gyantse on 8th September we had planned to do the 34 mile journey to Ralung in one stage, but the transport arrived late and we were, therefore, obliged to do a single-stage to Gobshi. Transport is normally provided for single-stages only, so when one undertakes a double-stage the transport has to be changed mid-way which takes two to three hours. Our transport requirement was four riding ponies, six pack animals and a mixture of ponies, donkeys, yaks and even cows. Each animal was accompanied by the owner and the traditional loading operation was interesting: firstly we placed the loads on the ground (two loads of about 80lbs each for one pack animal), secondly each owner offered one of his garters and thirdly some neutral personality was asked to cast one garter on each pack load, the pack animals were then each brought up to where their owner's garter had been cast and the loading up began.

We reached Ralung on 9th September and from there we proceeded at speed across open country, climbing under the enormous Nodzingkangsa glacier to the Karo La pass. After a night's rest at Dzara, a small cluster of hovels in a narrow gorge surrounded by peaks covered with perpetual snow, we carried on down to the Nangantse plain before climbing again to the Khamba La pass (15,400ft). From here we got a grand view of the Brahmaputra (Tsan-po) valley and started the 4,500ft descent. We crossed the river by ferry in yak-skin coracles, about 20ft by 10ft in size, and set off for Chosul 44 miles from Lhasa at an altitude of 12,000ft.

At Khotang we came across the longest span bridge we had yet encountered, logs spanning some 50ft on stone abutments. The weather then changed suddenly; we had been wearing shirts in blazing sunshine when suddenly the rain started accompanied by a very bitter wind and we were obliged to put on sweaters, scarves, mackintoshes and gloves, typical of rapid changes in Tibetan weather. After a walk up to the ruined Dzong we returned to supper at which was served rum-laced cocoa, now no longer a habit but a vice! An uncomfortable night followed, shared with many bed bugs.

When we eventually reached the village of Dongkar the track, with steps cut in solid rock, mounted a ridge from which a magnificent view is obtained in the distance of the two rock formations at the entry to Lhasa; on the one to the left is the Potala palace and on the one to the right is the Temple of Medicine; the gilded roof of the huge Potala was shining brightly in the sunlight. A mile and a half further on lay the Monastery of Drepung which houses between 7,000 and 10,000 monks; the other big monasteries in Lhasa are Sera (5,500 monks) and Gandea (3,300). Nearby is the residence of the State Oracle most of whose performances sadly take place in the Tibetan New Year, because we would very much have liked to have seen him in action. For the last three and a half miles we passed over marshy ground with the Potala looming ever larger before us.

Our journey had not been without transport problems. The motley collection of animals furnished by the local Headman at the start of each stage was rarely without one or two animals which could not be used because of open sores on their backs; on occasions, and after considerable delay, the Headman would round up the necessary replacements. But generally this was not the case and our riding ponies were converted into pack ponies, obliging us to complete the stage on foot. Pack saddles and girths were so primitive that the pack loads would often fall off. Riding saddles were sometimes unbearably uncomfortable, so one sometimes

Above: Guard Mounting, 1827. Re-enactment at unveiling of War Memorial 1927.

Below: Kabul Gate of Ghazni, Afghanistan 1839.

Above: The Blowing in of the Kashmir Gate, Delhi, 1857. (From an original drawing by Eyre Crow, ARA)

Left: The Kashmir Gate, Delhi after the bombardment, 1857.

Above: Post of 7 Company Bengal Sappers & Miners, Sherpore, Afghanistan, 1879.

Above left: Bridge at Safed Sang, Gandamak, Afghanistan, 1879.

Below left: Group of RE officers at Safed Sang, Gandamak, Afghanistan, 1879.

Above: Bengal Sappers – improvised bridging at Kundil River, Abor Expedition, 1912.

Below: War Memorial, Roorkee, 1927.

Opposite page: Bengal Sapper Uniforms c.1931.

Top left: Two Subedar Majors.

Top right: Naik Piper.

Below left: Tenor Drummer.

Below right: Sapper.

Right: Subedar Major Hon Lieut Nawab, IOM, IDSM. Winner of the Durand Medal, 1934.

Opposite page:

Top left: Everall Bridge, Akora 1934.

Second left: Folding Boat on Improvised Wagon, 1934.

Third left: Pack Mules, Kabul River 1934.

Bottom left: FBE with Breakdown Lorry, Kabul River 1934.

This page:

Top right: Inglis Bridge, Akora 1934.

Centre right: Folding Boat Raft, Kabul River 1934.

Bottom right: Pilgrim bridges built for the Kumbh Mela at Hardwar in 1930s.

Opposite page:

Top left: A Day's Food for the Elephant, c.1936.

Top right: Lt Col Martell mounting an elephant, c.1936.

Centre left: Outside the Mess at Roorkee (with tiger), c.1936.

Centre right: Subadar Sawan Singh, IOM, IDSM (later Subedar Major & Hon Captain), c.1936.

Bottom: One of the Lions on the Ganges Canal, Roorkee, c.1936.

This page:

Top right: Lunch break on the Sarital Pass (c.13,000 ft), Warwan Valley, Kashmir, 1940.

Centre right: House-boats on Lake Nagin, Kashmir.

Bottom right: Himalayan peaks from Lasht, north of Chitral.

Top left: Class 12 wooden trestle bridge in Kaphi Lui gorge on Tiddim Road, Burma, built by 70 Fd Coy, April 1943.

Centre left: Jeep suspension bridge over the Beltang Lui, Burma, built by 70 Fd Coy, May 1943.

Bottom left: Road demolition party of 70 Fd Coy on Tiddim Road, Burma, 1944.

Above: 70 Fd Coy's FBE bridge over Manipur river south of Imphal, Burma, May 1944.

Above: Sikhs of 70 Fd Coy around their bunker near Torbung, Burma, May 1944.

Top left: Bogged down in Burma, 1946.

Top right: Floating Bailey bridge at Myitnge, Burma, 1946.

Left: Ava Bridge over the Irrawaddy at Mandalay, Burma 1946 – with two broken spans.

Below: Double/double Bailey Bridge over River Aliakmon, Macedonia, Greece, built by 4 Fd Coy, July 1945.

Above: No. 2 Mess, Roorkee, 1944.

Right: Ante-room, No. 2 Mess, Roorkee, 1944.

Drawings by Desmond Henly.

Above: Stick Guard, Roorkee, 1996.

Above right: Mess Staff, Roorkee, 1996.

Right: The Officers' Mess, Roorkee, 1996.

Below: Officers' Mess, Roorkee, 1997.

preferred walking; girths and bridles were wont to part with dramatic consequences. Occasionally a pack animal feeling homesick would turn around and gallop back along the way we came. Anyway, all these problems should now be forgotten, our wildest dream had been realised; we had arrived at the Holy City, Lhasa!

In between the Potala and the Temple of Medicine there is a huge entrance chorten through which the Trade Route passes. There, awaiting us, was a Hindu servant of the British Trade Agent (Rai Bahardur Norbhu) who had come to meet us and guide us to the Residence at the Dekyi Lingka (Happy Garden). There we were given a warm welcome by the Rai Bahardur. With him was an Englishman called Fox who was responsible for the Rai Bahardur's wireless station. Fox had been in Lhasa for 18 months without seeing any Englishman, the previous record being held by Sir Charles Bell who remained in Lhasa for 10 months. We were to be accommodated in two handsome tents pitched in the garden and would have our meals with Norbhu, his wife and Fox. During the whole of our visit the Norbhus both proved to be the most wonderfully generous hosts. Norbhu then explained to us about the protocol governing our visit and informed us of the five official calls which he had arranged for us to make the following day the 15th September.

The Dalai Lama and the Panchen Lama are the two spiritual leaders of Tibet, the former in Lhasa, the latter in Tashilhunpo. There the similarity ends as the Dalai Lama has the political power to rule the country, whereas the Panchen Lama is purely a spiritual figure. The Dalai Lama rules Tibet with the aid of a Prime Minister (Lönchen) and a Cabinet composed of four members, one of whom is a monk; the Cabinet is known as the Kashag, the members as Shapés and they are all appointed by the Dalai Lama. Second and third rank officials are known as Dzasas and Tejis. Fourth rank officials are Depons and include Generals and Dzongpens of importance, the fifth rank are composed of magistrates and medium Dzongpens, the sixth of lesser Dzongpens, the seventh of Tax Collectors and other minor officials and the eighth of ungazetted officials. Ungazetted officials wear their hair in a single pigtail down their backs. Officials of the seventh rank and above wear their hair in two pigtails coiled on top of their head and those of the fourth rank and above decorate the coil with a turquoise ornament which faces forward. Monk officials, of course, all have cropped hair. Hats worn by officials vary with their rank and because of their size require to be securely tied down. Officials of the seventh and eighth rank, on approaching higher officials, are obliged to dismount, remove their hats, stick out their tongues and bow. Other officials just bow to each other from the saddle, though when they encounter the Dalai Lama, the Lönchen or a Shapé, they dismount and bow.

Our visits the first day were to important members of the Cabinet (Shapés), the most important being Bhondong Shapé; Norbhu accompanied us. Through Fox's wireless system Norbhu is well informed on world affairs and is able to pass this news on to members of the Cabinet, a service which they much appreciate. This morning the important news was about the Sino-Japanese dispute and the bombing of civilian targets by Japanese planes. We then rode on accompanied by a Tibetan official, who would follow us on all our outings, and a small mounted escort, to call on Kalon Shapé, the only monk member of the Cabinet. Our third call was on Kypup, a city magistrate, who spoke perfect English. He was one of four Tibetan boys whom Sir Francis Younghusband arranged to be educated in England during the First World War. They had all been sent to my old school Rugby, so this led to long and amusing conversations. After lunch we visited the oldest member of the Cabinet, Langchung Shapé. We were most interested to hear from him about the Lopchak Caravan which every two years brings a tribute, according to an ancient treaty, from Ley to Lhasa. The caravan travels for three months arriving at Lhasa in October, returning the following year as from October onwards the high passes are snowbound. Our fifth call was on Tehring Jigme. He and his wife, both educated in India, speak perfect English and are very pro-British; having been a General (Depon), he is now a Treasury Official. The five important people whom we visited on our first day could not have been more welcoming. The Norbhus are wonderful hosts. They serve us splendid meals which we eat together and we sleep peacefully in our tents pitched in their garden. We converse with Mrs Norbhu in Urdu.

On our second day of official visits we started with the Prime Minister (Lönchen) who was polite but rather cold. Then we met Ringang, a fourth rank official and the municipal officer of Lhasa. He spoke excellent English having spent some twelve years in England where, after Rugby School, he went on to study electrical engineering. Ringang had installed the small hydro-electric system which lights some 400 lamps only. Our last morning visit was to the third ex-Rugby boy, the monk Mondong, who is the monk magistrate (there are two lay magistrates) for Sho, that area which nestles below the Potala and is quite separate from the city of Lhasa. On the outside of his office were displayed a number of 'cat-o'-

nine-tails', for flogging culprits. Mondong is very tall and must have been a fine Rugby player in his school days and has a splendid sense of humour. Sadly the fourth ex-Rugby boy, Gongkar, died some years ago.

On the third morning we called on the Nepal representative and found that, surprisingly, he had a small escort of Gurkha soldiers. He told us that when the Chinese unofficial representative, a wireless operator, leaves his premises, he is always accompanied by two compatriots armed with revolvers. They are certainly not well regarded by the Tibetans. We next called on Doring Teji. He was a General, was then downgraded, but is now rumoured as becoming possibly the next Commander-in-Chief; he is a very wealthy landowner. Norbhu then hurried us on to the banks of the Kyi Chu, where our host, Trimon Shapé, had erected a number of decorated tents in which luncheon would be served for us and other guests. But first it was demanded of us that we swim in the river which was freezing cold and we were quickly in and quickly out. Trimon Shapé was a retired Shapé of some age but of most distinguished appearance. He had participated in the Simla Treaty of 1913. The meal was of outstanding merit, much of it composed of items imported from China: strings of peas in jelly, sharks' belly and sea slugs in slices; also huge bowls of thick vegetable and meat soup filled with metres of vermicelli! To accompany it all was served liberal helpings of 'chang', a beer-like beverage made from fermented barley. Some guests became rather the worse for drink, Tsarong in particular. Games of Mah-Jong were played at fast speed and for considerable (by Tibetan standards) sums of money. Three professional female Tibetan dancers performed on a narrow plank, two metres long, accompanied by a bizarre orchestra, two fiddlers (one a blind Chinaman), a bearded Moslem flute-player and a Tibetan drummer. The women remained in a separate tent throughout. Later in the afternoon the wind got up, one tent blew away and the party broke up.

On returning, Tsarong asked us into his house, an invitation which we could not refuse. Some European dancing ensued; Tsarong was rather drunk and I got him to repeat my Cambridge College toast 'In piam memoriam benfectorum nostrorum'. Two catastrophes ensued: firstly, as we left, a drunken servant swept some priceless pieces of Chinese porcelain onto the floor and they were smashed; secondly, on mounting my pony, the stirrup leather broke, the iron fell off, the pony took off in the dark, veered off into a ditch, where he collapsed on top of me. I was left with nothing in my hands except the head harness: the pony was drunk, I was sober!

On the following day we visited the magnificent Potala, constructed by the 5th Dalai Lama who died in 1682; it may be compared to some extent to the Vatican, the focus of the temporal and spiritual powers of the Dictator and Pope, the Dalai Lama. There the Prime Minister has his office and there daily come together all the Lhasa officials. It also houses a monastery, the Namgyal Choide, whose 170 monks are recruited from the more superior families. Here the Dalai Lamas are buried inside chortens of some size; that of the 5th Dalai Lama rises some 60 feet through three storeys of the building and that of the 13th Dalai Lama is even higher. These chortens are lit by holes in the roof and by butter lamps on the altar fronts and are also decorated with valuable antique china and cloisonné vessels. The roof and wall decorations are superior to anything that we had yet seen and the Assembly Hall was magnificent; it was here in 1904 that the Treaty with the Tibetans was signed by Sir Francis Younghusband. We mounted onto the roof from which there were superb views over the whole broad valley encircled by mountains. The golden-roofed cathedral shone out in the middle of the city and below us the monks were exercising themselves on the lower roof of their monastery. On descending, we were shown a hole in the floor covered by a slab, which gave access to a deep dungeon, food and water being lowered daily to the prisoners below.

Our official call on the Regent was scheduled for the really rather early hour of 8.30am. We arrived and whilst waiting on the ground floor of his residence saw his pet lioness sitting happily in a caged room; we wondered how pack animals had coped with bringing this animal from India and over the Himalayan range. There was no ceremony; we were escorted up to the first floor by a couple of monks where we performed, with both arms outstretched, the simple Tibetan ceremony of exchanging scarves with one's host. The reception room was richly decorated with gilded images and cabinets and the whole of one side consisted of windows overlooking the garden. There sat the Regent, who rose to receive us. He was a somewhat shy young monk but gave us a very warm welcome. The new re-incarnated Dalai Lama (the 14th) had not at that time been discovered. When this has been achieved he has to await his majority before coming to power and then the Regent stands down. We told the Regent how very pleased we both were, having been accorded the privilege of visiting Lhasa, and by the very warm welcome we had received from all the Tibetans we had met. We suggested that he would enjoy a visit to Britain for, being interested in animals (which he is), he would be fascinated by the London Zoo and, being interested in football (which very curiously he is), he would be fascinated to watch The Cup Final. He replied that he would much like to visit Britain, preferably by air, so long as he was satisfied that he wouldn't be sick. I was told that this young monk was longing to hand over his responsibilities and regain his personal freedom. On our departure the Regent presented us each with two scarves, a very special honour. (In 1941 this young monk, Reting Rimpoché, was obliged to resign. He had become unpopular and had developed a profound liking for money which it was claimed was being passed to him by the Chinese Government. In the Spring of 1947 the Reting Rimpoché attempted a 'coup d'état', supported by the monks of the Ché College of Sera Monastery, but this failed. He was arrested and 200 monks and fifteen Tibetan soldiers were killed. On 8th May it was announced that Reting Rimpoché, imprisoned in the Potala, had died; in fact, there is no doubt that he was executed).

The next morning, to our great surprise, the monk-magistrate paid us a return call at 7.30am so we gave him breakfast and on behalf of the Tibetan Government he presented us with some meat and a large number of eggs. We then set off on our arranged visit to Sera Monastery. We rode part of the distance along the Holy Way, a track of some six miles which encircles Lhasa and is much frequented by the very religious who walk round it daily. It must be followed in a clockwise direction, prayer-wheels being rotated similarly. The very, very religious sometimes pursue this route by standing up to say a prayer, lying face downwards, tapping the ground with their hands, standing up by placing their feet where their hands were, saying another prayer and repeating this performance for the whole circuit of six miles. There are also the professional performers, protected by pads on their hands and knees, who will willingly perform this task if paid by the more wealthy, who have neither the time nor the inclination for this pursuit.

Sera, a monastery with some 5,500 monks, consists of three Colleges. We were met outside by the two Proctors accompanied by two ceremonial mace-bearers and were shown a very fine Wheel of Life, just outside the Temple, and images of the Serpent Goddess, Chamba, the Protector of men and the much respected Fifth Dalai Lama. As we left the third college on our way to the Assembly Hall we witnessed in progress a 'viva' examination in divinity. Examiners sat on the ground, whilst in front of them each monk performed in turn, striding up and down making their theological point in a loud voice and occasionally advancing before the examiners in a menacing manner, thumping their closed fists into the palm of the other hand. We completed our third meal at the third college and then departed with friendly exchanges. Our daily tour finished with a visit in the City to the mint where the Tibetan money is produced.

We had left until our last day in Lhasa, the visit to the Cathedral which was erected in 652AD but to which subsequent alterations and additions were made up to the end of the 17th Century. We dismounted in front of the Cathedral, known by the Tibetans as the Jo-Kang, and were interested to see there a stone tablet erected by the Chinese at the end of the 18th Century engraved with instructions as to how to combat the dreaded scourge of smallpox. Near-by is a stone monolith recording a Treaty between China and Tibet. The Cathedral is the Holy-of-Holies for all the many thousands of pilgrims coming to Lhasa; they prostrate themselves before the entrance in large numbers, polishing the surface very smoothly in so doing. Above the entrance hangs a bell, but one wonders why it features in such a prominent position because it is a relic of the Capuchin Fathers' Mission to Lhasa in the 18th Century and bears the inscription 'Te Deum Laudamus'.

Mounting to the first floor we entered a gallery decorated with fascinating carvings, which is the most ancient part of the building. Here is the image of the first King of Tibet, Songtsen Gampo, who was converted to Buddhism by his two wives and who then, in the 7th Century, built the Cathedral. The chief shrine in the Temple contains one of the most famous idols in the world, that of the Gautama Buddha.

Mounting to the second storey we entered the small shrine of the Palden Lhamo (her Hindu equivalent is KaIi, the wife of Shiva). The Tibetans considered this goddess to have been incarnated in the person of Queen Victoria. The shrine contains two statues of the goddess: the first is a gilded, decorated, crowned figure smiling broadly in happy mood; the second shows her as a black-faced raging monster, clad in the skins of human victims and eating the brains of a defunct from his skull. The shrine was so small that in order to take a photograph we had to shut and jam the door to prevent others from entering. An extraordinary phenomenon was the mice who were scampering everywhere, over the statues, onto the altars, avoiding the lit butter lamps, and even onto the shoulders of a praying monk; the air was loud with their squeaking. A little further on we entered a room in which some fifty monks were engaged in a service with chanting and beating of Tibetan drums. This room was also dedicated to the Goddess Palden Lhamo in her evil role, for the statues were devilish and offensive. The walls had racks containing hundreds of ancient weapons: spears and muskets and even some chain-mail vestments and helmets. That this goddess represents Evil, War and Death there is no doubt whatsoever.

It was a considerable relief for us to mount a small ladder and emerge onto the roof, consisting of a number of gilded Pagoda-like structures shining brightly in the sunlight and with beautifully carved eaves below. In the distance the Potala looked more imposing than ever. The gilded roof of the Cathedral had been patched in various places: the damage had occurred on the occasion of the Chinese invasion of Tibet when the Chinese had opened fire on the building which was being defended by Tibetans. We descended to the ground floor, where in the open air a number of pilgrims were following the circuit, revolving all the many prayer-wheels in passing.

On returning to Norbhu's house we found more interesting mementos which we were tempted to buy. Officials came one after the other to return our calls, all bringing generous presents with them. A most friendly dinner brought our Lhasa visit to an end. Rai Bahardur Norbhu and his wife had been such very kind hosts and we had been remarkably warmly welcomed everywhere.

WANA TO THE KARAKORAM

by

Ian Lyall Grant

In 1939 I was stationed in Wana on the North-West Frontier. Wana, being in tribal territory and outside India's 'administrative frontier', entitled me to three months leave a year, a splendid perk, so I chose the most distant place I could see on a map of northern India, the Karakoram Pass, and decided to go there. As the junior subaltern in 3 Field Company I had no choice of dates and was allotted April, May and June. After the weekly convoy from Wana, a long train journey and a bus ride up to Srinagar in Kashmir, 10th April found me staying with the very hospitable parents of another Sapper officer while I made the arrangements for my trip. Dr and Mrs Rawlence were both doctors and missionaries, spoke several Indian languages including Kashmiri, and devoted their lives to helping the poor. They were delightful hosts, had many extraordinary stories to tell about their experiences and gave me much helpful advice.

Meanwhile I obtained a permit to visit Ladakh, bought a shooting licence and arranged with a local contractor, Bahar Shah, to engage a Kashmiri shikari/guide called Ahad Sheikh (Ahdoo) and his assistant and cook, Mahomedoo (Mohdoo). Together with Ahdoo, I hired two tents, cooking gear, hurricane lamps etc, medical kit, provisions and paraffin. For the first fortnight some local vegetables, dried fruit and flour would be available: after that we would be on our own. The contractor provided six ponies to carry our loads for the first two marches, after which we would have to change to porters because of the snow. The Himalayan Range catches the full force of the SW monsoon and in April there is still a great deal of snow about.

On 14th April I sent my bearer Abdul, who was too old for long marches, back to his wife at Roorkee, said goodbye to my kind hosts and started off up the valley of the Sind River. On the 16th we reached the edge of the snow, halted for a day, sent back our ponies and engaged sixteen porters for the next four stages. This would involve crossing the Himalayan Range by the Zoji La, a relatively low pass of 11,500ft but formidable at this time of year because of the heavy snow. We spent one night at Sonamarg, where we found the 'golden meadow' under seven feet of snow and the next day, having issued snow-glasses to the porters, marched in a snow shower and over many avalanche tracks to Baltal at the foot of the pass.

At Baltal the rest house was almost hidden under the snow. From the visitors' book I saw that I was the fourth traveller to attempt the pass that year. The first, a Gunner, had crossed ten days earlier. Ahdoo showed his mettle by getting the porters quickly settled in, fires going and hot food produced. Perhaps emboldened by this, the coolies formed up and asked if they might please have some tea. It turned out to be an opening gambit, for when I said yes, they said "what's the use of tea?" A bit more cash was the real idea, and from the back came the words "*Zoji La*", "*Sab Sahib log*" (all gentlemen), "*dastur*" (it is the custom). However, I reminded them that we had an agreement and that they would get baksheesh at the end, and they retired no doubt feeling that it had been worth a try. An unpleasant day and night followed, because the chimney was blocked in some way and the birch wood logs in the fire filled the room with aromatic and stinging smoke. My eyes streamed and it was impossible to read and difficult to sleep.

We planned to leave the next morning at 2am so as to cross the pass before the avalanches started but the porters weren't ready until two hours later. After we had gone about a mile it began to snow heavily and the visibility closed in, so we turned back and spent another miserable night in the Baltal rest house. The next morning, however, we got off successfully at 2.30am. It was a steep climb up the pass and there were two narrow gullies where it was best not to think about avalanches. Having reached the top soon after dawn we were met with a really bitter headwind and the next four hours to Machoi were hard going. I felt as though my face was being skinned by the wind and it was to remain sore for days. The porters, however, showed remarkable spirit and after an hour's rest agreed to press on the seven miles to Matayan which we reached, still in the snow, at 5.30pm. It had been a 16-mile march and because of the soft snow it had been necessary to trudge in single file in a narrow trench. For porters carrying 60lbs it was distinctly tough, but it paid off for the next day we covered the twelve miles to Dras in good time still through the snow. I heard later that John Smith, the Gunner who had crossed the pass first, had been obliged to stop at Machoi and didn't reach Dras the next day until 9pm when the temperature was -13° F and some of his porters had mild frostbite.

Both at Matayan and Dras the nights were bitterly cold but bearable because, heaven be praised, there were rest houses at each place and the fires didn't smoke. Having paid off the porters with generous baksheesh for they had done very well, we now switched to pony transport for the rest of the way to Leh. The next day's march was 22 miles and mostly a long traverse on a sloping hillside. This did my left knee no good and I was obliged to ride part of the way and to take a day's rest the following day as the knee had swelled up. It was to be a nuisance for the rest of the trip.

On 24th April we reached Kargil which was the first town in the province of Ladakh. Here a hitch occurred for I had mislaid my entry paper. The naib (assistant) tehsildar was a pandit and he was adamant. "Sir, you cannot go on without permit". So we were forced to rest another day while I wired Srinagar for permission to proceed. By the next morning no answer had come but fortunately the Tehsildar himself, a Balti, turned up and proved more flexible. I gave him a written letter assuring him that I had a permit and we set off with six fresh ponies.

Ladakh was very different from Kashmir. The people were Tibetan in origin and Buddhists by religion. The men wore their hair in a pigtail under a felt hat with ear-flaps, woollen trousers and one or two double-breasted woollen dressing gowns. Many of the women wore spectacular head-dresses shaped like the head of a cobra and studded with large turquoises. These were apparently family heirlooms and passed down through the generations. Women had much importance. They owned the land and polyandry was the normal system. If a woman married a man, she also married all his brothers. The British had recognised the very different nature of the province, and though Ladakh was no longer independent and was nominally a part of Kashmir it was in practice largely self-administered and there was a British Joint Commissioner responsible for seeing that all was well. There were no armed forces and very few, if any, police.

For the next three days we marched through hillsides of neatly-terraced fields and occasional apricot orchards, passing the very large monastery at Lamayuru and reaching Khalsi on the 27th. Here we crossed the Indus to the north bank via a suspension bridge and in three more pleasant marches reached Leh, the capital, on 30th April. On the last leg we passed a broad prayer wall, at least a mile long, with the top adorned with prayers carved on innumerable slates. The agreeable idea was that as travellers passed by they automatically said all the prayers. It had taken us 17 days, three of which were rest days, to cover the 226 miles from Srinagar to Leh. Nowadays, of course, there is a jeep road and the trip is an easy two days, but I doubt if modern travellers see quite as much of the country and its wildlife as we did.

Leh

Leh, at 11,500ft, was to be the base for the next stage of the trip and we spent five days there making the preparations. The first person I called on was Mr Asboe, the head of the Moravian Mission, to whom I had an introduction from the Rawlences. He was kindness itself and introduced me to the key men in Leh. They were the Aksakal, or Trade Commissioner, a fine looking man from Central Asia whose brother was said to be Aksakal of Yarkand; Mr Gautama the Government Customs Officer, a very helpful Indian; Mr Therchen, whose role I never discovered; and Kalon Rigzin, the Mayor and chief contractor for transport. I was told that the trade route over the Karakoram Pass had been closed since 1936, three years earlier. A major part of this trade had been in *charas* (cannabis resin) and formerly well over a thousand pony loads of this were imported over the pass every year, each pony carrying two 100lbs blocks. The Indian Government controlled this very profitable trade levying an import duty of Rs40 per pound and selling the *charas* through three outlets in the Punjab. Now a patrol of Chinese-led Kirghiz were stationed on the north side of the Pass; they not only blocked the route completely but made occasional sorties for two or three stages into Ladakh.

The next days were spent discussing routes and collecting supplies. To reach the Karakoram Pass, about 220 miles from Leh, we would have to cross the Ladakh Range. The Khardung La north of Leh was the nearest crossing but was currently impassable for animals, so we would have to cross by the Chang La, further south, and travel up the Shyok valley. On the way back I planned, if possible, to cross the Karakoram Range by the Saser La and return to Leh over the Khardung La, but there was some doubt whether animals would be able to cross these two passes, both about 18,000ft, even in a month's time. We would be three weeks out beyond any village, and in barren country, so all food for men and animals and all fuel, would have to be carried. Non-essentials such as a Roorkee chair, a canvas bath, some clothing and some tinned food, were left with the Asboes.

The Asboes had started a local blanket industry and I bought two fine blankets from them which were to prove invaluable. Every evening I went over to listen to their wireless and one day I borrowed a pony from them and, at their suggestion, paid a call on the Rani Sahiba of Ladakh in her palace at Stoke on the other side of the Indus. She no longer had any political power, but was much respected. Through a misunderstanding she was not expecting me and I found her dressed like a countrywoman among her servants and dogs. However, with charming manners, she sat in front of me on a carpet while I was served tea and biscuits and then retired to change while I was shown round her library and her private temple with its jewel-encrusted images. Soon she reappeared wearing a red velvet dress, an embroidered cloak, a magnificent turquoise head-dress and large pearl earrings. After this I was led on to a patio where there was a chair for me and cushions on a rug for her and her favourite Lhasa terrier, and I was served with hot milk and boiled eggs which she peeled with her own hands. It turned out that we had both met the same prominent travellers who had visited her recently and she was much amused at the feeble jokes that I made at their expense. I took several photographs (of which I later sent her copies) and after about half an hour made my way back, much impressed with her dignity and aplomb.

The next day was spent trying to arrange for our transport with Kalon Rigzin. I had worked out that we needed to start with thirteen animals. On the way back, if the Saser La proved too difficult for ponies, we would be stranded on the wrong side of the Karakorams and would need eight yaks or a number of coolies to come over the pass to pick us up. Kalon clearly thought that the whole project was a bit dicey and refused to agree a contract, so I walked out. Mr Asboe and Mr Gautama now came to my aid and, after two hours persuasion, Kalon changed his mind, a typed contract was drawn up and we both signed it in the Customs office. I was to pay Rs390 (£26) for the month's trip but was not to make any double marches. Any animals or men who died en route would be Kalon's responsibility unless I deviated from the route when they would be mine. On the 6th May, after saying goodbye to all my contacts at the gate of the bazaar, we were off.

The Karakoram Pass

We followed the Indus valley for a day and a half and then turned north-east for the climb over the Chang La (18,000ft). With our thirteen animals, we were quite a large party. As well as Ahdoo and Mohdoo, I had taken on a splendid Ladakhi called Punzuk as 'tiffin coolie' (odd job man), a tough old Yarkandi called Ghulam Khan as chief pony-man and three cheerful Ladakhi pony drivers, Tundup Tsering, Tsatta Tsering and Tashi Nurbo. "We've become a caravan" said Mohdoo with a laugh. We made a short stop at one monastery where a band was playing and a party was in progress and joined in the archery and refreshment of chang, a rice wine rather like cider. Later in the day I heard a curious buzzing sound which I couldn't locate and thought at first it was an aeroplane. Finally I found it was Punzuk, who, as he marched along, was repeating over and over again in a deep musical voice 'Om mani padme om, Om mani padme om ...', the Buddhist prayer, while spinning some sheep's wool into a thread.

The track now started to rise steadily and we camped at Zingrool (15,700ft) a few miles short of the pass. There was a wonderful view of the snow-capped peaks of the Himalayan Range and the next morning we left early and climbed up through the snow (where there were many snow leopard tracks to be seen) to cross the high but easy Chang La at 8am, dropping down to a camp site the other side at Tsoltah. Here there were two small lakes with two brahminy ducks sitting on one of them. At Ahdoo's request I shot one of them for his and Mohdoo's supper, cooked over a yak dung fire. I had brought with me a folding Westley Richards .318 rifle and about 25 rounds to shoot for the pot if a chance occurred. It was an excellent weapon but I had rarely used it and I had found on the march up that, with the cartridges I had, it shot about 6 inches high at 150 yards.

The march down to the village of Shyok, on the river to which it gives its name, was a very tiring one over the debris of an old moraine. The plan was for us to send back nine ponies and pick up here two donkeys and nine mules. These had duly arrived the day before from the Nubra valley, as agreed in my contract, but several were galled and in poor condition. I was furious and waited a day in Shyok to give them some rest before hiring three of the five ponies in the tiny village to accompany us up the Shyok valley for three days and thus allow the worst cases to travel without saddles.

There were four long marches, all well over twenty miles, up the Shyok valley to Kataklik where there was a camp site with grass. Each day we forded the river five or six times, the Ladakhis usually hitching up their dressing gowns and wading, thus revealing that they had very pale skins and were remarkably hairless. We passed a barren place beside the river called, most inappropriately, Chong Jangal (north forest). Ghulam, who had in the past been to Yarkand several times, said that indeed there used to be trees there but they had been washed away when the famous Shyok glacier dam broke. One evening, resting after our march, Ahdoo spotted three male burrhel, a type of wild sheep, about a mile away and near the confluence with the Changchenmo river. However, they saw Ahdoo and me crossing the Shyok and started moving away up the steep hillside. We clambered up after them and, heart pumping, I fired at one and missed it. They continued to move off in a leisurely way so we climbed further up, to about a thousand feet above the river, when I had another easy chance at the biggest one as they crossed a rock face above us. Alas! I had forgotten about the rifle shooting high and saw the bullet strike the rock just above its back. They disappeared round a corner leaving me feeling exhausted and foolish and we returned to camp.

We spent a day in Kataklik, resting the ponies, the Shyok ones having been sent back. The next day we left the Shyok valley and marched north-east up the gorge of the chocolate-coloured Murgo stream, eventually reaching the Murgo camp-site. As agreed before we started, I sent Tashi Nurbo, plus his share of food and fuel, off to Saser Brangsa, further up the Shyok. He was to cross the Saser La (17,500ft) when the weather allowed, and return with either 16 coolies or 8 yaks to reach Saser Brangsa on 27th May. This was in case the Saser proved impassable for ponies so early in the year and we were obliged to send them back down the Shyok. We dumped some stores (and buried the food because we had already seen one wolf nearby), meanwhile collecting eight sacks of burtsa. Burtsa was a small dry shrub, rather like a leafless pot-plant azalea, which burnt well and made a useful addition to our wood fuel. I expected that the round trip to the Karakoram Pass and back would take eight days, so we carried ten days of food for men and animals and eight days of fuel.

The march to Kizil Langar at 16,400ft was a hard slog uphill for 20 miles. It came on to snow and the wind was piercingly cold. We passed literally hundreds of corpses of ponies and camels and not a few heaps of stones marking the graves of their masters. That night at the foot of the Depsang Plains was extremely cold and the little stream by our camp froze solid. It was snowing the next morning as we climbed up on to the Plains and continued to do so as we marched across their barren undulating gravel. When it cleared for a little, Ahdoo and I pursued unsuccessfully a small herd of Tibetan antelope without getting a shot. For the last few miles it came on to snow heavily and there was a bitter wind, so the pony-men were glad to find two stone huts at our destination for the night, Karakoram Polu. One of the huts contained a skeleton. I had proposed making one more march down over the border into the Yarkand valley, but the pony-men protested, quite rightly, that they had come as far as their contract authorised, so the next day Ahdoo, Punzuk and I left them in camp and rode on ponies for the ten miles to the Karakoram Pass at 18,290ft. There was a good deal of snow and we had to lead our ponies most of the way. Finally we climbed up a low ridge to find a cairn which marked the summit of the Pass. The valley on the other side sloped down into China and Yarkand; we were on the India/Asia watershed and our main aim had been achieved.

The Shyok Glaciers

However, I had a secondary aim which was to find out more about the famous Shyok glacier dam. So instead of returning the way we had come, I decided to go, by a track marked on my map, to Gapshan near the head of the Shyok valley. After some grumbling, for none of them had ever been there before, the pony-men agreed. It was a fine but very cold day and we had a magnificent view of the north side of the Karakoram Range and the 24,700ft Mount Saser as we marched down the shallow valley of the Chip Chap river. Once settled in camp at Gapshan, Punzuk and I set off up the Shyok and I took some photographs of the snout of the Rimo glacier, its source.

Our white mule had been ill that day with a distended stomach and refused to carry a load. After asking for permission to cure it, Ghulam heated a horseshoe red hot and, after laying the mule down, burnt a cross on each flank while someone sat on its head. He then stuck a large needle into its nose and its tail. To my great surprise this worked, and the mule jumped up and appeared to make a miraculous recovery. There was now an argument about our route for the morrow. The pony-men wished to go back to Kizil Langar by the way we had come which would take two days. My map, however, showed that it was possible to cut the corner and go directly over the Depsang Plains to Kizil Langar in one day. Finally, with much reluctance, for they feared that we might get lost, they agreed to try my route.

Fortunately the next day was fine. There was no sign of a track nor of corpses as signposts and so I had some anxious moments until we successfully reached the main route and turned down it to Kizil Langar. On the way we saw five herds of the hornless female Tibetan antelopes but only one male. Ahdoo and I stalked one herd and I shot a female for the pot. Horns being the normal shikar trophy, I had to put up with ribald enquiries, on my return to Wana, about whether it was a record chest measurement. However, the meat cheered up the pony-men. Punzuk pulled the very fine wool off the skin, and on the way back, knitted a pair of socks with it.

From Kizil Langar we made our way back to Murgo where we recovered our dumped stores. At Ghulam's request we by-passed Saser Brangsa at the foot of the Saser Pass and made our way on the 24th to Aktash, a few miles further up the river, where there was more grass. This suited me as it was close to the southernmost of the three glaciers that I wanted to see. We rested a day at Aktash but it started to snow and the weather began to deteriorate. Punzuk went to Saser Brangsa and found that the sixteen coolies had arrived that morning, two days ahead of schedule, and they claimed to have only two more days' food left. The pass had been easy going for Tashi Nurbo eight days before but fresh snow had made the return journey more difficult.

On the 26th it was still snowing intermittently. Ahdoo, Punzuk and I rode up the Shyok valley, past the two horns of the Aktash glacier, now some way back from the river, and reached the Kichik Kumdun glacier. This was an impressive sight. It was about 50 feet high and stretched most of the way across the river-bed towards a vertical rock face on the east bank. However it didn't look as though it would ever make a very effective dam as the valley is wide there. Moreover the river was running underground for about a mile on either side. We were lucky. The weather cleared for a short time and I took some photographs. Then it began to snow again and so we returned to camp.

The poor weather continued, and although I managed to get some photos of the nearby Aktash glacier in a brief bright spell, it was no use attempting to visit the northernmost and most important glacier, the Chong Kumdun. Now the Saser La has the reputation of being a very dangerous pass in bad weather and Ghulam was becoming anxious about getting his ponies back over it in the fresh snow, so I decided that we would risk waiting only one more day and then return.

We were lucky. 28th May was a better day and we rode up to the Chong Kumdun glacier and took many photographs. It was clear that this was the glacier that formed the famous dam. The valley is much narrower here. The glacier was now about 150 feet high and about 60 yards from a vertical cliff of white marble on the east bank to which huge chunks of ice were still adhering. The river ran at the foot of this cliff and between it and the snout of the glacier was a mass of broken ice. We roped up to cross this and to take photographs from the north. I was to learn later that fifteen years before the glacier had been 500 feet high and when it reached the cliff had impounded a deep lake which stretched ten miles up the valley to beyond Gapshan. In 1926 the dam had partially broken and reformed; in 1929 the dam had broken fully and a flood, more than 70 feet high in some narrow places, had destroyed villages for hundreds of miles down the Shyok valley and raised the level of the Indus itself by 27 feet at Attock bridge 742 miles downstream.

Back to Leh

The following day, my second aim achieved, we moved back through Saser Brangsa and up to a camp-site near the foot of the saddle glacier which crowns the Saser La. It was a vile day, snowing, and with a bitterly cold wind blowing off the glacier. There were countless frozen corpses of animals from which some of our party cut pieces of hide to make shoes. The porters had not much shelter and six of them went down to Saser Brangsa for the night. At 4am on the 30th May we started off to cross this 17,500ft pass across the Karakoram Range. Only 10 coolies turned out so some of the ponies had to be lightly loaded. Climbing up on to the glacier through the fresh soft snow was a struggle for the animals, particularly for the two donkeys. After six miles the six errant porters joined us and things became easier. Fortunately the weather became better as we reached the summit and we arrived at the Tut Yailak *parao* (camp-site) on the south side at 11am, leaving behind us the black clouds over the Shyok valley. Here there was a fine view of the two spectacular sinuous median moraines on the Manostory glacier which descends from the 24,700ft Saser peak from which the pass gets its name. The first animal crossing of the year had been strenuous but not too difficult.

On the 31st we marched nineteen miles down into the Nubra valley. The south side of the range was very different to the bleak north. There was much more grass and we saw many herds of burrhel. Further down there were many wild roses but not yet in bloom. On the 1st June we made a short march to Panamik, the chief village in the valley, being inhibited from going further by our contract. Close by were some hot springs in which I bathed twice and felt cleaner and fitter. Continuing down this beautiful valley, we had lunch in the garden of Punzuk's father's house, set among fields and some fine big trees, and were hospitably served with *chang*. Punzuk went off to his wife's house and returned slightly the worse for wear, finding it oddly difficult to mount his pony.

That evening we reached Tegar and camped on Kalon Rigzin's land. Punzuk took us off to a big party being held by the lamas from a nearby monastery. Some fifteen lamas were seated on a dais in an orchard with an elderly and impressive-looking Head Lama in the middle. The archery over, the dancing was just starting. While the *chang* circulated freely, the men and women danced, but in separate areas. Then the men shuffled round by themselves in a rather dull ritual led by the Head Lama's son. After this the women danced, led by a very pretty young girl said to be his daughter, in a more graceful routine and making much play with their hands. The girl was beautifully dressed in a dark red velvet gown, white wristlets and a green shawl-cloak embroidered with roses and flowers, the whole topped by a fine turquoise headdress. The next day, however, I heard that the so-called Head Lama, though a rich man and much respected, was in fact no longer a priest, and the pretty girl who looked to be about twelve or thirteen was his newly-married wife.

At Sunur I paid a courtesy visit to the strict Yellow Sect monastery where one of Punzuk's brothers was a priest. The Head Lama greeted me outside the gate with a button-hole of roses and as I reached the inner courtyard all the lamas played a fanfare on drums and very long trumpets. I was then given another posy, and conducted upstairs for tea and dried fruit before being shown round the monastery. It was clean and well-kept but not very impressive except for a huge oil lamp with enough oil to burn for a year. Having taken some photographs of them all, I gave the Head Lama a small present and we went on to Satti.

At Satti the suspension bridge had been washed away in the 1926 Shyok flood and had not yet been replaced, so the next morning we forded the Shyok and marched to Khardung. That evening I finished the one book I had taken (a Complete Works of Shakespeare) and looked forward to a return to civilisation. However, Sanam, who was Kalon's brother and had accompanied us from Aktash, was worried about getting our ponies over the Khardung La, 18,380ft, and left to arrange for yaks and coolies if necessary. The Khardung is a 'knife-edge' pass and the last 800 feet or so on each side is very steep. We climbed up to the foot of the pass the next day and were joined by ten huge hairy yaks. On 6th June we left camp at 2.40am and had a difficult day. There was a lot of soft snow and the 'official' track was obscured. The ponies finally got stuck about 100 feet from the top of the pass and the yaks 100 feet lower down. I went on ahead and by great good fortune met an RAF type, Arthur Young, coming up the other side with yaks. He would not have reached the top until 8am, by which time it would have been very difficult to get his yaks down through the soft snow on the north side. So we agreed to swap transport. The loads were carried over the pass; he took my yaks and porters and I took his. Having said goodbye to the ponymen, Ahdoo, Mohdoo and I went down to Leh to the surprise of the locals for the bazaar rumour was that we had all been captured by Tungans.

Return to Srinagar

We spent four idle days in Leh before starting back for Srinagar. The Gunner subaltern, John Smith, who had crossed the Zoji La first this year, turned up, also homeward bound. One day Kalon Rigzin very kindly invited me to dinner and told me to bring my friend. It was a splendid evening. We started with Ladakhi tea with butter in it, followed by umpteen courses, mainly of meat in one form or another, and finally a huge pillau, all served by Kalon's brother and washed down by copious draughts of *chang*. Dorje, the local MES engineer, was there too and we had a most animated conversation in broken Urdu about Ladakh, Central Asia, and the iniquities of the Maharajah of Kashmir, always a popular subject in Ladakh. Then the arak started circulating and after one fiery glass we wisely concluded that the time had come to say goodbye to our very hospitable host.

On 11th June we started back with five ponies from Leh, having said goodbye to the Asboes, and having promised to advertise their admirable

Mission blankets. The countryside was now very different, with roses in bloom in all the villages. We passed two parties of men improving bad places on the road, always a sign that a VIP was not far behind. Sure enough, at Lamayuru we met the new British Joint Commissioner on his way up. He was interested in the news from the Karakoram Pass and asked many questions. John Smith had gone on ahead as he was worried about being late back from leave, but I caught him up on the 15th and we marched the rest of the way to Srinagar together. He was very good company and we often stayed up late, laughing and chatting.

At Dras we crossed the tracks of Mike Rolt from Roorkee; he had passed through some weeks earlier on his way to Skardu in Baltistan. Except for old avalanche tracks there was now little snow about and many flowers had appeared. Twelve days out of Leh we reached Srinagar on 22nd June. Here I parted from John Smith and our paths never crossed again. I hired a houseboat on the Dal Lake for two days while I returned my tents, settled my accounts and gave reference chits (very good ones) to Ahdoo and Mohdoo. Then back to Wana where I arranged for my photographs to be printed and in due course sent off 90 prints; some to the Himalayan Journal and many to my Kashmiri and Ladakhi companions. The whole trip, Wana to Wana, had cost just under two thousand rupees (£125), which included the purchase of two carpets in Leh. This was about my Indian Army pay for the three months. (Prices were then very different. The cost of my own food for the 70 days out from, and back to, Srinagar was £14!).

Some two months later World War II began and for the next six years such long leaves were naturally not permitted. After the war the Chinese unilaterally advanced their frontier. The Karakoram Pass, the Depsang Plains and the Shyok glaciers are now claimed as Chinese territory and are inacessible from the south. Possession of the Siachen glacier, at the head of the Nubra river, is disputed between India and Pakistan. I had visited an interesting and little-known area and fallen in love for ever with the great mountains. It was an unforgettable experience and typical of travels made by many every year in the pre-war era.

5
THE FRONTIER WARS

THE NORTH-EAST FRONTIER

As British rule expanded across the Indian sub-continent in the 19th Century, so the problems of boundaries arose with neighbouring countries such as Iran, Afghanistan, Russia, China, Tibet, Nepal and Burma. Wars were fought with some of these countries before agreement on boundaries was reached. The problem then arose of maintaining law and order within these boundaries. This was solved in some cases by helping to establish frontier groups as independent countries (eg Sikkim and Bhutan) and others as semi-independent states within

British India (eg Kashmir and Manipur). These states were responsible, with British help, for the security of their share of the Indian frontier.

The first serious dispute with a neighbouring country led to the war with Nepal in 1814–16. John Swinton, an outstanding Bengal Engineer, was then Commanadant of the Bengal 'Pioneers and Sappers'. He deployed eight companies in support of the various columns. It was a very tough war and the Gurkha forts were difficult to subdue without the use of heavy artillery. So the main task of the Sappers was to cut paths, and sometimes staircases, through the forested hills so that elephants could drag the guns up to the forts. Under an amicable peace treaty, Sikkim was established as a separate state and the districts of Kumaon and Almora reverted to India, while the Gurkhas began a long, friendly and very distinguished relationship with Britain.

There were many other small expeditions in the 19th century to establish India's North-East frontier, but until 1864 none were large enough to require engineer support. In 1864 and 1865, however, the 6th and 7th Companies of the Bengal Sappers and Miners took part in the campaign in the Himalayan forests which resulted in the establishment of the frontiers of Sikkim and Bhutan. While Sapper track-making was of vital importance to the expedition, the most memorable feature was a remarkable feat of bravery in storming a blockhouse at Dewan-Giri, for which two Bengal Sapper officers, Captain WS Trevor and Lieutenant J Dundas, received the VC. The citation for these awards appeared in the London Gazette of 31 December 1867 and read as follows:

'Major General Tombs VC CB, the officer in command at the time, reports that a party of the enemy, from 180 to 200 in number, had barricaded themselves in the Block-house in question, which they continued to defend after the rest of the position had been carried and the main body was in retreat. The Block-house, which was loop-holed, was the key of the enemy's position. Seeing no officer of the storming party near him, and being anxious that the place should be taken immediately, as any protracted resistance might have caused the main body of the Bhooteas to rally, the British force having been fighting in the broiling sun on the steep and very difficult ground for upwards of three hours, the General in command ordered these two officers to show the way into the Block-house. They had to climb up a wall which was fourteen feet high, and then to enter a house, occupied by some 200 desperate men, head foremost through an opening not more than two feet wide between the top of the wall and the roof of the Block-house.

Major General Tombs states that on speaking to the Sikh soldiers round him, and telling them to swarm up the wall, none of them responded to the call until these two officers had shown the way, when they followed with the greatest alacrity. Both of them were wounded'. (Captain Trevor went on to become a Major General, and his medals are in the Royal Engineers Museum, Chatham).

On the Burmese border there was unrest in several areas, notably with the Nagas, Lushais and Chins, all keen head-hunters. No Sappers took part in the hostilities against the Nagas, but in 1881–3 the 6th and 9th Companies of the Bengal Sappers built the first road, through a formidable gorge to Kohima, the capital of Nagaland. Ten years later, the 3rd Company joined two companies of Madras Sappers in extending the road from Kohima to Imphal, the famous Manipur Road. None could have foreseen then the vital strategic importance that this road would assume fifty years later.

Concurrently with these activities north of Imphal, several expeditions were launched against the Lushais and Chins to the south. Both tribes proved to be stubborn fighters in the guerrilla style and, although the main effort against them was launched from Burma, with Madras Sapper support, a southern column from Chittagong, supported by the 2nd Company of the Bengal Sappers, advanced to Haka. They were required to build a mule track through dense jungle. The steep hills and ravines, and the need for many bridges, made it a most formidable task. It took them two and a half months during which time nearly everyone caught malaria.

In 1899 the 5th Company took part in a small, but extraordinary, expedition to Mishmiland in the far north of Burma. The Mishmis had been attacking a neighbouring tribe and needed to be restrained. The hills in their country were so steep and unstable that tracks could not be cut and only porters could be used. It rained incessantly. The Sappers used tree trunks to cross the smaller streams, and suspension bridges, with the cables made from rattan cane, to cross the larger ones. Having crossed an 8,900ft snow-covered pass, the force reached the main Mishmi village to find it deserted. They then retired having made their point that no-one was beyond the reach of British-Indian law.

The expedition to Lhasa in Tibet in 1904, euphemistically called a military mission, in which the 3rd Company took part, was certainly the most ambitious operation connected with the North-East frontier since the war with Nepal. The 400 mile march included some stirring assault demolitions and two crossings, by flying ferry, of the great Tsang-po (Brahmaputra) at 11,000ft. However it was in reality an invasion, aimed at ensuring that a neighbouring state was friendly, rather than a frontier dispute and so is not part of the frontier story.

THE NORTHERN FRONTIER

After Sir Charles Napier's conquest of Sind in 1843, British forces for the first time encountered the problems of the north-west frontier with Afghanistan. This first contact at the southern end of the frontier was with Baluchi tribes, who were much less numerous and less warlike than the Pathan tribes further north. The latter were held in check at this time by the Sikh Empire with whom the British were allied. However, after the

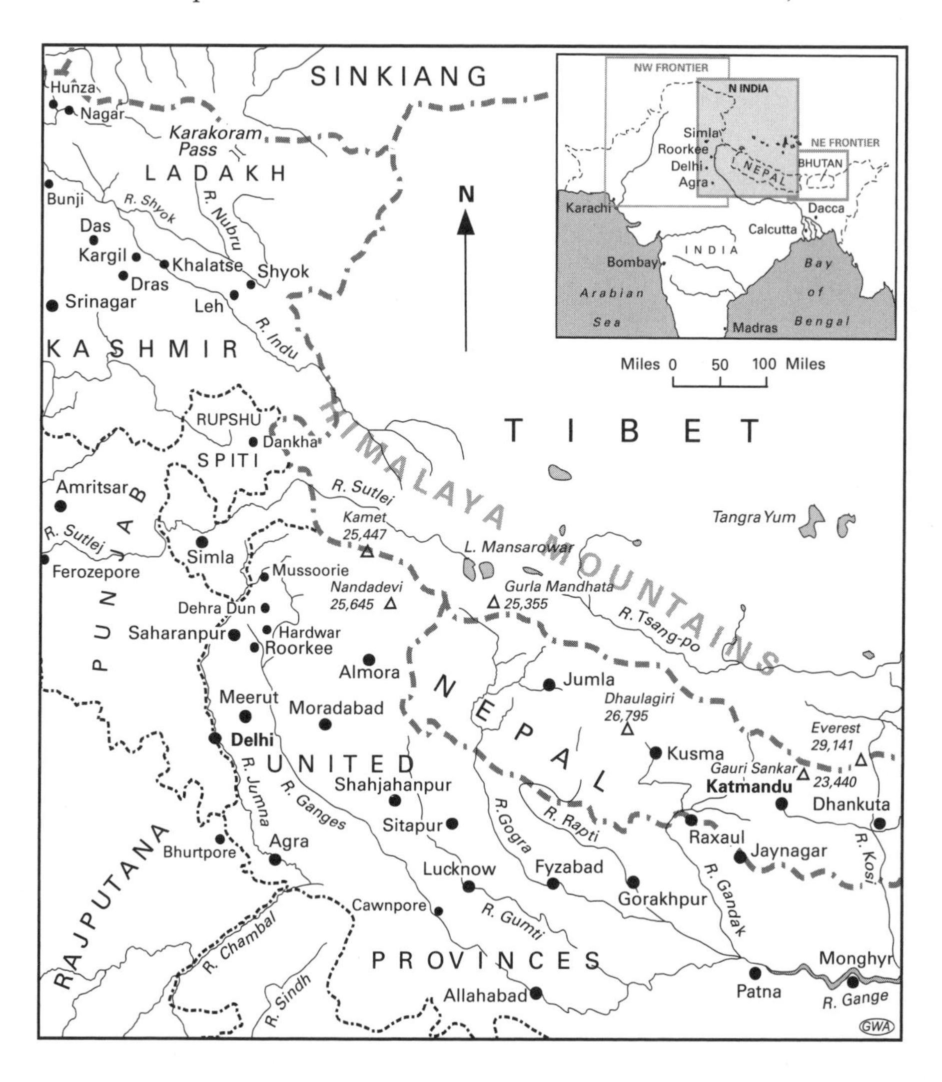

death of the famous Sikh leader, Maharajah Ranjit Singh, a power struggle followed among the Sikhs and the winner turned against the British. Two hard-fought wars followed. Finally successful, the British annexed the Punjab and in 1850 inherited the full problem of the boundary between India and Afghanistan. Aware that they had greatly increased the length of their frontiers, the British made a deal with a notable called Gulab Singh, whom they installed as Maharajah of Jammu and Kashmir. He would be responsible, with British help when required, for the security of the long northern frontier from Chitral to Ladakh.

This latter arrangement was first tested in a remarkable campaign in the far north of the country in 1891. The only two major passes over the Karakoram Range, which separates India from Central Asia, are the 15,000ft Mintaka Pass at the western end and the 18,000ft Karakoram Pass to China to the East. Astride the former route were the two little mountain states of Hunza and Nagar, whose inhabitants lived largely on apricots, and for hundreds of years had obtained their other needs by raiding the caravans on the Silk Road across Central Asia. Nominally subservient to Kashmir, but virtually independent because of their remoteness, they paid an annual tribute to their parent state: in the case of Hunza it was 20 ounces of gold-dust, two horses and two hounds, and for Nagar it was some gold-dust and two baskets of apricots! Fearful that these tiny isolated states might succumb to Russian bribes, the Government decided to establish a fort at the north end of a formidable gorge leading to their country and to bring them under British control. To implement this, a Kashmiri brigade was assembled at Gilgit in the far north of Kashmir and Captain Aylmer, OC 4 Company, and twelve Bengal Sappers, plus two companies of Gurkhas, were ordered to join them. The Hunza Nagar Expedition was a campaign waged almost on top of the world and spoken of as "a war of small parties, almost of individuals".

Aylmer's party joined the others at Srinagar and from there they set out for Gilgit. It was autumn and they had a tough time crossing the Burzil Pass over the Himalayas in a blizzard. Their next obstacle was a tributary of the Indus, crossed by an old cantilever bridge in very bad repair. Aylmer dismantled this and used the timber to build a low-level winter bridge. They then reached the Indus at Bunji where the resourceful Aylmer, who had brought from Roorkee a wire rope and traveller, built a raft with two country boats and made a flying ferry across the 500 foot river. Having joined the rest of the force at Gilgit, they found the ford across the Yasin River to be dangerously deep and the current fast, so

Aylmer decided to build a foot-bridge on piers made by cantilevering two strong men out over the water to hurl heavy stones into the river. A Kashmiri regiment supplied the stones and when one pier was completed the cantilever was pushed forward to build the next. Working from both sides the bridge was completed in five days. The force then moved on up the west bank of the Hunza River through a fearsome gorge to Chalt, where a fort was to be built. The path was totally impracticable for animals as it crossed an almost vertical rock precipice. In some places it zig-zagged up this rockface and in others rough ladders led from one ledge to another. Aylmer bypassed this portion in two days by building a wooden gallery suspended by wires attached to jumpers driven into the rock. However there was still one more bridge to be built, since the fortress at Nilt, the key to these hidden valleys, was on the East bank of the Hunza river. Having collected some pine logs, Aylmer dealt with this problem by building a winter bridge at a place where large boulders protruded conveniently from the river-bed.

The force now prepared for the assault on the formidable Nilt fort, whose massive stone walls were up to twenty feet high and twelve feet thick and well protected by towers. Colonel Durand's plan was for the Sappers, assisted by a covering force of Gurkhas, to blow in the main gate. This gate, however, was protected by an outer courtyard which was covered by a loopholed bastion. Aylmer and six Sappers, three with axes and three with guncotton, accompanied by Lieutenant Boisragon and twelve Gurkhas, approached by a nala and rushed the outer gate under a hot fire. They battered it down and while the Gurkhas fired at the loopholes of the bastion, Aylmer and three Sappers rushed across and laid their charges at the main gate, Aylmer lighting the fuse. However it went out, so although with a bullet in the leg and with one hand crushed by a stone, he went back and relit it. The gate was duly blown in but there was no sign of the storming party. Boisragon and a bugler went back to summon them, while Aylmer and Lieutenant Badcock, who had appeared with three more Gurkhas, were left with the survivors of the original party in the courtyard. Beyond the main gate was a tunnel through the massive wall, now filled with defenders. A Gurkha who tried to enter was shot dead, so Aylmer emptied his revolver down the tunnel to clear it and led a charge of Sappers and Gurkhas to the far end. The little party lost several men killed but they held their position until the storming party arrived and the fort was taken. Both Nagar and Hunza now submitted and a treaty was signed which was never broken. Aylmer and Boisragon won VCs, while two Sappers, Hazara Singh and Abdullah Khan, and several Gurkhas, won IOMs.

Aylmer then crowned his reputation as a military engineer by replacing the low-level bridges over the rivers Hunza, Yasin and Indus with suspension bridges before the rivers rose with the snow-melt in the summer. The passes being closed in the winter, no supplies were available, but he found some bundles of telegraph wire at Gilgit and Bunji and fashioned cables from them, while fir trees from the mountains provided the uprights. In describing this work, he wrote: "Without Naik Kala Singh of my company, I could not possibly have got through the bridging work. He was the ablest and most ingenious man in the Corps. Once I had chosen a site, made the calculations and started the work, I could leave him to finish any suspension bridge I had to make."

The following year, in an expedition commanded by Major General Sir William Lockhart, orders had been given to blow one of two towers. This was done most efficiently in the orthodox manner with a small charge of gunpowder. There was a gentle 'poof' and the tower subsided. The General, however, was furious. "That's no good," he burst out. "The tribesmen are all watching from miles around." Turning to Aylmer, he ordered him to blow up the tower 'properly'. "I took the hint," wrote Aylmer later, "and used a whole box of guncotton. A perfectly gorgeous explosion followed, and I am glad to say that none of the onlookers were killed, though there were some narrow escapes. Sir William was delighted."

Within the next few years there was another famous episode in which the guardians of the northern frontier were engaged. In 1895 an insurrection in Chitral led to the British force there of some 400 men being besieged in Chitral Fort. It was a famous siege, but for the Bengal Sappers the interest was in the forces sent to its relief. The first was from Gilgit and consisted of Lieutenant Fowler, Jemadar Lal Khan and nineteen Bengal Sappers. They crossed the 12,000ft Shandur Pass in February in heavy snow and joined Lieutenant Edwardes and 42 men of the Kashmir Rifles at Bunji in northern Chitral. The combined force marched south but were ambushed by a large force of Chitralis in a defile, so retreated to the nearby village of Reshan where they fortified a group of houses. Here they held out against repeated attacks for a week, Fowler leading a successful sortie, but their effective strength dwindled to 34. On the eighth day, Fowler and Edwardes, tricked by an offer of a truce, were captured, and the garrison after a stout resistance was overwhelmed. Twelve Sappers were killed including the redoubtable Naik Kala Singh. Fowler, Jemadar Lal Khan and seven Sappers, of whom three were wounded, were taken prisoner as well as Edwardes and a number of Kashmiris. They were released two months later, both Fowler and Edwardes being awarded DSOs, and Nabi Baksh and Chanda Singh IOMs. Naik Kala Singh would have got an IOM if he had survived. It was on this same campaign that Aylmer, still in command of 4 Field Company, saved the life of a soldier washed away on an overturned raft. Such action reinforced his reputation as a leader and enhanced the esteem in which he was held by the men he commanded.

THE NORTH-WEST FRONTIER IN THE 19TH CENTURY

The great problem on the North-West Frontier, which was never to be solved, was how to deal with the numerous Pathan tribes who inhabited both sides of the boundary between India and Afghanistan. These tribes were united only by a common religion and a common language. Their main groups were Mohmands and Yusufzais north of Peshawar, Afridis astride and south of the Khyber Pass, and further south Mahsuds and Wazirs. But these groupings were split into many sub-groups and their savage culture led to innumerable inter-clan and inter-family feuds. However, they shared a common interest in plunder and the murder of infidels, particularly if there were weapons to be obtained. When the British first reached the frontier they imagined that railways, roads, hospitals, schools, fair justice and good government would change this attitude. It was an illusion. In the next hundred years there was to be little change in Pathan activities. For part of the year they cultivated their crops and fruit trees, and the remainder of the time was spent in fighting each other, or preferably raiding into India.

In due course the British established an 'administrative boundary' inside which taxes were paid and civil administration flourished. Beyond this were the tribal territories and in 1894 an international boundary in the hills was agreed with Afghanistan and demarcated over the next few years. Many miles of rocky hills studded by the stone villages of the tribesmen lay on the Indian side between these two boundaries.

One of the first Pathan raids encountered by the British was in 1850 when a force of a thousand Afridis attacked a party from the 2nd Company who were building a cart-track through a pass near Kohat. Eight sappers were killed. A punitive brigade, which included the 2nd Company, was sent to the area from Peshawar and, after some stiff fighting, destroyed the villages from which the marauders had come. As the Pathans had no intention of ceasing their raids, this pattern was followed on some part of the frontier nearly every year for the next fifty years, and indeed sometimes twice a year. The Bengal Sappers supported the majority of these actions, all the companies from the 1st to the 8th being involved at one time or another. At first villages were burnt and destroyed, but this incurred the wrath of the Commander-in-Chief at the time, Sir Charles Napier, who regarded this as war on women and children. Consequently destruction

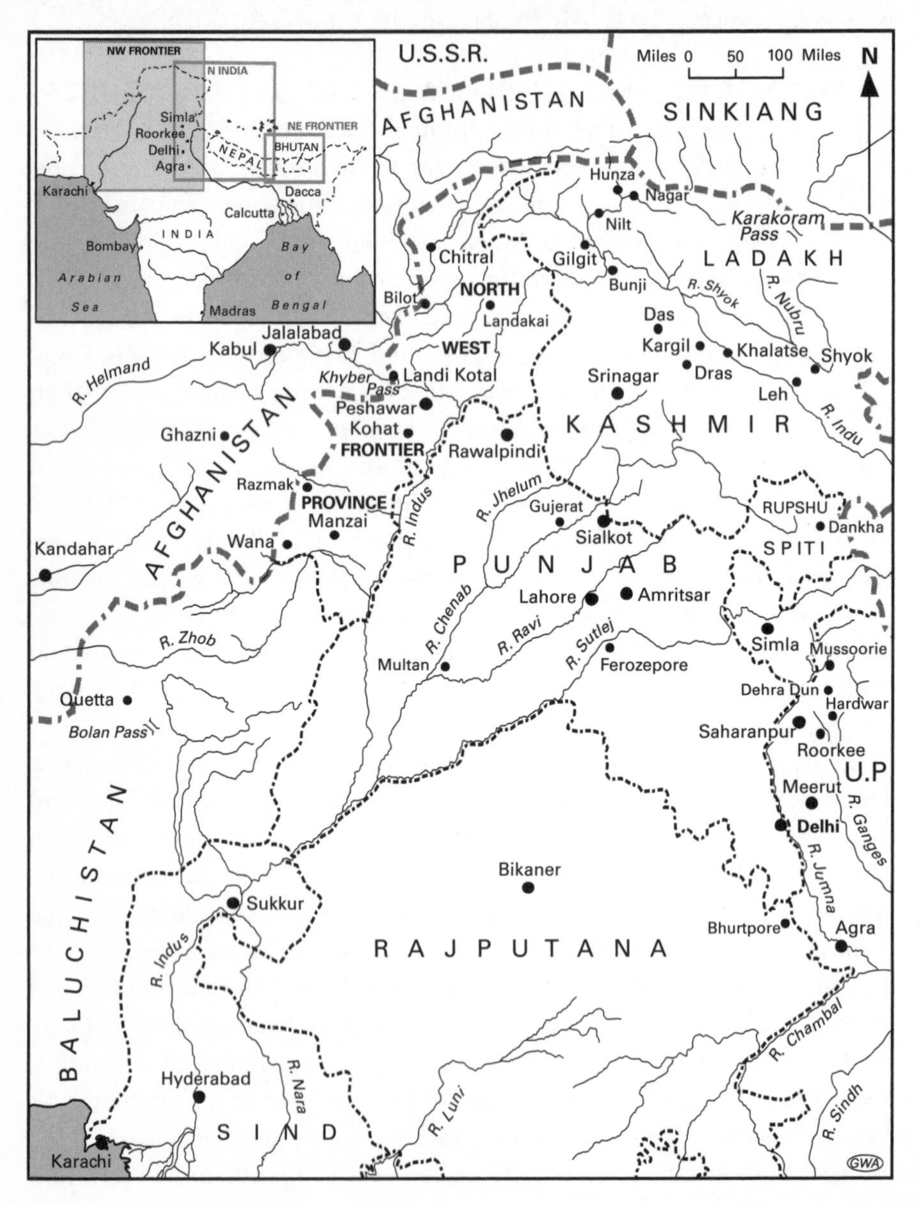

only of the towers, which formed a feature of the larger houses in each village, became customary. Apparently these towers were not so much fortifications as places where the owners could rest without fear of having their throats cut while asleep. In the early years only small parties of Sappers accompanied these columns, their task to blow up the towers and sometimes help with the water supply.

However, as expeditions grew larger and wilder areas were penetrated, more effort was required to improve the tracks, to bridge rivers and to provide larger quantities of water. Moreover, the tribesmen began to obtain modern weapons, and more elaborate forts and picquet defences had to be built. Hence more Sappers were needed. A typical example was in the Black Mountain expedition in 1868, when the best part of a Division was deployed and many miles of mule tracks had to be made in the steep hills in order to reach the main villages.

In 1877 General Sir Bindon Blood, at that time a Captain, saw active service for the first time when he commanded two companies of Bengal Sappers in the Jowaki Afridi campaign. They formed part of a strong brigade sent on a punitive expedition with the aim of taking the Jowaki's chief village which they found empty except for a young woman who had been left behind in charge of her elderly grandparents. Bindon Blood was ordered to look after her and found her in a state of alarm as she had been told that the British were 'a bad lot'! "However it was soon all right", he reported, "and when I sent her off in a 'dooly' in a day or two, she wept floods of tears and wanted to stay as one of my domestics, in what capacity she did not explain! I noticed that she was quite a nice-looking woman". There were, however, some more warlike activities to occupy him when it was decided to march through the hills to Kohat. Next day they halted in a valley with several villages, all walled and fitted with some very picturesque towers, which they were ordered to destroy.

In September 1879 Major Edward Thackeray, who had won the VC during the Mutiny, was selected to command the Bengal Sappers in Afghanistan during what became known as the Second Afghan War. For the next three months he was in almost continuous action, not a day passing without skirmishing or reprisal actions against local villages. Early in December, while General Roberts was besieged in Kabul invested closely by 100,000 Afghans, Thackeray was putting up a gallant defence himself against some 3,000 of the enemy in a small post at Jagdalak Kotal. He had only two companies of the Bengal Sappers, armed with carbines, one company of Bengal Native Infantry and twelve troopers of the 10th Bengal Cavalry. The Afghans attacked on 23rd December and poured in a heavy fire from all sides, but the little garrison showed such courage and fired so accurately that they held out for many hours and were only relieved after dark. Thackeray was severely wounded while standing exposed, the better to give his orders, and was eventually sent back to India, narrowly escaping the amputation of his arm. After leave in England he served as Commandant of the Bengal Sappers for seven years.

It would be tedious to mention all the many operations, exciting though they were for those who took part in them, for they had much similarity, but two more are certainly worthy of note. The first of these was the attack on Chitral Fort, already mentioned. This famous episode inspired the assembly, at Peshawar, of a Chitral Relief Force of divisional strength, which included the 1st, 4th and 6th Companies of the Bengal Sappers. Brigadier-General Bindon Blood, lately Commandant at Roorkee, was the Chief-of-Staff. Feint attacks being made on two other passes, the strongly-held Malakand Pass was forced on 3rd April, and the enemy were dispersed in a battle the following day. The fort at Chakdarra was then seized and, to speed the advance, some remarkable cantilever and suspension bridges were built over the Panjkora and Chitral rivers, Captain Aylmer again playing a prominent role. A trestle bridge, built by the 4th and 6th companies over the Swat river at Chakdarra in seven days, was no less than 1350 feet long. The steady advance of the main force alarmed the insurgents who began to disperse, and a force from Gilgit, under Lieutenant-Colonel Kelly, fought its way through to Chitral from the north and relieved the garrison.

In 1897 there was a good deal of unrest along the frontier, and in July some of the tribes north of Peshawar suddenly launched a series of violent night attacks on the brigade which was guarding the Malakand Pass. The attacks were repulsed, and it was decided to form a Malakand Field Force of divisional strength to enter the affected areas and restore order. Its commander was the newly-promoted Major General Sir Bindon Blood, and the campaign was to become unusually well-known because the young Winston Churchill accompanied it as a war correspondent and subsequently wrote a book about it. He wrote: "Sir Bindon was a striking figure in these savage mountains ... He liked these wild tribesmen and understood the way to talk to them ... He regarded the attempted stealing of the Crown Jewels from the Tower of London by his famous ancestor, Colonel Blood, in 1671 (possibly on behalf of the King) as the most glorious event in his family history, and in consequence he had warm sympathy with the Pathan tribes on the Indian frontier, all of whom would have completely understood the event in all its bearings, and would have bestowed unstinted and discriminating applause on all parties..... He had one personal ordeal in this campaign. A fanatic, approaching in a delegation, whipped out a knife and rushed on him from about eight yards. Sir Bindon, mounted upon his horse, drew his revolver, which most of us thought on a General of Division was merely a token weapon, and shot his assailant dead at two yards." It is easy to imagine how delighted everyone in the Field Force was at such an event.

In August the Malakand Field Force assembled in Malakand and Chakdarra and marching into Swat defeated the Swati insurgents at Landakai. The force was then ordered to go West into Bajaur where a large clan of the Mohmands had been prominent in causing trouble. A punitive sortie into a hostile valley by a part of the Force came under pressure during the withdrawal. A small party, which included the Brigade commander, Brigadier Jeffreys, some mountain guns, a few men of the Buffs and about 50 Bengal Sappers from the 4th Company, were cut off and, darkness falling, the Brigadier decided to hole up for the night on the edge of the village of Bilot. The Sappers with their two subalterns, Watson and Colvin, did what they could to form a perimeter round the guns, which came into action. Three companies of the 35th Sikhs were supposed to join them but did not appear. The party was soon attacked by hundreds of tribesmen, and Watson led some of the Buffs to drive off the enemy firing from behind a nearby wall. He was shot in the thigh and had to fall back, but then led a second attempt and was hit twice again. The mountain guns fired point-blank into the village, which was soon on fire. Colvin now led a party of eight Sappers to a house from which the dangerous wall could be enfiladed and, climbing on to a roof, succeeded in driving off the enemy. Returning to the gun area he found that he and a Gunner officer, Wynter, were the only unwounded officers. The Gunners with great spirit continued to fire sporadically at anything they could see in the dark, but before long Wynter was shot through both legs, leaving Colvin on his own. The sound of the firing was clearly heard at Brigade HQ further down the valley and, realising that there was a crisis, the risk was taken of sending out a relief force in the dark. In the early hours this force successfully relieved the beleaguered party. Watson and Colvin were both awarded VCs, and two Bengal Sappers, Havildar Mian Khan and Naik Natha Singh were awarded IOMs.

The Field Force stayed in this area for a month destroying towers and hostile villages. The Mohmands made a final massed attack on its camp and were beaten off with heavy loss. After this they accepted defeat, peace terms were arranged and, at a great jirga, the tribesmen handed in hundreds of rifles. During this procedure a curious incident occurred. Before destroying a tower in a captured village, the Sappers found, in an adjacent house, a woman who had just given birth to a child. They carried her out on her bed to a place of safety before destroying the tower and burning the village. At the great jirga, a fine old warrior and his stalwart son asked to see the "Captain Sahib of the Suffers and Miners" who had destroyed his village. When Captain Stockley appeared, the old warrior salaamed profoundly and thanked him for saving his wife and son. Out of gratitude he had brought with him his eldest son and begged that he might be enlisted in the Bengal Sappers, and so he was.

Sir Bindon Blood now moved rapidly to the East and invaded the Buner valleys, for the Buners had been supporting the insurrection, and brought them under British control. This completed the Field Force's mission. Further south there had been some very severe fighting with the Afridis south-west of Peshawar and they had not submitted until many of their crops and villages had been destroyed. By 1898 order had been restored and the Khyber Pass re-opened, but it had become clear to everyone that punitive actions were hardly the best method of winning the hearts and minds of the Pathans.

NWF ACTIONS IN THE 20TH CENTURY

The British still felt that it was necessary to defend India against the perceived threat of Russian expansion, and to extend the benefits of good administration to the Afghan border. They now decided that this could best be done by establishing forts in tribal territory and gradually extending railways and tracks to open up the remote valleys. It was a policy which provided plenty of work for the Sappers and Miners. Then, in 1907–8, the Afridis and Mohmands gave trouble and small expeditions were mounted against them. These operations followed the usual pattern, but some notable Sapper officers were involved. In the 1st, 2nd, and 6th Companies were Captains A H Cunningham, later a famous Commandant, J R E Charles, later Chief Royal Engineer, Lieutenants A J G Bird, later E-in-C India, L V Bond, later C-in-C Malaya, and P C S Hobart, later GOC of a famous specialist Tank Division. Apart from these inevitable small operations, there was a lull on the frontier in the early years of the 20th century, a friendly treaty with Afghanistan being signed in 1905.

Throughout World War I the Afghans remained friendly, in spite of overtures from Germany and Turkey, who were hoping to foment trouble which would pin down British forces in India. The British maintained a low profile on the Frontier and the Mahsuds, sensing weakness, took advantage of this in 1917 to force the evacuation of some of the forward posts, notably Wana. When the war ended there was political unrest in India. Britain had started the first moves towards Independence and Indian political parties began to stake their claims. Widespread riots broke out in the Punjab, but were soon brought under control. In 1919, the Amir of Afghanistan was murdered on a hunting trip and one of his sons, Amanullah Khan, seized the throne. Uncertain of the Army's support, he decided on the always popular plan of seizing the fertile vale of Peshawar and advancing the Afghan frontier to the Indus. Thus began the 3rd Afghan War, different from the previous two in that this time it was Afghanistan who was invading India. After a few anxious weeks as troops were assembled, the main Afghan advance through Afridi territory, although enthusiastically supported by the tribesmen, was held and then pushed back into Afghanistan. Large British/Indian forces, including many Sapper and Miner companies, were deployed, but the main engineer tasks were the usual ones of water supply and track construction and nothing of particular interest took place. After two months the excitement was over. However later in the year more serious trouble was to arise in Waziristan further south, and there was some severe fighting with the Mahsuds and Wazirs.

Although the life-style of the Pathans and their methods of fighting remained largely unchanged by World War I, aeroplanes and vehicles were now part of the scene on the British side. The early aeroplanes flew off grass or dirt fields and so presented no Sapper problem, but vehicles were another matter. Instead of pack-animal tracks, Class 10 roads were now required. A railway was to be built from Peshawar up the Khyber Pass to Landi Kotal, roads would be built into the tribal areas south-west of Peshawar, while a circular road would link the forward posts in Waziristan. The first equipment bridges now made their appearance in India. The best was the Inglis bridge, widely used in Europe in the later stages of World War I. The second was the Everall bridge, whose largest pieces could be carried on a camel. It was allegedly designed in case of a need to cross the Helmand River in Afghanistan. This meccano-like bridge was held together by innumerable nuts and bolts, all of which had to be tightened by hand. Though never used in action, it proved a useful tool in bridging camps for teaching the elements of bridge-launching.

A notable bridge was constructed across the Bara River in Afridi territory by Captain WM (Tubby) Broomhall (a famous Bengal Sapper, who later became a Major General) and the 2nd Company. A span of 140 feet was needed, but for class 10 the Inglis bridge could only manage 120 feet. The ingenious solution was adopted of adding 30 foot cantilevers at either end and loading them with concrete, thus reducing the strains at the centre of the 140 foot main span and enabling it to be up-graded.

Another Bengal Sapper who distinguished himself at this stage was Lieutenant M C A Henniker (later Brigadier Sir Mark Henniker). In 1933 he was engaged on roadmaking in Mohmand territory with the 2nd Company. Although the first bulldozer seen in India, and the first grader, made their appearance, it was clear that the work would not be finished before the winter. Now many Sapper officers had a smattering of Pushtu, but 'Honker' Henniker was fluent. His red hair and red moustache gave him prestige among the Pathans, and he did not hesitate to enter the local villages, uncertain though his reception might be, and to negotiate with the headmen to provide labourers. His confidence and courage paid off and he eventually built up a work force of some 2,000 Pathans and the job was finished on time.

The last drama on the frontier before World War II was in 1937 when a firebrand called the Fakir of Ipi stirred up trouble with the Mahsuds in Waziristan. Extensive operations were launched to restore order and try to capture the Fakir but he fled into Afghanistan. Bengal Sapper companies involved were 2nd Company, commanded by Captain G C Clark, the 3rd Company, commanded by no less than Major W F Hasted (later Chief Engineer 14th Army) and the 5th Company, commanded by Major W L D Veitch (later Engineer-in-Chief of the Pakistan Army).

LIFE ON THE NW FRONTIER BEFORE WORLD WAR II

There is no doubt that many young men enjoyed frontier life. It was professionally interesting, often arduous and occasionally dangerous. The Pathans are a charismatic race and their dark and cruel side was easily disregarded. Here are the impressions of a young Bengal Sapper officer newly out from England being posted to Wana in Waziristan in 1938:

"I left Roorkee by train in June, and after many hours and several changes found myself crossing a stony plain in a slow train aptly known as 'the heat-stroke express'. In spite of a hundred-weight block of ice placed on the floor of the carriage by some kindly station official, it was desperately hot, and arrival at Manzai at the foot of the hills and the edge of tribal territory, was a blessed relief. From here a road wound up through the hills to Wana on the Afghan border, but this road was only safe to use once a week, when a well-defended convoy made the 60-mile trip. I had to wait five days in Manzai for the next convoy and was made welcome in the battalion Mess of the 1st/13th Frontier Force Rifles, whose CO was Colonel Rob Lockhart, a famous soldier who was later C-in-C of the Pakistan Army.

My first night, there was a drama in the Mess after dinner, a Mahsud raid being reported. It was the first time I had seen a first-class unit in action. The Colonel called his officers together and, having explained the situation, quietly gave out his orders. "John, you take your company to ——, which is their probable goal, Clive you take yours round to —— and see if you can get on top of —— before first light and intercept them on the way back." Both officers left at once and an hour later were on their way. Not wishing to be left out I naively asked if there was any job for a Sapper. The Colonel was a kindly man. "Have you got any explosives with you?" "Well, er, no Sir." "Perhaps another time" he said with a smile.

The next day I heard that I was the only officer going up to Wana and so would be commander of the next convoy. This sounded exciting, particularly when other subalterns filled me in with details of how the convoy had been successfully ambushed by the Wazirs the year before in a three-mile gorge called the Shahur Tangi. It had been a very skilful ambush, the convoy being brought to a halt by an apparently innocent string of camels coming the other way. Seven British officers and a number of vehicle drivers had been killed, and it was many hours before a relief force rescued the survivors. So it was exciting to set off in charge of fifty lorries and three armoured cars with troops in support on some of the hills, and I scanned the high ground for signs of the enemy with great enthusiasm. Of course everyone, bar the commander, knew their jobs well. Nothing happened and we duly climbed up onto the Wana plain, high up in the hills, where a large notice greeted us:

WELCOME TO WANA!
THE LARGEST MONASTERY IN THE WORLD!
PARADISE FOR BACHELORS!
SANCTUARY FOR THE MARRIED!

Wana, originally a small mud fort, was now a brigade camp with its own water and electricity supply, and surrounded by two barbed wire fences lit by perimeter lights. Originally a tented camp, it was now in the throes of a development project. As contractors would not work in this area, three field companies, one from each Group, were building the new accommodation using hollow concrete blocks manufactured on site. The largest of the many different buildings were two-storey barrack blocks with corrugated-iron roofs. It was a popular task, giving the jawans a chance to practice their trade skills. The Brigadier was 'Piggy' Heath, who was wise, popular and a good mixer. In spite of a damaged left arm, he often turned out to play polo with the subalterns. Fate was later to deal him a very unkind hand in Malaya. Several other officers there were to have outstanding careers. Among the Sappers, John Bowring, a Bombay Sapper, would become Engineer-in-Chief. Tom Bostock, a Madras Sapper who was Master of the Hunt, was perhaps the most outstanding officer in the garrison and would surely have gone far if he had not been drowned trying to save one of his men who had fallen into the treacherous Kabul River.

There were hockey and football pitches inside the camp and a flat area of plain outside the western perimeter served as parade ground, polo field and landing strip. For officers, nearly all of whom had chargers, a main activity was the Wana Hunt. This Hunt, or more accurately Drag, took place every Sunday. First a platoon picquet would be established on a nearby hill and several armoured cars would spread out across the plain. A mounted officer with the drag would then set off and, after a pause, the smartly-dressed Hunt would emerge from one of the gates, the hounds would be put on the trail and off everyone would go. There were of course no fences, but there were plenty of deep ditches and small nullahs to jump over. Care was taken to vary the areas 'hunted' and, in spite of the regularity of the occasion, it was difficult for the tribesmen to interfere, although they tried to do so on one occasion during WWII. Occasional point-to-point races provided variety.

The weather was generally excellent, although cold in the evening. The Sappers and Gunners shared a cheerful Mess, and after dinner, while some retired to their rooms to study, others, clad in sheepskin coats, played poker under the stars at a pentagonal table placed outside the Mess. It was in many ways a very pleasant life for a bachelor. However, a feeling of claustrophobia could set in and the chance to 'go out on column' every now and then was relished. In due course I went on two or three 'columns'. These consisted of two battalions of Infantry (one being left to guard the camp), a Mountain Artillery battery and usually only one or two platoons of Sappers and Miners. The column sometimes went along a track, such as that to Razmak further north, and sometimes went across country. In the summer it was often extremely hot as the rocky landscape reflected the heat and marching on foot across the hilly and broken ground was extremely exhausting. Bar a few shots into the camp at night, the tribesmen kept a low profile in my year and so there was no chance to blow up any towers. Nevertheless there were some useful lessons to be learned. The goal for each day's march was a stream of some sort and I quickly learnt how vital water was for both men and animals. The camp routine of digging-in and dusk and dawn 'stand-to' was another lesson. Understanding the arduous picqueting technique employed by the Infantry and Gunners to protect the column on the march was a third. All were to be useful on the other side of India three years later."

THE NORTH-WEST FRONTIER IN WORLD WAR II

In World War II India was at full stretch supplying forces for action against the Germans and Italians to the West and against the Japanese to the East. On the North-West Frontier a belt of modern defences, concrete pill-boxes and anti-tank obstacles, was constructed in 1940–1 to obstruct any aggressor who might attempt a mechanised invasion, although it was not too clear until mid-1941, whether the invader was expected to be German or Russian. This work, subsequent generous subsidies and a passive policy, kept the Frontier quiet right up to the upheaval of Independence in 1947.

6 WORLD WAR II

PREPARATION FOR WAR

In 1939 the Indian Engineers formed but a small proportion of the Army in India. They had no transportation or survey units and virtually no Lines of Communication units. They had little or no bridging equipment, no mines or mine detectors and, with the exception of a few bulldozers and compressors, very little mechanical equipment. Indeed, so urgently were they in need of re-equipping that the Chatfield Committee, which met in 1938–9, considered the possibility of making funds available for this purpose by reducing them to one Corps. Finally the Committee recommended a reduction to two Groups, but fortunately this was not carried out because, only a few years later, the three existing Groups had to be reinforced by the formation of three more Groups at Lahore and others at Jullunder, Sialkot and Deolali. All these Groups were soon fully occupied in recruiting and training personnel for Engineer units of every type in the field. In the Bengal Sappers, for example, there were only five field companies and a few smaller units, all with emphasis on the North-West frontier, immediately before the war, a total strength of about 3,400 which rose to 23,850 by 1944.

War was declared on 3rd September 1939 and soon afterwards 4 Field Company, stationed at Roorkee, received orders to mobilize. This meant a change from four sections to three and for the mules and chargers to be returned to the Remount Depot. The following month the Company left Roorkee by rail, bound for Bombay and Egypt to join 4 Division but before they left they were inspected by the local District Commander, none other than Major General (later Field Marshal) Auchinleck, under whom they were destined to see much service. The garlands and best wishes of Roorkee went with them. It was the first of many farewells. For many the Indian Ocean offered an alarming experience. The 'lighted villages that floated on the sea' produced much sea-sickness, while the shortage of fresh water was to Indian troops a special hardship.

Roorkee was slow to react to the threat of war; indeed in 1939 the normal round of daily work had continued everywhere as if no clouds were gathering on the western horizon. The Commanding Officer of the Training Battalion went on parade early in the morning but never went back to the office after lunch. Training a recruit in peacetime took two years, covering drill and musketry, then fieldworks and finally a trade. Recruit parties came under an experienced Indian NCO and several parties were supervised by a Jemadar or a Subadar, so there was really not much for a British officer to do. Though the Club had closed in May, Roorkee still had a cinema but there were few parties. The Adjutant's Newsletter, written on the very day that war was declared, announced that "We have received no warning orders of any impending mobilization and it is not clear what effort the Bengal Corps will be expected to produce in any war". In actual fact all leave had been stopped and all ranks had been recalled, but life continued much as before for some time. In December a Sapper team had reached the final of the Meerut Polo Tournament and five officers had gone to Gulmarg in Kashmir for skiing. For a long time shikar continued, the jheels remained popular and weekend leaves were frequent. The war on paper grew fiercer than ever and everyone considered themselves very busy and overworked.

George Pearson reported that MT training was pursued 'with vigour and a great deal of smoke'. The most up-to-date types of vehicles being unavailable, fabulous prices were paid to contractors to supply what they could. As a result, an exciting circus of ancient buses, old private cars and a few lorries were gathered together, and these, puffing and shaking, made disjointed progress around the MT School's training area. Despite all the shortages, Roorkee began to assemble the Divisional Engineer units for 8th Indian Division in Iraq. In the following May, Aitken Lawrie was told to raise 69 Field Company and take it to join the Division. His first action, after indenting for stores, was to draw tents from the quartermaster and make a tented camp under the trees beside the canal so that the men would get used to living, washing and cooking under field conditions. For three months they were madly busy, but he managed to get everyone away on ten days leave before leaving Roorkee in early September 1941.

After a slow start Roorkee steadily went onto a war footing. One of the larger bungalows was renovated and became an additional Officers' Mess, the polo ground was converted into hockey and football pitches and the New Year's Parade on 1st January 1941 saw all officers on foot for the first time and men in field service dress in place of the former tunic, knickerbockers and blue hose-tops. It would have been difficult for any pre-war Sapper to recognise the Roorkee of 1941. By this time Colonel Obbard was Commandant, having taken over from Colonel Lee in August 1940. Indian officers under training at the Thomason College were withdrawn on the outbreak of war and the Academy at Dehra Dun became the sole means of normal entry for Indians to the King's Commissioned ranks of the Indian Engineers until the Engineer Officer Cadet Training Units (OCTUs) were established.

THE WESTERN DESERT, 1940

In Egypt, encamped near the Pyramids, the sappers of 4 Field Company were soon learning the techniques of desert driving. Men who had driven a lorry for the first time a few weeks earlier, now had to pilot their vehicles through the terrifying Cairo traffic and then drive over soft desert sand for further training.

Cairo had not yet felt the full impact of war and one of the features of the Christmas festivities was a big concert in aid of the Red Cross, attended by leaders of Egyptian society. At this, some Pathans of 4 Field Company performed with great enthusiasm what the programme described as "*Danses Indiennese-Khattak des Bengalis*"!

Italy entered the war in June 1940, and on 9th December 1940 the Western Desert force, in a brilliant encircling movement, surprised the sprawling Italian position south of Sidi Barrani just inside the Egyptian border. It was the first British land victory of the war. As soon as the Italian camps were entered 4 Field Company sappers began to collect enemy lorries and drive them to the rear, piled high with equipment and stores. They were also given the task of guarding some four thousand Italian prisoners who were only too glad to be out of danger and had not the least inclination to escape. Italian officers helped them by indicating the positions of mines and some of them must have been sorry to exchange their deep dug-outs for the stark realities of a prisoner-of-war cage, for the furniture, fittings and stores of wine and food were luxurious and profuse.

DEFEAT OF THE ITALIANS IN ERITREA, 1940

By the end of 1940, 5 Indian Division, with 2 Field Company plus 6 and 8 Army Troops, were in the Sudan. Their voyage from Bombay had not been without incident as Lieutenant Arjan Singh discovered. "I was acting as the Quartermaster and had to arrange for many types of kitchen in the restricted space available in a ship not specially built for Indian troops, for in those days Hindus, Mussalmans, Sikhs, Madrassis, Bengalis and Mahrattas were each entitled to have a separate kitchen. The ship's Chief Officer, however, had never heard of any such arrangement. 'There's the galley.' said he. 'Get on with it.' But after I had told him that I myself was an ex-sailor, he was persuaded to make certain alterations and, as it was impossible to have separate kitchens for every caste in each unit, it was decided that all cooking should be done in combined central community kitchens." It was not till much later in the war that such barriers were broken down in all units.

2 Field Company were soon working on ford crossings of the River Atbara, a tributary of the Nile, while 8 Army Troops constructed a boat bridge across the river and 6 Army Troops Company had begun to improve communications in the area, including five hundred yards of causeway over soft sand. On entering Eritrea from Sudan, several battles developed and a road block, formed by huge masses of rock blown from the overhanging hills, made two hundred yards of road impassable to wheel traffic: the whole of 2 Field Company worked to clear this block, despite sniping and a dive bombing attack.

By January 1941, 4 Division, having been transferred from the Western Desert, was also moving into Eritrea and the sappers of 4 Field Company were blasting rock and clearing a gorge of anti-tank mines. This was followed by making tracks up a rough and thorny hillside to gain a hold on Mount Cochen, 2,000 ft above Agordat. Once the summit was reached Agordat fell. The way to Keren now seemed open but the approach gorge was blocked by hundreds of tons of rock, covered by fire from the grim and forbidding mountains on either side. This was to be the scene of the final and most determined resistance by the Italian forces in Eritrea. On 10th February 1941 a divisional attack was launched against Keren. It failed and 4 Field Company suffered severe casualties, including the loss of a Jemadar.

An extract from the diary of Captain David of 4 Field Company illustrates the confused nature of the bitter battle:

"We were on the north side of the gorge and 3/1 Punjab Regiment were on Cameron Ridge with 1/6 Rajputana Rifles and were to take and hold a feature called Brig's Peak a thousand yards further on. Captain Penny, an officer from the CRE's staff, accompanied us and was a great help. There was a tremendous barrage for the attack and by 2100hrs we had completed a track of sorts but were then ordered to take over part of the line. We spent most of the night digging positions and wiring, and trying to get some sleep through rain, cold and intermittent firing.

We were told in the morning to stay where we were and to continue work digging in the Punjabi companies and wiring their positions, as well as making a new way up. It was a very hot day and there was much firing, including an accurate enemy 4 inch mortar, and we had two sappers killed and several wounded. The enemy was seen massing for a counter-attack and as the Punjabi companies were very much under strength, two other companies came to help. We were kept up in the line with one Bren gun while the rest of the company was in reserve.

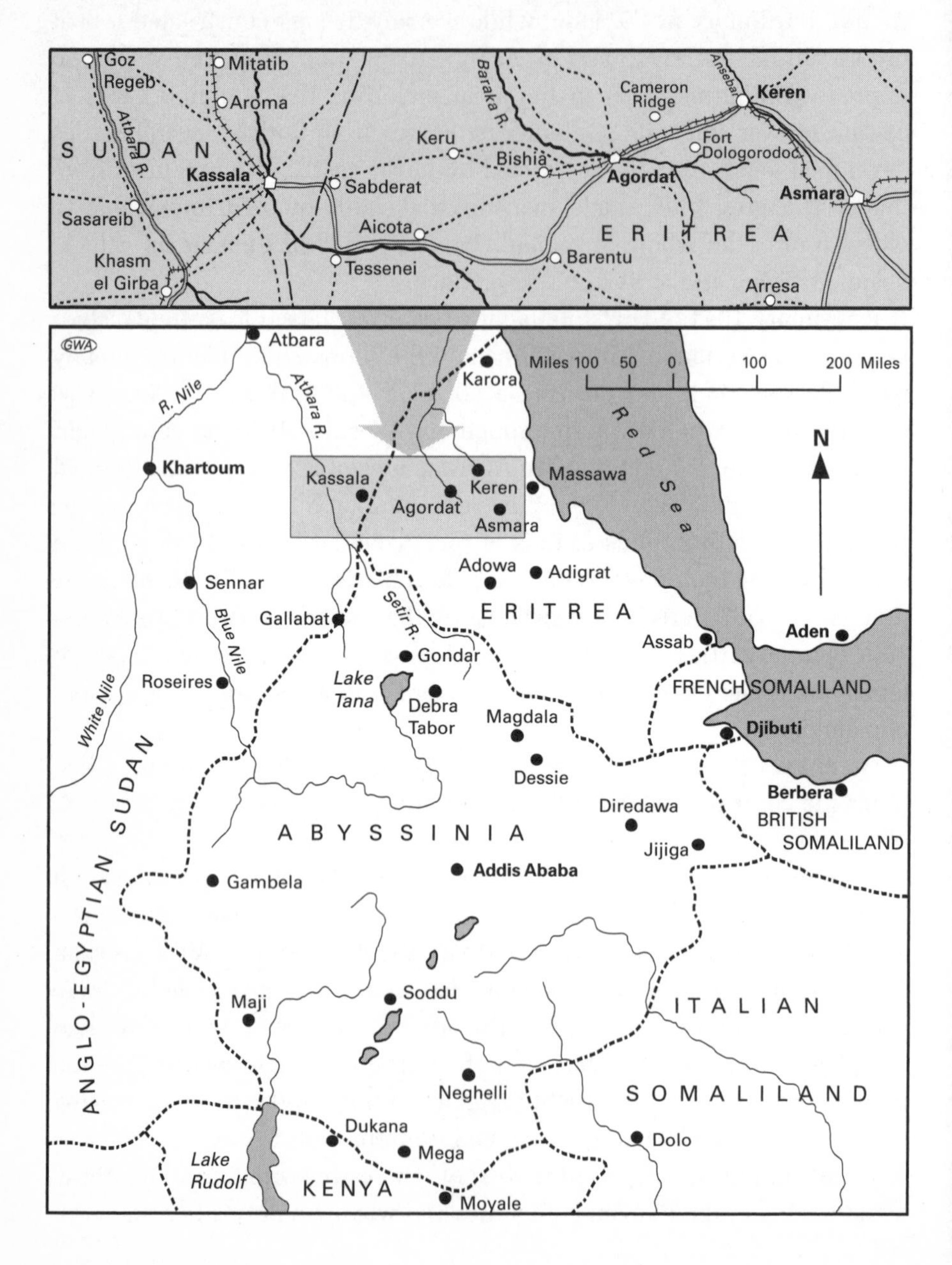

After 2230hrs sleep was impossible, shells from a pack battery and mortars bursting very near us. I was just below Battalion HQ and heard that A Company was down to twenty men and being heavily attacked. In the mortar and grenade attack that followed, I was hit in the leg and then in the eye and arm. I saw Penny, blinded and being led away. Eventually I found our Subedar with about twenty men holding part of the line around the Rajputana Rifles HQ and I stayed with them until we were ordered to withdraw." The Company had helped man the crest which for thirty-six hours was held against repeated Italian attacks. Not until the early hours of 12th February was the remnant of the Battalion forced back to Cameron Ridge.

Meanwhile 5 Division, with 2 Field Company, attacked Fort Dologorodoc on the south side of the Keren gorge. A detachment of 2 Field Company went to the aid of the infantry and Jemadar Kirat Singh led a bayonet charge to secure a machine gun post. For his heroism, he was awarded the Indian Order of Merit (IOM), the first decoration to be won by a Bengal Sapper in this war.

The fort was taken but it proved impossible to remove the road blocks below until a further mountain position could be taken. For the first time 2 and 5 Field Companies met as, in turn with other sappers, they laboured under fire, toiling day and night with picks and shovels and even hands to achieve the final clearance. Their work was typical of all the Sapper and Miner units in which officers and men constantly risked death or disablement as they formed the spear-head of every advance; and yet, unlike the other arms, they were seldom able to retaliate. No duty could demand greater courage.

On 26th February 1941 tanks and the rest of the column got through to Keren and were soon down the road to Asmara. 2 Field Company, following the broken Italian army, cleared road blocks and repaired road retaining walls. By April 1941, 4 Division and 4 Field Company were back in Egypt to help stem a sudden German advance. For some months the other units remained in Eritrea.

Back in the Western Desert the tide of Wavell's 1940 advance had ebbed fast. German tanks had appeared around Benghazi and were moving rapidly east. The threat posed by such fast moving armour can be illustrated by the fate of one Bengal unit, 35 Field Company. Such was the speed of the enemy tanks that their widespread forward unit was surrounded; and only by good fortune did two officers, on reconnaissance, manage to find a stranded lorry and avoid capture, whilst the remainder of the Company began a long period of captivity until the end of the war. A few days later Tobruk was also surrounded and General Neame, a former Bengal Sapper, then commanding Western Desert Force, was captured.

PAIFORCE, 1941–1942

By 1941 the oilfields of the Middle East were being menaced from within. Teheran had long been the base of German propaganda in the Middle East, whilst Baghdad simmered with intrigue against British interests. In April 1941 Rashid Ali, backed by four generals, overthrew the Iraqi government. His hostility expressed itself in an attack on the RAF airfield at Habbaniya, west of Baghdad, the sole defenders on the ground being 1,200 RAF Levies, comprising loyal Arabs, Kurds and Assyrians, later reinforced by a British battalion flown in from Basra. Luckily Colonel O L Roberts (later General Sir Ouvry Roberts), an ex-Bengal Sapper and Miner, was present and organised a stout defence for which he was later awarded the DSO. Though heavily outnumbered, bombed and machine-gunned by the Iraqi Air Force and shelled by the Iraqi Army, they held firm, ultimately defeating the enemy and thus saving Iraq and perhaps the whole position in the Middle East. Reinforcements were sent in to Iraq including no less than six Bengal Sapper units whose main job was to construct defences against any threat to the oilfields, a threat that became all the greater after Germany declared war on Russia in June 1941 and a gigantic pincer movement started to develop. Amongst these reinforcements was 41 Field Park Company, commanded by Major Mangat Rai: "We remained in the Basra area for the first few weeks; this being a relatively undeveloped country, there was much engineering work to be done. The unit was fully occupied with a miscellany of jobs at the base, the most important of which was the laying of a piped water system for Army camps. Outside Basra we were tasked with the repair of the railway line to Ur. The form the sabotage had taken was the removal of sleepers and the destruction of culverts. The repair party began work at the Basra end and moved up the line with a train following close behind. Work continued throughout the day under a blistering sun which reached 124 degrees in the shade, but the party lived in comfort at night for the train was equipped with showers and electric fans. As the job took longer than expected the party ran short of food. More food was then dropped from the air and this is probably one of the earliest instances of supply-dropping in the war."

The main oil pipelines ran from Kirkuk, north of Baghdad, westward through Syria to Tripoli and Haifa on the Mediterranean coast. The main task for 41 Field Park Company was to maintain a water supply along the chain of pumping stations. This included lifting water from the River Euphrates. Soon, however, they were back on Iraq's eastern mountain border with Persia, in support of Divisional activities. Here was a mountainous road with steep gradients on either side which had to be defended against a clearly developing German threat.

About the same time 5 Field Company, having moved from Eritrea, was busy at Basra replacing the bridge across the Shatt-el Arab which had been burnt by the retreating troops of Rashid Ali. Built in two sections on either side of Coal Island, the bridge was the second longest boat bridge in the world at that time and enabled one thousand vehicles to cross each day, where previously only 80 could be ferried. Later the bridge took vast quantities of petrol en route for Russia.

Other Bengal Sapper units had come to Iraq in September 1941. As they drove to the northern frontiers of Iraq and Persia, the men found sand, desolate and unbroken, stretching for mile upon mile, across the desert. Travel by lorry depended on proper engine maintenance as the drivers soon realised during this 500 mile convoy journey. The major task on the frontier was to improve the natural defences around a 5,000ft high Pass in Iraq and a precipitous gorge leading into northern Persia. There the sappers worked day and night, blasting hillsides for pill-boxes, laying tank obstacles across the stony valleys, repairing and improving old roads, building concrete gun emplacements and camouflaging the anti tank defences. Not having any bulldozers, much of the work was carried out by local coolie labour, with the attendant problems of communication and much thieving. However, boredom was perhaps the chief enemy, although by no means the only hardship. Winter in Iraq was the bitterest in living memory and an entry in 1 Field Company's War Diary recorded that "snow started to fall early and continued all day. This was a miserable day for everyone and work was called off at 10am ... The next few days were bitter, being especially hard on those men who had not yet received woollen underclothing. There were 20 degrees of frost one night and great trouble was experienced in keeping the MT vehicles going. Ten coolies died one night of cold. By day the sun shone and melting snow turned roads into a quagmire but work continued, though at a slower pace."

Altogether a vast amount of defensive work occupied the various units until May 1942. The principal enemy was the weather: frost and snow in January, sandflies and sand-storms in April. At all times there was audacious thieving of stores, mainly rifles. One CSM, whilst sleeping, found his greatcoat being drawn off him.

Major Mangat Rai, by this time commanding 5 Field Company, told of their work on field defences north of Baghdad, in intense heat, and the difficulties in controlling a large body of contract labourers of heterogeneous composition: mainly Iraqis, but also including Persians, Kurds, Armenians and Jews. After preparing all the major road and rail bridges in the area for demolition, the Company moved to cooler climes in Persia, where they were camped at 6,000ft, preparing defensive positions on a mountain pass. He reported that: "While there Lieutenant-General Mayne, the Corps Commander, inspected the site and stayed with the unit for a couple of days, living in a caravan which was parked below the Officers' Mess. A small 'ablutions' tent used by officers had been pitched below the Mess, and one morning, while the General was inside, it was pelted with a fusillade of earthen clods thrown from higher up the hill. The whole tent shook. Naturally surprised, the General emerged only to discover that the culprit was the junior subaltern of the unit who, on seeing him, was greatly alarmed. However, the subaltern apologised and explained that he had thought it was a friend of his who was in occupation and the General received his apologies with good humour. Nevertheless, when he went to the tent next morning, he placed his 'brass hat' carefully on the apex."

In September 1942, PAIFORCE – Persia and Iraq Force – was born, principally for work in Iraq but also as a corridor for supplies to Russia. The oilfields had been secured from local sabotage but German armies striding into the Caucasus threatened them as much as Rommel's drive into Egypt. With Stalingrad surrounded, the passes on the northern frontiers became outposts against possible German entry.

Persia and Iraq became a vast training ground for Bengal Sapper units and many others. However when on 21st February 1943 the German armies surrendered at Stalingrad, defence works were no longer needed. Several units moved into Syria and Palestine where the change of scenery was much appreciated. Despite the exodus, several units were left in Iraq to build up supply depots and it was not until May 1943 that the Bengal Sappers were free of Iraq.

MALAYA, 1940–1942

At the end of 1940 the sappers of 3 Field Company and 43 Field Park Company were in Kuala Lumpur turning out standard sets of shuttering for pillboxes. They then moved north to Sungei Patani and began making sets of mobile timber bridges and concrete road blocks, while others were employed constructing huts among rubber trees, creating new roads and footbridges and camouflaging pill boxes. Nevertheless it cannot be said that the main defences were fully prepared against any attack from the north.

On 7th December 1941 the Japanese flood broke loose and their soldiers poured into every creek and every island of the East. A Japanese air attack was made on the airfield at Kota Bahru on the east coast of Malaya and 3 Field Company were ordered south to prepare a demolition belt, but not before a foray was made over the Thailand border to delay any Japanese

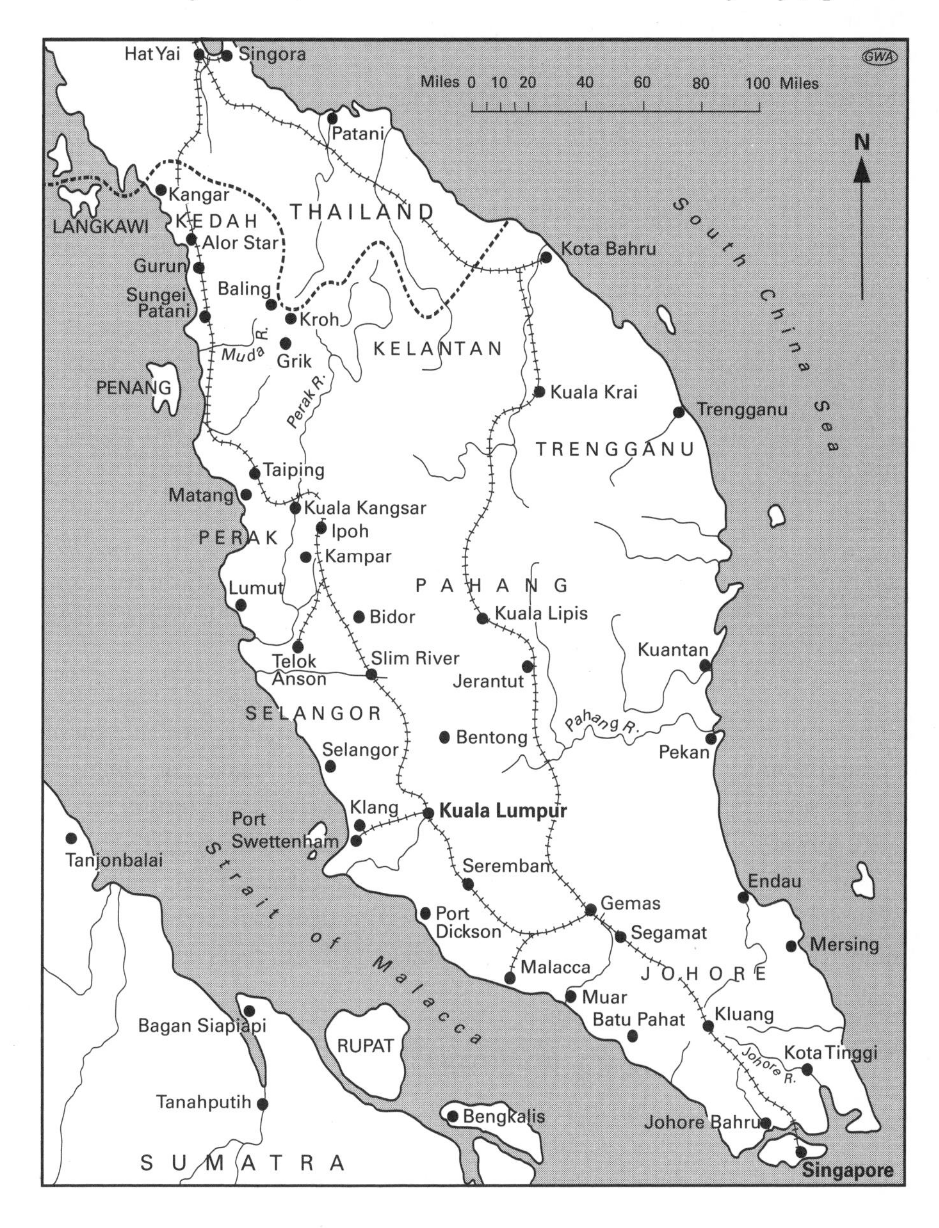

advance. A road column set out, also an armoured train, keeping in touch with the road column by wireless. To guard against derailing and booby-traps, Lieutenant Poyser of 3 Field Company went with the train, lying on the front of the leading truck inspecting the line as the train proceeded and signalling back to the driver. After the train had travelled about ten miles beyond the border it came to a very large girder bridge which Poyser decided to prepare for demolition. Though the work was not completely finished, he heard firing far in the rear and decided to blow the bridge at once, his first attempt failing, but the next succeeded and the bridge was left with two halves precariously interlocked.

On the west coast the main road ran through a vast paddy area and from there south, the country consisted of a large forest of rubber plantations covered by a network of estate roads. A strong position had previously been selected for a demolition belt, but when the British and Indian troops reached it, they were not only very tired but they also lacked the time required to reorganize and defend it successfully against the speed and thrust of the enemy. Within 24 hours the defenders were driven completely from the field. The long retreat had begun.

Clad only in vests and shorts, the Japanese soldiers moved rapidly, almost invisibly. Jungle swamps and rivers did not hinder them and the British and Indian defenders never succeeded in securing control of a situation conditioned by such versatility and daring. On 7th January 1942 the Japanese made deadly use of fifty or so tanks. A losing battle took place on the Slim river and 11 Division practically ceased to exist. It was a fate which most of 3 Field Company sappers shared.

As retreat by the remnants continued towards Singapore, 43 Field Park Company, in Singapore, successfully carried out systematic destruction of materials most likely to assist the enemy. However once the Japanese landed on Singapore Island the remainder of the British and Indian forces were quickly forced to surrender. This was on 15th February 1942.

During the retreat, over three hundred bridges and culverts had been destroyed by the two Bengal companies. But this distinguished record was small consolation for men now condemned to long years as prisoners, their misfortune intensified in captivity.

BURMA WITHDRAWAL, 1942

Back in Roorkee, Major Ian Lyall Grant had been raising a new Field Company destined to go to the Middle East. "After nine months as adju-tant of 2 Training Battalion in Roorkee, I had had my fill of training and was desperate to see some real service. In October 1941 my chance came and I was appointed to raise and command 70 Field Company.

70 Company was to be a three-class unit, that is it would have three platoons one each of Hindus, Sikhs and Mussalmen. As a start I was allotted 16 VCOs and NCOs and about 60 sappers, mostly straight out of the training battalion, and my first preoccupation was to get as good a lot of VCOs and NCOs as possible. My subedar, that key man in an Indian unit, was a large and corpulent Sikh with a grey beard and many, many years' service. He was a nice fellow, shrewd and with a good sense of humour but far too old for active service. When I remonstrated about this I was rebuffed with the remark that an old subedar matched well with a young OC (I was 26, but Roorkee was rather old-fashioned in some respects). However, there were several good NCOs and one outstanding VCO, Jemadar Bachittar Singh, who was to prove a tower of strength.

At first there was only one other British officer to help me. He was a municipal engineer of rather fixed habits and perhaps not ideally suited to the rough and tumble of a field unit. I gave him the difficult task of trying to obtain the extraordinary variety of equipment that a field company was supposed to need in those days. In 1941 this, as a result of many years of peace when field companies were often far from any depot and had to rely on their own resources, was of bewildering variety.

Innumerable indents for equipment had to be prepared and dispatched to various ordnance supply depots. Some stores arrived and a few vehicles, but the vast majority of the indents were returned, marked 'not available'. Equipment was very short in India and it was clear we had a low priority. However there was plenty to do on the stores side. At that time the Middle East was the fount of all battle knowledge and we acted on two recent recommendations. The first advised making a general purpose tool set for each section (there were four sections, each of a corporal and twelve men, in each platoon). Accordingly our carpenters built twelve coffin-like wooden boxes each containing 6 pickaxes, 6 shovels, a crowbar, 2 saws, a sledgehammer, a mallet, some augers and a few other items. They were to prove invaluable. The second piece of advice was that any fool could be uncomfortable, so one should have a well-furnished officers' mess. So we built a folding trestle table, six folding chairs and a beautifully fitted box which held a complete set of china bought in the local bazaar. They were made by our first rate carpenter, Havildar Raj Din, out of some fine old seasoned teak planks found in a training store and we were very proud of them. However, in our case, this turned out to be not such good advice.

Meanwhile I continued to sort out the necessary promotions and appointments in our personnel and was lucky enough to get another exceptional VCO in Jemadar Dharam Singh, a Hindu of warrior caste from the hills of Kumaon. Like Bachittar Singh he was from 3 Field Company, in which I had started, and I well knew how very good he was. After a few weeks four more British officers were posted in, all straight from OCTU. One, Wally Valsler, was a lieutenant by virtue of previous service in the

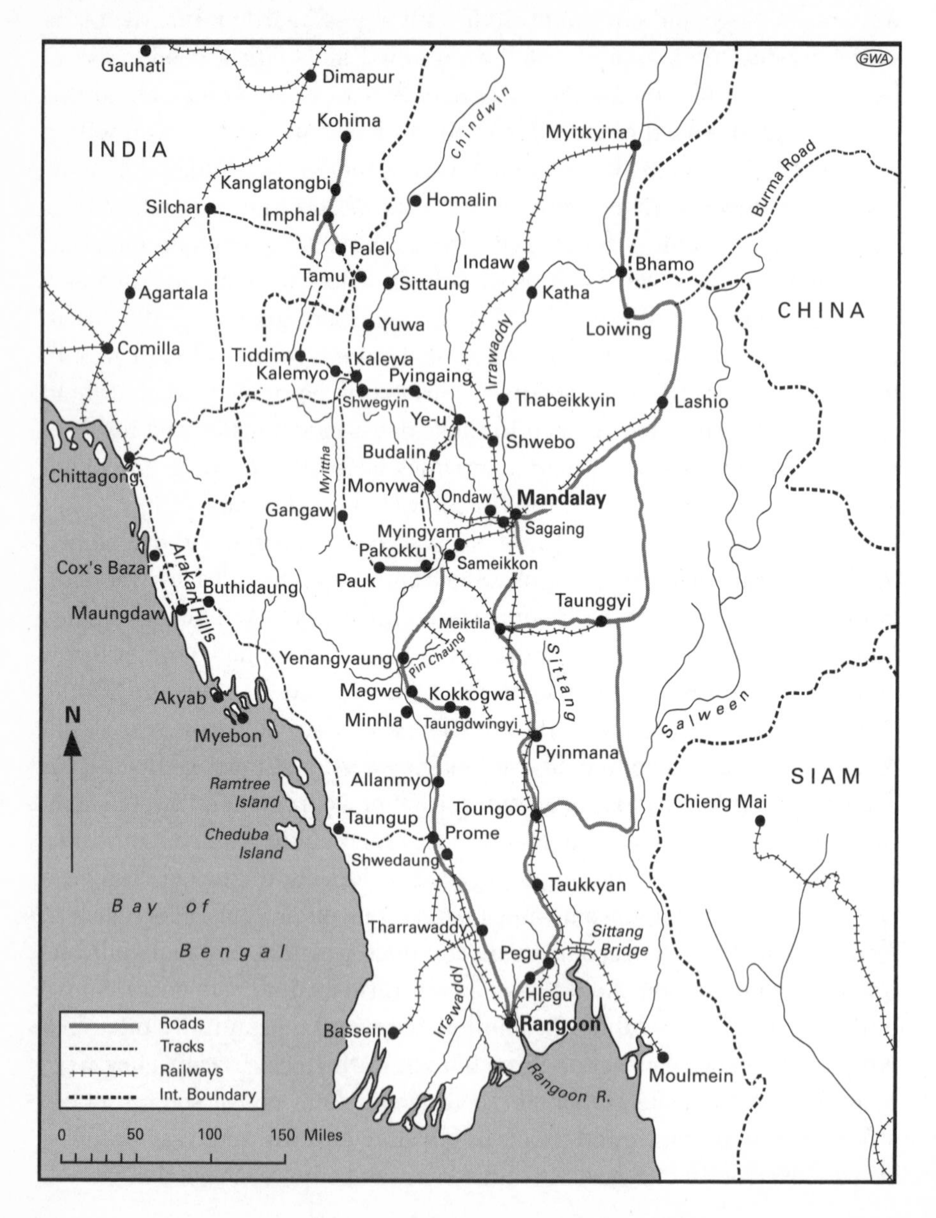

ranks, the other three were second-lieutenants. Wally could speak a little Urdu but the others knew none. I was very lucky; they were good companions and were soon to prove themselves excellent officers.

About this time my second-in command was posted to another job and I had to choose his replacement from among the officers that I already had. Hugh Kelly at 26 was the oldest and was the obvious choice. He was a lively and likeable ex-mining engineer, experienced, adventurous and a born leader. His promotion to captain was popular and upset no-one. On his shoulders now fell the burden of wrestling with the ordnance depots for our stores and the purchase of whatever could be obtained in the bazaar; no easy job for someone unused to Army bureaucracy and he had to work very long hours to compete with it.

In December came the dramatic news of the Japanese attack on Malaya and it began to dawn on us that we might not have to fight in a desert after all. So far our men had done a certain amount of musketry, fieldcraft and marching, but very little else. Now something more was required and I decided we should do some training in watermanship and wet bridging. The watermanship training was great fun and the VCOs who did the bulk of the training (for the officers were still struggling to learn Urdu) were very good at it. The Ganges Canal ran close to our Lines, and was ideal for training as some skill was required to cope with the current. Inter-platoon competitions in rowing and making rafts and flying ferries began to give everyone a little more confidence in their own and their comrades' abilities.

Towards the end of our training, in mid-January, I was asked quite casually by our Regimental HQ to put on some form of demonstration for a senior Sapper officer from GHQ at Delhi who was due to arrive in a couple of days' time; anything would do. This seemed quite easy and we just arranged for each of the platoons to run through one of the watermanship competitions that we had been practising. On the day, everything went smoothly and the great man seemed pleased. He mentioned that he had just returned from Burma where he had watched a field company operating ferries across the River Salween.

About a week later the Commandant appeared unexpectedly on our morning parade and told me that our late visitor had written to say that 70 Company was to go overseas in about three weeks' time. He had added that he had seen all the other companies forming in India at the time and had decided that 70 Company was the most suitable and although it was unusual to send so new a company into action he did not think he was mistaken.

Of course this was a great break for us and entirely due to the happy chance of having done a little watermanship training. The exciting news had a dramatic effect. At once a flood of men were posted in from the training battalions to bring us up to full strength. At the same time the ordnance depots began to swamp us with stores of every description. Many of these lacked some vital part, necessitating violent telephoning to the depot concerned and nearly driving Hugh Kelly demented. GHQ had decreed that 70 Company was to be reorganised on a new scale. The company was to be a marching one, with only its equipment carried in vehicles. There were to be some mules in case part of the company was required to operate across country. This new scale changed the 'magic number' of the company. This was our name for the total personnel strength and was vital for Hugh Kelly to know so that he could order the correct number of rifles, tin helmets, gas masks etc. As far as I remember it was 318, which included the ten per cent extra men who were to accompany us overseas as 'first reinforcements' but not the 18 camp followers. The latter included some cooks and a tailor. Only 26 of the soldiers in the whole company had been enlisted before World War II started.

It is difficult to recall all the doings of those last few hectic weeks. Our elderly subedar was transferred and Subedar Kanwal Khan, a very fit Mussalman, took his place. All our men, including the two hundred new ones had to be sent on leave for a last visit to their homes, thus making it extremely difficult either to get them organised, equipped and inoculated or to get any work done. Then all our vehicles had to be collected from Delhi by Godfrey Wood, our sixth officer who had arrived in Roorkee ex-OCTU some ten days before, and brought back by our very inexperienced drivers. They were new Chevrolets, painted desert sand colour, and by some miracle all arrived intact. Eighteen mules and five horses arrived from the remount depot at Saharanpur. The horses were meant as chargers for the officers, none of whom, except myself, had ever ridden before. For the sea voyage all equipment had to be boxed or crated. No wood was provided and we had to scrounge what we could. Some of the men were of poor physique (the rapid expansion of this great volunteer army had been a little indiscriminating at times) and the Commandant kindly agreed to change fifteen of the least fit. This was a great help to me later but I wished I could have made it thirty. Everyone worked throughout the day and late into the night. Even though other units and officers in Roorkee all did their best to help, I can't think how it all got done.

Our final orders came on the 16th of February. The vehicles and mules were to go by train to Calcutta on the 21st and the Company was to entrain at Roorkee on the 22nd for Madras. Last parties were held. Godfrey Wood, quiet and competent, departed with the transport for Calcutta. The Company, hot and dirty from loading stores, had a last parade before the Commandant. Finally, led by the band of the Bengal Sappers, we marched down, happy but rather scruffy, through crowds of cheering sappers to Roorkee station. There we entrained in our special train in a siding and settled down for the night. As dawn broke the next day we were off."

Victoria Point, at the southern extremity of Burma, had been occupied by the Japanese on 15th December 1941 and by mid-January 1942, when the southern and eastern frontiers of Burma lay open to the enemy, 17 Indian Division and 1 Burma Division were driven back towards the Sittang river. The disastrous withdrawal over the Sittang Bridge took place towards the end of February and it was hoped to be possible to hold the west bank. Reinforcements, including 70 Field Company, landed at Rangoon in March 1942, but it soon became apparent that even Rangoon could not be held. Ian Lyall Grant described his first few days: "On 3rd March we sailed the twenty miles up the narrow Rangoon River to the docks. There was an unmistakable tension in the air. The houses and jetties on the banks of the river were all deserted and two columns of smoke rising high into the blue sky almost obscured the glorious golden spire of the Shwe Dagon pagoda. The only people to greet us on the quay were a group of officers, some red-hatted, who fell over themselves to fasten our mooring lines and then rushed on board to adorn the ship's bar.

In the evening we marched through the bombed and deserted city to our billets in the Engineering College of Rangoon University, about five miles from the docks. The next day we investigated the docks and found some large warehouses crammed with boxes of American stores destined for China. Everyone was helping themselves. It was a lucky dip as the boxes gave no indication of their contents. Nevertheless, over the next three days we acquired a ton of guncotton, some compressor tools unavailable in India, some green and brown paint with which to repaint our desert-coloured vehicles, a brand-new jeep and a magnificent ten-wheel GMC truck.

We had been put under command of the Chief Engineer at Army HQ for 'essential services'. I called on him and was told my task would probably be to build hutting in North Burma for the monsoon. It didn't sound very exciting. However I was given a paper map of Burma at a scale of 32 miles to the inch, quite invaluable as this was the only map we ever had. Meanwhile I was to report to the Commander Royal Engineers (CRE), Rangoon, whom I found having afternoon tea in his bungalow with his officers.

The CRE told me politely that he didn't need any help so I returned to my unit and we set about repainting our trucks which had arrived in the meantime. I assembled our VCOs and NCOs and passed on what little I knew, including that we would be fighting some people called Japanese, who might be helped by Siamese or Burmese but were not to be confused with Gurkhas, Chinese and Burmese who were fighting with us. Meanwhile our 63 Brigade moved towards the front. A reconnaissance party of the Brigadier, his brigade major and the three battalion commanders went up the road to Pegu to see the form. On the way back they were ambushed and all killed or seriously wounded. At a stroke the Brigade had been decapitated.

On 6th March things looked up as we were given the task of preparing for demolition an oxygen and acetylene factory, the only one in Burma, and also providing protection for a party of Burma Sappers who were to demolish the big main-line railway bridge over the Pazundaung creek.

General Alexander had now taken over command and he decided to abandon Rangoon the following day, the 7th. On this day we were ordered to march out of Rangoon and join 17 Indian Division at Taukkyan. During the day all the demolitions took place, including that of the great Syriam oil refinery which produced a vast cloud of smoke hanging over the city. 70 Field Company having reached a 'harbour' in a rubber plantation about a mile from Taukkyan, I went in search of the CRE of 17 Division. We could hear the rattle of automatic fire and the thud of bombs and shells two or three miles to the north, the usual racket with which we were soon to become familiar.

The CRE introduced me to the Divisional Commander, Major-General 'Punch' Cowan. The interview was brief as the General seemed to have something on his mind. Not surprising, as it turned out that General Alexander and Army HQ, the Rangoon garrison and the battered 17 Division were now trapped with Rangoon destroyed behind them and a Japanese roadblock across the only road to the north.

A long hard march looked probable the next day but I was happy that all our work to organise and equip the Company had now borne fruit. This was the culmination of our effort. We had joined the Division and were ready to go.

After dark we received our first message from Divisional HQ. It said simply, 'The attempt to break through the roadblock this evening has failed. A further attempt will be made tomorrow morning. If that fails you are to break your unit up into parties of twelve to make their way out to India individually.' I passed this message on to the officers, with the valuable information that India was about 750 miles away somewhere to the north, and then lay down and went to sleep. We had begun to realise that fighting a war in Burma would certainly never be dull."

Alan Hiscock, one of the subalterns in 70 Field Company, remembers the tense atmosphere in the almost deserted city of Rangoon. "Most of the population, whether Burmese or Indian, had fled after the bombings and those who remained were largely engaged in looting or incendiarism. Fires were being lit all over the place, odd shots ringing out as the military fired at looters; every shop was broken open with its contents thrown out; burnt-out cars were everywhere; and here and there lay an unclaimed body."

The Japanese battalion holding the road-block to the north had suffered heavy casualties, and General Sakurai, intent on his main aim of capturing Rangoon, lifted the block, much to the surprise and relief of the British, who marched north in two days to Tharrawaddy. These two marches were 28 and 31 miles in temperatures of about 100 degrees. 70 Company had each day to send on its trucks, dump its equipment, and bring the trucks back to ferry the sappers for the last part of their march. No-one got much sleep. At Tharrawaddy the CRE wisely decided that the Sappers must somehow become motorised, so much equipment was either dumped or sent back to Mandalay. Fortunately 70 Company had twelve 15cwt pick-up trucks and for the rest of the campaign each of these carried a section of 14 men, their fieldworks tools, all their baggage and a 20-gallon drum of petrol. A 30cwt truck per platoon carried platoon HQ, specialist tools, cooking gear, rations and explosives.

The British now fell back to Prome, the Sappers, including 70 Company, demolishing saw-mills, rice-mills, railway bridges and stations, as well as many large road bridges. More than 400lbs of gelignite were used to cut the bridge girders. The gelignite sticks being used here and elsewhere had a tendency to weep unstable yellow nitro-glycerine.

Careful handling was essential! It also stained one's hands yellow and produced terrific headaches. Sappers soon discovered that it prolonged one's active life if Japanese snipers failed to hit the gelignite whilst it was being fixed in position for blowing.

At Prome, a long and scraggy town surrounded by dense scrub jungle, it was intended to make a stand, but there were too many 'Chiefs' and some unwise theories were tried out unsuccessfully. Some attempt was made to safeguard large dumps of petrol, ammunition and stores, but it was a quite indefensible location, especially after a Japanese air attack practically wiped out the Allied air force. 70 Company was again reorganised, this time onto a mule and bullock-cart basis, vehicles being sent to the rear. Further retreat became urgent but not before the Company had demolished most of the river shipping on both sides of the Irrawaddy, and the power supply. The Company suffered its first killed and wounded here while holding part of the perimeter. When the withdrawal was ordered, they blew the main road bridge behind the rearguard. The next two days revealed the futility of the bullock-cart idea, and 70 Company became motorised again, their vehicles augmented by the Prome fire engine.

The retreat continued and, for the Sappers, followed the same pattern of track-making and demolitions. In the course of this, Alan Hiscock went to Magwe and saw the sad remains of the Royal Air Force on this, their main airfield outside Rangoon. Unaware of the strategic problems of the RAF, the soldiers had been highly critical of the lack of air support, especially after being heavily dive-bombed a few days previously. The remnants of the RAF had now been withdrawn from Burma but, fortunately for the army, the Japanese Air Force expended most of their effort on bombing major towns. 70 Company was detailed to support 48 Brigade in a rearguard action at Kyaukse, just south of Mandalay, designed to hold up the advance of the Japanese long enough to enable British and Chinese troops to cross the great Ava bridge, the only bridge on the Irrawaddy which would allow every vehicle, tank and gun to cross. It was a tough assignment.

48 Brigade was well under-strength and heavily outnumbered by the Japanese advancing on Kyaukse, the country being a mixture of paddy fields and banana groves but well suited for defence, although the town itself had been heavily shelled and was ablaze. Nine large bridges were demolished, four during the 24-hour battle. There were dramas with several of them. The main road bridge was to be blown at 1800 hours, leaving two tanks deliberately on the enemy side. The Infantry holding

south of the river were to thin out half an hour earlier and cross the river by footbridges. There was a large overcharge of explosives (courtesy of a Chinese dump) on the two-span bridge, the charges being connected by cordtex and initiated by safety fuse. The two fuses were lit, one by the OC (Ian Lyall Grant) and the other by Havildar (later Lieutenant Colonel) Aurangzeb and were burning merrily when a truck-load of Gurkhas came bumping very slowly along the far river bank. The truck stopped at the end of the bridge while the driver carefully changed gear, and then came slowly up the road. They were lucky. A few seconds later the bridge blew up with a deafening explosion. The effect was electric. All firing stopped. For a moment the silence was eerie and uncanny. Then down came the guns again, the two tanks circled the town and came in ten minutes later over a reinforced concrete canal bridge. After the tanks crossed, it took another ten minutes for Naik (later Colonel) Vakil Singh to insert the detonators in the many charges and for Tom Valsler to blow the bridge, by which time the rearguard was far up the road conducting an orderly and perfect withdrawal. General Slim described this small battle "a really brilliant example of rearguard work". 70 Company was complimented by the Brigadier and was to remain affiliated to 48 Brigade for the rest of the war in Burma.

On 2nd May 1942, along with other troops, 70 Field Company reached Ye-U, fifty miles north-west of Mandalay, where further reorganization was possible. All packs, respirators and surplus tools were destroyed. The 120 miles of winding track northwestwards from Ye-U appeared impassable, especially as the monsoon was due to break at any moment and this could easily turn the forest tracks into a quagmire. The stocks of food grew smaller and the Japanese, using the river, had time to get ahead of the force to ambush it. However, the troops, grateful for the concealment which the jungle gave them from air attack, got through and concentrated at Shwegyin on the east bank of the Chindwin River. 48 Brigade was still the rearguard and in all this movement 70 Company and its sister Company of Madras Sappers and Miners had played a vital role, not only in demolitions to hinder the Japanese advance, but also in repairing roads and tracks and bridges to enable the force to retreat in good order, and in providing drinking water at every stage. They also destroyed hundreds of abandoned vehicles that got stuck along the track, as well as quantities of ammunition and mines.

When the rearguard moved on to Shwegyin, they were given the task of repairing the improvised jetty there which had been swamped by a sudden rise of several feet in the river level. This was a vital task as the Chindwin was about half a mile wide at this point and flowing fairly fast. The only method of crossing was by paddle steamer to Kalewa, six miles upstream. With the aid of some nearby palm trees to make crib piers, Jemadar (later Lieutenant Colonel) Bachittar Singh raised the jetty and extended it onto a half-floating bay made from a handy barge and that night a number of steamers made the round trip from Kalewa. However at dawn the next day the Japanese attacked. The attack was held and although the jetty came under sporadic mortar and rifle fire the Sappers continued to work on providing a second pier. However the civilian steamer crews refused to come downstream any more. It was now impossible to withdraw the vehicles and so, when night fell and more vehicles and guns had been destroyed, the British withdrew through the forest and next morning crossed the river to Kalewa.

The Japanese did not follow up and after marching for seven days 70 Company crossed the Pass into India. Ian Lyall Grant, their OC, wrote: "thanks to some really first-class VCOs, the morale of the Company was surprisingly good. Most of us had lost up to two stone in weight, and had lived in one set of clothing for many days, but the men not only carried all their rifles, but also a few tools and six extra Bren guns jettisoned by other units. On the last day we met General Slim, sitting in a jeep and watching the units intently. He called me over and asked who we were, and I must confess that I half expected a compliment, but the truth is that all he said was 'Stick to it!' It was good advice, for that night we were deposited in an area of scrub jungle without any blankets, cover or hot food and, as darkness fell, the monsoon started." The men though were increasingly distressed by the Indian refugees, the majority from Moulmein and Rangoon. Many thousands walked all the way to India, suffering terrible hardship. Occasionally they were able to get lifts from the railway or from the army and they often received food from the soldiers. They were a pathetic sight and many died on the way from exhaustion, cholera, dysentry, fever and Burmese dacoits. The really dreadful sight was that of the vultures circling around the dead and dying, even feeding on those still warm from life.

Four fifths of the retreating army were now in India, with many lessons learnt. Training based on these lessons would produce soldiers who, two years later, would inflict on the Japanese an overwhelming defeat. 70 Field Company were to return later to share in the victory they had done so much to make possible.

DESERT VICTORY, 1941–1943

In three breathless weeks of 1941 the British were hustled out of Libya and by May Tobruk was besieged by Rommel. The German armour roamed the desert between Tobruk and the Egyptian frontier while both opposing armies awaited reinforcement. Working on the principle of 'Twice blest is he who has his quarrel just; but three times he who gets his blow in fust', Wavell launched a pre-emptive attack to destroy all the enemy forces east of Tobruk but met heavy resistance, particularly in the area of Halfaya Pass. Many of the tanks were knocked out and gradually the force was brought to a standstill. Some tanks entered an uncharted minefield under heavy enemy fire and it now became a Sapper's job. Before the tanks could be moved, the extent of the minefield had to be discovered, but there were the tanks, stuck among the mines and only 500 yards from the enemy. Lieutenant Thomas of 4 Field Company carried out a reconnaissance alone, under intense fire. Coolly and deliberately he searched the ground, the tank commander being killed while actually listening to his report. Then the Sappers came forward and removed the mines – dangerous, cold-blooded work – and during the following night the tanks were recovered. Thomas won an immediate MC for his gallantry and he brought back with him the first Tellermine to be seen by Western Desert Force.

There followed a period of apparent inactivity, but during this period 4 Field Company evolved a drill for locating mines by prodding with bayonets which was provisionally adopted by the Division. Later the CRE 4 Division conceived the idea of the knotted cord drill for minelaying, which eventually became the standard method of the British army. In September 1941 4 Field Company began work on laying a minefield over nine miles in length, with some fifty thousand mines laid, according to the new drill.

Meanwhile new Divisions were arriving in Egypt. With great foresight the new Commander-in-Chief, General Auchinleck, had selected a position at El Alamein on which the army could cover the Delta, if ever the desert fighting went against us. His thoughts were not entirely defensive; indeed an advance began on 19th November 1941. However, in the mobile desert warfare that followed, there was little engineer work. The Eighth Army, joined by the Tobruk garrison, eventually swept into Derna where 4 Field Company cleared some 800 mines from its northern perimeter and restored the water supply with 'the assistance of an Italian plumber.'

It was not until early January 1942 that Benghazi was reached and 4 Company had plenty of work there – at the power station and a pumping plant nearby; also restoring the harbour facilities and exploding huge quantities of enemy bombs.

In the meantime, a great tank battle at Agedabia had gone against the Allies and a rapid withdrawal became necessary. A new defence line was formed east of Derna and here 4 Field Company helped to create extensive minefields. One night three thousand mines were laid in just over twelve hours. Not until 22nd February was the Company withdrawn to Egypt for a short period of rest, refitting and training. There the blackout was practically non-existent, fresh food and limitless water were available.

On 28th May 1942 the Germans launched an attack in the Western desert and a huge tank battle developed, the British armour being forced back and a few days later Tobruk was again occupied by the enemy. Further retreat became necessary, all the way back to El Alamein, the men

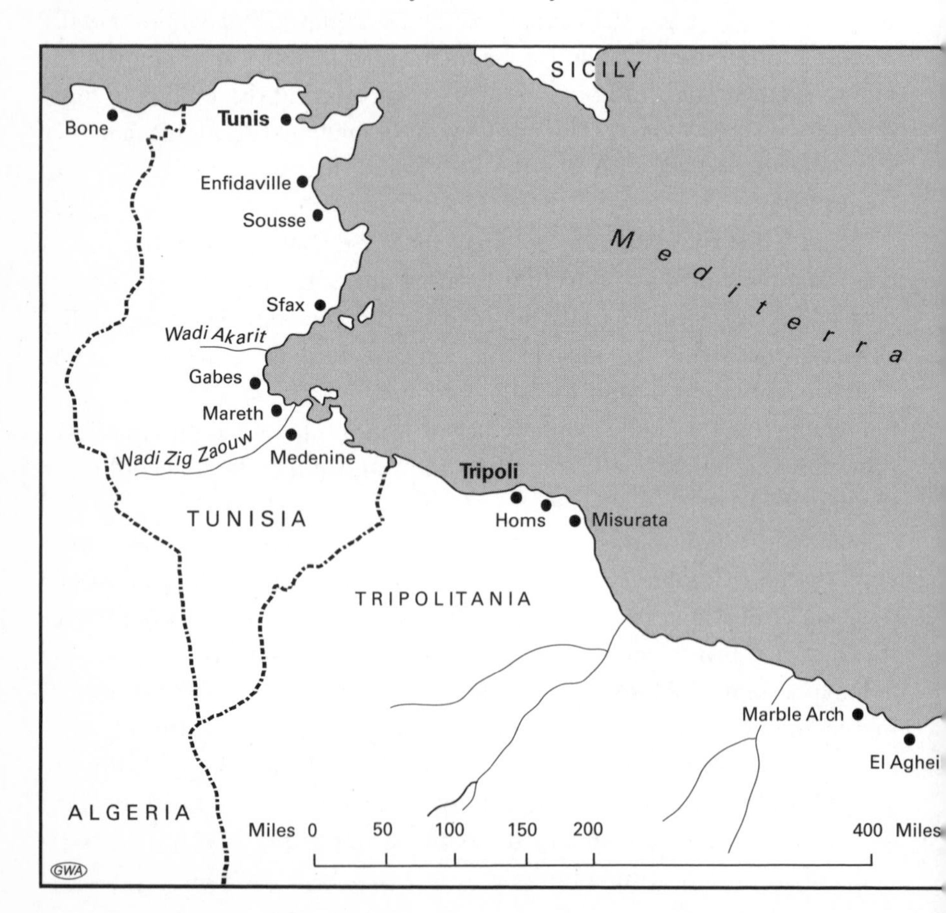

of 4 Field Company making a night dash in their vehicles through the enemy lines.

41 Field Park Company, however, were not so lucky and less than half got through to El Alamein. Havildar Chanan Singh recorded his experiences: “We were given the task of demolishing supply dumps but the enemy was now quite near and began to shell the supply area continuously. At 4pm German bombers set all the petrol dumps on fire but we continued our work. By 8pm, the supplies had been prepared for demolition but we were cut off by the enemy and our Platoon Commander told us that we had to withdraw without support but the enemy was not to benefit from the supplies. The demolitions were then started and terrible explosions rent the sky with fire all around us. We withdrew, having orders to push straight towards the desert for forty miles and then turn north and seek the main road. This had to be done in impenetrable darkness, lit only by huge enemy fires, and without maps as we had received

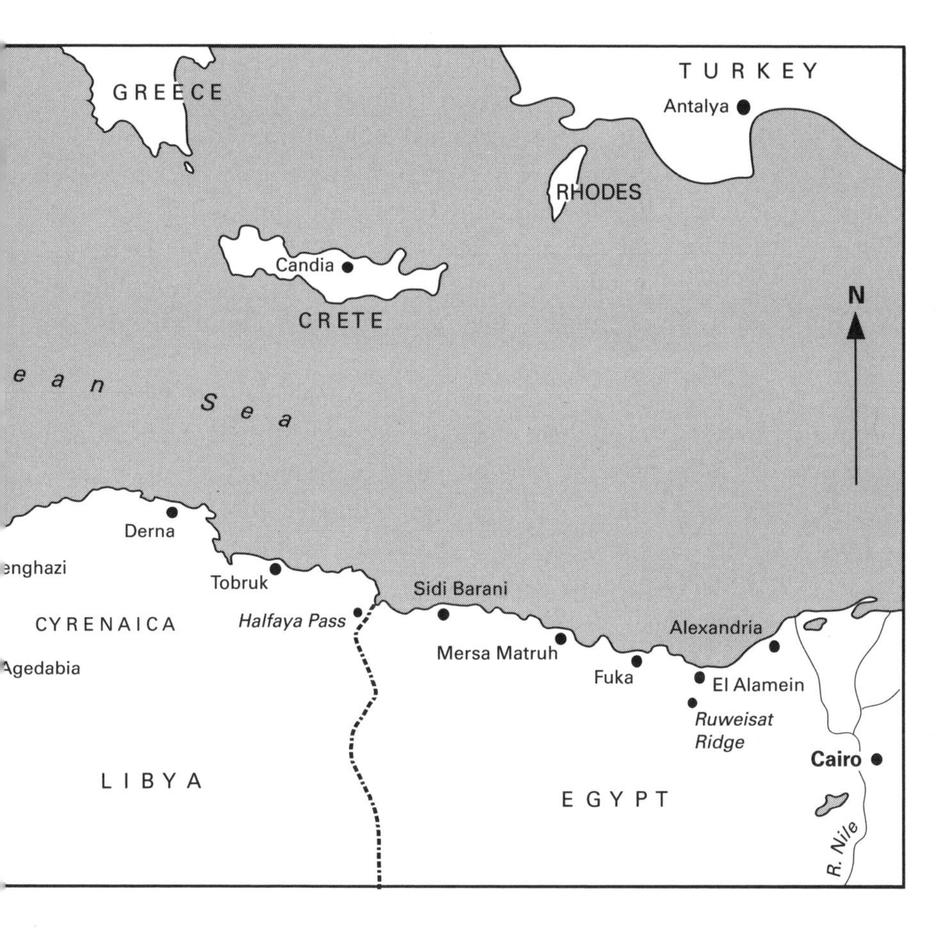

none from Headquarters. Every track, road and field was new to us. We started with heavy hearts but determined to slip through the enemy lines. Every man had to act on his own initiative. Three times, I, with my party of five in a truck, found ourselves very close to the enemy and pushed our way through in hand to hand fighting, but we never failed to regain the truck though we lost two men. By 4am most of the other columns had been captured. Many times our troops clashed with each other. Exhausted Germans and Italians were attacked while asleep. The thick morning fog added to our difficulties and sometimes we had to stop to regain direction. At dawn I found myself leading four other vehicles of my unit about 20 miles south of the main road to El Alamein, the rest of the convoy having vanished. I stopped the vehicles and went to each one. I found two wounded sappers, so we did first aid and then pushed on. We had covered only a few more miles when two armoured cars were seen standing 400 yards away to the right. This made us believe that the road was clear and that we had contacted our own troops, but as my vehicle passed the cars it was fired on heavily. Those in rear promptly turned back and I told my driver to do the same; but all in vain for my truck was immobilised. The enemy cars approached and we were taken prisoners. The other four vehicles managed to escape. We were taken back to Mersa Matruh, reaching it by nightfall, and I saw the supplies still burning. When we asked for food and water the Germans took us round the devastated area and asked whether we were worthy of being given anything at all. 'You should die of hunger', they said. Yet, in spite of all this, we survived."

Slowly, at El Alamein, a more closely knit defence was evolved. Reinforcements arrived, among them 66 Field Company, who in one week had come over 650 miles from the Arabian desert into action. Unhappily, their Brigade was quickly overrun and was never reformed; but most of 66 Field Company escaped and returned to the mountain pass defences of Iraq.

However, 4 Field Company took part in 5 Division's attack on Ruweisat Ridge, an action which forced the enemy from both sides of this 'hog's back'. Later, the Company was largely responsible for opening and closing gaps in minefields. The defences required constant attention; gun pits were dug and blasted among dead bodies and incessant flies, whilst the noise of gunfire and small arms fire went on all night. On one occasion 3,500 mines were laid in three hours, just part of the total laid. 2 Field Company helped in the defence of the Ridge and by the end of July the position was stabilised.

The Alamein line, '*once no more than groups of desperate men, was now as tight as a bowstring with an arrow in it.*' A new over-all Commander, General Alexander, and a new spirit, typified by his Army Commander, General Montgomery, began to tip the arrow for release.

September passed and October began with chill winds, sandstorms and rain. Then on 23rd October 1942 the signal was given. '*Under a brilliant moon, a crash of ten thousand guns broke the fitful silence of the arena. A vast crescent of flame raked the enemy front in depth*'. As the desert filled with vehicles all moving westward, 4 Field Company, despite grievous casualties from booby traps and mines, were in support of infantry patrols. From Ruweisat Ridge a wedge was driven into the enemy positions and by 6th November 1942 the victory of the Eighth Army had exceeded all expectations. Forward units were already west of Mersa Matruh.

Lieutenant Ivory of 2 Field Company described the battle: "With the last of the light a Rajput patrol led us to the enemy minefield fence which we cut, sending in a sub-section of sappers shoulder to shoulder searching with bayonets for anti-tank mines, while pretending to ignore desultory enemy small arms fire, some of it uncomfortably close. After locating and marking a batch of Tellermines near the front wire and then nothing for some yards beyond, we changed to a fresh row of searchers deeper in the minefield, while we marked the sides of the gap with broad white tape and checked that we had not missed any mines between our cones. After locating a further batch of Tellermines near the far fence and marking them, we placed a charge of gelignite on each mine, salvaging our cones and connecting all the charges with detonating fuse, and cleared the area of sappers. We destroyed all the mines with one stroke of the exploder handle, linked to an electrical detonator; this seemed the safest way of dealing with any booby traps under the mines, about which the South African troops had warned us.

Rather unexpectedly, at a time when Radio Newsreel had claimed RAF mastery of the skies over El Alamein, we were attacked from the air. We were at lunch when we heard the moan-wail-scream of a Stuka bomber's siren approaching fast. The two officers sitting close to the open tail of the mess lorry made a lightning exit, hampered by a table. I opted for the lorry floor. A stick of bombs fell across the Company lines, the fourth and loudest exploding close to the lorry. I lost my hearing for a few seconds but became aware of my heartbeat drumming on the steel floor. Then I heard the diminishing noise of the Stuka, looked up and into the sun shining through the shredded canvas canopy of the lorry.

One officer (Neilson) was walking away and calling for the doctor; another (Sandford) was lying in the mess vehicle pit, unable to use his legs. The mess waiter, who doubled as my orderly (Mohammed Sharif), was dead, shattered from head to foot. The mess cook (Budu) had been disembowelled. The water carrier (Maqbool) had one hand severed. Scott, the Company 2 i/c, arrived from the office lorry and told me with admirable sang-froid, 'You'd better get going for the Argylls' outpost; remember you won't have any cover from the heat haze after three o'clock'. So I straightened up and joined my truck and driver in B Section lines. We found the gap in the minefield where traffic had caused a thick layer of dust and thence the route to the outpost, marked by a field telephone cable. After reporting to the commander, I made notes on the work necessary to make slit trenches – newly excavated by blasting and the limestone left jagged – more habitable without using any more explosive. This work was never done.

We heard our own 25 pounder guns open up and wondered briefly what target they had; then the shells fell amongst us ... Two of the Jocks were killed and the commander on the telephone to his HQ gave a forthright opinion of the Brigade's staff work. I returned to 2 Company lines to learn that Budu had spent three hours dying; Maqbool and Sandford had been evacuated to hospital. It transpired at the Brigadier's '0-group' the following morning that the Argylls had abandoned their outpost during the night without authority, and a blazing row ensued. Thus, in less than 24 hours my war adventure had deteriorated into a squalid experience."

By December 1942, the immediate threat to Egypt and the Suez Canal had been removed and 4 Field Company found themselves in Benghazi again, with a variety of work to be done. Some five lighters, stuck on rocks by a recent storm, were refloated; roads were reconstructed and a wireless mast erected. Their OC, Major Murray, wrote that: "we are asked to open up a water-point at the Lete Grotto, 6 miles from here. It is a wonderful place, an underground reservoir composed of three lakes about 120 feet below the surface. It is quite dark down there and it would be easy to get lost if one pushed off in a boat without a life-line for retracing one's route. We have found a well-shaft on the surface leading down to the lakes and have decided to have our pumping engine on the surface. The 'Waters of Lete' (or Lethe) are famous and it is said that anyone partaking of them forgets everything." (*According to Greek mythology, the Lethe was a river of the nether regions from which departed spirits drank to obtain forgetfulness of the past. The name itself implies forgetfulness.*)

Relaxation was provided by occasional ENSA entertainments and by Indian films. It was a very pleasant interlude. The War Diary commented: "Benghazi's white buildings glistened in the sun and the two domes of its cathedral dominated the skyline. The blue skies overhead are dotted with silvery balloons, about twenty in all, the only outward sign that we are at war".

However, by the middle of February 1943, the Company was on the move again for Tripoli. It was a long way from Benghazi, yet it seemed a joyride with the desert so full of flowers. On the way, though, they had to pass through El Agheila where they found many examples of the latest German booby-traps. According to Murray, "the retreating enemy had shown the utmost ingenuity in planning these devilish devices. Large craters would be blown in the coastal road and anti-personnel 'S' mines buried beneath the metal splinters lying around the edges. These splinters prevented the use of mine-detectors. Again, an abandoned vehicle might have booby-traps fixed to the brake or gear lever so that when an attempt was made to tow the vehicle clear of the road a mine exploded beneath it. Alternatively, the vehicle might be left clear of traps and several mines buried in the only empty space off the road to which it might be towed. Sometimes the enemy prepared a sham grave near the road with a cross leaning crazily to one side. The short path to that grave was sown with 'S' mines and any attempt to straighten the cross caused a mine beneath it to explode. Yet again, the side of the road would be undermined and a couple of Tellermines inserted beneath the metalling. A few vehicles might then pass safely, but when the crust of the undermined portion collapsed under further traffic the mines exploded. Occasionally, trip wires, as fine as gossamer threads and almost invisible, were attached to a barbed wire barrier across the road. The wires led to 'S' mines buried beneath the barrier. Oil drums, half filled with rubbish, were often strewn across the road, each with a pull-ignition arrangement attached to a Tellermine below. The lessons learned on the Agheila Road made the Sappers so suspicious that it is surprising that they could ever bring themselves to move anywhere or touch anything, but move they did and with remarkable rapidity. Fortunately, they were no novices at the game and consequently they suffered few casualties."

Some hundreds of miles further west, in Tunisia, Rommel was preparing the Mareth line. Just east of the little town of Mareth, the most abrupt of a number of deep wadis cutting the coastal plain was Wadi Zig

Zaouw, a formidable obstacle 50 feet deep and 70 yards wide with a muddy bottom. Here the crossing had to be done by steel mesh stretched over fascines: it was a crossing bravely achieved by 4 Field Company with a Madras Field Company, amongst continuous gunfire and without any armoured protection. The Sappers were, in fact, leading the attack on the Mareth line. But sadly German counter attacks and heavy rain later brought their labour to nought.

A curious incident occurred at the Wadi Zig Zaouw. While 4 Field Company were laying their fascines in the bottom, help was requested to extricate a wounded Indian soldier who was buried beneath a blown-up truck. A Sapper dressed in an overcoat, and with his face covered in mud, immediately volunteered to rescue the man and did so at considerable risk. A few days later the OC received a message stating that Army HQ wanted to know the name of this Sapper. He made enquiries but could not trace any such man in his unit and replied accordingly. However the British officer who had asked for help insisted that there was such a man and an identification parade was arranged so that the wounded man could pick out his rescuer. Still there was no result; but as the wounded man was leaving the parade ground he happened to pass an officer whom he saluted smartly. Then an expression of the utmost amazement came over his face. "Wuh admi!" (that's the man), he shouted, and pointed to Lieutenant Colonel John Blundell. The 'Sapper' who had saved him was the CRE of 4th Indian Division.

4 Field Company was next needed in the Hallouf Pass, where a whole Division was being held up. Compressors and a bulldozer were taken down a narrow trail to cut away rock, and slowly they built a retaining wall, thereby allowing twelve thousand men and two thousand vehicles to edge their way forward and to link up with the other Divisions. The Company spent some days improving this road and bartering with the local villagers. It was recorded in the War Diary: 'One lieutenant obtained six eggs for showing them how to disarm a Tellermine'.

Another, more lighthearted, view of the Alamein and Tunisian campaign comes from Major Gerrie who rose from subaltern to become OC 4 Field Company, serving from October 1942 until August 1945: "I had a most unusual introduction to the Bengal Sappers and Miners. On Sunday 18th October 1942, accompanied by two fellow subalterns, I arrived at HQRE of the 4th Indian Division in the desert at El Alamein. We were welcomed by the CRE who carried out a friendly interview before allocating us to his three field companies.

We loaded our kit onto a 15cwt truck and were taken to our appointed units. I was the last to be delivered. I got out of the truck and started to unload my camp kit and suitcase but the driver said, '*Nahin sahib, yeh mera kam hai*' (No Sahib, that is my job) and he unloaded my belongings at the back of the truck, saluted smartly and got into the driving seat. Unfortunately he engaged reverse gear and before I could shout a warning he had crushed my suitcase."

At this point Major Murray, his future OC, and Captain Penny (recovered from his wounds in Eritrea) observed his plight and offered help in the shape of a large steel ammunition box for his belongings and then a large whisky to drown his sorrows.

Later on Major Gerrie found a discarded black wooden box of German manufacture almost identical in size to his late suitcase, extremely well made with dovetailed edges and steel caps on all corners. "It had a stout handle and a pair of catches to secure the lid. With the fittings removed I had a first class suitcase and a useful camp stool into the bargain.....The box came home with me when I was demobilised in January 1946, and I have it still!"

Major Gerrie also described his later adventures in North Africa. "Early in 1943, 4 Indian Division was concentrated around Benghazi. During this period I was nominated to attend a course held in the Canal Zone near the town of Ismailia. On the last week of the course I learned on the amazingly accurate source of information popularly referred to as 'The Wooden Wireless', that 4 Indian Division had moved up to reinforce the 8th Army and were now somewhere in Tunisia.

I realised that I now faced a journey of some 1,200 miles before I could rejoin the Company. The usual system was to report to a transit camp and await a suitable opportunity to join a supply convoy going west to Tripoli but this was a long and tedious business. Troops in the Middle East often referred to Movement Control as 'all control and no movement!'

Just alongside where the course was held there was an airfield operated by the United States Army Air Force. I had often seen their aircraft landing and taking off. It occurred to me that if any of their flights were going up to Tripoli I might get a lift.

On the final day of the course I walked along to the airfield and was directed to an enquiry office where I met a very friendly American Top-Sergeant to whom I explained the reason for my visit ... He told me that if I returned the following afternoon he might be able to help me. Next day

I duly returned and was greeted by my friendly sergeant who said, 'Right Lieutenant, you be here tomorrow morning at eight o'clock and we will fly you up to Tripoli.' This they did with no formality. They did not even ask my name.

The Dakota aircraft took off promptly and flew to Heliopolis just outside Cairo where it picked up a load of material and personnel. It then flew on to Benghazi where it refuelled before going on to Tripoli where it arrived in the late afternoon. I was accommodated overnight in a transit camp and in the morning was able to contact 5 Indian Division Infantry Brigade's transport who were loading supplies.

I stayed overnight with them at their HQ and after breakfast the first person I saw was 4 Field Company's quartermaster who had arrived to load rations for the sappers. By mid-morning I was back with the Company in their campsite not far from the Tunisian town of Gabes." It had taken the Lieutenant just over twenty four hours to rejoin his Company 1,200 miles away.

Twenty miles north of Gabes there was a replica of the Mareth line in the shape of the Wadi Akarit. After the initial crossing, 4 Field Company was sent forward to complete one of the crossings and Lieutenant Colonel Blundell was standing on the bank talking with some of the officers when two shells in quick succession struck the group, killing the CRE, OC 4 Field Company and several other officers and men, wounding many others. It was a sad day for the Bengal Sappers but, in the crossing of the Wadi Akarit, and for work done later, Havildar Babu Singh and Havildar Mutant Ram, each of 4 Field Company, won the IOM.

The following day, 7th April 1943, British and Indian forces broke through the Wadi Akarit on the coast and the enemy was in full retreat. In the hills the Indians linked up with the Americans and the two fronts became one in a glorious advance over the rich Tunisian plain. On 11th May 1943 the campaign in Tunisia was over.

ROORKEE'S WAR, 1941–1945

Prior to 1932 the Bengal Sappers had been responsible for their own recruiting, a simple matter because there was no lack of applicants of the very best type to supply the modest needs of the Corps, but after war broke out all recruiting was done through Recruiting Officers controlled by the Adjutant General's Branch. Though recruiting was accelerated, the real flood of recruits did not begin until 1941. Family tradition and personal selection went by the board and were replaced by a cold, though highly efficient, regime which was better designed to meet increasing demands. Despite these restrictions, Aitken Lawrie managed to visit villages not reached by Recruiting Officers and was able to select first class men from the many hundreds who presented themselves. The initial slowness of expansion was probably due to a feeling that Indian troops were unlikely to be used against Germany in Europe and also the fact that Japan was neutral and not seen to pose a threat, but there was also a general shortage of equipment, which inhibited expansion, and an acute lack of officers.

In the early stages of the war the Bengal Sappers were required to raise various specialist units such as Road Roller Platoons and Line of Communication units, but soon the enlarging scope of the war forced the Corps to concentrate on field units and the raising of specialist units became the responsibility of other, newly formed, Groups. More than a dozen new field companies were raised in Roorkee during 1941 and 1942 and as fast as they were trained, they disappeared eastwards towards Burma.

The raising of new units naturally depended on a greater output of men from the Training Battalion, the Workshops and Fieldworks, and on drawing manpower from other sources such as the calling up of reservists and re-enrolment of pensioners. All this resulted in a huge expansion which included two further Training Battalions, the last being authorized in September 1941. Regularly the orders went out: 'The following units will be raised forthwith', or 'The following personnel will he transferred to such and such a Company'. Soon there were men on the ranges learning to shoot or, off the canal 'hard', practising watermanship, men marching to and from training, occasionally letting loose concerted battle cries, men going garlanded to the station and, beneath the wild skirling of the pipes and the determined beat of the drums, wondering a little what was ahead of them.

The Depot Battalion had been separated from the Training Battalion in 1940 and in April 1944 it became a Depot Wing, comprising a Reinforcement Battalion and a Specialist Battalion which held all MT and Workshops trainees as well as permanent staff and people passing through the Depot Company: arrivals, leave personnel, medically downgraded men etc. A Boys Battalion was raised in 1941 to recruit boys between the ages of 15 and 16 years and to train them as tradesmen. After eighteen months training, they passed out as Sappers.

At the beginning of 1942, in accordance with orders issued in the previous October, the three Corps of Indian Sappers and Miners were re-named 'Groups'. Previously, Sapper and Miner units had not been shown as belonging to the Indian Engineers, but now they were required to adopt the suffix 'I E'. The title 'Royal' was accorded in February 1946 in recognition of their war service. The appointments of 'Colonels' of the three Sapper Groups was abolished in 1942 and replaced by those of 'Colonels Commandant', the first for the Bengal Group being Lieutenant General Sir Ronald Charles. 'Don Carlos' to his friends, Charles had won the DSO in South Africa and took command of 6 Field Company at Kohat in 1902. He had been a Divisional Commander in France in 1918 and after the war he was GOC Waziristan, where his former frontier experience and fluent Urdu were great assets. He retired in 1934 after being a member of the Army Board back in London and later became Chief Royal Engineer. He had a reserve, a gravitas about him which made him seem to many in later life as stern and forbidding, but in fact he had a strong sense of humour and was an excellent raconteur.

By 1942 most of the empty spaces in the Cantonment had been built over, as was the Grass Farm and right out to the Rifle Ranges, with two new ranges beyond them. The old monsoon polo ground near the Malakpur estate was covered with Thomason College buildings, new married quarters appeared in the area between the maidan and the Garrison Church and also on the spur above the Slaughter House. A branch of the Women's Voluntary Service(WVS) organisation was established and did excellent work. A Supply Depot, with its own railway siding, was also built and occupied the area between the railway and the old Range Road, with a new railway station called 'Dandhera'. On the sporting side, very few people were able to get to the jheels, no one shot a tiger and polo was only played on the odd day when sufficient players were forthcoming. An innovation in aid of War Funds was a Race Meeting one Sunday afternoon in which all the horses in the Station turned out. Some refused to start, some decided to run the course the wrong way and some just parked their riders on the ground. However, sufficient finished to ensure a decision in each race and the War Funds benefited by over a thousand rupees.

Aitken Lawrie was recalled to Roorkee in 1943 to run the OCTU as the previous OC had died. He found cadets sitting in classrooms listening to boring lectures on accounts and military law so he moved the whole set-up fifty miles into the jungle, where they had to build their own accommodation and learn to live there. The Forestry officials were glad to provide a site alongside a river, provided they could have roads and bridges built in return. There were at that time two OCTUs in Roorkee for which the Bengal Group had to provide Instructors and Staff, and cadets were trained for about seven months in engineering subjects before being posted as officers to one of the Engineer Groups.

Later that year Aitken took over the Workshops which expanded into all the buildings formerly used as Fieldworks Stores, and a new Stores building was built extending up to the Hill Cut. The instructors were Indian NCOs, under the supervision of some thirty RE Sergeants and Warrant Officers who were responsible for setting standards and carrying out trade tests in each trade. With some two thousand men under training they were invaluable. Though a few tradesmen, such as carpenters and blacksmiths, were enlisted, they were low caste and not considered eligible to become NCOs, though on active service they were often promoted. The ordinary sapper, though, had no idea of any trade and had to be allocated to what was thought suitable for him and where there were vacancies. The Workshops were in need of modernization and the new Chief Instructor began by altering the layout to make it more efficient and then had samples made up in each trade of the standard to be achieved for each grade. These were prominently displayed, together with Standing Orders for the Workshops, and they were still in use when Aitken Lawrie went back to Roorkee in 1988. "As you see, Colonel Sahib "said the Head Clerk, "There have only been three amendments since you wrote these Orders."

Aitken Lawrie's next appointment, in 1944, was as Military Adviser to the Indian State Forces' Sappers and Miners. One third of India had never been conquered by the British and remained in the hands of some 560 Indian Princes who had signed treaties of eternal friendship and cooperation with Queen Victoria. They were loyal supporters of the Crown and had always offered their own armies to help in any war in which the British were engaged. Six of them had their own Sapper and Miner units but it was clearly out of the question to send them straight from guarding a medieval palace, where their standards were somewhat old-fashioned, to fight the Japanese in Burma. An Indian State Forces Training Battalion (ISFTB) was therefore set up in Roorkee where 2,000 State Forces personnel were trained by Bengal Sapper NCOs in Field Engineering and Trades until they were considered ready for Burma. Under their British officers they all did very well there and the additional manpower they provided was most welcome.

Roorkee was kept busy with the training necessary to keep all the field units supplied with men and there was a constant movement in and out of the Centre. Such was the demand for men that in 1941 the training period for recruits had been reduced to only nine months and ended with the completion of a Fieldworks course. By 1943 jungle training had become a fine art and all men underwent a strenuous course with a great degree of realism in the Battle School before being posted to units. Early in the year the first Bailey bridge appeared in Roorkee and sappers soon mastered the new equipment and were to use it later with conspicuous success. The bulldozer was already achieving in Burma miracles of road-making; now the Bailey bridge transformed bridging operations.

By March 1943 the strength of the Corps reached a peak of nearly 24,000, a seven-fold expansion of the pre-war strength. Early in the year the Corps assisted in the establishment of a School of Military Engineering (India) in part of the Thomason College and many of its courses were subsequently attended by officers of the Group. 39 Training Division settled nearby at Hardwar and the Group had two field companies there. Platoons, complete with VCOs and NCOs, were sent out from the Reinforcement Battalion at Roorkee and did nine weeks' training. A week was spent in watermanship and improvised jungle rafting on the Ganges, and the last two weeks were devoted to tactical and Engineer schemes in the jungle with platoons of other field companies. This system continued until April 1945.

THE INDO-BURMA BORDER

The Central Front, 1942–1943

Any large-scale map of Burma before 1942 showed red-lined roads from India petering out on the Burma border and a fresh network of red lines beginning in the Ye-U and Shwebo area north-west of Mandalay. The road system from India ended at Dimapur, and between Dimapur and Shwebo, 250 air miles twisted on the ground into more than 450 miles. It became the task of the Sappers to join the ends of the two road systems and fashion roads which would bear the weight of modern armour.

In the late 19th Century, the Sappers had improved the footpath over the mountains from Dimapur to Imphal and Palel in Manipur State into a track that could take horse or mule drawn carts, their feat commemorated by a village subsequently calling itself 'Safarmaina', near the highest point. By early 1942, a pack-horse track had been extended over the hills from Palel to Tamu on the Burmese border, some 60 miles away. It was clear though that any link with Burma must take this route, so the track had now to be turned into a two-way all-weather road with Class 30 bridges. In six weeks a Sapper task force built, at remarkable speed, a fair-weather motor road between these two places, completing it just in time to provide supplies and an exit for the retreating Army in Burma, and many thousands of refugees, before the monsoon in mid-May. In January, 71 Field Company had erected a six-bay Inglis bridge over the Lokchao river which bisected the road and, after everyone had passed back into India, 414 Bridge Construction Section (later to become 414 Field Park Company) dismantled and recovered it. This was no easy task as, the monsoon having arrived, the road deteriorated and they suffered severely from malaria, no preventive measures, other than mosquito-nets at night, being available. Meanwhile throughout that summer 71 Company struggled to keep the road open.

Terence Tinsley, a subaltern in 73 Field Company which had just arrived in Ranchi, en route for the Arakan, was ordered to move in advance of the rest of the Company to Assam in order to destroy oil installations, should the need arise. "I had a short briefing from an expert on such demolitions and he handed me a map which was marked 'TOP SECRET'. It showed a number of circles, connected by a network of lines and a mass of symbols. 'It's quite simple,' he said. 'The circles represent the oil tanks in their bunded enclosures. The lines are the detonating fuses, and the symbols give the details of the time-delay igniters to be used at each point, the quantities of explosive to be put in each charge and the places to which the detonating party have to run after they have let the things off. It's a doddle really.'

He then drew my attention to the classification printed at the top of the map. This was the only real problem. The Army was very touchy about the word 'retreat' and the civilian population of Assam was likely to be even more sensitive. Nobody was to know that people were worrying about the Japanese coming any closer and we wanted all the oil we could get from these wells. Any whisper of worry and the operators of the drills and pumps might pack up and leave.

So off we went to Assam. The oilfield was at Digboi, but we were not allowed to go within fifty miles of the installations so we set up camp at a little place called Mariani, a small village in the centre of a group of tea plantations. The managers of these estates had organised a small club-house beside a well-tended field on which they had been accustomed to play polo, but the Chief Engineer's staff had requisitioned the far end as a camp site. We also had the use of an open-sided shed beside the club-house as a monsoon-proof store for our gear. This shed had been built to serve as a garage for club members and was a simple corrugated-iron roof on a steel framework.

I collected the stores which, for the most part, came in boxes marked 'Gelignite: High Explosive'. We were to be particularly discreet so I moved the section as inconspicuously as possible to the polo ground and set up camp. The boxes of gelignite were off-loaded into the open-sided shed and we took care to turn all the marks which showed the nature of the contents to the inside of the stacks so that they looked like simple wooden crates of military stores. The space inside these walls of wooden boxes was ample for my camp bed so I moved in. I reckoned I could safely tuck myself up at night with my hurricane lamp and I hoped that when the tea-planters saw me stagger into the shed after club-nights clutching my lamp, they would have no idea of what was in the plain wooden boxes. We carefully buried the primers and detonators at a safe distance apart. If the gelignite began to deteriorate, I expected that I would begin to suffer from headaches which were unattributable to club-nights. So far as I know, this mild deception worked and nobody asked me about what was in those boxes of 'engineer stores'.

We set about making ourselves comfortable in our tents with a supply of bamboo provided by the Military Engineering Service (MES). Bamboo saws easily across the grain and is easy to trim to size and shape so we were able to raise floors in the tents and put thatched roofs over them, thus making the tents cooler in the heat and proof against the torrential rains of the monsoon. We had two types of bamboo, 'jahti' and 'mooli', the former being the stronger, with a thick wall of tough wood round the hollow core. This hollow core closed across at each nodule up the stem and the nodules grew close together. Jahti was used for all the parts of a structure which were load-bearing, such as struts and beams. The other type, mooli bamboo, was thin-walled, with the nodules more widely spaced. Pieces of mooli bamboo split easily along their length, rather like chestnut paling. When these were hammered flat at the nodules they made strips which were pliant enough to weave into a strong form of matting. The process was similar to the making of hurdles and the 'taza' matting made an excellent flooring. With the polished green side uppermost it was decorative and felt as if it was sprung. The open weave allowed air to pass through and this helped to keep the tents cool inside.

We carried out a programme of normal sapper training, naturally emphasising subjects connected with demolitions. Every now and then I set out circles of white tracing tape in the middle of the training ground and we practised setting out charges with time-switches, detonating-fuse and other devices. I knew what the circles represented, but I kept that to myself and I do not think anyone connected us with the oil field.

Two sappers did all our cooking. They certainly coped well with their task and I never heard any complaints about the food they cooked on the section's regulation cooking gear, as supplemented from the local bazaar. They worked in a bamboo and thatch lean-to in an agreeable haze of curried wood-smoke and formed the social centre of the camp. Anyone off-duty would probably be found squatting on their hunkers gossiping with the cooks. I made regular checks of the 'langar' (cookhouse) to see that the rules of hygiene were being followed and that the gear was kept clean and complete. It kept the cooks on their toes and improved my knowledge of Urdu.

I was very fortunate in the choice of a batman, Chandar Mandi, who stayed with me for the next three and a half years. He was very quiet and very serious and it was with difficulty that I ever got him to smile. He looked after me like a mother and I could rely on him to be on the spot the moment I had finished all that I had to do, ready to see to my needs. He organised my bath every night, which did a lot for my morale in the heat. It was a primitive yet effective arrangement utilising a bit of the camp kit which was issued to officers. The bath was green canvas, rather like a child's paddling pool, about two feet square and some nine inches deep. The canvas was supported by a folding wooden frame which cunningly did double duty as the frame for a smaller canvas shape. Stood upright this formed a hand-basin. I never used the basin but that bath was a god-send. Chandar Mandi heated the water in a large canister, the universal ghee-tin of so many uses. He had persuaded the unit carpenters to fix him up with comfortable carrying handles to a pair of tins, and when I called for my bath he would appear at the trot, with one tin full of piping hot water and the other full of cold. I could truthfully claim to be supplied with running 'H & C'. He had my bath ready for me every night in the room formed by the boxes of gelignite.

We settled in and waited for things to happen. I expected the rest of the company to follow us to Assam, or the Japs to arrive when the monsoon ended but, after about six months, I was informed that I was to pack up as the danger of a Japanese attack reaching as far as Digboi had receded and I was able to rejoin 73 Field Company who were now in the Arakan."

The Arakan Front, 1942–1943

In July 1942 on the Arakan front, few communications existed south of Chittagong, a small sea-port some 250 miles south-east of Calcutta, other than the waterways of the country, the tidal chaungs which intersected the plains and were extensively used by local sampans. From Chittagong there was a railway to Dohazari and a few tracks out of the town. From the narrow coastal strip, dotted with paddy-fields and villages, rises the Mayu Range with the Arakan Yomas further to the east, anything up to 25 miles in width and 2,000ft in height. Like the Mayu Range, this barrier is a wilderness of jungle intersected by ravines and with knife-edged ridges ideal for defensive positions. The heat and dust during April and May are very trying and during the monsoon period from the middle of May to the end of September life becomes almost unbearable. The jungle sprouts visibly in the humid atmosphere, deluges of rain fill every ravine with a roaring torrent and roads are obliterated by mud. Mosquitoes and leeches abound. The only relief was afforded by the winter months from December to March when the sun shone on a wonderfully beautiful scene and the nights were cold.

14 Division, ordered south to make contact with the enemy, reached Maungdaw, but Japanese landings along the coast soon forced a withdrawal and the unusually heavy rain produced a stalemate. Even so, throughout October 1942, 73 Field Company, despite the fact that it was still equipped for the Western Desert, worked on the track from Dohazari to Ramu in a general effort to improve the road as far as Maungdaw. It was a road which ran partly through paddy fields and partly though undulating jungle. The transport of stores was difficult and several bridges were destroyed by heavy rain. However, a number of pile bridges were built by men of the Company, of which that over the Pruma Chaung was the largest – well over 400 feet in length and required many days for completion.

In October 1942 two of the Field Companies extended the track beyond Ramu to Bawli Bazaar. Excavating machinery was unknown, so local coolies did most of the work. Indeed at one time each section had a thousand or more coolies who were paid on a daily basis. Keeping the accounts was one of the biggest headaches for all officers and as Terence Tinsley commented: "time had to be allowed at the end of each working day to let the villagers return home and also for us to take up positions for the evening 'stand-to'. At the right moment we would order work to stop, collect stores, and the work-force would line up for pay. It did not take us long to realise that the number of payments made were beginning to exceed the morning's head count. Some of the labourers were plainly sneaking back into the line for a second hand-out. We solved this problem by using the purple office stamp on the out-stretched palms and the colour lasted just long enough (until next morning)."

On 16th December 1942 the first offensive operation against the Japanese converged on Maungdaw and on Buthedaung. However the Japanese withdrew without firing a shot, so the advance continued towards Akyab in order to capture the important airfield on the island before continuing onwards. In this operation 74 Field Company built several bridges and pushed a track some way south of Buthedaung, but it soon became clear that Akyab could not be taken before the monsoon broke.

Sadly, with enemy infiltration increasing, two officers of 74 Field Company were killed in one night as a withdrawal took place. Despite this, the Company continued to work on bridges and ferries right into March 1943 when a complete withdrawal to Buthedaung became necessary. In the Arakan mosquitoes often put more men out of action than Japanese bombs or bayonets and by April 1943, 74 Company, greatly under strength as a result of malaria, were back in India at Ranchi.

Meanwhile 73 Field Company continued to improve the roads south of Maungdaw and by the end of April an all weather road had been pushed as far south as Indin. Country boats, some thirty feet long and eight feet wide, were used to cross the numerous chaungs, often joined together to form rafts. There were very few vehicles and mules were the normal means of transport, but Terence Tinsley described how "they did not take kindly to boat trips and it was necessary to provide rafts with sides, built above mule-eye height, made of bamboo matting. This helped once the mules were aboard, but it still left the awkward task of getting them up the ramps to start with. Our sappers learned fast and soon became experienced mule psychologists. With the help of the mule drivers they learned that there were two methods to adopt, depending on the particular mule. It was simply a matter of knowing the direction in which the animal preferred to kick when annoyed or frightened. Some kicked out sideways and others kicked backwards. For the back-kicker you grabbed the right ear and pulled the mule up the ramp while he lashed out to the rear. For the side-kicker you grabbed his tail in a bunch in your hand and pushed from behind while the animal kicked away to port or starboard. I admit that I use the word 'you' deliberately. I never put the theory to the test myself, firmly agreeing with Kipling's words 'You are a better man than I am, Gungha Din'."

By May 1943 72 Field Company at Bawli Bazaar, north of Maungdaw, had begun to learn how to cope with the ways of the jungle and the conditions of war imposed by Japanese jitter parties. Gradually they realized the need for concealment and strict track discipline. There were no lights and no talking after dark. They learnt to stifle curses if they put their face in a thorn bush and to restrain their amusement when others did the same. Company offices were often just a palatial hole in the ground, deep enough to be sound proof and light proof when covered by a tarpaulin. Their main work during the monsoon included the bridging of chaungs during very heavy rainfall: in six days thirteen inches of rain fell. Malaria also weakened the Company strength, ten per cent being an average daily toll, but by December new anti-malaria orders, including the wearing of trousers instead of shorts and long-sleeved shirts, were of some help.

The Central Front, Burma, 1943

Meanwhile, back on the Assam-Burma border many miles to the north, by December 1942 Allied reconnaissance had begun to extend as far as Kalewa, a hundred miles down the Chindwin. In February 1943, infantry patrols frequently crossed the Chindwin river to gather information and parties of 68 Field Company often went with them, spending up to twelve days behind Japanese lines. Meanwhile, the remainder of the Company were working on the Kalewa road supervising the construction of heavy log bridges of teak, cut by coolie labour and positioned by elephants directed by local men. Earlier in the year they had been busy making a fair-weather road for 15cwt lorries. Here bulldozers were very busy, advancing tottering towards the face of open cuts, lurching in for a grip and as often as not sinking wildly in treacherous mud. Way ahead, intermittent explosions blasted the sandstone and removed large trees to reduce the work of the machines. Among the many timber bridges built in the area was Skew Bridge, laid upon 56 piles and completed by April 1943. A month later, 68 Company, having suffered much from fever brought on by hard work and low rations, moved back for watermanship training on Waithou Lake near Imphal.

Once the fair weather had returned, several Bengal Companies were again at work on roads south of Imphal, either towards Tamu or along the Manipur valley to Tiddim. The risk of malaria during the second monsoon was now being more effectively controlled by proper training and by the use of mepacrine but nevertheless it had taken a heavy toll. In September 1943 one Field Company had only thirty men available for working parties but still they strove to improve an old bridle path between Palel and Tamu to make it passable for jeeps. Although barely twenty miles apart on the map, the two places north needed fifty miles of road to connect them. Even after four or five months work, jeeps could only crawl along it and drivers considered it a nerve-wracking experience, only eased by the local rice beer.

71 Field Company, based nearer Tamu, maintained lengths of road, much of which was timber corduroy, and fair weather bridges were rebuilt to withstand the monsoon season. The work around Tamu also included shingling part of the Sittaung road. Not until June 1943 did 71 Field Company withdraw for a rest and further training, which included bunker attacks and the use of the new Bailey bridge equipment.

A tremendous amount of engineer effort was also employed back on the main road from Dimapur to Imphal as well as the new road to Tamu. Rock crushers were set up at various quarries and up to two thousand local coolies were employed. A visit from the Viceroy and frequent visits from the Army and Corps Commanders served as reminders of the road's importance. Work continued through the monsoon of 1943 and, despite the heavy rain, one way traffic enabled the forward troops to be kept supplied.

The path to Tiddim crossed the Manipur river 126 miles from Imphal. The last 17 miles of this lay through a steep and rocky gorge. Much of this being unsuitable for angledozers, 17 Division, with two brigades and two field companies, was in March 1943 given the task of building this stretch. While the Infantry and Gunners did the digging and blasting, the Sappers built the bridges and culverts, 47 of which were in 70 Company's eight-mile section. Lieutenant Urwin wrote that "equipment was always in short supply and much improvisation was necessary. Our transport was often limited to a jeep and about thirty mules per platoon. The Sappers had to be prepared to attack and defend. The terrain called for toughness and the work was exhausting. Most of the work was done with axe, pick and crowbar, assisted where possible by compressor trucks. The road was cut into the mountain side and every re-entrant had to have a bridge or culvert, local timber being used for the former. The road surface was always a problem; during the monsoon, only 4-wheel-drive vehicles could be sure of getting through, and in the summer the dust rose in choking clouds. Although there was always water in the deep valleys, the supply to the troops was a difficult problem and it was a familiar sight to see mule-drivers taking their animals down as much as 1,000ft to bring up water."

On 1st May 1943, the Tiddim Road was declared open for 15cwt vehicle traffic as far as the Manipur River crossing, but beyond that point there was still only a precarious jeep track to Tiddim. Many thousands of Chin coolies were employed on the upgrading and though it was appallingly difficult country through which to drive a road, the scenery was indescribably beautiful. Range upon range of forest-clad hills stretched to the horizon. Some of the peaks rose to 8,000ft and in the dim distance Kennedy Peak soared to nearly 9,000ft. The final stretch of the road to Tiddim involved a climb of 2,000ft in four miles and had thirty hairpin bends. This was known as 'The Chocolate Staircase', so called because, viewed from below, it appeared as a series of golden-brown steps hewn out of the purple jungle. Tiddim itself was a straggling village 5,600ft above sea level.

Their work on the gorge completed, 70 Company drove back to Shillong with 17 Division, leaving one platoon to support a battalion in Tiddim. This was their first relief from the forward area since marching out of Burma exactly a year before. However after two weeks in Shillong they were recalled to Tiddim, along with 48 Brigade, for the Japanese had started an advance into the hills.

In their absence there had been a drama at the Manipur river. While Roger Urwin with half a platoon was supporting operations at Tiddim, Jemadar Dharam Singh with the other half was busy keeping an improvised floating bridge in operation at the key river crossing. With the monsoon the river started to rise and one dark night in June it suddenly rose three feet and became a raging torrent, breaking six of the bridge's eight holding cables. Dharam Singh instantly took the decision to 'break' the bridge and save the boats, in these conditions a most difficult and dangerous task but one which he successfully accomplished. Although one petrol-barrel raft with four sappers on it was swept away, they managed to scramble ashore further downstream. Dharam Singh then built a 'flying ferry' for jeeps with some of the remaining boats. According to the Jemadar, when General Cowan came by a couple of days later, he shook the Jemadar's hand for "qariban ek minit" (almost a minute).

It soon became apparent that the Japanese were making a serious push into the Chin Hills. A most successful Gurkha attack at the end of May overran a strong Japanese position on the East side of the hills, but the British later decided that it was impracticable to hold so far forward and withdrew to the crest of the range. In August, 63 Brigade relieved 48 Brigade and, supported by 70 Company, attempted to repeat the original Gurkha success. Dense forest covered the approaches but the crest was rough and bare. As the sappers moved along a mule track, the rain was so heavy that visibility on a dark night was less than three feet and contact with each other could only be kept by means of phosphorescent leaves stuck in their packs. Sadly surprise was lost, the Japanese were well dug in and the attack failed, but not before the sappers had impressed the infantry by their courage and steadiness under fire. Shortly afterwards the Japanese brought up reinforcements and captured a peak overlooking Fort White, south-east of Tiddim, which they rapidly fortified.

Over the next six months 70 Company supported several attacks on this position, in one of which they succeeded in blowing in a Japanese bunker with its occupants inside, but suffered ten casualties including two good NCOs killed. The enemy's bunkers, made of timber and earth, were very elaborate and had interior blast-walls so that a grenade thrown through a firing slit would probably fail to dislodge the defenders. This was where the Sappers came into their own and an assault party, usually consisting of an NCO and three men, each man carrying a 20lb explosive charge with the NCO responsible for the firing mechanism, would crawl forward and destroy the bunker. In the intervals of supporting operations and several deep raids, the sappers worked hard to build a jeep track to the top of the range, eleven miles beyond Tiddim, overlooking the Burmese plain, and on to Kennedy Peak. These months of sporadic fighting were to prove excellent training for all arms for the severe test that lay ahead.

Along both the Tamu and Tiddim roads throughout 1943 the infantry, astride the ridges overlooking the Chindwin, were supported by the sappers. Leave was a very rare and doubtful privilege, such were the distances and difficulties of travelling. Yet new roads had been launched into Burma which had set its defenders on the frontier hills ready for the challenge of 1944.

INTO ITALY, 1943–1944

Allied landings in Sicily took place in July 1943 and, with scarcely a pause, the Eighth Army leapt the narrow straits onto the toe of Italy on 3rd September, the day the Italians signed an armistice. Meanwhile the Fifth Army stormed ashore at Salerno, south of Naples. The Germans, however, determined to turn Italy into a battleground and, eighty miles north of Taranto, they prepared to defend a series of natural obstacles that increased in difficulty as the Allied armies progressed.

The mountain chain created watersheds which directed rivers east and west across the paths of the invader. This terrain demanded a new type of warfare. 8 Divisional Engineers landed in Taranto in September 1943 and reached the battleground just south of the Biferno River on the eastern side of Italy. They brought with them two new tools, bulldozers and Bailey bridging. Bulldozers began to push northwards, impressing everyone with the amount and speed of their work, whilst the Bailey Bridge, its versatility equalling the simplicity of its construction, began to create temporary diversions and roadways as well as crossing the river gaps with astonishing ease, though not without casualties from enemy fire.

To the natural difficulties of the country were added two further obstacles, mines and mud. Rain turned streams into torrents overnight, sodden roads crumbled under unaccustomed traffic, retaining walls slid away from steep hillsides and earth churned into mud. All the bridges had been systematically destroyed by the Germans and likely diversions had been heavily mined, so that distances were now measured in hours rather than by miles. The programme of the engineers was therefore filled with road mending, mine clearing and continual bridging.

7 Field Company opened the programme in October 1943 by bridging the Biferno, a minor stream, and here the Bailey equipment and the bulldozers began to show their value. In order to send the stores forward, the Company built a long mud skidway down to the temporary river crossing and 69 Field Company, improving the roads to the rear, built many diversions. 66 Field Company cleared the river approaches of mines and booby traps, crossed the river with a trestle bridge of Folding Boat Equipment (FBE) and went on to search for obstacles on the far side. 7 Field Company and 69 Field Company went forward to assist in mine clearing and to launch small Bailey bridges for more permanent use. Soon the routine was almost commonplace.

The next obstacle of importance was the Sangro river. Here the Sappers toiled unceasingly to combat the weather and the broken roads. 7 Field Company launched one of many bridges but most of the Sappers' work consisted of mineclearing and improving the approaches with Sommerfeld track. North of the river the ground was so thick with minefields that a party of 47 Field Park Company removed two hundred and sixty one Tellermines in a day.

Aitken Lawrie, who earlier had commanded 69 Field Company for two years, described what happened next. "The Allied armies were advancing up the east coast when they were held up a few miles further on by the River Moro which ran along the bottom of a thickly wooded ravine 800 feet deep. The Germans had blown up the old masonry bridge and they had evidently considered that there was no feasible crossing place since they left no troops on the site.

The engineers of the British, Canadian, New Zealand and Polish Divisions evidently agreed as they had declared that no vehicle crossing was possible, but when the Sikh Subedar of 69 Company had a look at it, he at once said, "*Achchi bat, Sahib. Thik hai. Ham banaenge.*" (That's alright, Sir. We can do it.) That night all the parts for a Bailey bridge were silently carried by hand down the gorge and across the river, which was little more than a trickle, and laid out along a white tape on the far bank. Before dawn a 120 ft Class 12 Bailey bridge had been built and launched across the gap from the enemy side and our troops streamed over and soon established themselves north of the river. The Army commander was delighted and handed the flag from the bonnet of his staff car to the new OC, Major Higham, as a memento. This is now proudly displayed in the Regimental Museum in Roorkee."

7 Field Company then added another truss and the classification was thereby increased to Class 30. Later 66 Field Company took it over, added 30 ft and put it on new bank seats to keep it from sinking. The bridge was a triumph for 8 Divisional engineers, all Bengal Sapper companies, and was proudly known by the whole Division as 'The Impossible Bridge'.

The winter months in the area just south of the river were spent widening roads, clearing up mud, providing ditches and retaining walls, and laying Sommerfeld track. Six inches of snow fell in February 1944, and rain, slush and sleet were endured until the spring. Meanwhile many forces were gathered on the other side of the country to attack Monte Cassino, the keystone of the German defences. Already five separate offensives, including three by the Americans, had failed to move the central obstacle. 4 Indian Division, who had landed in Italy early in 1944, was sent to the scene and with them went 4 Field Company and 5 Bridging Section. As soon as they arrived the Company came under heavy shelling. Then, after twelve days of laborious spade-work in wet weather, they made mule tracks into the hill positions and completed a jeep track, known as 'Roorkee Road'.

7 Field Company's part in the Cassino attack is illustrated by the account of Major Thornton MC, at that time a platoon commander. "7 Field Company's involvement in the Cassino assault started with the preparation of roads towards the Rapido river. All this work was done at night and the off-loading of crushed rock from tipper trucks made such a noise as to send shivers down our spines but it had to go on with only a few interruptions.

On the night of the final offensive, I can recall only my own B platoon's part which was initially to construct assault boat pontoons and rafts to get the 1/5 Royal Ghurkas across the river for their attack on San Angelo, a short distance upstream from Cassino itself, in full view of the monastery. We worked under smoke a lot of the time with a long porterage of the equipment from the off-loading area to the river. No enemy fire was directed at us although there was plenty about. I had led my working party down to the river and then, returning to the off-loading point to chivvy up the sappers, I had found a group of them collecting fireflies in their hands – there were thousands of winking lights that night – rubbing them together, then throwing them upwards to form an additional fireworks display. Children could not have been happier in a playground.

This pleasant interlude was followed by a move some distance upstream to look after a Bailey bridge which had been constructed by another unit and was now under continuous smoke for 36 hours with the enemy lobbing 177 mm shells at the bridge. After each salvo my NCOs and I took it in turns to run out quickly to inspect the bridge. It was one of our most nerve-wracking experiences."

March 1944 brought even heavier shelling until Cassino town crumbled under concentrated bombing. On 15th March, as 7 Brigade tried to take Monastery Hill by way of a heap of masonry, the task of 4 Field Company was to prepare a route for tanks up to Castle Hill and thence to the Monastery. In reconnoitring this route, Lieutenant Murray and a New Zealand sergeant accidentally passed into the German forward positions. They took cover behind a house for over an hour; they then entered the house and went down to the cellar where they ran into a party of Germans. The sergeant was killed but Lieutenant Murray managed to shoot three of the enemy and got out of the house. Outside he met and shot a fourth German before making his escape up the road to Castle Hill. He was awarded the MC for this exploit.

By 18th March 1944, with Castle Hill besieged, every supply column ran the gauntlet of the enemy guns. During the assault 4 Field Company suffered fatal casualties and many men wounded. Jemadar Abdul Sadiq, though wounded and in great pain, insisted on completing his mine clearing task and was subsequently awarded the IOM.

However, as the rains stopped, rivers abated and the mud dried. Allied aircraft took to the air in great numbers and the increased speed of movement made a flank attack on Monte Cassino more likely to succeed. Another great assault was planned and 8 Indian Division was given the task of forcing the Rapido river south of Cassino town and fighting their way north-east to turn the Monastery defences. Three crossings of the swift flowing River Gari, part of the Rapido, were required and minesweeping parties went ahead to clear the approaches. All the work had to be done at night and 66 and 69 Field Companies were each in great danger as they built three bridges, code-named Oxford, Cardiff and Plymouth. With two of these bridges secure as supply routes, the infantry west of the Gari river were able to be reinforced. Smoke was often so thick that parties were occasionally lost in the fog. When visibility returned the work had to be done under heavy shelling. In these days Jemadar Sher Ali of 69 Company won the MC in rafting operations.

With Cassino finally taken, a swift retreat had begun and in the Allied pursuit the chief problem was bridging. Much of this work was carried out by 7 Field Company, but both 66 and 69 Field Companies were similarly involved, or else busy with demolition work or mine-clearance. Soon, so swift was the advance, thanks largely to the sappers, that Monte Cassino was left far behind and bridges prepared by the Germans for demolition were sometimes captured intact.

In five weeks the front had advanced two hundred and twenty miles, well to the north of Rome. But enemy resistance was stiffening in the mountains and a great effort was still needed. 10 Indian Division had landed at Taranto in March 1944 and while the attack on Cassino was at its height, its sappers were improving roads and bridges on the Adriatic side of Italy. At the end of June 1944, 8 Divisional Engineers moved back to rest, 10 Division took over and came up against the enemy in the Upper Tiber valley. The Division, who had trained for mountain warfare, began to press northwards along both sides of the Tiber, with 5 Field Company and 41 Field Park Company constructing tracks for jeeps and for tanks.

By August 1944, sapper patrols had reached Florence, where the only intact bridge was the Ponte Vecchio, its approaches blocked by rubble and mines. 7 Field Company cleared these approaches and forded the river. Meanwhile a part of 47 Field Park Company succeeded, where others had failed, in opening some sluice gates, so dropping the water level sufficiently to allow the infantry to ford the river unopposed.

Lieutenant KC McCallum of 7 Field Company was at this time involved in a gallant rescue which was recorded in the Divisional newsletter. This told how a party of Bengal Sappers under the lieutenant was working on road construction when an Italian civilian who was hanging about slowly drew near him and took out a cigarette from his pocket. Instead of smoking it, he proceeded to tear it open. Shaking off the tobacco, he showed the paper to the lieutenant and there, scrawled in broken English, was a request from Contessa Donna Maria Adelaide Borghese to send a British officer with troops to conduct her into the British lines. The Italian explained that the Contessa was the leader of the partisans in that area.

McCallum, with a small party of sappers, crossed the River Arno and soon appeared below her castle, which overlooked the ground across which the Contessa had to be conducted in broad daylight. The Germans had turned the castle into an observation post and defended it with four machine guns. Before the enemy could know what was happening, the Contessa had slipped out of the house, under cover of her orchard trees, and was well on her way, escorted by McCallum. Carrying her across the river in his arms the gallant lieutenant saw her safe to Brigade HQ. The grateful Contessa declared that her ambition was to see her castle used as a HQ where she could act as housewife to the Brigade staff and provide all the comforts of home.

She tried British gallantry once again when she requested that her maid who had been many years in her service should be rescued likewise. The rescue was accomplished with but one incident – the havildar escorting her to the Contessa was arrested by a Military Policeman on suspicion and had himself to be rescued. The 'Gallant Lieutenant' (as he became known) kept the Contessa's cigarette paper as one of his prized war trophies.

At the end of August 1944 an all-out offensive began on the Gothic Line. There was still a long way to go.

GATEWAYS TO BURMA, 1943–1944

The Arakan

Aware that the British planned to invade Burma in 1944, the Japanese decided to make a pre-emptive strike. Its aim was essentially defensive. They would strike first in the Arakan and draw the British reserves to that area and then 'burst like a torrent' into the Imphal plain, capturing the airfields and depots there, and thus preventing any major British advance that year.

In November 1943, out of the jungle of the Central Provinces of India, 77 Field Company brought specialised jungle training to meet any Japanese threat. They moved via Chittagong to improve roads for 7 Division which was slowly forcing the Japanese back to the Maungdaw-Buthedaung road. Work also began on the Ngakyedauk Pass, just to its north, along with a Madras Company, to make it possible to take jeeps; this involved extensive blasting of the rock face, but by 15 December the road was pronounced good by Lord Mountbatten who drove a jeep over the new alignment. The pass was later ranked as one of the best miniature engineering achievements of the Burma War.

Roads, mule tracks and bridges remained the chief tasks of the sappers and they all worked on the road down to Maungdaw as well as supervising coolie labour on roads elsewhere. It became clear that the Japanese were preparing an offensive, but it was not until February 1944 that the attack came.

The Mayu range was a tangle of precipitous ridges. Subsidiary spurs herringboned off the spine. The whole range was thickly wooded, with bamboo and elephant grass on the lower slopes and trees higher up. Reconnaissance was therefore very difficult and silent movement through the bamboo well nigh impossible. On 3rd February 1944 the leading elements of the Japanese task force, under cover of the morning mist, penetrated 7 Division's forward positions and, swiftly advancing, overran the Divisional Headquarters. The staff fought their way out and withdrew into the old Admin Base at the foot of the Ngakyedauk Pass. 74 Field Company covered the withdrawal to their own Brigade's Box, where despite serious casualties, they manned positions against further Japanese infiltration. The Admin Box was an open area of paddy fields surrounded by hills which had been the old Corps base. Now it swelled from a few score to thousands of men, with the infantry in a minority. On 10th February 1944 it was encircled and for eighteen days enemy aircraft, infantry and long range guns hammered at its position. The main Dressing Station was taken and retaken. At night every shadow seemed to be a Japanese soldier.

Dakotas flew over with supplies and, as 5 Division began to force a way over the ridge, a relief column from 26 Division came down from the north. HQ 7 Indian Divisional engineers, who were now Bengal Sappers, later wrote: "The food situation was very good, supply planes came over every day and the men were greatly impressed. We were short of nothing except sleep." In the Box men learnt to hold their fire against Japanese jitter parties who, using English, Urdu and Punjabi words, tried to make the sentries answer and so expose themselves. But soon the enemy found only walls of silence. As the tide of battle swirled around the Box 33 Brigade with 77 Field Company stood their ground. In one crisis, when the perimeter of the Box had been penetrated, Hugh Kelly, OC of 77, led a Sapper counter-attack with the bayonet. He was badly wounded himself and Peter Higgins his second-in-command was killed, but the enemy were either killed or driven out. For this feat Hugh Kelly was awarded an immediate MC.

Slowly a concentrated effort was made to open up the Ngakyedauk Pass as the infantry blasted and winkled the Japanese from bunkers and positions on top of the Pass, and so enabled 74 Field Company to start to clear the road of obstacles, filling in craters, cutting new paths and repairing blown culverts. On 24th February the Pass was clear again and the first tank got through. The tenacity of the defenders had baffled the enemy whose rations now began to give out. When late in February 1944 the tanks of 5 Division and 26 Division linked up with the Admin Box, the Japanese rout was complete. Hardly one in four escaped from these operations which only ended when the monsoon broke in June.

During February 72 Field Company, in support of 26 Division, had turned a jeep track to the Admin Box into a 15cwt road which was, it was said, 'the lifeline of the Division and the Brigade'. A tremendous artillery concentration gave them no sleep at night and when a tank overturned on the Ngakyedauk Pass 72 Field Company made the necessary diversion to enable the advance to continue.

The Japanese task force had been defeated but with the monsoon approaching the victorious troops could go no further. Another more pressing factor was that men were desperately needed to stem the hordes of Japanese thrusting up the Manipur river into the Imphal plain.

During ten hectic days in mid March 1944 the troops, guns, jeeps and mules of 5 Division were loaded into transport planes and flown north to Imphal, nearly four hundred miles away. By this new daring method, a large formation was lifted bodily out of the Arakan to fight in another place.

Back in the Arakan, however, the 14th Army's spring task was still incomplete as they had not yet reached their objective of the narrow, all-weather road running between Maungdaw, which was only a little river port consisting of some twenty or thirty 'bashas' set around an open area leading down to a simple jetty, and Buthidaung, another small river port about sixteen miles to the east over the Mayu Range. Back in 1918 a company had been formed which planned to open up trade in the area by linking these two ports with a light railway and two tunnels were constructed in order to cross the Mayu Range, but the scheme did not succeed and the railway was converted into a road. It was important to secure this road so that the advance could continue south towards Akyab, but the Japanese stored ammunition and supplies in the tunnels and surrounded them with a maze of defensive positions and it was not until March that Tunnels West fell. But Tunnels East, the strongest natural position in the area, the capture of which was essential for the security of the road, was still held by the Japanese. In May 72 Field Company joined in the bitter fighting which finally wrested the road from the enemy.

While this fighting was going on, a plan was being made to move a force by sea to a village on the peninsular opposite Maungdaw and Terence Tinsley was instructed to construct a jetty for the troops to disembark. He wrote later that "In addition, some temporary facilities were asked for ashore, such as a couple of cooking shelters and some latrines. These were to be set up under cover of the trees and when I was siting them I came across some piles of what looked like brown tennis balls. They were just at the spot I had chosen for the latrines, so it looked as if some elephants had been issued with the same pocket book on hygiene that I was using. Elephants are, I believe, creatures of habit and I did wonder if any of the troops were due for a shock in the middle of the night while using the facility." No casualties were reported.

The Central Front, 1944

The Japanese offensive on the Central Front was launched more than a month after that in the Arakan, partly to give time for the British reserves to be committed there, and partly because one of their divisions was delayed. Their aim was to capture the four airfields and many supply depots on the Imphal plain and so forestall the looming British advance into Burma. To do this they would first cut off and destroy 17 Division in the area of Tiddim and then attack Imphal with one division from the south and another from the north. Meanwhile a third division would seize Kohima and a long stretch of the road from Dimapur, thus isolating Imphal and preventing its reinforcement.

The British also had three divisions and their plan, if a Japanese attack came, was to withdraw to positions around the Imphal plain. 17 Division, however, was deployed in the mountains some 180 miles south of Imphal. To withdraw it prematurely would be unforgiveable and so, perhaps inevitably, the order was given too late and the Division had to fight its way back. When the warning order for the withdrawal was received, 70 Company was given the task of destroying the 11-mile road which rose 2,500 feet up from Tiddim. Using massive charges dug down into the rock over the previous three days, they blew the road away behind the rear-guard in four places, as well as laying mines and booby-traps. The Japanese light tanks and heavy field artillery were held up for six days and this was to be critical in the race to reach the bottle-neck of the vital bridge over the Manipur River, some 40 miles north of Tiddim, which the Japanese were already threatening.

Any satisfaction felt by 70 Company was dissipated the following night. 48 Brigade and divisional troops marched down the 'Chocolate Staircase', ten miles north of Tiddim, and harboured in two Boxes beside the river. 70 Company was split between the two. In the centre of one Box some administrative troops lost their heads when the Japanese jittered the camp. They started firing automatic weapons straight into a sapper platoon holding the perimeter and caused several casualties. Jemadar Dharam Singh and a Naik courageously went to try and stop them and both were shot dead. It was a tragic end for a very fine VCO who was widely admired in the division, and it was a blow to the whole company for he was very popular.

414 Field Park Company had been sent back across the river a few days earlier and harboured at the Forward Supply Depot (FSD) at milestone 109 from Imphal. They were unlucky. This was the target for a Japanese brigade which had crossed the river south of Tiddim and marched up the west bank. The FSD, in a valley and surrounded by hills, was indefensible. The garrison made a gallant attempt to defend it but were overrun. 414 Company survivors made their way back along forest paths and the Japanese seized ten miles of the road behind our lines.

Although two more Japanese divisions were now approaching, General Scoones at Imphal took the high risk of deploying his last reserves and sent two brigades of 23 Division a hundred miles down the Tiddim road to help clear the block. Meanwhile, 63 Brigade successfully held off the Japanese brigade attacking the Manipur bridge while the rest of 17 Division crossed, and 48 Brigade, in a brilliant operation in which 70

Company played its part, recaptured the FSD and in the process virtually destroyed a Japanese battalion. Reckoning their casualties too heavy while their main objective still lay ahead, the Japanese withdrew from the road and the British forces all passed through to Imphal, 71 Company destroying the bridges on the way.

Lieutenant Urwin recorded his impressions of the withdrawal. "It was a sad business blowing up the road and the bridges that had been made with such labour. We didn't really know what was happening. Nerves were taut and we had to grow accustomed to the idea of being surrounded. It was three months before we could feel that the Japs were only in front and not everywhere else as well. Certain things stand out in my mind: the slowness of the convoy as we moved away from Tiddim; a piece of rock falling on my tin helmet after a demolition; being badly 'jittered' by the Jap in camp at night; a reconnaissance at a ruined camp; finding a tin of milk and drinking it straight off; marching a very long way one night and finally being shelled when we reached the Imphal Plain."

On 4 April 1944 70 Field Company reached Imphal after 183 miles of continual withdrawal. A week or so later they went south again to villages on either side of the Tiddim road to seek out and burn as much of the rice stores as possible. The importance of the day's work was realized later when, after the siege of Imphal, it became clear that one of the main reasons for the Japanese defeat was that their rations gave out.

While these forces were fighting their way back, a severe crisis had developed in Imphal and at Kohima, there being no infantry reserves and strong Japanese forces approaching both places. Three brigades were hastily flown up from the Arakan, and the Japanese advance was halted. Now began three bitter months of savage fighting before the Japanese were forced to acknowledge defeat and to withdraw the remnants of their shattered 15th Army.

Six Bengal Sapper field companies took an active part in these operations. There were many memorable feats but only a few can be mentioned here. 2 and 77 Field Companies were in the savage fighting at Kohima. Lieutenant John Wright of 2 Field Company was involved in one stirring episode. A stubbornly defended Japanese bunker was causing great difficulty and he led a party with prepared explosive charges and blew it in, killing the occupants. For this he was awarded an immediate MC. He later designed the war memorial which stands there, with its infinitely moving inscription:

When you go home
Tell them of us and say
For your tomorrow
We gave our today.

North of Imphal, Captain Ivory of 74 Company recalled one incident at that time: "During May 1944 we received a consignment of Argentine mules, all rated at 140lbs carrying capacity, and set out on a series of expeditions cutting jeep or mule tracks on hillsides to facilitate supplies to forward infantry. Lieutenant Neilson designed and supervised a successful suspension bridge over the Imphal river which was in monsoon spate, using salvaged wire ropes. It could carry a single jeep or two loaded mules with drivers. Most mules would not venture onto a swaying bamboo bridge deck without a leader and usually there was only one lead mule available who crossed and recrossed the bridge until he led the whole column across, one by one. Hessian screens had to be erected on each side of the bridge, so that the animals could not see the torrent below."

South of Imphal the whole of 70 Field Company supported 48 Brigade, less a battalion, in a bold attempt to turn the tables on the main Japanese forces advancing up the Tiddim road. Secretly assembling south of Palel at dusk, the Company put a Folding Boat Equipment (FBE) bridge across the Manipur river. The brigade then crossed and lay up in two villages, the bridge being removed before dawn. The next day the brigade put in a block on the Tiddim road twelve miles behind the Japanese front line. It provoked a violent reaction for vital enemy reinforcements were on their way. The Japanese 15th Army Commander had passed through two days earlier, having come up to direct the final attack on Imphal. The Gurkhas, however, held the block successfully for six days against repeated attacks. The Sappers in the block mined the road, accompanied patrols and scraped an airstrip from which light planes evacuated the seriously wounded to Imphal.

Ordered to withdraw, the Brigadier decided to return up the road and through the Japanese front line, so the brigade seized a village near the road, five miles to the north. That night the monsoon broke, and one light and three medium Japanese tanks, supported by a fresh battalion, launched an attack on the Gurkha battalion holding the block on the road. They had many casualties and would have been in grave trouble but for the mines laid by Roger Urwin which knocked out two tanks and blocked the road. The Sapper platoon in the block had, like the rest, a very unpleasant night as their slit trenches filled with water and the tanks blazed away at anything they could see.

For the next four days the brigade fought its way north, the Sappers protecting the rear against the tanks by laying mines and demolishing bridges. Enemy shelling was severe on the last day, but the planned Japanese advance on Imphal had been emasculated by 48 Brigade's activities and failed.

Throughout June there was much hard fighting as the Japanese were worn down and forced to accept defeat. Then began a British advance which would not stop until Burma was recaptured.

The Advance on the Tiddim Road

By mid July, in one village, nothing was left but 'a sea of huge waterlogged craters, shell holes and sticky mud, with not a house and scarcely a tree or bank standing.' In the early stages of the advance, Sappers were active in bunker-busting and fought with the infantry as, one by one, the hill features on the road to Tiddim were retaken. The decision to pursue the enemy during the monsoon season doubled the obstacles of terrain and jungle. In front of them were huge craters, mile upon mile of mud, treacherously steep hills and the Manipur river swollen by rains to a powerful roaring torrent.

It was fully expected that the existing bridge, crossing the river further south, would be blown by the retreating enemy and the site heavily defended. Captain Ivory, by now 2IC of 74 Field Company, was ordered to reconnoitre the Manipur river for an alternative crossing-place: "Naik Avadh Behari Singh was to accompany me on the intended week-long absence in the Chin hills and we were to attach ourselves for at least part of the journey to a Gurkha patrol of 'V-Force', a cloak-and-dagger outfit which spent most of its time in enemy-occupied territory. Progress was good at first, downhill to the valley bottom; there the jungle was so thick that the Gurkhas took turns to hack a passage through, while the rest of us picked leeches off each other's backs. Then came the climb to the opposite side of the valley and I was glad I had declined the invitation to arm myself with a heavy Tommy-gun instead of my Smith & Wesson revolver. After a brief pause on the ridge, we plunged into the next valley, halting at a village which we surrounded until we were sure it was clear of Japs. Then we took zu (rice beer) with the headman. We were cautious with the zu which had a reputation for anaesthetising the legs.

The next day was much like the first and we spent the night in another village of only eight huts, where we were entertained with more zu, and chicken and millet. We were loaned blankets which had been abandoned by 17 Div in their withdrawal a few months earlier. Under the floor of the hut allotted to us there was a store of other military equipment including British rifles and ammunition. The following morning we were soon reminded of the enemy's presence when we found a Japanese mess-tin on a wood fire beside our path. My Gurkha escort pointed to tracks downhill in the long grass where the Japs had escaped, but I pointed to the ridge ahead of us on our route and I suspect the Lance-naik was disappointed in me for denying him a Jap-hunt.

On Day 5 we reached the Manipur river and Avadh Behari and I set about measuring the river. Being deep and very fast, we calculated the width by the time-honoured 3-4-5 triangle (to make a right-angle) method using the knotted string which I had had the supreme foresight to bring. The speed of flow was determined by that other time-honoured method, adopted by Winnie-the-Pooh, of timing the passage of sticks.

Our return journey was much the same as the outward and we stayed again in one of the villages we had previously visited. This time a young woman came into the hut with an offering of dried fish. As well as bearing the fish she was breast-feeding a baby and smoking a portable 'hubble-bubble'. The fish was acceptable; the smoke was foul.

Back with 74 Company I shaved off a nine-day stubble and wrote my report on an alternative crossing of the Manipur river. Next day I felt ill and the following day I was evacuated by field ambulance to a tented hospital near Imphal. There I was nursed through scrub typhus fever and nurtured on champagne for the last five days of it, before being flown out to Comilla for convalescence. I was not to see the Division again until the year 1944 was nearly over."

The main supply line was now the Dakotas, dropping bundles from the sky which blossomed into rations, stores and medical supplies. The Sappers set the pace of the advance, bulldozing the craters full enough for vehicles to pass over, opening the drains, laying trackway over seas of mud, building short spans of Bailey bridging and, wherever necessary, using pick and shovel to repair the roads. Huge landslides blocked the way, the result of both enemy action and the monsoon. Again and again with explosive and bulldozers, followed by gangs of labouring shovels, another sticky road was exposed and remade.

Captain Leslie Beswick related with stark reality something of the horrors of being shelled on the Tiddim road and dealing with a Japanese night attack: "In the afternoon we put panjis (varying lengths of bamboo, sharpened at both ends and placed in the ground at an angle) around the perimeter, in lieu of barbed wire. Booby-traps were set to reinforce the panjis and everyone roofed over their slit trenches with thick pieces of wood, covered with turf.

By five o'clock we had made our plans for the next day when from the opposite hills came a muffled bang followed by a rushing noise ending in a crash right inside our perimeter. We ran towards our trenches shouting to the men to take cover before the next shell. I was sharing my trench with my orderly and another sapper. My orderly was quiet, I was quietly scared and the sapper was babbling prayers to himself. From outside came horrible screams which told of hits on trenches. I found that I was shaking and sweating and the thought that I must not appear to be afraid, and so let the men down, kept hammering through my brain.

The ground was shaking and as I heard the whine of each shell I was silently praying 'not this one, please', and the words of the 23rd Psalm, remembered from my choirboy days, ran through my mind. Suddenly I saw stars and lost consciousness.

I became aware of my orderly shaking me in pitch darkness and for a moment thought that I had been blinded. Then I realised that the wood and earth roof had been brought crashing down upon our trench and that one of the logs had knocked me out. With bare hands we moved enough debris for me to crawl out but, as the shelling recommenced, I quickly flopped back. There were more screams and I heard shouts of 'the Major Sahib is dead'. Eventually the shelling ceased and I climbed out shaking like a leaf. All around was the sour smell of cordite and from time to time screams came from the first-aid dug-out. I walked round as calmly as I could to try and create confidence and visited each trench asking '*sab chiz thik hai*?' (everything OK?). A few cheery words sufficed, but I had never felt less cheerful nor more scared.

We agreed that we could expect an attack an hour or so after nightfall. My platoon manned the inner circle of trenches and formed the second line of defence. We were to use bayonets and knives and not bullets to deal with any Japs breaking through the outer ring. We were to fire only if a whole section of the outer defences was overrun. The two Dogra infantry companies we were with had also suffered several casualties and were now thirsting for revenge.

As darkness fell we watched headlamps coming from the direction of Tiddim and the gunner FOO tried to phone the mountain guns but enemy scouts had cut the wires. Eventually he established a wireless link, not always easy after nightfall, but before he could bring down any gunfire the vehicle lights went out. For a time there was silence then a muttering on our left gradually extended above us until we realised that we were surrounded.

The sharp whang of one of my booby-trap grenades was followed by screams, then silence. Suddenly shouts of 'Banzai Nippon' and 'Don't fire!' in English and Urdu heralded the first charge. As the yells came nearer the Dogra VCOs were calling on their men to hold their fire. Then, as the Japanese blundered into the panjis, our perimeter burst into a sparkling and flashing ring as the Bren guns chattered. As the enemy got closer the noise of hand grenades thrown on command by our riflemen was followed by muffled screams, and again silence.

Now the enemy could be heard concentrating on our left again and the mountain guns were called into action, supported by the mortars from our position. Japanese mortars were fired in reply and on they came again. Very lights were fired to help our Bren gunners and the attack was broken again. When a third attack from a different direction was repelled we began to feel certain of being able to keep them out.

The attack continued at intervals with diminishing force until, an hour or so before dawn, there was silence. I snoozed in my trench until dawn when I was woken by the usual order to 'Check on ammunition and report!' An early morning mist screened us from the prying eyes of enemy artillery spotters as I went my rounds. September the 19th had begun."

By the second week of September the Manipur river itself now challenged 2 Field Company as they struggled to span its raging torrent. A platoon had crossed by boat, but various efforts to conquer the flood failed. A sapper who tried to swim the current was rapidly swept away, whereupon Jemadar Jahan Dad, although he knew that six people had been drowned in the river that very morning, ran down the bank and plunged in to save the man. Despite the current he reached the sapper, grabbed hold of him and then, inch by inch, dragged him back to safety. Jemadar Jahan Dad won the George Medal for his bravery.

On 19th September, platoons of 2 Field Company completed a FBE ferry which on the first day, in competition with the Bombay Sappers, averaged ten to twelve crossings every hour. Next day 2 Field Company took over both ferries but two days later the river had risen so high that ferrying continued only with pontoon rafts. By 4th October not only had the main body of the Division, with many tanks and a great load of equipment, been taken over the river but the personnel and the needs of two hospitals had also been safely ferried over.

Meanwhile 74 Field Company had bridged the raging Beltang Lui, a tributary of the Manipur river running directly across our front, and then on reaching Tiddim ten miles further on had restored its water supply. 2 Field Company then joined them to labour under fire to repair the cliff roads to Kennedy Peak and beyond, work which was to take them to Kalemyo, nearly sixty miles beyond Tiddim and approaching the Chindwin river. In mid November the East Africans and units of 5 Division met in Kalemyo to celebrate a joint victory over both the Japanese and the monsoon weather. The time had come for rest and re-equipping, so both 2 and 74 Field Companies flew out of Burma, after fourteen months of working and fighting, leaving a springboard for the advance on Mandalay and Rangoon.

Down in the Arakan the rainy season was no fun for anyone. During three weeks of July 1944, the monsoon rains totalled four feet and roads were closed, even to mules. Companies, which had spent the spring watering the roads to keep down the dust, now found it impossible to keep themselves dry and, with malaria prevalent and the work continual, there was little to raise the spirits. However, with explosives and bulldozers the Sappers eventually opened their road and in August, 25 Divisional Commander could say: "The fact that the road – Maungdaw to the Tunnels – has not only weathered the monsoon but is in good condition for bearing the strain of future operations, reflects great credit upon your troops."

Farther east, as 5 Division made its monsoon advance to Tiddim and Kalemyo, the Corps Troops Engineers also came out of their defence 'Boxes' and began work again on the supply roads. When the Japanese faded away one night, 75 Field Company began work on two Bailey tasks, allotted to them before being switched to the Tiddim road, to help maintain the road to the Manipur river where 2 Field Company ran the ferry. The stretch of road at Milestone 91 contained the world's finest 'Slough of Despond' where a bulldozer shifted muck continually. The drill here was to collect about five vehicles going in the same direction and then, using the bulldozer as an engine, make a train and pull them all through. There was much spadework too: one day the Company Subedar announced that the Company had now moved "at least half Assam".

Also on the Tiddim Road were 80 Field Company whose roadworks enabled 5 Division to move forward. At Bishenpur, fifteen miles south of Imphal, they felt some satisfaction that the Japanese were only five miles down the road but there was less enthusiasm when the work required of them was hand shingling the road among the stench of dead Japanese. After lording it over thousands of coolies this was not very lively work. As the Japanese retreat continued, platoons went down the road replacing old bridges. Soon 75 Field Company were the only Corps Troops left on the Tiddim road and orders were expected daily for the road to be abandoned. In December 1944, as prophesied, the road was closed and 5 Division relied thenceforth on air supply alone.

The Advance on the Tamu Road

Meanwhile on the parallel Tamu Road 33 Corps Troops Engineers began to assist the Division going down to Kalemyo and Kalewa. Actually 80 Field Company got there first, removing large trees from the path of the bulldozers and giving the drivers protection as they worked. The road eventually reached a speed of advance of nearly four miles an hour. The monsoon being over, sappers found that the road was now so dusty that nine inches of dust could rise to twenty feet which threatened safe driving. The remedy was water-carts to keep down the dust and one enormous improvised water carrier was made out of a tank transporter. The Company also improved the road with stretches of elephant bridges, causeways made of green timber felled in the jungle, which actually carried weights double the normal specified load.

In November when 75 Field Company joined 80 Field Company on the road, the CRE of 7 Division seized the chance of another Field Company and they were soon in support of 7 Division's crossing of the Yu river which runs down the Kabaw Valley to join the Chindwin at Kalewa. The Mintha approach track to the Chindwin was due to take both 19 and 20 Divisions on the road to Mandalay and everyone from General Rees downwards seemed to be lending a hand.

The main task on the Chindwin was the bridging of the river at Kalewa. Other Sapper units had been brought in and construction of the main Floating Bailey Bridge started at dawn on 9 December 1944 when equipment for the eastern bank was rafted across. Both the eastern and western landing bays were finished by nightfall and the first floating bay was towed into position very early next morning. When the remaining bays were brought into position there was an error of just seven inches, so the west floating bay with eleven floating bays attached was pulled back over timber bank seats and at 1450 hours on 10th December the longest floating Bailey bridge in any theatre of war at that date was complete. The bridge, a triumph for Bengal sappers, was named 'Grub Bridge'. Two days later an air attack was made but every bomb missed. The mastery which the Allies had achieved on the Chindwin is illustrated by the manner in which 75 Field Company joined 4 Corps. In eight days river sailing the Company safely travelled 139 miles down the Chindwin, from Tonhe to Kalewa, bringing, in a convoy of rafts, stores, bridging equipment, petrol and one jeep.

NORTH ITALY AND GREECE, 1944–1945

By the end of August 1944 not only the German High Command but the enemy rank and file also seemed to know that the war could not be won. Behind the formidable defences of the Gothic Line they were aware of the supreme confidence of the assaulting troops.

The Gothic Line was cracked north of Florence. The terrain was so difficult that the enemy could not believe that an attack in strength could be maintained. The engineers' work on the roads was therefore decisive. All the Bengal Sappers of 8 Division played their part, filling in craters, making diversions and pushing jeep tracks after the assaulting troops. 47 Field Park Company sent out bulldozers to brave shellfire and to repair broken culverts using five gallon drums that came out of their workshops. The rains had made ford-crossings of the Arno impossible. There was mud everywhere. 5 Bridging Section had reported laconically: "result of the day's work, four lorries extracted from the mud."

At the beginning of October 1944, 4 Field Company built a Bailey bridge over the Rubicon near Rimini where history records that Caesar burned his boats, indicating to his Roman legions that his advance was to continue and that there would be no retreat. 4th Indian Division assumed that it would follow Caesar's example and continue to advance northwards to the Austrian frontier but events were to decide otherwise.

News arrived that the Division was to be withdrawn from the Eighth Army and sent with 4th British Division to Greece from where the German Army of Occupation had withdrawn. The Greek Government returned to take over the running of their country but found that they were opposed by a strong Communist movement, collectively called the ELAS, who wished to overthrow them and establish Greece as a Communist state. The Greek Government appealed to Britain for help in preventing the Communists from seizing power.

5th Indian Infantry Brigade, including 4 Field Company, landed at Piraeus in the second week of December and began the unpleasant and dangerous task of evicting the ELAS forces from the maze of back streets and alleyways of the Piraeus. In this situation there was no recognised front line, active ELAS supporters looked like any other Greek civilians and their snipers could appear anywhere at any time. Fierce street fighting ensued but the ELAS forces were steadily pushed back and by the beginning of January they were finally evicted. The city of Athens was also cleared of their activities by the other British formations.

6 Army Troops Company had arrived in Piraeus somewhat earlier to rebuild the docks and run the town's generators. At one time the Company was besieged by ELAS forces and found it was out of touch with the

sappers operating the town's lighting plants. Captain Hawkins relates that: "In charge of the sappers running the plant for the HQ and hospital buildings was Lance Naik Mohammed Imait Ullah. He spoke no English and could not make the British Army Signal Office understand that he wished to speak to his OC in Piraeus. Undefeated, he just stood on the pavement outside the HQ building saluting every officer who passed and greeting each with '*Salaam Sahib*' until an officer returned his greeting with '*Salaam Bhai, ap thik hai*?' (Greetings, how are you?). Problem solved and message sent!"

At the end of the hostilities 5 Brigade began to move northwards through Greece towards the Albanian and Yugoslav frontiers. 4 Field Company went to Volos to begin work on road repairs and create diversions around the bridges which had been destroyed, allowing vehicles to get forward. The airfield was also cleared for use by small aircraft.

On their way north, the sappers passed through Larissa, Elasson and Trikkala, leaving the roads open behind them, before reaching the Aliakmon river at Servia where a three span bridge with a length of 510 ft had been demolished. A 'flying ferry' was constructed on the crossing allowing vehicles to move to and from Athens and Salonika. It also became very popular with Greek farmers moving their livestock to summer pastures. The Company finally moved to Kozani, a small town about sixty miles south of the Yugoslav border, where its headquarters were established. Work then began on an extensive programme of road works and bridge building.

The main task ahead was the building of a large Bailey bridge over the Aliakmon river. Work began immediately on the abutments and the equipment began to arrive on site on 22nd June, the bridge being named 'Red Eagle' in honour of 4th Indian Division, and stands as the special contribution by Bengal Sappers to reconstruction work in Greece. It was opened on 31st July when Commander, 5 Indian Infantry Brigade handed the bridge over to the Governor General of Macedonia. He formally declared the bridge open and it was duly blessed by the Bishop of Kozani. The Company then enjoyed a few days rest at Katerini on the Aegean Sea which, after the hectic activities of the past months, was much appreciated.

Meanwhile back in Italy, 10 Division carried the offensive into the knife-edged northern reaches of the Apennines. Sappers cleared oak and poplar trees to open up a field of fire for the artillery and their bulldozers ploughed a way through heavy clay to maintain the roads. Late in October, 5 Field Company were given the task of bridging yet another river but this time it was done by converting an old aqueduct to a bridge. At one time shells were falling there at the rate of about two every second. However the walls of the aqueduct gave some protection to the sappers and the bridge was completed before daylight next morning. For his direction of this operation Lieutenant Hare of 5 Company was awarded the MC.

By mid-September 8 Division, back into action, had broken the Gothic line and the sappers concentrated on the development and maintenance of the routes forward. Heavy rain and the narrow passages afforded by the Apennine barriers completely halted the initial progress. Moreover the Germans had retreated skilfully leaving no bridges and many mines.

The Bengal Sappers now faced a huge programme of bridging. 47 Field Park Company found their task heartbreaking, as bridging lorries often slipped their loads and sometimes had to be pushed over the side of the road to let others through. On one occasion a bulldozer fell over the side of a cliff, turning ten times before it landed with engine and track undamaged. Many new tracks had to be blasted for jeeps. The principle was to get jeeps through to the other end as quickly as possible so that they could take supplies and ammunition forward and bring back the wounded.

From late November until early January 1945, over four thousand feet of Bailey bridging was launched, thirty four miles of road were opened and many more miles maintained. In all, the Bengal Divisional engineers built more than twenty large Bailey Bridges and a dozen smaller ones. All the piers were also of Bailey construction and one bridge had a pier 70 ft high, the highest in Italy, and was opened for traffic on Christmas Day, 1944. When that sector was stabilized in mid January 1945, 8 Divisional Engineers rested. The campaign in the mountains was over.

The Sappers with 10 Division now began preparations for a new kind of terrain where every road was flanked, usually on both sides, by a deep irrigation ditch; the main roads made of tarmac were few, and the countryside was intersected by a network of third class roads which were narrow and without foundations. Constant road maintenance was required of all sappers.

Bitter weather was followed by equally bitter fighting. Not until February 1945 could work on the approach roads to the River Senio be resumed. This was a new type of river flowing between flood banks raised perhaps thirty feet above the level of the plain. The enemy had fortified both banks thereby making three obstacles out of one river. Detailed recces were made and March was spent in various trials and rehearsals for the Senio. The Senio and the Santerno rivers were just over three miles apart on the Divisional sector. 8 Division now returned to the area and looked to the sappers to construct a large number of assault bridges. On 9th April 1945 the drone of bombers signified the commencement of the attack on the Senio. The infantry waded the river with flamethrowers in close support. Soon three out of five bridges were in use and the armour swiftly reached the banks of the Santerno. This was a wider and deeper obstacle than the Senio and the problem was to get tanks across by daylight in order to hold the bridgehead and to construct sufficiently strong bridges to pass through the wheels and tracks of the follow-up Division.

The end was in sight. The artillery hurried forward and in the swift advance to the River Po the Field Companies replaced damaged bridges and opened up roads. When the river was finally reached, its great width put an immediate Bailey bridge crossing out of the question. Instead an assault crossing was planned for the night of 25th April with 8 Division the first to try. The infantry did not wait but were ferried across by amphibious tanks, the ferries and rafts of the Sappers being hardly used. The rafts of 7 Company, though, proved useful and they put more than thirty lorries across the river early on 26th April and averaged four trips an hour across the 1,000ft gap despite a three knot current.

All the Field Companies were across the Po by the end of April and reaching for the Adige River, a formidable river fifteen miles beyond the Po. 7 Company improvised rafts for jeeps and platoons of 66 and 69 Field Companies completed a 460ft FBE bridge across the river. The infantry were still ahead. With a sense of finality the bridge was named 'Roorkee.' Throughout the crossings from the Senio to the Adige rivers 47 Field Park Company were hard at work moving advance dumps, not only for 8 Divisional sappers, but also for three other Field Companies. Over two hundred and fifty lorry-loads of Bailey were moved by the Company's transport and as soon as each battle ended salvaging began. Clearing up the area afterwards was also a task of some magnitude.

Meanwhile as the massive Eighth Army assault succeeded, 5 Field Company cleared mines and in April 1945 completed the biggest Bailey bridge they had yet built. Two more large Baileys were launched by them and others delaunched. They also built a high level Bailey on existing masonry piers over the Adige.

On 29th April 1945 when the Companies were due to go over the Adige orders were cancelled and everyone told to stay put. Rumours of victory were in the air.

BURMA: THE ADVANCE DOWN THE COAST

The defeat of the 1944 Japanese offensive made a general advance possible, both in the Arakan and from the Chindwin River. On the coast 15 Corps was soon into its stride. The Divisions began to leapfrog down the coast of Burma and in three months they were halfway to Rangoon.

25 Division led off with landings on Akyab island, the first large-scale amphibious operation in Burma, and Major Beaumont, OC 78 Field Company, described the scene on landing: "When I approached the mansion allotted to my Company I found that it had been burnt to the ground and there was a dead dog in the well. I toured the looted and deserted town which had been abandoned by the inhabitants for at least two years to escape the Allied bombing. In the main street the vegetation had grown up between the road and the buildings so that it seemed as if one were walking along a jungle path."

Lieutenant Adrian Sandes, also of 78 Company, had an exciting landing: "We had been disembarking down scramble-nets and were practically all aboard the 'Z' landing craft when I saw an aeroplane diving straight at us. A small black object dropped from it and hit the water about a hundred yards to starboard. Realising immediately that this was a Jap air attack, the Subedar and I lay down on deck vaguely aware of machine-guns firing and the splash of bullets around. We heard no sound of the bomb. Soon the plane was back again followed by another. They concentrated on our ship but failed to do any damage although one bomb fell very close. Our anti-aircraft guns opened an ear-splitting barrage and the Spitfires joined in, six enemy planes being shot down."

The Company was soon installed in a camp near the derelict aerodrome outside the jungle-covered town. "Jap bunkers were everywhere" continues Adrian Sandes "and so thick was the undergrowth that one literally could not see them even when standing on them. Their average field of fire was only a few yards. The town seemed deserted and we settled down and built corrugated-iron shelters and pitched tents in some aircraft dispersal bays. Akyab was delightful, so beautiful with its fine trees, European houses and tarred roads. In the miles of derelict rice-factories one could find anything from furniture to water pipes. Our jobs were mostly water-supply and road repair. The bathing was excellent – off vast sandy beaches in clear water with rolling breakers and here we stayed for a month. Akyab was coming back to life before we left with cinemas and ENSA shows. I even met a few nurses from a nearby hospital. Our only lack was cigarettes which were always scarce."

Three days after the initial Akyab landing, 3rd Commando Brigade, including a platoon of 78 Company under Lieutenant Francis, landed at Myebon, 32 miles to the south-east. The Sappers helped the Commandos to consolidate and afterwards lifted a number of 120lbs Japanese mines of a new type. They were hemispherical in shape and each had a couple of horns, made of lead, which projected above the sand when the mine was buried in a beach. Francis sent some of these mines back to Akyab where Adrian Sandes spent many hours in experimenting on them. "There were two methods of disarming the mines. The first was to remove the horns which unscrewed with a left-hand thread. The second was to lift a small brass plunger thereby breaking an electric circuit by which the mine would be detonated if the horns were crushed. The plunger had a little tapped hole in the centre and I found that it could be raised easily by screwing into the hole a piece of soft copper wire which engaged the threads. Francis, I believe, had raised a plunger by hooking it with a piece of bent wire inserted through one of the horn sockets." The experiments were carried out in a corner of the camp where it is said that Sandes' friends seldom cared to visit him. However all went well and a regular disarming drill was evolved for future use.

26 Division then made a bold leap to Ramree Island which had an excellent harbour and much needed room for airfields. 72 Field Company went with the Division and its first task was to construct fighter and Dakota air-strips. Usually it was considered advisable to provide new air-strips rapidly rather than spend time on clearing existing airfields, but in this case the airfield site was tackled first. Though it was studded with sharpened stakes to deter parachutists and intersected by deep ditches, the Company was not deterred. The ditches were filled in by bulldozers, the stakes extracted by coolies, trees were cut down and bricks for metalling brought from derelict houses. Sommerfeld track was laid in the worst places and in five days part of the airfield was ready for use. The airfield was aptly named 'Ditchfield' and the final touch was a wind-sock made from the white-washed pagris of one of the platoons! On 27th January 1945, the first plane came into land, a shining Dakota carrying General Wheeler, the deputy Supreme Commander, who congratulated the Company on their efforts. The Company then turned to road repairs and began to create other airfields for all-weather landings.

THE ADVANCE ON THE CENTRAL FRONT

On the Central Front General Slim originally expected that the Japanese would oppose 14th Army's advance north of the Irrawaddy and he planned to fight a main battle with his two Corps on the Shwebo plain. Sensing, however, that the Japanese were going to withdraw and fight from the south bank, he changed his plan and sent 4 Corps secretly down to cross the great river south of Pakokku and from there to seize the nodal point of Meiktila on the Japanese L of C. As the Japanese record, "it was a master-stroke."

The sappers of both 7 and 17 Divisions now combined to support the Irrawaddy river crossing. Major Bill Adams sets the scene: "The British advance into Burma from the end of 1944 up to the recapture of Rangoon in May 1945 provided everything a sapper could ask for. I had taken over command of 75 Field Company in early December and from early January our main task was to assist the move of 4 Corps 230 miles down the Gangaw Valley track from Kalemyo to Pakkokku. It was hard but fairly routine work with the aid of an Elephant Company for culverting and such mechanical equipment as we could get hold of. The difficult task was to get the worn-out vehicles of 854 Bridge Company, which were carrying the floating bridge equipment, through the hill section of the track, and it was becoming clear to us that we were to take part in a very major river crossing operation."

The Irrawaddy was wide and treacherous with shifting sandbanks. Happily the enemy were surprised by both the location and the strength of the approaching forces. The plan was for 7 Division to seize a bridge-head through which 17 Division could pass to seize Meiktila. Under cover of smoke, the small boats nosed their way across the river and safely grounded on sand. The infantry swarmed up the beaches and, with early reinforcements, were able to secure the opposite bank. With rafts of stores and ammunition following quickly, three battalions were holding the beach-head by nightfall.

Bill Adams continues: "The crossing took place on 14th February and was only partially successful at first. Outboard motors failed to start or cut out at critical moments. Although the crossing was secured, light enemy opposition inflicted heavy casualties on both sappers and infantry. Two days were occupied in making the crossing-place secure, by which time there were sapper units involved with an establishment of some 3,000 men, though there were somewhat fewer in reality. Failure of Sommerfeld Track to arrive added to the problem of crossing the sandy beach but by the 18th access tracks, landing stages and rafts were all ready and the crossing began to gather momentum.

Class 18 pontoon rafts were used by my Company and each sortie took about an hour as the crossing distance was a mile. Night-ferrying was, for many reasons, not possible and the problem was how to achieve the maximum number of sorties each day between dawn and dusk. The Gunners were in charge of traffic regulation and the shortest possible time was spent loading and unloading the astonishing variety of vehicles and home-made trailers used by 14th Army.

There was no time to be wasted on temperamental engines and a workshop for outboard motors and propulsion units had been set up on the beach. From the start it was obvious that this arrangement would cut across our own system of maintenance and Ken Sink, my South African second-in command, accordingly found a spare pontoon which he anchored in mid-stream and used as a workshop, changing motors in motion to a programme as rafts passed. This was a complete success and we had no breakdowns during the whole operation. There was so much going on that our unorthodox operation wasn't discovered for two or three days but we were allowed to continue.

An unusual feature was that all three Groups of Sappers and Miners were represented in the crossing and this made for terrific competition between them. Each raft flew its own 'house flag'; a control tower housed the 'Clerk of the Course of the Irrawaddy Regatta'; and a large noticeboard gave 'form' at a glance. The scene may well have resembled Margate-on-Sea on a Bank Holiday but the results achieved were impressive: during the entire operation 20,000 vehicles were ferried across in one of the largest river crossings in any theatre of the war."

17 Division advanced east from the crossing to Meiktila where savage house to house and bunker to bunker fighting took place until 4th March 1945 when Meiktila could be said to be controlled. The trap was now closed. Later in the month, when 7 Division took Myingyan and 19 Division took Mandalay, the Field Companies were still busy ferrying across the Irrawaddy at various points. The Army Commander expressed his appreciation of 'the splendidly organized ferry service'.

With most of Meiktila taken, the airstrip nearby became the focal point of Japanese counter-attacks. The strip was put in order by 414 Field Park and a platoon of 70 Field Company. Despite heavy shelling the airfield also became a huge storage area for both 17 Division and part of 5 Division.

The rest of 5 Division, having rested in Assam, entered Burma again by travelling more than a thousand miles by road through Imphal, Kalewa and Monywa. 2 Field Company found it an exciting journey: the long trek to the Chindwin, the bridge at Kalewa, pagodas at Ye-u, the ferry at Pakokku and golden pagodas just beyond, at Pagan, until they were within the sound of guns. 74 Field Company on a similar journey enjoyed much the same experience.

By April 1945 the situation allowed a general advance on Rangoon. However, when 4 Corps left Meiktila in April, Rangoon was still over three hundred miles away and the monsoon could be expected within six weeks. It was decided that the main effort should be made along the railway axis via Toungoo and that airstrips should be the vital factor in making swift progress.

70 Field Company advanced from Meiktila initially with 17 Division, but when 5 Division took over, the Company continued to assist, mainly in clearing an enemy stronghold which had dominated the road from the east. 2 Field Company also went forward helping to create a giant diversion, their bulldozers preparing a route across sand and paddy fields and several crossings over a 500 yard wide chaung. A furious battle developed with heavy shelling and enemy snipers hiding in foxholes and trees.

17 Division then took over again. 2 and 74 Field Companies followed closely upon the leading armour and by mid-April both were in Toungoo a hundred and sixty miles from Rangoon. The general advance was now so swift that a contest to reach Rangoon before the break of the monsoon began between 17 Division and a seaborne landing out of Ramree Island by 26 Division. By 29th April, three days before the sea assault, the men of 17 Division were on the outskirts of Pegu, just over fifty miles from Rangoon.

There were three bridges over the Pegu river: the road, the main railway line and the diversionary railway, all held by the enemy. Suddenly a tropical rainstorm broke over the town, the country rapidly became waterlogged, all the bridges were blown and the Pegu river, up to then fordable, rose in spate washing away even the piers of the wrecked structures. However 48 Brigade with 70 Field Company had managed to ford the river and despite further heavy rain a platoon of 70 Field Company was able to launch a Bailey bridge in place of the Pegu railway bridge enabling most of the Division to pass over. Unfortunately some thirty two miles from Rangoon a wide tidal chaung held up most of the Brigade. The infantry swam across but the vehicles were far behind. 70 Field Company was called forward to the new obstacle where amid deep mud and heavy rain they began to prepare the approaches for a new bridge.

That afternoon troops of 26 Division landed in Rangoon. A recce party from 73 Field Company landed on the soggy undefended beaches ten miles south of the city. What had seemed a risky Combined Operation met with no opposition. Meanwhile, fortified by a rum issue, 70 Field Company completed their bridge. News then reached them of their failure to reach Rangoon first but that disappointment was soon overtaken by the good news of the end of the war in Europe.

In Rangoon, as 73 Field Company began repairs to warehouses, railway sidings and jetties, 72 Field Company arrived and began to restore the city's water supply. Adrian Sandes, by now a Captain and second-in-command of 78 Company, reached Rangoon on 6th May and wrote: "As we sailed up the river the city presented a picture of the most complete desolation it is possible to conceive. Miles of riverside wharves were deserted and lined with sunken boats. Some of the jetties were mere masses of wreckage and many of the houses just rubble. On landing we walked straight into our allotted area near the Mayo Club and you may imagine our delight on seeing great sheds, with roofs on, for the men and a fine house for our Mess. Of course the whole place was in a disgusting state owing to the looters. Exploration revealed miles of dumps of every conceivable kind. There were vast engineering workshops and shipyards, timber mills, rice mills, piles of steel joists and stacks of piping but almost everything was rotten, rusty and broken. The streets were covered with litter and strewn with worthless Japanese currency notes. I have never seen so much money in my life. The cranes were out of order, the railways overgrown with vegetation and the stations masses of twisted metal and debris. There were no trains, water-supply, or electric light. Here and there lay dead bodies and the stench of rotting rice was abominable. Exploring the place was an eerie experience. Doors hanging open, creaking in the wind; piles of ashes stirring in the breeze; smashed furniture lying about; everywhere deserted and derelict houses. The Japs had placed fire-bombs in some buildings but these had already been extinguished. Wherever you went you could see Jap money, abandoned motor cars, lorries by the hundred stripped of their parts, wrecked bulldozers, rusty steel helmets. I entered the Secretariat looking for mines. The Japs, in their inexplicable way, had used this beautiful building as a warehouse. There were great halls full of rice, rooms filled with broken packing-cases, others piled with rotting State archives and others again full of old boots. Never have I seen such confusion. And the smell!"

Meanwhile on the Irrawaddy axis 7 Division had occupied a key town on the way to the oilfields and by mid April they were at Yenanyaung, the main oil town. The way was open to Prome and, in company with 20 Division, the town was reached early in May 1945. Once the biggest river port on the Irrawaddy, Prome was only a shell when retaken. 332 Field Park Company spent most of May restoring some of the services there, including getting the town's water supply working again.

By June 1945 contact was made between all the Divisions in the Burma offensive. Any Japanese remnants were fleeing eastwards or making pockets of suicide resistance. A period of mopping up kept the infantry busy, while the work of supplying the many units congregating in the area still provided many tasks for the sappers.

On 6th August the first atom bomb was dropped. The second followed and on 15th August 1945 the war in the east was brought to a sudden end. The news brought mental relief to all troops but there was no early discharge of the engineers' responsibilities. There was still much to do.

EPILOGUE

Throughout 1945 and 1946 the field companies came back, one by one, to Roorkee for disbanding or regrouping according to need. For some the wheels of demobilization began to revolve and men gratefully returned to their villages after many years of army life, carrying with them tales of many a famous battle, of leave in wonderful cities and of different customs and ways. Prisoners of war came back from the horrors of Japanese prison camps and from the prison camps of Europe. On Roorkee station there were men who could carry on a conversation in German, French and Italian, as well as Urdu and English, and excited sappers who could demonstrate the master flanking attack that wrested Cassino from the Germans as easily as the General himself.

In many homes in Britain and under the banyan tree in many Indian villages, individual and unknown heroes will have doubtless made amends for the shortcomings of any history, and will have told the tale of the great Chindwin Bridge and the Irrawaddy crossing, or be proud that they fought at Keren, Imphal or El Alamein. In their memories, no matter what changes have since occurred, the comradeship and triumphs of the Bengal Group will surely endure.

7
SOME POST-WAR EXPERIENCES

THE FLYING JEEP
A Cautionary Tale from the Greek Mountains

In 1945, immediately after the end of the war in Europe, 4 Field Company was stationed in Greek Macedonia building bridges and generally repairing communications between Salonika and Athens. As a very junior subaltern, with precious little experience, David Alexander had the happy chance to be posted from Italy to join the Company in Kozani. As part of his induction to the work which they were undertaking and to familiarise him with the local terrain, he was sent in the company of a brother officer, Lieutenant Peter Bromhead, on a reconnaissance into the mountains to the North. They were to travel by jeep and as there were two officers to share the driving they decided to dispense with the normal driver. This is David's cautionary tale.

"Little did Peter know how little driving experience I had and personal pride prevented me from revealing the truth. It was a failing that was to have somewhat disastrous consequences. We set off on a clear morning following the mountain road towards Kastoria. As with many roads in immediate post-war Greece, it was narrow, precipitous and very badly maintained. Indeed it was in part the poor state of this particular road that we needed to observe and report on. We were to find out in a dramatic and near fatal manner.

The road continued to climb and we bucketed over the broken surface, thankful for the robustness of our vehicle and mindful that we were not in wireless contact with Company HQ, nor with the Gurkha detachment that was encamped some twenty miles further on. The road became narrower still with hairpin bend after hairpin bend, a sheer rock wall on one side and a frightening drop on the other to a river-bed some 400 feet below. The hairpins were sharp and had no parapet to restrain a skidding vehicle. But the sun shone, we were free of military discipline and life was very good. It is conceivable that the changing of gears might even have been accompanied by a snatch of Gilbert and Sullivan or an aria from Verdi. Heads were high and attention on the lowish side.

Peter had asked me if I would like to take over the wheel for a spell and I was rather congratulating myself on the way I was negotiating the hairpins. Blithe might well have characterised my attitude to things at the time. Then we rounded a corner and started to descend to a particularly sharp bend, only to encounter a shepherd driving a flock of goats towards us up the slope. Now your ordinary calibre of goat is not endowed with a surplus of grey matter and it behoves a vehicle passing a flock of such animals to proceed with more than a little caution. This I did and crept past on the mountain side of the road giving a cheery wave to the goatherd as I did so. The last of the goats were strung out to the left and I began to accelerate away to the heart of the bend. As I did so, the very last goat panicked and leapt across the road directly in front of the jeep.

Now I have never been of a murderous turn of mind and my instinct on the whole is to avoid doing gratuitous injury to other creatures. In an endeavour to avoid the leaping goat I wrenched the steering wheel to the right and stamped on the brake. With the hindsight of nearly 60 years neither action was wise. The jeep swerved towards the rock face where it made contact with loose stones at the roadside and slewed back to the left. My attempt to bring the jeep to a halt had exactly the contrary effect. The climbing nails attached to the outside of my right boot (a fancy in the height of fashion with young officers at the time) clipped the accelerator pedal and we roared forward to hurtle into space off the road with little but clean mountain air between us and the glistening river below.

Well – whether the Greek gods who still look down in those parts on the antics of the human race relented, or whether it was just good fortune of a more common kind, I do not know. What I do know is that we took off over the edge with such speed that the natural tendency of a jeep to be affected by the weight of its engine and to turn turtle was overcome by our forward movement. The jeep flew the first 20 feet before Peter managed to bale out, breaking a tooth and spraining a knee on the way. The jeep and I landed rear first, gouged our way through the scrub for another thirty feet and crashed into a fortuitously placed pine tree in a cloud of dust and steam.

I was pinned in the driving seat, smashed the windscreen with the top of my head and bent the steering wheel with my chin. I did not know till many years later that I had been knocked out by the impact and Peter's polite enquiries as to the state of my health met with little response. Eventually I came round and climbed out. I confirmed that I was in a tolerable state of health until I saw Peter looking aghast at my shorts which were soaked and dripping with blood. On more intimate examination it was revealed that I was bleeding profusely from the tip of a very private part. Fearing some frightful internal injury, Peter helped me back up the slope, parked me bleeding at the roadside and gallantly hobbled off to fetch help from the Gurkhas, unknown miles away.

Whether I passed out again I do not know but I was suddenly alert to the sound of a truck grinding its way from the direction from which we had come. I staggered to my feet – a blood-spattered figure waving wildly above the steaming wreck of a jeep lying in the gully below – and to my astonishment what was approaching but an army ambulance complete with doctor and crew. Immediate attention was given to my bleeding parts which were swathed in bandages and off we sped to the Gurkha camp, picking up an unbelieving Peter Bromhead on the way. A more miraculous piece of luck could hardly have been scripted by a Bollywood screenwriter.

There were three sequels to this not very meritorious affair. There was first a good deal of well-justified ridicule to be endured on arriving back at HQ swathed in bandages to all parts (the injuries proved to be trivial). Secondly, an equally well-earned rocket to be received from the gentle Bill Gerrie, the Acting OC of 4 Field Company. Lastly, the Divisional Commander judged my conduct to have been negligent and ruled that I would have to pay for the jeep which was a total write-off. I think that the gods even smiled on this sentence and I believe that somewhere in the dusty archives of Army HQ Delhi there may still rest an unactivated payment order blessedly detained by a benign bureaucracy. At all events, no deductions were ever made to my account at Cox & Kings, Bombay – and I vowed thenceforth to give up all attempts to fly a jeep."

ESCORT FOR A GENERAL

Sapper units were kept fully occupied in the months following the end of the war in the Far East on the reconstruction of communications, power supplies and repair of water pipelines. In all these tasks they were assisted by parties of Japanese prisoners awaiting repatriation. Their attitude to life caused some surprise, as Lieutenant Reggie Sfakianos discovered. "I got to Burma by a long and roundabout way – Omdurman on VE-Day, Halifax on

VJ-Day, and an assortment of transit camps in Moascar, Bombay, Kirkee, Roorkee and Barrackpore – arriving at Rangoon in early 1946 in an ex-Polish troopship, the SS *Kosciusko*. Looking forward to rejoining a unit at last, I was less than pleased to arrive at yet one more transit camp where I was told that the Bengal Sapper Company to which I had been posted had already returned to India. No doubt our paths had crossed somewhere between Rangoon and Roorkee.

Most of my fellow-campers were, of course, going the other way and the usual transit camp round of meals and trivial administrative jobs were more than usually irksome. It was therefore a great relief to be told that I was to escort Japanese General Honda to Prome as part of the exercise designed to repatriate Japanese troops from Burma.

I was rather less than happy when I was presented with a 15cwt truck and an Indian driver for the journey. Bumping about in the back of a truck for a hundred miles or so of Burmese roads, communicating with the driver by shouting in a language of which my knowledge was limited to what I had learnt in a few weekly sessions with Wajid Ali, the Bengal Sapper and Miner munshi, was not quite what I had volunteered for when I had left the Middle East.

When the General arrived with his Military Aide, I began to get a taste of the cultural differences between the two armies. The first surprise was to be saluted by the General before I had a chance to salute him – as a subaltern, it was not an experience I had had before and it was not to be repeated in the next twenty-odd years. The second surprise was to be told that General Honda wished to inform me that he and the Military Aide would travel in the back of the truck while I travelled in relative comfort in the front.

For me at least the journey was pleasant enough. We arrived in Prome after nightfall to find the PoW Camp in the charge of what were technically its inmates. The British staff, I was told, were at the cinema in Prome! My charges were borne away and the driver and I were left to make our arrangements for the night. There appeared to be no facilities for casual visitors and the offer by a kindly Japanese soldier of a tin of processed cheese with a lid bent back and a spoon stuck in did not augur well for our stay.

At about this time the lights went off as the electricity supply in Prome was, as usual, cut off at night and it was something of a relief when a Japanese officer, Captain Kitamura, arrived. A tall, well-built man, he had swum, as I recall it, in the 1500 metres freestyle in the 1936 Olympic Games in Berlin and spoke perfect English. We talked for a time while arrangements were made for the driver and me to move to a West African Brigade for the night

I was again made to realise how different our military systems and attitudes to them were. Though Kitamura of course knew of the bombs on Hiroshima and Nagasaki, no details or personal news had been given to individuals. Fixed overseas tours did not exist and the welfare and postal services which our troops took for granted were sketchy or non-existent. Even notification of casualties was limited and might, he said, be no more than the arrival in Japan of a soldier's ashes."

A SMALL WAR IN JAVA

The sudden capitulation of Japan in August 1945 left South-East Asia in turmoil. The Dutch authorities, though they were in no position to do so, had expected to reassert control over their colony without question, but the Indonesian National Movement in Java and Sumatra, formed in the 1930s under Sukarno, had been encouraged by the Japanese and declared independence as soon as the war was over. A large number of Dutch ex-prisoners of war and internees, having been ill-treated, overworked and close to starvation were living in camps, sometimes deep in the jungle, awaiting repatriation. British forces moved in as soon as possible to take the surrender of the Japanese, rescue the Dutch, provide for their immediate needs and medical care, and evacuate them home with due speed. Meanwhile the British had de facto responsibility for law and order.

Though many Indonesians, thinking that to gain independence too soon would be disastrous, wanted the protection of the Dutch, at any rate for a time, Sukarno was resolved that Indonesia should become an independent Republic as soon as possible. A number of uprisings took place and the Indonesian volunteer force, with arms and ammunition provided by the Japanese, carried out a remorseless series of vendettas. The British forces, seen as fronting for, and helping, the return of the Dutch authorities, were treated as an army of occupation and harassed at every turn. There was constant bombing, mortaring and machine-gunning, especially in the port city of Batavia, now known as Djakarta, at Bandoeng in central Java and in Sourabaya, well to the east. 23 Indian Division were to suffer 1,500 casualties in a campaign which lasted just over a year, on a mission which was essentially humanitarian. This type of operation, now familiar as 'peace enforcement', came as a complete and unwelcome surprise after the long, bloody and ultimately successful war against the Japanese.

On the arrival of 49 Brigade, part of 23 Division, at Sourabaya, Brigadier Mallaby conferred with Dr Moestopo, the local Indonesian leader, who had been instructed by Sukarno not to oppose the landing, and accordingly the Brigade occupied all the key points in the town without bloodshed. Sourabaya was a large town of about 300,000 inhabitants and on 27th October 1945 the first units moved inland to Darmo, a residential area six or seven miles south of the harbour, where there was a large Dutch civilian internment camp. The Indonesians at once suspected that Mallaby intended to hold them down by force until he could hand over to their previous masters, the Dutch. They had 12,000 soldiers, trained and armed by the Japanese, supported by an armed mob 75,000 strong, and next day this mob poured through the town, murdering isolated parties of British and Indian soldiers and many Dutch women and children. Street fighting began in earnest, Brigadier Mallaby was murdered and the Brigade lost 400 officers and men before it withdrew to the dock and airfield area in the north until reinforcements arrived.

The first troops to set foot in the town were some men of 71 Field Company commanded by Major Nigel Holmes. They had a sullen though not too unfriendly reception and a subaltern was sent to reconnoitre the airfield next day, meeting with much obstruction from the Indonesian officials because they thought he was Dutch. Most of the Company moved to the Darmo suburb where all was quiet to start with and Indonesian soldiers saluted our officers, but serious trouble was obviously brewing. It started soon afterwards when there was much fighting in the centre of the town and some of the Company transport in the docks area was ordered

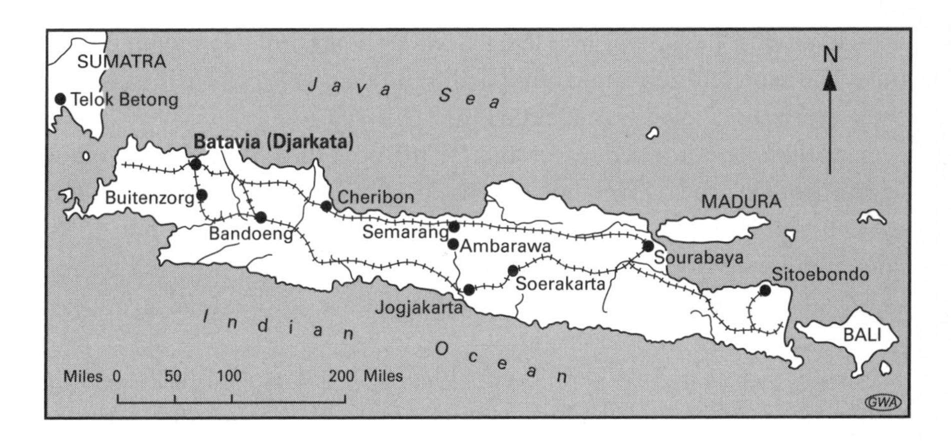

to move to Darmo. This it did after dusk under heavy fire. News came that a convoy of nineteen trucks carrying women and children to safety had been ambushed while being escorted by men from the Indian Army Service Corps. Many of these women and children were bayoneted. Others perished when the houses in which they had taken shelter were set on fire. Only thirty survived out of two hundred. The Indian drivers put up a great fight and all but eight were killed at their posts.

Early next morning, fire was opened on 71 Field Company's position in the Darmo barracks. The Indonesians crept up to within fifty yards and casualties began to mount. Nigel Holmes then asked for artillery support which was given promptly. Captain Floyer, from a very exposed position, directed the fire onto the enemy's positions and many of the Indonesian troops who tried to escape were killed. At 3pm some Thunderbolt aircraft came over and fighting ceased, but not before the Company had lost two killed and eleven wounded.

30th October was another exciting day. A detachment of Rajputs in the Darmo Railway Station was short of ammunition so at 10am Nigel Holmes despatched a party to the station in a lorry. Heavy fighting was in progress but the ammunition was delivered and several wounded Rajputs evacuated to hospital before the party returned to the barracks where the situation was becoming increasingly serious. The Indonesians swarmed on all sides, waving flags, shouting "Don't shoot", and demanding that 71 Company should surrender. Floyer then set out, unarmed, with the Indonesian commander to the rebels' headquarters, six miles away, to discuss matters. He returned safely, two hours later, in an armoured vehicle, having been forced to abandon his 15cwt truck. Meanwhile Holmes had waited calmly outside the barracks facing an excited crowd but with four machine-guns placed in convenient positions behind him. Floyer's return fortunately coincided with the arrival of a letter from Dr Soerkano enjoining moderation. The rebels were sufficiently pacified to disperse to their homes and soon afterwards Floyer was awarded the Military Cross.

Supplies were dropped by air and for the next three days all was quiet at Darmo. On 2nd November a convoy of vehicles transported 1,400 women and children to the docks area. 71 Company followed four days later and joined in minor offensive operations during the next few weeks until, on 25th November, it embarked for Batavia, in Western Java, very glad to see the last of Sourabaya.

Meanwhile, 68 and 78 Field Companies, who had landed in Batavia in October-November 1945, had been equally busy. By the time they arrived, the country was already in the throes of a popular uprising. The Indonesians had taken charge of all public utility services; they ran the railways, the post and telegraph services, and the water-supply in Batavia. They commandeered any vehicle they fancied and seized any building they desired without any interference from the police. The local Press hurled abuse at the Dutch. Ships lay unloaded in the docks. Shooting began in the streets and barricades appeared overnight.

The work in Western Java resembled that carried out in the eastern territory, except that there was more to be done in the evacuation of internees and the repair of airfields. Roads needed constant attention and every convoy had to be provided with a detachment of Sappers to lift mines and clear road-blocks. Much attention had to be paid to Batavia itself where the public utilities had to be repaired and operated. Labour was scarce because the Indonesians refused to work under Dutch or even Japanese supervision, but an urgent task was the clearance of drainage canals choked with silt and obstructed by a growth of water-hyacinth. The canals also contained many corpses which blocked the sluice gates and had to be removed and buried.

68 Field Company, under Major Bob Allen, had one unusual task which was the printing of *The Fighting Cock*, the Divisional newspaper, produced curiously enough with the full cooperation of the Indonesians. A few months later the Company helped with the renovation of the Concordia Club in Bandoeng, which was turned into an Officers' Club with an English-style pub named *The Crippled Chicken*, complete with appropriate inn sign.

By the time Hugh Beach arrived as a platoon commander towards the end of January 1946, the work of 68 Field Company had lessened, being confined mainly to the thankless task of endlessly filling potholes. A more interesting job was the construction of a short Bailey Bridge on a main road some 60 miles inland from Batavia. As Hugh reported: "Protection was not lacking: we were accompanied by a battalion of Seaforths, some Patialas, troops of guns, Sherman tanks and armoured cars, all overseen by a Brigadier with his headquarters. Bob Allen came along to see I did not make a bog of it. There was no interference from the Indonesian rebels, construction went well and we all trailed home in the evening."

A considerable amount of time was put into road reconnaissance and repairs and in support of convoys which were often ambushed. Culverts and bridges were sometimes damaged and at times destroyed, and occasionally whole lengths of road would be dug up overnight to a depth of several feet as anti-tank ditches and in an attempt to delay convoys. The use of light aircraft proved invaluable in the prompt identification of such obstacles. One rather different task involved the taking down, without causing damage to a nearby HQ, of six very tall wireless masts made out of bolted timber sections, part of a former Japanese wireless station.

The company lines were often fired on, but only at night, from the kampongs on the other side of the deep nullah and river in front of the lines. George Franklin, one of the platoon commanders, used to marvel at the complete disdain with which his Sikhs treated the shots frequently fired at them, wondering whether it was sheer bravery or a lack of imagination!

At the end of June the Company moved a short distance to a place called Depok where good use was made of Japanese boats for recreational purposes, with visits to some of the small islands nearby. Also, using explosives, the Company was able to keep local units well supplied with fresh fish, with catches of up to 150lbs. The officers divided their free time between the Box Club, the pre-war English club in Djakarta, and the Hotel des Indes, a famous colonial hotel to rival the Raffles Hotel in Singapore. Sadly, some years later, the Indonesians demolished the Hotel des Indes and replaced it with a modern multi-storied monstrosity!

APPROACH TO INDEPENDENCE

The end of the war in Europe made little difference in Roorkee except that a few British officers were allowed to go home as replacements arrived. The number of recruits was gradually dropping and this eased life a bit, but demobilization plans were in the offing and nobody knew what was likely to happen in either the military or political fields. When the war against Japan ended in August 1945, people felt quite guilty at stopping the evening parade and resuming some peacetime activities such as Athletic Meetings and Games. Life in Roorkee in 1945 was described by Lieutenant Colonel Dick Connor who had just returned from Burma to become Assistant Commandant after an absence of three years. He found two Messes, each filled almost to overflowing, and people working very long hours. The hot weather programme was 6.30am to 2pm with a break from 8.15 to 9.15am and then from 4.30 to 6.15pm, so there was little time for relaxation.

During the cold weather of 1945–6, Dick Connor managed to visit the jheels fairly frequently, but found they had changed for the worse since

1942. The Solani River was flowing through Panchli Jheel, which had silted up, and the jheels which remained would only take four or five guns.

With vast distances to he covered, train journeys necessarily took some days. Meals were usually taken during lengthy halts at the larger stations and bunks on the train were made up at night. At this time, female officers travelling by train had to he escorted by a male officer. I recall a duty group of male officers assembling for a journey at Saharanpur; a fearsomely large female officer bore down on the smallest member of the waiting group, grabbed his hand and said "Come along, laddie…." .We never knew what happened to him.

(Related by Chris Popham)

The characteristic feature of the years 1945–7 was a feeling of impermanence. In the effort to do their best, everyone worked at the highest pressure. The circumstances were rendered more difficult by the release and repatriation of many British Officers, although most of these held only temporary commissions and could not adapt themselves easily to peacetime conditions. There was a scarcity of almost every commodity – food, drink, clothes and cartridges – and what could be obtained was very expensive. Good servants were also rare. The men, when off duty, had to walk out in uniform because Hindustani clothing was only obtainable at a prohibitive cost. The average sapper, however, was more intelligent than his pre-War counterpart; he spent more, but in return he expected more in the way of food, recreation and welfare generally. His family was already discarding the purdah and the Commandant was always sure of a warm welcome when touring the family quarters or visiting the Womens' Institute. The Joint Magistrate, though a Muslim, was very popular with the Hindus and Sikhs. Good feeling permeated the countryside and the area round Roorkee was little affected by the disturbances elsewhere. The VCOs, especially the senior ones, were the mainstay of discipline. When it was found in 1945 that few Sikhs were volunteering for service as parachutists with 33 Field Squadron, the fact was mentioned casually to the senior Sikh VCO at the SME Roorkee. On the very next day the Commandant was informed that the entire Sikh strength of the Corps were anxious to become parachutists!

Demobilization plans were put into effect as soon as the war in the Far East ended. It was planned to be carried out in three phases, the first men to be released being recruits with less than six months' service.

The second phase involved the release of trained soldiers and by the middle of 1946 more than half the men in the Bengal Group had gone. The third phase was intended to secure a reduction to peace-time strength but was postponed because of problems arising from the probable partition of the sub-continent between India and Pakistan. No 2 Training Battalion was converted into a Demobilization Battalion, under the command of Lieutenant Colonel Bill Adams, and in addition to demobilization duties, gave instruction in useful peacetime occupations to men destined for release.

On one occasion the following year, when a visit of inspection was pending from the GOC Lucknow District whose chief idiosyncrasy was known to be a terror of flies, DDT disinfectant was poured into every hole and corner for hours and it was hoped that all would be well. But when the General came, he spotted a couple of flies in the Dining Hall and at once started a harangue on his pet subject. A bad report seemed inevitable. The new CO, however, was equal to the occasion and, in a broad Scots voice, declared "Ye need na' worry, Sir. I've noted these particular specimens for demobilization tomorrer." In the resultant laughter, all was forgiven and forgotten.

With the bestowal of the title 'Royal' on the Indian Engineers in February 1946, Major General Sir Horace Roome became Colonel Commandant of the Bengal Group. The post-war composition of the Group was also announced at this time as 50% Mussalman, 40% Hindu and 10% Sikh, and it was decided that all post-war units were to be of one-class composition. These changes came gradually into force, and by the end of 1946 there were four Mussalman units (2, 4,and 5 Field Companies and 35 Field Squadron) and five Hindu units (1, 3, 67 and 74 Field Companies and 6 Army Troops Company). 7 Field Company had become an all-Sikh unit. Meanwhile, many other units had made great progress towards integration and had got all classes to mess together. Sadly this all fell apart at the time of Partition in 1947.

It may now be a suitable moment to discuss the relationship between officers and men during the period between the start of World War II and Partition. Prior to the outbreak of war there were relatively few officers in Roorkee, a great deal of power rested with the VCOs who commanded all platoons, while the British Officers carried great responsibility as company commanders at a very young age. Officers were encouraged to go on trek, on shikar or a combination of the two and officers also had plenty of time and opportunity to learn the languages of their men.

Traditions were strictly upheld, not least in the Officers' Mess, and officers spent much of their career with the Group. Pre-War officers like Bill Veitch, with their great grasp of the language, were inclined to consult VCOs and even NCOs, especially the ones they could trust implicitly, over the heads of their officers. This did not always meet with the approval of other British officers, especially when Bill Veitch would get men to come to his bungalow and sit on the porch and gossip, but it was almost commonplace before the war and indeed for some time later. This was hardly surprising, though, especially with young officers who did not know the language and customs of the men; this was exacerbated by the arrival of so many new officers on the outbreak of war. These officers had difficulty in supervising the execution of their orders, they could not effectively judge the morale of their men, detect grievances at an early stage and effectively nip in the bud any developing trouble. Great efforts were made to teach officers to speak Urdu and officers spent many long hours with their munshis in efforts to gain proficiency in the language. There were also financial incentives for passing the various exams. Later in the war, as more officers passed through the OCTU in Roorkee, as well as those in Bangalore and Kirkee, language proficiency improved as they could not gain their commissions unless they had passed the initial Urdu exam.

The Regimental Munshi comes every morning and I take lessons from him at 10.30. He is short and fat, and wears glasses and a little topi, like an inverted soup plate, and khaki shorts, and brown stockings and shoes. He arrives on a bicycle, sitting bolt upright and reaching down with his toes so that his foot does not lose the pedal when it is at the bottom of its circuit.

He waits on the verandah till asked to come in. He then removes his topi, holds it in both hands in front of his tummy, and seats himself in an upright armchair looking like Buddha might have done if he had retired and gone to live in Los Angeles. His legs are so short that they appear to wave about in the draught from the fan until he makes a great effort and points his toes so that they touch the ground. He then leans over and puts his topi on the floor beside him, the fat under his hairy brown little knees squelching out as if to distribute the weight over as much of the seat of the chair as possible.

Finally, he pulls a shabby little grammar from his pocket, looks hopefully at me and says in a cultured and effortless voice "Well now, perhaps I'd better hear your words".

The men were very easy to amuse. They had never known radios, cinemas or TV. Most of them did not smoke or drink. 'Crime' in the military sense was unheard of. Their food was simple and monotonous, but that was what they were used to in their own villages. In their spare time they played or watched hockey or football, played cards or simple board games, chatted or made their own music – singing well known country songs and beating time on an old tin can. This was just as well in view of the ineffectiveness of newly arrived officers.

Thinking about his time as a Bengal Sapper, Graeme Black summed it up in a letter written over forty years later: "When I look back at my own ignorance and ineffectiveness as a young officer, and the responsibilities thrust upon my units, I realise all too well how much was owed to the long service and experience of my VCOs and NCOs who uncomplainingly supported me. I am also appalled at the assumptions of superiority which were made by young war conscripts like myself just because we were British and officers and I am amazed at the cheerful acceptance of us by our troops. And yet it worked. Great work was done. Great affection flowed both ways."

To the young wartime officer arriving in Roorkee for the first time life seemed almost unreal. It was unsettling enough to arrive in the middle of the night, to be met at Roorkee station by the Orderly Officer, and to undergo the ritual treatment next morning of breakfast in the Mess – almost complete silence, one's own bearer standing behind one's chair. Then one was expected to attend Riding School, as if it was still pre-war! What was worse it started at some unearthly hour, before dawn, when, particularly in the winter months, it was freezing cold. This was compensated for by the wonderful early mornings, when one could see for literally hundreds of miles and watch the sun glinting on the snows of the Himalayas and particularly Nanda Devi at over 20,000ft. George Cooper remembers the dreaded words of command "Right, Gentlemen, grip, and cross your stirrups" as some fiendish exercise was started, to strengthen non-existent thigh muscles and was the precursor to another meeting at close quarters with mother India. Fortunately for him he was excused further torture after one particularly mad gallop along the bed of the Solani River when he ended clinging to the neck of his horse. Determined not to he beaten, he purchased his own horse, Lancer, bought under an Army scheme for a hundred chips (rupees) and shared with Jimmy Haddock who only wanted to ride at weekends while he spent the time on shikar. This was a good arrangement and it was far more fun to go on a quiet early morning hack along the banks of the Ganges Canal than being tortured by the Riding Master.

Amongst the returning Officers was Lieutenant Colonel Rosco Adami, who had been in 1st Field Company before the war. His reputation had preceded him and it was said that he had won his DSO at the Rhine Crossing, standing on the top panel of a Bailey bridge as it was being launched, urging his men on and brandishing a bottle of whisky in his hand. Certainly he enjoyed his drink and on one famous occasion he entered the Mess during a cocktail party, heard one of the recently returned wives complaining about her new dress which she had bought at Fortnum & Mason shortly before leaving England. Lurching up to her, rather unsteadily, he exclaimed "Madam, what do you expect if you must buy your clothes at a grocer's shop?"

PARTITION

The appointment of Lord Mountbatten as Viceroy was announced on 20th February 1947 and he was entrusted with the task of transferring responsibility for the government of British India in a manner that would best ensure the future happiness and prosperity of the country. Army Headquarters had already begun to arrange for the nationalisation of the Army and it was anticipated that this would be complete by June 1948, but plans had to be swiftly revised when it was announced that Independence would take place nearly a year earlier on 15th August 1947.

The Day of Independence, 15th August 1947, was a cause of great joy and jubilation throughout the sub-Continent. Celebrations in Roorkee went on well into the night with plenty of fireworks and crackers. The new National Flag of India appeared everywhere. The British officers maintained a low profile and let the Indian officers have their historic event to themselves. The day was, however, tinged with sadness and there was a sense of apprehension and indeed foreboding. Nothing was going to be the same again.

Everything had been done in such a hurry and few of the problems had been thought through properly. In the division of the three Groups, the Bengal Group would be the chief sufferer, not only in general strength – it was over 40% Muslim – but also in terms of equipment and property. As the Royal Pakistan Engineer Centre would have practically nothing at the start, it had been decided that about one third of the available engineer equipment should be transferred there from India, and that, partly because of convenience of transit, it should be drawn mostly from Roorkee. It was fortunate that Roorkee had certain equipment in excess of the peace scales which had been left over from the war, for otherwise the cupboard would have been swept almost bare.

The Officers' Mess, unlike the Madras Group at Bangalore and the Bombay Group at Kirkee, was a Royal Engineers Mess and although the Commandant was always President it was not a Sapper and Miner Mess. Some of the Mess silver and other assets at Roorkee might therefore be regarded as the property of the Royal Engineers but, before Partition, the RE Corps Committee had agreed, with the consent of RE officers serving in India, that all Mess silver and assets should he presented to the Engineer Messes of the two new Dominions. Despite this agreement, some officers in Roorkee were determined that 'Winged Victory', the most prized piece of silver in the Mess, should not be handed over and it was packed up and sent to England where it was presented to the Headquarters Mess at Chatham. The inscription says "Presented to the Officers Royal Engineers to mark the long association of the Corps of Royal Engineers with the KGVsO Bengal Sappers and Miners by the Officers KGVsO Bengal Group Royal Indian Engineers 1803–1947". The Chief Royal Engineer thanked the Commandant at Roorkee (still a British Officer) for 'this generous token of goodwill'. No reference was ever made to the decision of the RE Corps Committee that all silver should be handed over to India or Pakistan. 'Winged Victory' had of course been purchased originally by the (British) Officers after World War I and was inscribed "Presented to the RE Mess Roorkee by the Officers past and present of the 1st KGO Sappers and Miners", which indicates it was a gift to the Mess. Over the years as more and more Indians were commissioned and became members of the Mess it was quite rightly considered the de facto Bengal Sapper Mess, though perhaps legally it might have still been a Royal Engineers Mess. Whatever the rights and wrongs of the case, the Indian Officers did resent the removal of this cherished piece of silver.

The technical training of Indian Engineer officers took place at the School of Military Engineering which had been established in part of the Thomason College, but early in 1946 the Education Department asked for the return of the College accommodation which had been lent to the Army. This meant that the SME had to leave and a new site was selected at Kirkee, but the move was delayed by the imminence of Partition to the end of 1947. One of the complications concerned the disposal of the Army equipment installed in the SME, but as the College had provided the School with free accommodation during the war, most of the workshop equipment installed by the military authorities was left for the use of the

College, a portion only of the fieldworks equipment being allotted to the Bengal Centre to replace some of that transferred to Pakistan.

On the assumption that the assets at Roorkee included the value of Government buildings and other static property, Pakistan's share involved the transfer of almost everything that was mobile. Almost all the workshop equipment and masses of fieldworks stores and mechanical transport were to be transferred to the Royal Pakistan Engineers Centre at Sialkot, though the requirements of the Bengal Group were to be kept in mind. The Workshops were especially hard hit. The printing machinery was removed en masse in a single day and the engine sheds and machine shops were soon completely denuded. The MT School had to relinquish its most serviceable vehicles. Training in trades came practically to a standstill. Instruction in fieldworks had to cease for several months because of lack of equipment and tools. The Scientific Library was emptied, Regimental funds were halved. Roorkee still had a well-equipped Indian Families Hospital, a Women's Institute, the Knox Memorial School and Hostel and a Girls' School, all with some equipment, but as a counterweight there had to be a transfer of over 5 lakhs of rupees to Pakistan. Practically all the moveable assets of the Roorkee Officers' Mess vanished. Carpets, curtains, furniture, silver, crockery and cutlery went to Sialkot. The VCOs' Messes suffered similarly. The instruments, music scores and funds of the Band also departed so that Roorkee had the players but no instruments and Pakistan the instruments but hardly any players.

It was a traumatic time for everyone but by the beginning of November the last train had left Roorkee and things slowly returned to some semblance of order.

What do you remember of the Depot at Roorkee?
The clinging dark blue hose tops, puttees, shorts and wide topi;
Tonga wallahs, bhistis, the sleeping chowkidar;
And officers with time enough to travel on shikar?
Tree-lined shady rastas with bungalows tucked away;
Learning Urdu from the Munshi for an hour at break of day;
Sleeping on the charpoi under swathed mosquito net;
Waiting for the monsoon, to stand out in the wet?
Dinners in the Mess, served by your khidmatgar;
Porridge over-salted and the silver, port, cigar;
Pipers circling proudly round the table – 'bahut shor!'
Music after dinner, lights flickering once more

LAST POST

Shortly before the great day of Independence, Alan Sloan of 71 Field Company, was given a secret briefing in Delhi and told to take a section of Muslims to Lucknow. The Residency there had withstood a siege lasting some six months during the Mutiny of 1857 and had kept the Union Flag flying day and night throughout as a symbol of defiance. To commemorate the Relief the Union Flag was allowed to fly twenty-four hours a day in perpetuity. It was regarded by India though as a symbol of British Imperialism, so it was decided to have a special parade on Independence Day when it would be taken down and replaced by the new Indian National Flag. Alan Sloan was ordered to remove, not only the flag but the flagpole as well, at midnight, thus thwarting the people of Lucknow. Such an episode seems petty today – indeed it would be unthinkable – but at the time it had seemed a perfectly logical thing to do. In the event, it very nearly didn't come off as, to his consternation, Alan Sloan found that instead of being made of wood the flagpole was a metal one! Rising to the challenge, he managed to remove it and when dawn broke this symbol of British rule was no longer there. Returning to Roorkee, he discovered that the Union flag was in fact two flags sewn back to back to make them last longer. One of the flags was sent to Field Marshal Auchinleck, the Commander-in-Chief, and one was forwarded to Mountbatten. The top of the flagpole was cut off and kept by Alan Sloan who was killed sadly a few months later in the aftermath of Partition.

Meanwhile the Army remained staunch. Its great traditions held all ranks, classes and creeds together until the crisis was past. Blood was certainly spilt – sometimes oceans of it – but not the blood of serving soldiers. These did their best to minimize the massacres which occurred in the border areas between India and Pakistan even to the extent of taking action against armed bands of their own faith and thus they shortened the period of unrest. At the lower level, though, things began to be uncomfortable. Mixed units which had fought together, lived together and eaten together were now being broken up. The news, and more often the rumours, in the boundary area led to ever-increasing rioting, murder and arson and inevitably had an unsettling effect on those units still in Roorkee. Each side blamed the other and it was depressing to think that there had only been one 'side' a few weeks before. Taking 70 Field Company as an example, they lost their Sikh and Hindu platoons and their Hindu Subadar favoured his own kith and kin. This was quite natural but led to an uncomfortable atmosphere and sadly relations became strained.

Deep friendships were eroded and replaced by suspicion and there was something of a sense of relief when the reorganisation was completed.

The attitude of Indian officers in Roorkee was ambivalent. On the one hand many felt that the sooner the British officers left, the sooner they could get on with running their own country. These were sensible aspirations but others realised there would be a lack of expertise if there was a sudden exodus of British officers. There was concern, though, at what many Indian officers perceived as the majority of British officers favouring Pakistan and volunteering to go to Sialkot, the proposed new Centre for the Royal Pakistan Engineers. In fact most officers were given no option. In the case of 70 Field Company, they had arrived back from Burma only a few weeks before Partition expecting to be disbanded, but they were suddenly told to re-form as an all-Muslim Company destined to be part of the new Pakistan Army. Their OC, who had been expecting to go to Palestine, found that his posting was amended: 'for Palestine, read Pakistan'. No option!

With Partition taking place at such short notice, decisions had to be made swiftly and everything to be moved to Sialkot was placed securely in the old Supply Depot at Dandhera where it was prepared for transport by road and rail to Sialkot. OC 70 Field Company was made responsible for moving everything to Sialkot. The movement of men and stores was hindered not only by the tense communal situation in the Punjab but by heavy rain and floods. On 29th September Major 'Timber' Wood and Captain Chris Popham took a convoy of 200 men and 35 vehicles over to Sialkot, a three day journey through the troubled areas of the Punjab. Heavily armed, and with detailed orders in the event of trouble, they survived numerous tense situations and were quite proud that they lost nothing more than a small bulldozer on the way. Trains loaded with equipment left Roorkee at irregular intervals and were guarded by soldiers, not only to stop looting in transit but also to prevent countless refugees climbing on board in an effort to flee the communal rioting. Crowds of people eager to leave Roorkee would gather round the Supply Depot offering large sums of money to be allowed on the trains but also to leap on the trains if an opportunity presented itself. Wherever possible trains would gather speed inside the Depot, the gates being kept closed until the last moment to prevent unauthorised boarding. It was not a nice situation to be in.

Much the same happened to John Green, who recorded that: "Partition had been announced and things were happening. I was interviewed by the

Commandant in Roorkee and asked what I wanted to do about continuing service in the sub-continent. I said that, all things considered and looking to a career as a regular officer, I would prefer to return to the UK. My request seemed to have been ignored, or somebody erred, because I was ordered to go with the first train out of Roorkee, taking a large number of Punjabi Muslims of the Bengal Sappers to the newly forming Pakistan, destination Sialkot.

It was a full train-load, soldiers armed with ball ammunition in bandoliers, also a dozen Bren guns, NCOs with Sten guns and to cap it all a modest supply of No. 36 grenades. No radio sets, none of the prescribed kit usually carried if one was liable to act against civilian attack, which was a possibility. As a junior officer, barely fledged, I had had no briefing for this excursion and looked therefore to the OC train for my orders and guidance. I found that he was a Major Quartermaster, who told me he was travelling with his family (wife and two nubile daughters), that he was non-combatant and was going to lock himself into his compartment until we arrived at Sialkot. I was nonplussed but told the OC train to keep out of the way and to look after his family because I was taking charge. I called an 'O' group of the six or so VCOs on the train, laying down orders, procedures and communication in the event of trouble from outside the train or even inside it. I positioned myself in the centre of the train with the senior VCOs.

In normal times the train journey would have been completed in half a day but progress was so slow that it took three whole days. We travelled through a countryside with bloated bodies along the track and in ditches, people suffering from dysentery and other miseries at stations, a nightmare with the movement of the refugees from east to west and vice versa.

We were delayed in Lahore station and lost our locomotive, taken away I presumed for refuelling and watering. It was quite common to see severely wounded people; there was nothing we could do about it. Parked on the other side of the same platform was what I thought a strange composition. It was a medical carriage manned by two British ORs with a rail flat at either end with sandbag emplacements, which had served as firing points. These BORs could at least make a decent cup of tea! Still no appearance of the OC train except to enquire what the delay was in departing from Lahore. After something like 12 hours of a hot and worrying wait, I went looking for the station administration and eventually found a somewhat obese Anglo-Indian, was rather rude to him and rattled his inkwells. It seemed to have the desired effect because we got a new locomotive and set off.

It was a horrible journey, fraught with danger and seeing all the dreadful results of attacks upon earlier civilian trains and the pitiful state of the souls who had been involved. It has all since been documented and I need not, therefore, expand but I have never seen anything approaching that situation. At least we arrived without trouble and not having fired a shot.

Sialkot was a troop-empty cantonment; except for a few remnants of I know not what. There was a detachment of airborne Pakistan Sappers who were part of Lieutenant Colonel (Honker) Henniker's Command, based in Lahore. We set about finding barracks for the men and got them settled in and fed. I had the immediate problem of what to do with the weapons and ammunition we had with every man plus the reserve ammunition. I found an unsuitable building with barred windows, logged all the weapons in and posted an armed guard over it. This 'arms kot' was to be a thorn in my side for weeks, because I was not happy about its security, particularly as one morning I found that large numbers of Pathan tribesmen with henna-dyed hair had arrived after dark and were camped all around the kot. I quickly organised an armed show of strength in the area and eventually they went on their way. At some time after our arrival, there came a road convoy of Pakistani Sappers from Roorkee and other places bringing much-needed transport. I made my base in the area in which they were parked.

A Pakistani Colonel had arrived with his wife and they established themselves in one of the many empty bungalows. He was the only officer I could see and I relied on him for orders. These he often gave me from his charpoy, whilst his wife was in bed beside him, which I found a bit strange. I met a second train up from Roorkee with Colonel Dick Connor on board, who brought some order to the situation and became the first Commandant of the Engineer Centre.

There were no organised bearers in Sialkot at that time but there was always a queue of people offering to undertake the duties. For the most part they were a disreputable looking selection but I took on a young female who served me well. Almost too well because once when I had a fever for about three days, she tended me by washing me down in bed with cold cloths to reduce my temperature and she used to come into the bathroom night and morning bringing me fresh towels and buckets of water to rinse me down after washing my hair or whatever. And since you may wonder, no, I didn't!"

Back in Roorkee, 68, 70 and 71 Field Companies, all destined for Pakistan, were not allowed to go out on Internal Security operations but fortunately had plenty to keep themselves occupied. Colonel Rex Holloway, the Commandant, returned from leave in Canada and found that the division of spoils had already been agreed and all items destined for Pakistan had been moved into the Supply Depot. He questioned some of the decisions and one day came out and gave instructions to OC 70 Field Company to return certain items to the Cantonment. This placed the OC in a difficult position as he had very specific orders that everything under his charge was to go to Sialkot. He explained his predicament, whereupon the Commandant said that this was an order not a 'request'. Taking a deep breath he replied that he could not obey the order. Eventually, in danger of being placed under arrest for disobeying the direct order of a senior officer, he said that he would only obey the order if he was given it in writing. The Commandant stormed off to his office and half an hour later a *chaprassi* (messenger) arrived back with the written order. The items specified were then returned to the Cantonment and the Commandant's letter was forwarded to the Engineer-in-Chief in Rawalpindi with a covering letter saying that he had only obeyed under duress. This whole episode was symptomatic of the tensions that had built up, even in Roorkee, but all the same it was a foolhardy thing for a young Major, aged 21, to have done. He later went on to become a General!

Towards the end of 1947 many British officers, who had only stayed on after Partition to help with the transition, began to feel that they were no longer needed. Some were disillusioned by all the bloodshed and the effect it was having on the two new Dominions. Most were overdue to return to England at the end of their normal three years overseas. John Green's experience of leaving was similar to so many others leaving both India and Pakistan: "I left Sialkot towards the end of 1947 by jeep. The journey by road still showed signs of the troubles and as I approached Lahore there was a huge refugee camp near the Ravi River. It was difficult to cross the bridge because of the bullock carts etc and the thousands of moving people. After a few days we were marshalled to move and assembled at a rail siding with all our kit to entrain. The train had come from elsewhere and there were a few families in the compartmented sections, whilst single officers were herded into open carriages in which Indian Other Ranks would usually travel and we were to sleep in tiers on plain wooden bunks."

There were many such trains heading to Bombay or Karachi full of British officers leaving their Regiments. George Cooper's experience was much the same as that of John Green; a long, dusty, tedious journey by train down to Karachi in extreme discomfort. There was no restaurant car and meals were taken beside the train at various halts. Everyone queued with their mess-tins, from the General downwards, for their ration of bully-beef stew. The train was swiftly called 'The Pale-face Special' and it felt as though the British were silently creeping away. There was no fuss, a few days were spent in the Transit Camp at Karachi until the troop-ship arrived and then everyone embarked for the cramped voyage home. At least there was a send-off at the docks and the ship drew away to a Lament from the Pipe Band of the Black Watch, the main body of which was to leave Pakistan a few weeks later, the last British Regiment to serve in the new Dominion of Pakistan.

Everyone was sad to be leaving but the British left the Indian sub-continent proud of their achievements and the many lasting friendships that had been forged. We had left behind two new nations, with first class armies, firmly rooted in traditions going back many decades. Our footprints were left behind for future generations to follow.

8
POST INDEPENDENCE

THE BENGAL ENGINEER GROUP

The Fateful Year

On Partition, Roorkee, being the nearest to Pakistan, had to bear the brunt of providing their new Engineer Centre at Sialkot with equipment and funds. Some of the main features provided being entire Workshops, Field-works equipment and stores, including MT and Plant. Fifty per cent of the funds were transferred as well. In the case of the Officers' Mess, practically all movable assets in the way of carpets, curtains, furniture, books, silver, crockery and cutlery were allotted to the Pakistan Centre. Havildar Mathai Lal and his swing boys were unable to perform for quite some time as the entire brass band equipment and its funds were sent away.

Planning and implementing all this had begun in July 1947, the actual physical movement of personnel and stores being hindered to a great extent due to the break down of communications resulting from the tense communal situation in both East and West Punjab. To crown it all, when the whole country was making every effort to complete the partition, there were very heavy rains in Northern India which cut communications even further. Roorkee had 14 inches of rain in three days. The Solani rose above all previous record levels causing havoc all round, including silt on the golf course, where, apart from the first, third and fourth holes, it was a case of 'boundless and bare, the lone and level sands stretch far away.' At one time Roorkee was completely cut off from the rest of the world. A sigh of relief was heaved when, on 7th November, the last 'Pakistan Special' steamed out of the Engineer Stores Depot at 1530hrs, four and a half hours behind schedule, thus completing the partition, but leaving the Centre reeling from all the depredations.

These depredations were hardly unexpected, given the decision that Roorkee was to bear the brunt of transferring assets to Pakistan. Furthermore, with the disbandment of the Lahore and Sialkot wartime Groups, the strength at Roorkee was about 6,000, a majority of whom were Muslims destined for Pakistan. By chance all the plant experts were Mussalmans and as a result considerable difficulty was experienced in finding the right type of men for the Plant units. Great efforts were made to remedy the shortage and a successful Plant training camp was run at Chilla, near Hardwar. The removal of all the equipment and machinery from the Centre eventually proved to be a blessing in disguise as the deficiency was made up by the provision of the very latest that was available.

The class composition of the Group was completely upset and by the end of the year the Sikh percentage was increased to 35% and Hindus to 65%, which corresponded with six Sikh and 12 Hindu units. With the departure of so many British officers, over twenty VCOs were commissioned as 2/Lts in December and joined the Officers' Mess where they found the life there "very interesting"!

Life in Roorkee slowly returned to normal, but there were numerous changes of appointment. By November, Col Rex Holloway had returned from leave in Canada and Dick Connor, who had been officiating in his place as Commandant, was about to go to Sialkot as Commandant of the Pakistan Engineer Centre. Col Mohd Anwar Khan had also left for Sialkot and Major YR Puri took his place as Assistant Commandant. The Adjutant's Newsletter of Nov 47, also recorded that among those leaving was Major Harold Andrews from the Records Office who had served the Group for more than fourteen years and retired on pension. 'Though a stern man, he was very pleasant to get on with and we miss him a lot'(Ibid.). Another old stalwart to leave was Major R A T Moss, destined for Pakistan.

Rex Holloway, with his renowned calm and efficiency tried to hold the disintegrating organisation together. Life was not easy, especially in the Training Battalion which had been stripped of all training publications and aids except for a single copy of the recruits' syllabus. By dint of hard work and selfless effort on the part of all, a semblance of order and normality was reached by the time the first Indian Commandant, Colonel Dhillon, took over in February 1948.

Joginder Singh Dhillon (or Jogi Dhillon, as he was affectionately called) had first come to Roorkee in 1936, after being commissioned from the Indian Military Academy where he was the Senior Under Officer and gained the Sword of Honour and the Gold Medal for being the best all-round Cadet. He first saw active service in 1941 in Iraq with 5 Field Company and then went on to command 75 Field Company in Burma. He saw further active service commanding 2 Field Company at Sourabaya in Java in 1945 before joining the Engineer-in-Chief's Branch at Delhi where he was heavily involved in the problems and aspirations of the new nation. He was thus eminently suited to become Commandant on promotion to Colonel.

In the aftermath of Partition leave became a great problem, especially when so many soldiers wanted to see their families with their own eyes.

In particular men who had been living in West Punjab had lost their homes and a percentage of all ranks became refugees. A Refugee Office was set up to deal with problems such as tracing of relatives, evacuation, provision of accommodation, clothing, funds, fuel and rations. A Refugee Camp was also set up in South-Gazani Lines where families could be accommodated, with an office dealing with registration, following up claims and all correspondence. At the same time a substantial fund was set up with donations from all units. The Gudwara was exceptionally generous and the Boys Battalion did its share in raising funds with the performance of numerous very successful dramas. By the middle of 1948 the number of families had gone up to 120 and plans were being made to open a Cottage Industry Centre to teach such skills as weaving, spinning and tailoring. Arrangements were also made to supply clothing, ata (flour), firewood and vegetables at cheap rates and a sense of security was gradually restored. In subsequent years a number of institutions were created for the welfare of Other Ranks and their families, and widows of war casualties. The two major ones are 'Sarvatra', under the aegis of the Army Wives Welfare Association, which provides vocational training-based commercial ventures, and the General Krishen Soni Widows Home and School. These institutions have been constructed beyond Manglaur. On the new Roorkee by-pass is the Yadav Puri Colony which was initiated by Colonel Yadav Puri to provide housing for refugee families from West Punjab.

On the more lively side, Guest Nights continued in the Officers' Mess though rather less frequently. Brigadier Williams was one to be well and truly dined out on his appointment as Chief Engineer Southern Command and after responding to the toast, everyone present stood on their chairs, with one foot on the dining room table, and toasted "The Bengal Sappers." Bill Williams had first joined the Bengal Sappers in 1918 and devoted a life-time of service to India. He had become Corps Adjutant in 1929 and then spent three years at the IMA at Dehra Dun before returning to Roorkee as Professor of Civil Engineering at the Thomason College . He had a wonderful faculty for friendship in dealing with all creeds and levels of society, princes and politicians, soldiers and servants. He was particularly popular with the junior Indian officers and was early convinced that India should some day gain her independence and sought to help in any way he could. He became Engineer-in-Chief India in 1948 and held this post until his retirement eight years later. Such was the esteem in which he was held that he was appointed a Knight of the British

Empire and given the honorary rank of Lieutenant General by the Government of India. He died on 17th October 1971 at Mussoorie and was buried with full military honours in Roorkee where his grave is still honoured by visitors of all ages and creeds. One of his ex-students said that "Roorkee was his Shantiniketan and his Sevagram – and finally his Samadhi", which translates, rather inadequately, from the poetic Hindi as being his 'home from home, the heart of his selfless service and his final resting place'.

By April 1948 the last three British officers, Lieutenant Biggs, Captain Mee and Captain Coulson had been dined out and left Roorkee, bringing to a close a long association but with the hope that the British officers would continue to take an active interest and keep in touch with the happenings in the Group. As the Group Adjutant at the time wrote: "We should always be grateful to British officers for creating such a magnificent army in India and specially to those who were the pioneers of this Corps for making such a fine Group" (Newsletter, June 1948).

Towards the end of 1947 an infantry battalion was stationed in Roorkee. 4 Dogras came over in small packets from Pakistan and occupied the whole of North Range Lines, with No2 Officers' Mess and the Training Battalion's VCOs' Mess for their officers and VCOs respectively. Their arrival was most welcome as they were able to relieve the Centre of much of the burden of Internal Security duties. Nowadays an Armoured Brigade is permanently located at Roorkee but the Centre Commandant continues to be the Station Commander.

The School of Military Engineering finally moved to Kirkee after Partition and a number of British officers moved with it including Rex Holloway who took over command of the School in February 1948 after leaving Roorkee. This enabled the Thomason College to get all its accommodation back and it was soon busy on new construction. It also made room for the Punjab College of Engineering which had been uprooted from Lahore and came over from Pakistan with a number of professors and students, occupying some of the quarters deserted by the SME and being renamed The East Punjab College. The Thomason College continued to expand until it achieved University status. It is now a major centre of higher technical learning, catering for a vast array of engineering disciplines. The old polo ground and the area to the west of it, towards Roorkee town and below the Principal's bungalow, encompasses the University complex. No longer part of the old United Provinces of the British era, Roorkee now falls under Utranchal, the newly created hill state.

ROORKEE RESURRECTED

After a year of intense activity and hard work, with equipment, tools, vehicles and training stores being obtained from various depots and stores, Roorkee was once again humming with its usual activity and the ambience and élan of the Centre was restored. Independence Day was celebrated in style on 15th August and a lively account followed in the "Sunday Statesman", a copy of which is appended. Diwali that year was celebrated with all the pomp and show worthy of the occasion, the Quartermaster General taking the salute at a Ceremonial Parade on 1st November. The whole of the Cantonment was illuminated for the first time in the history of the Centre. This included the Corps War Memorial and one could see jawans reading out names of the heroes of previous wars to their wives who had never been there before. This was followed by a further Ceremonial Parade on 25th November under the command of Colonel Dhillon, to celebrate the restoration of Roorkee. He led the parade in a perfect march past with the Band playing 'Wings' and Prime Minister Jawaharlal Nehru taking the salute. He was much impressed with what he witnessed and in deference to his wishes the honour of commanding the first Republic Day Parade in New Delhi was given to Colonel Dhillon. On several occasions since, the Bengal Sappers Contingent has won the Best Marching Trophy at this Parade.

It was not long after Partition before the Boys Battalion was reorganised into a Military School with the aim of producing future leaders for the Army. The Training Battalion was also reorganised with a new syllabus and a lively and interesting programme. At the same time the Commandant's Fund released large amounts of money for the welfare of the troops. This included hot water in the winter, reconstruction of messes, furnishing and decoration of dining halls, better sports grounds, improvements to the welfare centres and schools, as well as more amenities in the Lines and improvements in the jawans' living conditions.

In November 1948 the Commandant held a Conference of all unit commanders and announced the observance of a Group Day. After taking soundings throughout the Group and setting out his reasons, the Commandant decided that this would take place every year on 15th October. Colonel Dhillon had made his mark on Roorkee and been responsible for laying the post-Independence foundation of the Centre, so it came as no surprise that he was to be promoted to Brigadier and given command of 161 Infantry Brigade in the Uri Sector in Kashmir. He then went on to command 82 Infantry Brigade in Rajasthan and later 26

Infantry Division before becoming Deputy Chief of the General Staff. He commanded XI Corps in the 1965 war with Pakistan, followed by Army Commander, Central Command until 1970 when he retired. He was Colonel Commandant of the Bengal Sappers until 1976, one of the truly great Bengal Sappers.

On 12th January 1989 the Bengal Sappers were the first among the three Engineer Groups to have the honour of receiving 'Colours' from the Supreme Commander, the President of India. The battle honours selected to be emblazoned on the Colours range from Ghazni 1839 to Meiktila 1945, all ten being pre-Independence.

In the resurrection of Roorkee the Officers' Mess received close attention. The Mess building was the private property of the Bengal Sapper Officers so in order to provide funds for refurbishment it was decided to sell it to the Military Engineering Services. The wall between the dining room and the old bar was removed to extend the dining room and a new bar was added at the head of the entrance lounge. The Ladies Room was also enlarged. Hard and soft furnishings were purchased and several silver trophies, linked to significant historical events, were designed and crafted and many new ones were presented by individual officers, units and institutes. There are still some of the old shikar trophies on the walls, together with new paintings of key people and events over the past fifty years

Over the years the Mess building has gone through extensive renovation. All the rooms have been panelled in teak and the lawns have been extended, beyond which lie an orchard and a rose garden. Its stock of rose varieties has made it second only to the National Rose Garden in New Delhi. For the needs of visiting officers and families, several charming residential suites have been put up in the vicinity of the Mess, maintaining the overall architectural harmony. Adjoining the Swimming Pool a covered Band-stand has been constructed to cater for inclement weather.

On Partition, the Centre band passed to Pakistan and the gap was filled by the induction of the Sirmoor State Band. New instruments were procured for both brass and pipe bands; the men were suitably kitted for winter and summer and put through an intensive course of training at the School of Military Music at Panchmarhr. Many new tunes have since been composed and introduced into the band's repertoire, the most popular being 'Saare Jahan se achha Hindustan Hamara' which has now been immortalised by its humming in space by Wing Commander Rakesh Sharma, the first Indian astronaut, while he relayed a message of greetings to the Prime Minister from his orbiting spaceship! The Centre bands are often called up to New Delhi for Rashtrapati Bhavan functions held in honour of visiting Heads of State and high dignitaries. They also take part in the yearly Republic Day Parade and are conspicuous by their stirring performance and colourful dress. In addition they visit all Regiments during their Raising Days and while at Roorkee they regale its military and civil audiences with their music on festive occasions.

LANDMARKS IN ROORKEE

Among the Roorkee landmarks, the Parade Ground has been bituminised and extended up to the War Memorial. The Colonnade leading to the Ghazni Tower now has a large 'Sapper Grenade' chiselled in black granite under a canopy and a fortress wall in keeping with the Indo-Saracenic architecture of the Memorial. On each Group Day it is the venue for a 'Son-et-Lumière', staged to depict acts of valour by the units of the Group in various operations. Identical architecture has been adopted for the new Quarter-Guard building.

A fine stadium, with a stand capable of seating 1,500 spectators, has been constructed on the old Military Transport training ground and alongside this an Olympic size swimming pool. The earlier pool in the Fieldworks area has been abandoned. These are venues for inter-regiment, regional and National level sports events.

The entrance to the cantonment is through the imposing Cawnpore Gate, to commemorate the raising at Cawnpore (Kanpur) in 1803 of the Bengal Pioneers, the predecessors of the Bengal Sappers. There is now a by-pass round Roorkee from the Ganeshkand bridge to the Roorkee–Dehra Dun road, and the approach to Hardwar takes off near the Canal Workshop. Not far from the Military Hospital on the Roorkee–Meerut Road a bridge has been built over the railway line. All these have brought radical change to the geography of Roorkee.

A major attraction for visitors to the Station is the Museum and Archive located in the old No 1 Training Battalion and Depot Battalion office block. With much effort, many war trophies, flags, colours, battle honours, medals, bravery decorations and medallions, together with related photographs and sketches, have been collected and housed therein. A gallery of portraits of prominent war heroes and Colonel Commandants has a high place of honour. The front of the building is given a sense of heraldry with a nine foot high bronze statue of Lord Kitchener which faces the War Memorial. He was the only Sapper to become C-in-C of the Indian Army (1903–1907). The statue was previously at the Dubela Museum in Madhya

Pradesh, having been cast in Sydney in 1930, and was carefully transported to Roorkee in January 1995.

The Headquarters, the administrative hub of the Group, is now located in an imposing new building, though the old one, of comparatively modest dimensions, is still retained and houses the offices of the Commandant and Group Adjutant. The Records Office, an important part of the Group's administration, also serves the MES and Military Survey units. Besides these, the Border Roads organisation also draws its staff from the Group.

Several enclaves have come into being to provide residential accommodation, with all the necessary infrastructure facilities, for single and married personnel. A number of retired Officers and JCOs have also settled down in Roorkee. Schooling facilities have been vastly improved at kindergarten and nursery level, while higher secondary levels are on a par with any reputed Public School in the country. The Knox Memorial School has been expanded and St Gabriel's Academy flourishes in the old No 2 Officers' Mess and the ante-room, with its stout pillars and domed ceiling, is now a Catholic Chapel. In addition, there is a Central School, reaching up to the 10+2 level (equivalent to the British O level). To keep the Station's health services at a top functional level, the Military Hospital and Dental Centre are well equipped and have specialists in all major disciplines.

The old Sergeants' Mess is now the Junior Commissioned Officers' (old VCOs) Mess and for them a second Mess has been constructed in the old No 2 Training Battalion area. Their dining strength is over 150. Ever since 1948 there has been a Clerks Mess which has been a great success with its own TV and radio room and library.

The Other Ranks' kitchens and dining rooms, which earlier had demarcations according to the established social norms of those times, are now integrated spaces equipped with everything necessary for efficient service. In these areas many innovations, like a perforated griddle for puffing chapattis on a mass scale and a steam cooking system, have been introduced, and a number of cafeterias provide a variety of cuisine and have replaced the erstwhile 'Wet Canteens.'

Following the customary pattern of integrated architecture, the places of worship for Hindus, Sikhs, Muslims and Christians are adjacent to each other and all ranks join in celebrating every festival with equal fervour. St John's Church, which was at one time boarded up, has been reopened with regular services in Urdu. Aitken Lawrie was particularly pleased to see this on one of his many visits to Roorkee, since this was where he was married and his children baptised.

SPORTS AND SOCIAL ACTIVITY

In the late 50s, due to the imposition of a total ban on the shooting of birds and wild animals, the Shikar Club was closed. However, when the going was good, several impressive trophies were added to the earlier collection in the Officers' Mess. In the immediate aftermath of Partition, birds were fairly plentiful in the neighbourhood of Roorkee and a few parties went out on shikar, but the well-known jheels had been covered with sand from the Solani floods and duck were far from plentiful.

The Roorkee Olympics, in association with the University of Roorkee, were revived. To provide wider opportunities for sports, under the Sapper Adventure Foundation, other avenues were explored. In the field of mountaineering, the Bengal Sappers have been the leaders. Major Nandu Jayal and Colonel Yadav Puri were, in fact, pioneers in this field. The Himalayan Mountaineering Institute at Darjeeling was set up by Major Jayal. Continuing in this tradition was Major MP Yadav, who led many national and international expeditions and was Principal of the Nehru Institute of Mountaineering. Starting in the early fifties, the first two peaks to be scaled successfully by the Bengal Sappers were Mount Kamet (25,447ft) and Mount Abi Gamin (24,130ft). These were followed by regular forays into the mighty Himalayan Ranges year after year. The most difficult peak, Nanda Devi (25,796ft), was climbed in 1993. Major Jai Bahuguna VSM and Bar KC SM was another outstanding mountaineer but sadly lost his life in an attempt on Mount Everest. Lieutenant Bhagat, Colonel Yadav Puri and Major Jayal had earlier lost their lives in this exciting sport.

The Bengal Sapper Centre has a fully fledged Equestrian Club, with a dozen mounts in its stables, and the Club has sent a number of competitors to the National circuit Horse Shows and other equestrian events. A Four-in-Hand and a 'Tum-Tum' are still in use by the Centre Commandant.

Sailing, in particular, has attracted considerable interest among the Bengal Sappers. Besides the yearly cruise along the Western Coast and to neighbouring Sri Lanka, several voyages have been undertaken to the east coast of Africa and to destinations in South-East Asian countries. The epoch making event was the first round-the-world cruise of 30,000 nautical miles carried out successfully in 1987, in a small, seventeen-year-old yacht christened TRISHNA, through literally the Seven Seas. Its crew included Major AK Singh, a Bengal Sapper with an amputated leg, the injury being sustained while hang-gliding. He created a world record by this daring feat and earned the National Adventure Award, Kirti Chakra and Sena Medal. Nine Arjuna Awards (the highest National awards for Sports) have been earned in Diving, Squash, Basketball, Boxing and Weightlifting.

Taking advantage of being located near the upper reaches of the river Ganges (Ganga), the Bengal Sappers have been pioneers in the field of rowing and have dominated the National scene right from the beginning. Nb/Sub Inder Pal Singh represented India in Rowing at the Sydney Olympics in 2000. Other exciting sports events which are popular are paragliding, white-water rafting, kayaking, canoeing and fencing. Participation in these events is by both Officers and Other Ranks.

A Nine-hole golf course has been laid out in the 'Hill-Cut' area, with green fairways and putting greens. The golf course has hosted several events and is popular both with Officers and their families. Next to it is the Three Feathers Institute, the Officers Club and a Golf Hut, off Garden Road and overlooking the greens, which caters for golf addicts from outstations.

All in all, Roorkee is considered one of the finest cantonments in the country, an achievement of which the Bengal Sappers are justly proud.

THE FIELD FORCE

All the Field Force units were kept extremely busy in the aftermath of Partition and, as part of the integration of the erstwhile princely states, Field Companies from Teri Garhwal, Sirmoor and Faridkot joined the Group in 1950, followed by the Malerkotla Field Company in 1951 and the Mandi Field Company the following year. The merger of these units added about 2,000 to the strength of the Group and political developments compelled the expansion of the Group to over 10,000 by the end of 1957. Most of this expansion was due to the intensive road building in the border areas of Nepal and the North-East Frontier Area, and the Chinese confrontation in these areas called for special task forces. The sudden Chinese invasion in October 1962 shattered the smug complacency within the country and came as a shock to the Indian people who were caught on the wrong foot. The Group was called on to increase recruitment from an annual rate of 1,100 in 1960 to 4,000 in 1962 and 11,000 in 1963. It peaked to more than 21,000 in 1965.

As far as operations are concerned, fighting broke out in Kashmir within weeks of Partition and units were deployed in support of the Army, an ongoing task to this day. Contributions, in cash and kind, were quickly put to use and the Ladies Welfare Committee was soon producing sweaters, pullovers, mufflers etc for the jawans. In Hyderabad, the Nizam had established an independent sovereign state at the time of Partition and his forces began a gradually escalating reign of terror which resulted in the Indian Army invading the State in September 1948. 7 Field Company, in support of the only Armoured Brigade in the Division, led the advance the entire way from the border to Hyderabad, clearing mines and road-blocks, constructing air-strips and carrying out bridging operations. Though the Government played down the whole operation, calling it a 'police action', it was known in more enlightened circles as 'Operation Polo' and OC 7 Field Company felt it was possible that the last chukka had yet to be played. Fortunately the operation was soon concluded.

Indian engineers were involved in all the various operations of the next few years: Nagaland in 1956, Goa in 1961, the Chinese aggression of 1962 and the conflicts with Pakistan. Operations continue, of course, at many locations, including a Mission to Mozambique to provide transport, police cover and clerical aid to Force and Regional HQs and to assist the United Nations in the enforcement of the peace agreement and the holding of elections. This is not the place to recount their stories; suffice to say that the black year of Partition lies decades in the past and new generations of Bengal Sappers have only a prospect of achievement and progress in front of them. The best summing up of the men who restored "God's Own" to its old glory is that they have truly lived up to the motto given them by their first Indian Commandant: "*Ekta: Seva: Ilam*" (Unity: Service: Inspiration).

INDEPENDENCE DAY, ROORKEE, 1948

by

"BENGAL SAPPER"

(Reprinted from The Sunday Statesman, Delhi, 22nd August 1948)

We dined together in the Mess the evening before. The line of easy chairs on the lawn, the Pipe Band marching to and fro, servants in smart white uniform, pleasant easy conversation, the Mess Silver. "The King", "India", and one's thoughts continually drifting back to Guest Nights of years gone by. After dinner, games, "Gentlemen! Gentlemen, please!", the Umpire calling vainly "Keep your seats and hands on the floor" as, feet in the air, the ball is tossed from end to end of the ante-room. Tomorrow some bones will ache a little, and some seats will need a dab of Iodine, but tonight: 'Football', 'Cock Fighting', and 'Are you there, Moriarty?' All the old, familiar fun.

Next morning, the Parade: the long drawn up line of soldiers at attention. 'Present Arms' as India's flag is broken at the mast-head. The feu-dejoie, the one solitary round which should not have gone off echoes about the ground before the zip-zip-zip of the volleys themselves. Three jais for the Governor-General and then the march past. The horses have gone, the men's hats are a poor substitute for the Pugrees we knew, but the bearing and pride of Regiment remains and as Company after Company swings past the saluting base a lump rises in the throat.

Breakfast: less poring over papers and more light talk than an older generation favoured, but just as great a range of dishes. Afterwards "howdy dos" with old servants on the lawn. The Head Mali who came 23 years ago, the Marker whose grandfather ran one round the squash-courts has now a third son, an old syce, 82 and almost blind, the "grave digger," grumbling and bent with age.

Later, Prayers, where men of all classes sit densely packed in the temple compounds. From a platform the Colonel leads "Beseeching Thee to accept on this self-hallowed day of Independence our thanks and dedication to Thy service ... Give us Thy light to guide us in the troublous times ahead ... Give us soldiers of India strength to play our part in the building of this New India. Help us to live as Brothers side by side, to fight shoulder to shoulder, and when the call comes, cheerfully to make the supreme sacrifice for our cherished Motherland."

Then tree-planting at the Regimental School. Lines of small boys watch one fumbling with a spade: a sapling which one day they say will be a magnificent flowering tree. Then small boys from each class plant their trees, Mangoes this time, which the Subedar-Major has chosen, and there is some talk about who will eat the first fruit. Some smiling and giggling in the Ranks. The boy in the yellow coat is Jiwan Singh's son and though he looks an angel now, the Master says: "Like his father, always in mischief." We walk round, much joking as the names and tales of different boys are told, a drill display, with marching songs by some and choruses by others. How John, in whose memory the School was built many years ago, would have enjoyed it!

Then a JCOs party at the Mess. A Subedar, whose father was mine 30 years ago, gives the latest news from home. His hair is slightly grey and the wrinkles on his face bring back sharply the memory of his father with all the Company seated about his chair, listening while he told a young Subaltern how men must be handled if things are to go well in tight corners. And Captain Rehmat-Ullah Khan, now the only Muslim officer with the Regiment, who joined it before I did, runs through the names of those who played their part in times gone by, and there is much old soldiers' talk. Then a large and gay lunch party, each one helping himself to endless varieties of Curries and pulaos.

Afterwards, old friends from Cantonments and the City came to call. Kanaya Lal has long since ceased to be the Regimental Contractor and now devotes his life to running a local School, a Muslim friend asks advice about the future, for Partition has not made his position easy. Though he wants to stay himself he wonders how his son will fare.

Then a display of physical training for the townspeople, and again the Pipe Band, all the old tunes and a clown who did the exercises best of all and made small boys and girls scream with delight at his efforts. Everywhere the green, white and saffron flag of India, and everywhere good humour and great friendliness.

Later, to see the men's dinners: great feasts of curries, sweetmeats and fruit, specially large and imposing to mark the day and a decision to do away with all forms of special langars in the Regiment, and my thoughts go back to all the difficult problems which caste and food had raised in days gone by. Here and there a man answers: "The food is good but we could do with more atta because we work hard." An old grey-head Sikh, every inch a farmer from Ludhiana, is sitting among the boys. In broad Gurkhali, he tells me that he has brought ghee for the lad and his son who sits beside him is clearly not forgotten.

Then to the Mess again where officers and their ladies assemble to close a long day's celebration with supper and games, and when I slipped away hours later the fun was still fast. Down the long road which leads to Delhi, and as the car speeds through the night, thoughts race through the mind of what we thought Independence might mean and of the reality. Disorder, discontent and disillusionment, we said, but never this. Trouble and want there is in plenty still, but on one day, Independence Day, all India rejoices and her people's friendliness and joy and pride are witness of her greatness.

DÉJÀ VU: RETURN TO ROORKEE

Many of us have been fortunate enough, and indeed privileged, to have visited Roorkee in the years since Independence. To pay a sentimental visit anywhere after an interval of 40 years or so is a risk. It is to court disappointment, either that the place will have changed so much or that one's reception will be somewhat off-hand. All of us must have wondered in advance whether any changes had been for the better. India had rightly celebrated our departure in 1947 and it would be hardly surprising if many had felt that the sooner we left the sooner the sooner they could run things in their own way. What would our reception be like? We need not have worried. After all they are still the Bengal Sappers and still refer to themselves as 'God's Own'.

Young officers on joining probably still find that the train arrives in the middle of the night and that they arrive at the Mess in a tonga. Most visitors, on the other hand, drive up by road from Delhi. The road is now built up all the way but the main difference is that the bullock carts – surely the same ones we all remember? – are now fitted with rubber tyres. They would probably fail any UK or Indian police check but they are only travelling at the same old two miles an hour, so what the hell? The point is that when they move off the road they no longer break up the edge with their metal-bound wheels and that pall of fine, talcum powder dust that used to envelop us is kept at bay by car windows and perhaps air-conditioning. Reaching Roorkee, crossing the bridge over the railway, turning right up Dhillon Marg , observing the side road marked God's Own Marg, one swings into the garden of the Mess.

The warmth of our reception left us in no doubt that we were indeed welcome. We found ourselves amongst friends who were intent on surprising us with their hospitality and the genuineness of their feelings towards us. It was as if we had never been away. Whisked off to a Guest Bungalow, we were given a chance to wash and brush up, a bearer hovered in the background, ready to help us unpack and take any clothes to the dhobi that needed washing. A Liaison Officer was appointed to brief us on the programme for our visit and to advise on the appropriate form of dress, to warn us of any possible pitfalls and to introduce us to people we might expect to meet. Then off to the Officers Mess for a cool drink and perhaps lunch.

The Mess facade is unchanged from what we remembered in 1947 and the garden is beautifully looked after, with a lush, weed-free lawn that would be the envy of any gardener at home. George Cooper was there for a full-blown Guest Night in his honour (in August 1982), with no concession made for the time of year so Mess Kit overalls soon became incredibly uncomfortable. "The table was glistening with silver, the Mess Staff were immaculately turned out, the Band played in the background, conversation flowed and, at the end of dinner, the President stood up and announced "Mr Vice, The Queen"! Everyone rose, the Band played our National Anthem and we all drank the Loyal Toast. It was as if nothing had ever changed and was a most generous and moving gesture. The next toast was their traditional one, to the President of India, both toasts being, of course, in water.

Generous tributes to their British predecessors were made in subsequent speeches, reciprocated by the guests, and followed by presentations. On the conclusion of the formal part of the evening, everyone moved outside, where the Band continued to play light music until, shades of the 1940s, the lights went out. The Band continued playing as best they could but gently faded away, rather like an old-fashioned gramophone running down, until, all of a sudden, the lights came on once more and the Band struck up again as if nothing had ever happened. There were no Mess games and there were blank looks when the young officers were asked the whereabouts of the small brass cannons that used to be outside the Mess. Billiard balls were exactly the right calibre and a generous helping of black powder made them a wonderful projectile. The nostalgic evening ended with the Band playing 'Wings' and I retired to bed feeling that I had never been away."

After breakfast in the bungalow, (having been woken of course with 'chota hazri' and the familiar sounds of the band practising, bugles blowing and rifles firing on the ranges, not to mention the brain-fever birds shrieking), a tour of the Cantonment was on the agenda. Of course there had been changes. Perhaps the most obvious was that everything seemed so much bigger than one remembered, hardly surprising when one realised that the Corps has expanded from something like 3,000 in 1947 to approximately 50,000 today. Not only have the trees and vegetation grown up to obscure what one recollected as being wide views across the surrounding countryside, but there has also been a great deal of new building. Alas, one can no longer see across the plain to the Mussoorie hills and the snow-capped peaks of the Himalayas beyond. The old Thomason College is now a fully fledged University with some 4,500 students from all over India and the Far East, with teaching carried out in English.

Every visitor wishes to see some particular place associated with long ago, be it a boat trip up the Ganges Canal to renew one's acquaintance with the massive lion sculptures by the town bridge (now a City), or to see the great aqueduct carrying the Canal over the Solani River, or to visit the Cemetery with the grave of Lieutenant General Sir Harold (Bill) Williams, with its memorial stone of black marble, a fitting memorial to a man who gave so much of his life to the Bengal Sappers. All these wishes, and many others, were catered for by the long-suffering Liaison Officers. Hugh Balston, in 1978, was anxious to see the grave of his wife's aunt, who had died in 1946 and found it a peaceful spot and well tended. By extraordinary coincidence the entry for her burial in the cemetery book was signed in the column headed 'officiating clergy' by 'H Williams, Brigadier – in the absence of a priest'!

But much is still as it was: the wide tree-lined avenues, the fine War Memorial, the magnificent parade ground, the general air of efficiency, of controlled activity and purposefulness. At every road junction, Regimental Police, immaculately turned out, were directing traffic. The officers may not be wearing the pale blue 'mazri' shirts, khaki shorts and dark blue hose-tops that we wore in winter 40 years ago, but in their smart modern uniforms all ranks display the same pride of bearing, the same efficiency and the same cheerfulness and friendly behaviour it was our privilege to know and be part of so long ago.

The old Workshops still have their vital role to play in the training of Sappers, but have been comprehensively modernised for the needs of today's army with all its new technology. Psychological and other tests have replaced the more haphazard selection methods of 40 years ago which amounted to little more than a casual conversation between the Company Commander and his Subadar, with perhaps a word or two of recommendation (or rejection) from the Platoon Commander and his Jemadar. Not very scientific perhaps, but it seemed to work without too many errors! India, however, has always been adept at making equipment last and it was no surprise to find, in the 1980s, some Folding Boat Equipment (FBE) on the Bridging Hard beside the Ganges Canal, probably the last of the equipment mentioned in the Adjutant's Newsletter of June 1934 as having just arrived! The comment at the time was: "Opinion was unanimous that the folding dinghy (sic) would make an excellent duck punt for the Jheels". Perhaps that is why it was still being retained?! Sadly, such shooting is no longer permitted, so doubtless it has been replaced at last.

There were no signs of bicycles still being used by officers to get around the Cantonment and thus no opportunity for coming to grief like the young officer cycling to work, crossing the flooded wooden bridge over the monsoon drain with his feet up on the handle-bars, only to realise, far too late, that the bridge had been swept away in the night. And what of the 'pi-dogs'? The elderly Sikh who used to march round the Cantonment, shotgun under his arm, ready to dispose of any strays, must now be long retired, if not long forgotten. His career was somewhat chequered, with frequent dismissal for habitual drunkeness, but he was always reinstated when nobody else could be found to undertake this somewhat tasteless task.

Those fortunate enough to visit Roorkee in 1997 were treated to a performance of Son-et-Lumiere on the War Memorial Lawns. A brilliant potted history of the Bengal Sappers, from the raising of the Companies of Bengal Pioneers by Lieutenant Wood at Cawnpore in 1803, through to the raising of six Companies of Sappers and Miners at Allahabad in 1819 as part of the Bengal Presidency Army and on to more modern times, was described, with each major incident briefly illuminated in the darkness. Part of the Commentary was spoken by Lieutenant Dolly Kushwah, the first female Engineer Officer in the Bengal Group.

Ceremonial Parades follow the same format as a British parade and Ian Lyall Grant described one he attended as "first class; I don't remember having seen a better parade. Although the band played several Indian tunes, the Colours were slow-marched back to their position to 'Bonnie Prince Charlie' and the parade marched off to 'Wings'." The battle honours selected to be emblazoned on the Colours stem from Ghazni 1839 to Meiktila 1945, all ten being pre-Independence. Very naturally, no battle honours won inside India were chosen though these are all (including Delhi) shown on full lists. 'Ubique' as a motto has been replaced by its Hindi equivalent 'Sarvatra' and the new crest is the Indian Engineer one showing the gate at Ghazni in the centre. The old crests, however, particularly the Prince of Wales' feathers, are still much in evidence. Colonels Commandant are all serving officers and are elected to their posts by their contemporaries.

Farewells are always sad occasions and saying goodbye to all those who have looked after us on our nostalgic returns to Roorkee are particularly painful. No account can really convey the wonderful atmosphere that prevailed and the affection held for all those past members of the Corps of Bengal Sappers and Miners. Such a heartwarming experience makes one proud to have made the long journey back to 'God's Own' country.

RISALPUR

Though this anthology is about the Bengal Sappers, it may be of interest to readers to know what happened to those Bengal Sappers who went over to Pakistan on Partition in 1947. Both countries were undoubtedly pleased to achieve independence, but the initial months were overshadowed by the internal security situation on either side of the border between the two countries. Many British officers stayed on for a while to ensure that the new countries got off to a good start, but there was a quite natural desire in both armies to run their own organisations as soon as possible, despite their lack of expertise in many spheres. Often disillusioned by the terrible internecine slaughter on both sides, and by watching the break-up of former happy multi-cultural units, few British officers remained for more than a few months; many were long overdue anyway to return home from wartime service. It was a very busy period, but not an altogether very happy one.

The first home of the Pakistan Engineers was at Sialkot and it soon became a hive of activity. Apart from a few buildings, there were no engineer facilities of any sort. Though many engineer stores and much equipment had come over from India and in particular from Roorkee, there were shortages everywhere and much to sort out. There were plenty of 'Braves', but very few 'Chiefs'. George Cooper, commanding 70 Field Company, often had up to a thousand men on parade with plenty of work for them all but only a Jemadar to supervise and no other British officers. "My Company was very short of equipment so I took myself off to Army Headquarters in Rawalpindi, bluffed my way into Engineer Branch and demanded my entitlement. Unfortunately a Colonel appeared, I was given a lecture on priorities and promptly shown the door!

On my way back to Sialkot, I planned to call in at various villages to meet the families of some of my jawans. Wending my way through the crowded suburbs of Rawalpindi as darkness was falling, I found myself a figure of curiosity: hawk-eyed Pathan tribesmen with sun-blasted skin, heavily armed, bandoliers of ammunition slung around their shoulders, peered into my jeep and shouted 'Azad Kashmir'. I realised they must be so-called 'Freedom Fighters' who had crossed over from the tribal territories of the North-West frontier and Afghanistan and were heading for Kashmir where they were intent on fighting the Indian forces in that territory. Music was blaring from loudspeakers, interspersed with cries of encouragement. The authorities were taking no steps to quell this enthusiasm and it was evident that the tribesmen had their tacit support. The atmosphere was electric. I quickly drove on.

Next day I stopped off at a village, only half a mile or so from the Kashmir border, and was immediately welcomed and invited to sit down for a meal. Everyone was excited, falling over themselves to regale me with their latest successes. Pride of place was given to the shooting down of an Indian plane the day before. Sitting opposite me was a young-looking tribesman with his arm in a sling, the result of a bullet wound a few days earlier. The young man commented that, prior to Independence, he would cheerfully have shot me and there would never have been an occasion when we could have sat down at the same table. However, now we were 'bara bhais' (brothers in arms), united in opposing the illegal occupation of Kashmir and wouldn't the Sahib come with them that night when they were going on a raid behind the Indian lines? Deciding that discretion was the better part of valour, I swiftly made my excuses and wended my way quickly back to Sialkot."

A few years later, being so close to the frontier with India, the Engineer Centre was moved to Risalpur, where they had to start again from scratch. They now have a magnificent set-up with the Headquarters, two Training Battalions and their School of Military Engineering, all together in one place. Visitors from England are received with great hospitality and shown round with justifiable pride.

The Army Engineers soon became heavily involved in the Frontier Works Organisation (FWO), the largest construction agency undertaking various tasks all over Pakistan. They were involved in the completion of the 805km Karakoram Highway and continue to be responsible for its maintenance. It has brought the factories of western China 1,000kms nearer the sea, at Karachi. With the success of that immense operation behind them, the FWO has undertaken further road building projects in Skardu, Chitral, Baluchistan, and other roads for oil exploration. Apart from roads, the FWO has also constructed airfields, canals, dams and major drainage schemes. The driving of the Lowari Tunnel was the responsibility of the FWO and it has assisted in the construction of five units of thermal power stations.

Mention must also be made of the huge contribution of the Pakistan Engineers to the clearance operations in Kuwait following the Gulf War. Mines, wire and other obstacles, ammunition, missile bunkers, burnt-out tanks, any and all abandoned war material and defensive positions received the expert attention of the Pakistan Engineer Force sent out to assist. The Task Force won the highest commendation from the Kuwait Government and the diplomatic corps generally.

It is little wonder, with all these major operations to support, not to mention the tension on the border with India, that the training undertaken at Risalpur assumes such importance. The officers and men have of necessity to be of the highest calibre and capable of responding as readily to the demands of peaceful operations as to any more warlike activities.

BIBLIOGRAPHY

Allen, Charles *Plain Tales from the Raj*. André Deutsch, 1975

Allen, Charles Raj, *A Scrapbook of British India 1877-1947*. André Deutsch, 1977

Beswick, Capt L S *Two Roads in Burma*. Privately published

Blood, Gen Sir Bindon *Four Score Years and Ten*. G Bell & Sons Ltd, London, 1933

Baird Smith, Lt Col R *Report of Proceedings at Roorkee*. RE Journal, Vol X1X, 1914

Churchill, WS *The Story of the Malakand Field Force*.

Corrigan, Gordon *Sepoys in the Trenches. The Indian Corps on the Western Front 1914-1915*. Spellmount, Staplehurst

Cunningham, Col AH *A Short History of the Corps of KGO Bengal Sappers and Miners during the War 1914-18*. Roorkee, 1930

De Santis, Lt Col E *Life of Maj Gen WLD Veitch*. Privately published, Columbia, USA

Hambleton, Joan Mary *The Old Tin Trunk*. Privately published

Henniker, Lt Col M C A *Memoirs of a Junior Officer*. W Blackwood & Sons, 1951

Hibbert, Christopher *The Great Mutiny, India 1857*. Penguin Books Ltd, 1980

Lethbridge, Katharine *Forthrights and Meanders*. Merlin Books, Braunton, Devon

Keay, John *The Honourable Company*. Harper Collins, 1991

Lyall Grant, I G *Burma: The Turning Point*. Zampi Press, 1993

Lyall Grant, I G, & Kazuo Tamayama *Burma 1942: The Japanese Invasion*. Zampi Press, 1999

Mason, Phillip A *Matter of Honour*.

Nunnely, John (Edited) *Tales from the Burma Campaign*. Burma Campaign Fellowship Group

Pearson, George A *Brief History of the KGV's Own Bengal Sappers & Miners Group, RIE*. Roorkee, 1947

Roberts, Maj OL *Notes on Castes and Tribes*. KGVO Bengal S & M, Roorkee, 1938

Sandes, Lt Col EWC *The Military Engineer in India*, Vols I & II. Institution of Royal Engineers

Sandes, Lt Col EWC *The Indian Sappers & Miners*. Institution of Royal Engineers, 1948

Sandes, Lt Col EWC *The Indian Engineers 1939-47*. Institution of Indian Engineers, Kirkee

Scott Moncrieff, Maj Gen Sir George *Canals & Campaigns*. BACSA, London, 1987

Sita Ram Pande, *From Sepoy to Subedar*. Edited by James Lunt. Routledge & Kegan Paul, London, 1970

Stocqueler, J H *The Old Field Officer*, Vol I

The Institution of (Indian) Military Engineers, *History of the Corps of Engineers 1947-1972*. Palit & Palit Publishers, New Delhi

Tinsley, Terence *Stick & String*. Buckland Publications, 1992

Warner, Philip Auchinleck, *The Lonely Soldier*. Sphere Books Ltd, 1982

INDEX

INDEX OF MILITARY UNITS AND FORMATIONS

THE BENGAL SAPPERS 1803–2003
ROORKEE CANTONMENT
Circa 1931–32